THE *Middle East* COLLECTION

THE *Middle East* COLLECTION

ARABIA
of the
WAHHABIS

H[arry] St. J[ohn Bridger] Philby

ARNO PRESS
A New York Times Company
New York—1973

Reprint Edition 1973 by Arno Press Inc.

Reprinted from a copy in
  The University of Illinois Library

The Middle East Collection
ISBN for complete set: 0-405-05310-X
See last pages of this volume for titles.

Manufactured in the United States of America

———◆———

Library of Congress Cataloging in Publication Data

Philby, Harry St. John Bridger, 1885-1960.
  Arabia of the Wahhabis.

  (The Middle East collection)
  Reprint of the 1928 ed. published by Constable,
London.
  1. Arabia--Description and travel. I. Title.
II. Series.
DS207.P52 1973   915.3'04'4   73-6297
ISBN 0-405-05355-X

ARABIA OF THE WAHHABIS

MARZŪQ *ALIAS* RUMMĀNĪ (ROMANY).

Frontispiece.

ARABIA

of the

WAHHABIS

By

H. S^tJ. B. PHILBY, C.I.E.

B.A. (Cantab.), F.R.G.S., M.R.A.S.

Late of the Indian Civil Service
Formerly Adviser to the Ministry of the Interior, Iraq, and
Chief British Representative in Trans-Jordan; Founder's
Medallist of the Royal Geographical Society and
First Burton Memorial Medallist of the
Royal Asiatic Society

Author of
The Heart of Arabia

LONDON

CONSTABLE & CO LTD

1928

PUBLISHED BY

Constable & Company Limited
London W.C. 2

.

BOMBAY   CALCUTTA
MADRAS
LEIPZIG & COPENHAGEN

Oxford University
Press

.

TORONTO

The Macmillan Company

by the same author

THE HEART OF ARABIA

A Record of Travel and
Exploration

in two illustrated volumes

Times Literary Supplement : " The whole
book is a wonderful record of exploits
crowned with astonishing success. . . .
Indeed, it is impossible to speak with too
high praise for the industry, the care, and
the high sense of duty with which Mr.
Philby kept his records."

D. G. HOGARTH in the *Observer* : " Mr.
Philby, the most fortunate and favoured
Christian who has penetrated to the heart
of Arabia, now offers us one of the half-
dozen best accounts of the Peninsular
ever written. A book packed with novel
experience fully and faithfully set down,
and with information about the heart of
Arabia more comprehensive and exact
than any Briton has collected except
Doughty."

PRINTED IN GREAT BRITAIN BY ROBERT MACLEHOSE AND CO. LTD.
THE UNIVERSITY PRESS, GLASGOW.

AD

PHILOMENAM

[V. A. P.]

L'amico mio, e non della ventura,
  nella diserta piaggia è impedito
  sì nel cammin, che volto è per paura ;
e temo che non sia già sì smarrito,
  ch' io mi sia tardi al soccorso levata,
  per quel ch' io ho di lui nel Cielo udito.

DANTE

PREFACE

THIS volume continues and completes the record of my sojourn in Arabia during the years 1917 and 1918. In effect, therefore, it forms a third volume of *The Heart of Arabia* and, with the two volumes of that work, can at any rate claim to present a picture of Arabia at the end of a perfectly definite period of its evolution. I was, I think, the very last European to sojourn in *Wahhabi* Arabia before its desert spaces were desecrated by the advent of the motor-car, which made its first appearance in the territories of Ibn Sa'ud within a twelvemonth of my departure. The invasion was at first tentative and timid, but motor-transport is now a recognised factor in the life of the Arabs. It will become increasingly so in the future and Arabia will slowly but surely lose that air of mystery which has lured so many to its deserts.

The Great War found the desert peninsula still sunk in the restive torpor of a patriarchal stage of development and its people constrained to the nomadic life imposed on them by the very nature of their desert country. The sporadic advent of the high-velocity rifle had been a shock to its pastoral system and had necessitated some modification of method in the national pastime of civil war. But these changes were slight enough to be scarcely perceptible. The Arabia I saw during this period was in all essentials the Arabia of Doughty and Niebuhr. The Arabia of to-day is a very different country. It was, may be, the operations of Lawrence in the North that roused the Arabs from their long sleep to take part, as a giant refreshed, in the race of the modern world. But, whatever the cause, it were well to recognise that the canons by which formerly we were wont to judge Arabian events and tendencies are no longer applicable. Strange as it may seem, Arabia of the *Wahhabis* is already almost established in the comity of the world's nations.

The few steps, short and decisive, which led to this transformation will some day demand the attention of the historian. The present volume may serve as an introduction to that thrilling story. In it the curtain rises on the first insignificant scene of a drama which was to culminate on 8th January, 1926, in the coronation of the *Wahhabi* monarch in the Great Mosque of Mecca as King of the Hijaz. The first attack on Haïl in September, 1918, was a failure if not a *fiasco*, but it committed Ibn Sa'ud to a policy of imperial expansion. He had thrown down the gauntlet to the most dangerous of his rivals—the issue lay on the knees of the Gods. Never probably in all his long career of steady progress was he more distracted with doubts and fears as to the wisdom of his action. Yet no single act of all his career led so inevitably to the final glory. This volume is a record of the anxious months and weeks which immediately preceded the casting of the die.

The long delay in the publication of this work, the inception of which dates back as far as August, 1920, is largely due to the indulgence of my publishers, who have never pressed me to turn from the absorbing activities of the post-war years to my diaries of past events. To them my gratitude is due for such consideration, which happily brings its own reward, for the events of recent years have amply justified the estimate of Ibn Sa'ud's character and capacity on which I ventured in my earlier volumes. And this volume provides me with an opportunity of drawing the reader's attention to a prophetic passage in the first volume of *The Heart of Arabia*. ' The events of the following year,' I wrote,[1] ' made me regret bitterly that circumstances had not permitted of a longer sojourn at and closer inspection of a locality [Khurma] destined, for all its seeming insignificance, to a fateful share in the making of history, perhaps indeed to be the earthly grave of the Utopian ideal of Arab unity, perhaps, who knows ? to be the anvil on which that ideal may yet be hammered into reality.' If Arabian unity is not a Utopian ideal, it is through Ibn Sa'ud and through him alone that it will be realised. It is for the Arabs themselves to meet their destiny.

The system of transliteration adopted in this volume is roughly that prescribed by the Permanent Committee on Geographical Names set up by the Royal Geographical Society in 1920. I have not, however, been able to bring myself to assimilate the *Lam* of the Arabic definite article to the

[1] *H.A.* vol. i. pp. 167-8.

first letter of the word it qualifies—in cases where assimilation occurs in pronunciation—and always transliterate this article as *al*. In other respects I conform to the P.C.G.N. system without, however, taking advantage of the *e* and *o* allowed by it in some cases as alternatives to *a* and *u*.

The map at the end of the volume is identical with the International Million Sheet, North G. 38, Riyadh, for permission to use which I am indebted to the War Office. The plan of Buraida was prepared by the draughting staff of the Royal Geographical Society, which I have to thank for permission to reproduce it. And, finally, the figures and diagrams illustrating architectural and other features of Arabian life have been prepared from my own very rough notes and sketches by my son, H. A. R. Philby, a King's Scholar of Westminster School.

JIDDA, *August 1st*, 1928.

CONTENTS

CHAPTER IV

HOMEWARD BOUND

APPENDICES

ILLUSTRATIONS

MAP, PLAN AND DIAGRAMS

CHAPTER I

RIYADH AT MIDSUMMER

1. THE GREAT FAST OF RAMDHAN

IT was on the 24th June, 1918, that we re-entered the *Wahhabi* capital on our return from the South ; the 15th day it was according to the official reckoning, of the month of *Ramdhan*, for the young crescent of the moon had been observed in the Qasim the night before we had first beheld it in the uplands of Tuwaiq and the *Wahhabi* calendar had been adjusted accordingly by decree of the ecclesiastical authorities. The month of penance was but just half spent and the exhausted citizens of Riyadh looked back on the trials of the past fortnight as the measure of those yet to be suffered ; the worst, indeed, was yet to come, for in Arabia the sting of *Ramdhan* is in its tail.

Once in a long generation the month of *Ramdhan* falls astride Midsummer's day and the devout *Muslim*, wherever he may be, must gird up his loins to face, with what stoicism he can muster, the extreme rigours of an ordeal never, perhaps, intended to be more than a reasonable test of the adherents of the true faith under the conditions obtaining at the time of its inception by the Master. It was a winter [1] month that the Prophet, perhaps scarcely conscious of the inherent defects of the lunar calendar, selected for the first *Ramdhan* ; it was moreover for Arabia that he legislated, little realising perhaps that his creed would ever penetrate beyond its frontiers, but certainly ignorant that the span of daylight differed at different latitudes. ' What would you do,' I once asked Ibn Sa'ud, when he had been complaining of the severity of the ordeal at such a season ; ' if you were at the North Pole, where the sun at this season never sets ? ' For a moment he looked at me askance, thinking that I had

---

[1] December A.D. 623, vide *Life of Mohammad*, by Sir W. Muir, pp. 192-3.

presumed to jest at the expense of *Islam* ; but, finding me
serious, he quoted the scripture as proof sufficient of the daily
rising and setting of the sun throughout the world. ' But if
a true *Muslim*,' he went on, ' were to find himself during this
month in a place where the sun did not set, he would fast for
twelve hours out of every twenty-four and treat the remaining
twelve as if they were hours of darkness.' Such a solution
of the problem seems scarcely compatible with a literal
interpretation of Quranic precepts, and I do not know how
the doctors would tackle it ; but Ibn Sa'ud, well-versed as
he was in matters pertaining to the faith, was content to
limit his curiosity to matters within his ken.

Ever and anon he would make enquiries of me regarding
the various countries of the world. The status and financial
circumstances of the Indian princes were a favourite theme ;
our relations with Afghanistan another, and our generosity
to the King of the Hijaz a constant source of irritation ; but
at times he would go further afield. Once, when Ahmad Ibn
Thunaian was present, he asked me what was the language
of the Americans ; I told him that their speech was English.
' What, then,' he asked, ' are they of English stock ? I
thought they were of Indian origin.' I explained about the
Red Indians and the term ' West Indies ' in reply and asked
if America was mentioned in the *Quran*. ' Yes,' said Ahmad
without hesitation ; Ibn Sa'ud came to his rescue when I
hazarded the suggestion that the New World had not been
discovered in the time of Muhammad. ' But God knows
everything,' he said, ' and the *Quran* is his word.' That was
somewhat disconcerting, and I could only cover my confusion
by suggesting that God would not necessarily display the
whole of his knowledge to ignorant mortals. Ahmad caught
nobly at the straw and, admitting that America was not
expressly mentioned, quoted some vague but comprehensive
passage as doubtless intended to cover all countries not known
to the world in those days. I immediately plunged into
another morass : ' Do you know,' I asked, ' that you can
reach America both by travelling westward and travelling
eastward ? ' Ibn Sa'ud was puzzled, but Ahmad reminded
him of the ' *kurriyat* ' or ' orbicularity ' of the earth, though
even that failed to satisfy him of my complete sanity, when

I assured him that by travelling eastward or westward round the world he would come again to his starting-point without retracing his steps. ' *Wallah,*' he declared, ' I do not weary my head with such speculation, for I have enough to do to rule this land righteously in the fear of God until my time comes to die. Assuredly there is no difference between humanity and the animals except that the former have a conscious idea of God and religion and the future life ; for the rest they are both alike, having eyes, noses, mouths, teeth and limbs ; they eat, drink, wed, sleep and wake alike.' ' Have you,' I asked, ' ever seen a monkey ? ' ' No,' he replied, ' but once at Kuwait I saw a Persian cat.' Ahmad, however, had seen monkeys at the Zoo at Cairo, and agreed that they bore a remarkable physical resemblance to man ; and so we passed on to talk of Egypt and its past glories, the great pyramids [1] and the like.

As the Passover is to the Jews, Lent to the Christians, *Muharram* to the *Shia's* and the Great Pilgrimage to orthodox *Sunnis,* so is *Ramdhan* to the *Wahhabis,* the season *par excellence* for a general demonstration of the sincerity of their faith. From sunrise to sunset none may eat or drink or indulge in sexual intercourse ; smoking is of course at all times forbidden to the *Wahhabis* and liquor is not to be found in their midst; in these respects, however, they are on common ground with their fellow-*Muslims* of all sects—at least nominally. They differ from others in the rigid observance of precepts, which their brethren profess but do not always follow ; they differ again in eking out the weary hours of the long day in prayer, contemplation and the reading of the scriptures, for ' prayer is better than sleep ' ; but above all they differ from their fellows in their manner of spending the short hours of the night. ' *Lailat ul Qadri khairun min kulli lailatin*—the Night of Glory is better than all nights,' for which reason the nights of the month of *Ramdhan* are more excellent than the nights of any other month of the year, even as the first ten days of *Dhil Hijja,* the period of the Great Pilgrimage, are more excellent than other days. And, proceeding in ever-narrowing circles toward the central feature of *Ramdhan*—the ' Night of Glory ' itself—the last

[1] *Ahrām,* pl. *Haramān.*

ten nights of the month are better than the rest, while the
nights of the odd dates—21st to 29th—if only they could be
known with absolute certainty, are better than the others.
The special merit of the ' Night of Glory,' almost equivalent
to our Day of Resurrection in its significance, derives from
the fact that it is then that the Almighty releases the greatest
number of souls each year from the tribulations of Hell. But
the exact date of the month preordained for this great night
was never revealed to the Prophet, who was therefore unable
to convey to his followers more precise information than
that it would probably fall on the 29th, though it might fall
on any of the four preceding odd nights. And the uncertainty
is rendered the more uncertain by the fact that the lunar
months, depending for their beginning on the actual appearance of the moon to human eyes, are always liable to an error
of one day, one way or the other, in respect of their component
days. Thus the 20th may be the 21st or *vice versa*, and
Wahhabi practice, to be on the safe side, ordains a special
programme of rigorous religious exercise for all the nights of
the month from that of the 20th until the end. And thus it
is that, should the Night of Glory manifest itself suddenly
and unawares, the *Wahhabi* congregation will be found ever
ready—in the very act of prayer and adoration—to enter the
portals of Paradise. The annual admission of souls, of those
already gone before and sojourning in Hell to purge away
the sins which have tarnished the basic virtue of true belief,
is curiously suggestive of the Catholic purgatory and is
perhaps unique in its observance of the anniversary of an
event yet to come, which, though dateable within the *Muslim*
year and within the narrow limits above described and preordained as to the year of its occurrence from the beginning
of time, will occur without warning. And on that night there
will be the final gathering into Paradise of all true believers,
the dead and the living, except perhaps such of the latter
as may be caught in the act of sin or neglect of God's precepts.

The whole theory of the *Wahhabi* faith seems to be outwardly
and visibly concentrated in its observance of the *Ramdhan*
rites, and I count myself fortunate to have had the privilege
of witnessing them at close quarters in the *Wahhabi* capital
itself and at a season which contributed to make the ordeal

imposed on the faithful as severe a test of their fortitude and physical, as well as moral, capacity to endure as could well be devised. And through it all one figure stood out prominently—an example of fortitude and zeal to his subjects literally groaning under the penance of these terrible days,—for Ibn Sa'ud himself, though he held no regular public audiences as at other times, never failed to sit twice a day—once immediately after his morning sleep and again after the afternoon prayers—to transact public business, to receive complaints and petitions and the like. And not content with this, he seldom failed to send for me twice during the day—morning and afternoon—to discuss the many matters which constantly demanded his personal attention. The intervals he spent in enjoying short snatches of sleep and in religious exercises. The object of the great fast being by bodily abstinence to purify the soul for admission to Paradise, it is held by the *Wahhabis* that, to be fully effective and acceptable, it must be accompanied by prolonged periods of prayer interspersed with periods of reading from the *Quran* and by a complete distraction from the affairs of the world and from all sorts of wickedness. The more often the *Quran* is read [1] through from cover to cover during the month, the greater is the credit in one's favour in the final reckoning. Devotees like the aged 'Abdulrahman managed to repeat this stupendous performance as many as thirty times in as many days, but Ibn Sa'ud confessed that necessary and unavoidable attendance to affairs of state made it impossible for him to achieve more than four or five such readings during the month.

With the first streak of the false dawn,[2] occurring at this period about $7\frac{1}{2}$ hours after sunset, the signal for the coming day of fasting was given to the residents of the capital by the hoisting of a great arc-lamp on a sort of gibbet-shaped ' flagstaff ' on the roof of the royal palace and a simultaneous preliminary call to prayer. The whole population then roused itself from its slumbers to prepare for the day. Without appetite they eat and drink after a period of private prayer,

[1] ' Reading ' the *Quran* includes ' having it read before one by a professional reader.'

[2] *Fajr al Kadhib.*

until the true dawn [1] is heralded in by the *Adhan* proclaimed from the various mosques. Prayers follow, whereafter no food or drink may be touched until the sunset *Adhan*—a period at this time of some 15½ hours in the hottest and driest and dustiest season of the year. Under such conditions sleep was the natural refuge of the weaker souls, but Ibn Sa'ud's own allowance was strictly rationed to an hour immediately after the dawn prayer, two and a half hours before midday, and an hour before the afternoon prayer, with about two or at most three hours during the night—not a large amount of complete rest, but all through his life he had disciplined himself to indulgence in little sleep divided into short periods. Every now and again he would confess to not feeling very well, but in the main he praised the fast as a sovereign remedy for the ordinary ills of the human system.

About a quarter hour before sunset it was his regular practice during these days to repair to the roof of the private apartments of the palace, where he would be joined by various members of the royal family. Thus assembled they would await the first sound of the *Adhan* announcing sunset, each man holding a date between his forefinger and thumb while repeating the phrase '*Astaghfir' Allah* ' [2] again and again in accordance with the practice and precepts of the Prophet. The dates were committed to the mouth at the first words of the call [3] in token of the formal breaking of the fast ; a draught of water was then taken to slake the day's thirst, and this was followed by the appearance of great trays of sliced melons which were consumed to the extent permitted by jaded appetites. The sunset prayer was the next item on the programme, and the evening meal followed immediately afterwards, though few were able to do justice to it owing to the quantity of liquid—water and melons—consumed immediately before.

The party would then break up, each man retiring to the privacy of his home to resume the companionship of wife

---

[1] *Fajr al Sadiq.*   [2] ' I demand pardon of God.'

[3] The *Adhan* appeared to be proclaimed immediately after the disappearance of the sun in strict accordance with *Wahhabi* tenets. It seems that the *Shia's* (generally termed *Rafidhis*) wait until the first star appears, while the *Wahhabis* treat the term sunset quite literally and regard any delay as likely to vitiate the day's fast.

and children interrupted by the fast—it would seem that the
ritual embargo on actual sexual intercourse is interpreted
by the *Wahhabis* as involving complete abstention from
female society—until the call of evening prayer [1] reunited
them once more in the palace mosque, while the general
public of course assembled in the various mosques of the city.
And the evening prayer in *Ramdhan* is followed by a course
of *Quran*-reading, which, after a short interval—during
which Ibn Sa'ud generally visited me on the ' flagstaff ' roof,
which was assigned to me for the night and from which I
was able to study the devotions of the congregation in the
mosque below—was itself followed by a further course of
prayers known as *Tarawih* or special supplications for the
salvation of the soul from the dangers surrounding it. These
took place every night during the month and generally lasted
about an hour, the *taslim* or prosternation being repeated
more frequently than in the ordinary prayers and lasting in
each case several minutes. During the last ten nights of the
month a further item was added to the programme, the
Tarawih being followed after a brief interval by the *Qiyam* [2]
or ' resurrection ' prayer, the culminating phase of the
Ramdhan ritual. This prayer lasted through the whole night
until the *Suhur* or pre-dawn meal already mentioned, and
consisted in inclinations and prosternations terribly prolonged
—often for as long as a quarter hour at a time—and so
exhausting that human frailty had to be supported in the
intervals between each set by coffee and tea actually served
round in the mosque precincts.

Such is a bare outline of the ordeal of *Ramdhan*, which
completely dominated the stage during the first fortnight
of my sojourn at Riyadh after my return from the South.
Social activities being at a discount, the time passed pleasantly
enough for me in semi-idleness, which left me plenty of leisure
to deal with the arrears of official work which had accumulated during my long absence and to take stock both of the
results achieved during my last journey and of the political
and military situation arising out of recent developments in
various directions. During the first week, in fact, I only left
the palace once—and then very unwillingly—to attend a

---

[1] *'Asha* or *Akhir*.   [2] Pronounced *Jiyam*.

dinner party arranged by Ibrahim al Jumai'a to celebrate
the safe return of our party from the expedition to Wadi
Dawasir. The memory of some incidents of that journey
was, however, too fresh in the minds of most of us to make
the occasion an unqualified success. The distribution of
bounty was yet to come, and some of my companions were
acutely aware that they had scarcely earned the share they
nevertheless expected on the general Arab principle that the
past was not worth worrying about. On the whole it was a
distinct relief to get away from the feast and to proceed, as
some of us did, to the house of the slave, 'Abdul Razzaq,[1]
where I had the pleasure of making the acquaintance of a
fellow-slave, Mukhaiyit by name, who was very severely
wounded at the famous battle of Jarrab,[2] and was still, and
probably for life, a hopeless cripple, unable to move owing
to his right leg being permanently doubled up. His cheery
disposition made amends for his sorry plight, and it was
pleasant to observe the sincere friendship and admiration
which he seemed to inspire in his visitors.

Later in this same week the ordeal of the distribution of
bounty to my recent companions took place. Tami, being
suddenly ordered to proceed to young Turki's camp on the
Shammar borderland, was the first to receive his allotment
and went away satisfied. And Ibn Jilham, having come at
my invitation to dine with me the night before he was to
start off for Aflaj and Sulaiyil with a party of 25 men under
'Abdulrahman Ibn Thunaian to collect Zakat on the Dawasir
flocks and herds, received the same sum. He accepted it
gratefully and suggested that an Aba would be a welcome
addition to the gift, but I replied that he would not have had
to ask for it if he had been more actively helpful to me in
connection with certain incidents of the journey. I added,
however, that, bearing him no ill-will on that score, I would
give him an Aba on his return from the South, and he went
forth destined to see me no more. The following day I
summoned Rushaid to help me in the preparation of a list
of awards to the rest of the party, and, the news of this having
got abroad, the whole party appeared in my room to save him
the trouble. At that moment, however, I was summoned

[1] H. of A. ii. 17.   [2] Idem, i. 384-6.

away for an interview with Ibn Sa'ud, and the actual distribution of presents took place the following morning. Mitrak,
having tried to deceive me over the alternative return route
from Haïr, and 'Ubaid,[1] who had left the Wadi without my
permission, had been warned that they would get nothing
and wisely stayed away to avoid the mortification of seeing
the rest rewarded. But Ibrahim, nothing daunted by the
knowledge that he was in like case, walked in while I was
paying the rest and sat down against the wall until the last
payment had been made and the recipients of my bounty
had vanished. ' Ma ili shin ?—nothing for me ? ' he then
asked. In reply I upbraided him, the leader of the party,
for his constant efforts to spoil my enjoyment of the expedition. The past was past, I admitted, but if I rewarded good
and bad service alike I should get nothing but bad service in
the future. And the future was my present concern. So
there would be nothing for him. He was probably genuinely
surprised and, rising from his place with a characteristic
series of grunts and groans, he shuffled out of the room
disconsolate and disappointed. Rushaid had previously
made a vigorous effort to deter me from my purpose lest
Ibrahim might complain to Ibn Sa'ud, but I was prepared to
take that risk though not the greater risk of being saddled
with him again on my next journey. As events proved, this
incident finally closed all accounts between Ibrahim and
myself. During the years that followed I was destined to see
him again from time to time and to appreciate his worth from
a more detached point of view than was possible during the
two great journeys I made under his guidance. We have
even with the passage of time been able to discuss and laugh
over the petty incidents of travel which divided us of old,
and it is with genuine satisfaction that, far removed from all
risk of ever travelling the desert again under his leadership,
I can record that we are now as ' friends once parted grown
single-hearted.' Since those days he has received promotion
to high office in his master's service and to-day he is Chamberlain in a king's court.

Rushaid Akhu Hasana practically stepped into Ibrahim's
shoes from this moment onwards, and it was on a visit to his

[1] *H. of A.* ii. 302.

house for coffee that I issued from the palace for the second
time during this period. I found him alone with his brother-
in-law, Muhaimid, in his tiny, stuffy parlour, where, as he
admitted without shame, he spent the whole of his time,
except for brief intervals of attendance at Ibn Sa'ud's
audiences, dallying with his wife. He declared himself to be
perfectly contented with his present lot, and added that he
had recently refused a personal invitation from Ibn Rashid
to return to Haïl, his original home. The household consisted
of his wife's mother and two sisters besides Muhaimid and
himself, and a somewhat extraordinary thing had occurred
a short time before our return to Riyadh. His wife had
suddenly been seized with an epileptic fit which had lasted
five days and during which she had remained speechless and
like the dead. Rumour also had it that she had approached
Ibn Sa'ud to arrange for her divorce on the ground of her
husband's inability to provide her with a child. In this case
rumour may have been malicious, taking advantage of the
man's childlessness to charge him with impotence. But
time brings its own revenge, and when I met Rushaid seven
or eight years later in the Hijaz, it was to hear that he was
the proud father of a son, already three or four years old, by
an Armenian woman whom Fate had brought down into
Arabia and into the fold of *Islam*. And that son,[1] in memory
of these days of which I write, had been named by my name !
Rushaid, for all his intrinsic worthlessness and gross material-
ism, had a sensitive side to his character and was even something of a poet by the modern Arabian standard, but his
chief merit lay in the fact that his retentive memory was a
veritable mine of modern poems. I was able to get from him
in writing a poem by the famous Hamud Ibn 'Ubaid of Haïl
and another by a ' slave ' called Mufadhdhi, but his elementary transcription of the words defeated the experts at
Cambridge, and I have always regretted that I did not
prosecute my studies of such literature on the spot with
greater vigour. But I regretted more than anything else my
failure to make a representative collection of the poetical
works of Tami, who is now no more.

My next outing was to the house of Muhammad Ibn

[1] The child died in 1926.

Shilhub, Ibn Sa'ud's Treasurer and Accountant-General. Whether acting under the orders [1] of Ibn Sa'ud or not, he came by arrangement to fetch me away for coffee, and I spent a pleasant hour in his parlour with some half a dozen other guests, all of whom seemed to be content to sit there in stolid silence and to leave the conversation to my host and myself, while tea and then coffee were served round and followed by the production of large dishes of sliced water-melons and delicious grapes. The proceedings closed with a round of incense, after which Shilhub and I returned to the palace together as he had to join Ibn Sa'ud for the evening prayer. By birth a native of Riyadh and by religion of course a *Wahhabi*, he was a man of great charm of manner, and was always on terms of friendliness and frankness with me. He seemed indeed to be entirely devoid of the cant and bigotry so common in the ordinary citizen of Riyadh, and his own or his wife's—I think he had two separate establishments at this time—taste were abundantly apparent in the almost luxurious furniture—*i.e.* rugs and cushions—of a really cosy parlour.

And so the month of *Ramdhan* dragged on slowly but surely to its weary end. On 7th July, equivalent to 28th *Ramdhan*, Ibn Sa'ud was talking generally of the severity of the fast and wondering whether the moon would appear on the following night. Having already carefully studied the Nautical Almanac and ascertained that the moon would be old enough to show under favourable conditions, I made bold to predict that the following evening would usher in the *'Id* in spite of the expectation of the local ' wise men ' that there would be a thirtieth day to this *Ramdhan*. And just before sunset the next evening there was a great concourse of people assembled on the housetops craning their necks in the direction of the jagged lip of Tuwaiq set off by a sunset of unusual splendour. Many of the crowd were women, who are credited with keener sight than men, and I had an uncanny feeling that my prediction of the probable appearance of the moon was known to many of the watchers who, in spite of the extra day's fast involved, would be almost glad to have the infidel's impudence confounded by a manifestation of divine arbitrariness.

[1] I had complained of the lack of social diversions.

And as luck would have it a band of wispy clouds lay over the moon's position throughout those critical moments. The sun went down in a blaze of yellow flame piercing the flimsy clouds and turning them slowly to a lovely tint of rose-colour, lying in thin bands across the sky which showed between them in transparent streaks of the clearest light blue. But as the darkness gathered about us it was clear that the moon was not to be seen that night, and disappointed figures crept down from their roofs to break the fast which was to be endured for yet another day. Yet their disappointment was as nothing compared to mine, for my ' books ' had failed me under a crucial test ; and it was with a feeling of weariness of mind rather than of body that I lay down to sleep that night on the palace roof. I was startled from my slumbers by a cannon-shot, which was followed by another and another —some six or seven shots in all—at intervals. It was 2 a.m., and below me in the mosque I could hear the droning intonations of the *Qiyam* prayers. Something out of the way had clearly happened, and if I had had any difficulty in guessing the nature of that occurrence, Salih, the lamplight, coming up to the roof to change the arc-lamp—which incidentally was alight throughout the night during these last ten days—lost no time in telling me the glad tidings. Some *Badawin* of Dakina had come in post-haste to report that they had seen the crescent of the new moon and had been sent to the chief *Shaikh*, 'Abdullah Ibn 'Abdul Wahhab, who had immediately assembled an ecclesiastical court consisting of himself and two *Qadhis* to take the evidence of the new arrivals. They had pronounced themselves entirely satisfied, and the gunshot, which had awakened me, was the first announcement to the people of Riyadh that the morrow would be celebrated as the *'Id*. The *Qiyam* prayer continued to the completion of the *Taslim* on which the congregation was at the moment engaged. And it is impossible to imagine the inward rejoicing of a whole people when they rose to their feet from the last syllable of the last word of the last verse of that last *Taslim*—the great fast over and done with for another year, and a year of unfettered enjoyment of the good things of life before them. *Allahu Akbar !* It would be difficult to imagine a more stupendous exhibition of worship and ritual than the keeping of the great fast of *Ramdhan* by the people of Riyadh.

The sun rose next day on a population decked out in its best garments in anticipation of a festive day to be begun with the customary service of thanksgiving. At a very early hour—about 5.30 a.m.—I was roused from my slumbers and warned to get down to my apartments before the crowd returned from its devotions to the palace. For a few moments I dallied on the roof gazing out over the city from the palace battlements. A haze of dust hung like a pall over the scene with a feeble sun struggling to pierce it. The city wore a look of utter desolation and desertion, broken only by the bleating of myriad goats, whose release to their pastures waited upon the return of the shepherds from the thanksgiving service and the banquet which would be served to them immediately afterwards in the palace. The whole male population of the city had gone forth to the special enclosure reserved for the '*Id* prayers outside the north-east gate. The service itself, begun at sunrise and including an address by Ibn Sa'ud, lasted about half an hour. The crowd then streamed back to the palace, where countless trays of rice and mutton awaited the guests in the great courtyard of the section of the palace in which were my apartments. As each man finished he rose from his place, licking his fingers, which, as he passed through the small courtyard in front of my window, he dipped into a great cauldron of water placed there for the purpose. And so, one after another in a never-ending stream, they passed on, drying their hands on their holiday garments or against the mud-walls of the courtyard, to the great audience-chamber, where Ibn Sa'ud sat in state to receive their homage.

Ibrahim al Junaifi celebrated the occasion by breakfasting with me to assist in the preparation of a list of presents, which custom required that I should distribute to the palace servants. The rest of the day, apart from a very brief interview with Ibn Sa'ud in the afternoon, I had to myself, well content with the fortnight of enforced idleness which had enabled me to get on terms with my work but hoping, nevertheless, that life would be more varied and amusing than it had been under the shadow of the fast. Apart from

the few visits I have recorded, I had divided my time in
almost equal portions between my apartments and the
' flagstaff ' roof, to which I ascended regularly with my books,
papers and writing material as soon as the sun was low enough
to give me the shade of the battlements, and from which I
descended with equal regularity each morning when the
same battlements failed to screen me from the risen sun.
During the day-time a standing dish of excellent melons and
grapes of fair quality was always at hand for my refreshment,
and my meals were of course served regularly from the palace
kitchen in spite of the fast. In fact the kitchen was scarcely
less active than in ordinary times, for there was always the
stranger within the gates, on whom the fast was not incumbent. The great water-melons of the neighbourhood
seemed to be the staple article of food during this season,
especially during the evenings, and, as they were said to cost
as much as one rupee each, the palace expenditure on this
item alone must have been prodigious. One evening, for
instance, as I was passing by on my way to the roof, I observed a group of about twenty slaves gathered round an
enormous tray of sliced melons eating with enormous gusto,
and, wherever one went in the evenings, there was always the
same dish to partake of after the usual tea and coffee. And
the melons of Riyadh, or rather of Masana' and Manfuha,
are famous in Arabia for their great size and delicious flavour.

The festivities of the 'Id on this occasion were unfortunately
marred—though after the event—by an untoward and
unusual incident. According to the Wahhabi tenets the great
and obligatory feast of Ramdhan may be followed up after
the celebration of the 'Id—on that day fasting is not per-
missible—by a secondary and purely voluntary fast of six
days from the 2nd to the 7th of Shawwal. And it is held that
those whose fortitude is equal to this extra penance are
practically assured of admission into Paradise in due course.
And the Ikhwan, leaving nothing to chance, had duly started
on this second bout of fasting when one of the chief divines
of Riyadh—Ibn Nimr by name and Ibn Sa'ud's chaplain-in-
ordinary during his travels—created something in the nature
of consternation in their ranks by upbraiding them for
fasting on a day which was in fact the 'Id. His wrath had

been roused by the omission of the chief *Shaikh* to summon him to the court which sat in judgment on the evidence of the Dakina *Badawin* already mentioned. And he had chosen this form of revenge which involved the imputation of a double sin to the innocent *Ikhwan*, who, if he was right, had not only erred by fasting on the *'Id* but had committed the unpardonable offence of feasting on the last day of *Ramdhan*. The accusation was too serious to be disregarded. Ibn Sa'ud himself was appealed to by the bewildered *Ikhwan* for the solution of their terrible dilemma and he disposed of the matter in characteristic fashion. Ibn Nimr was sent for to explain his attitude. He appeared unrepentant and adopted an attitude that was both impertinent and defiant. And he found himself without further ado inside the jail, where incidentally the Turkish officer, Qudsi [1] Effendi, captured on his way from the Yaman across the desert to Syria during the previous April, was apparently still eating out his heart in solitary confinement. A few hours of a similar experience were sufficient to persuade Ibn Nimr of the error of his ways, but his piteous screams for mercy found no path to the heart of Ibn Sa'ud. He was released a few days later a sadder and a wiser man, and his example served to warn the *'Ulama* of Arabia that the creation of distress in the minds of the public was not a legitimate weapon in the controversies arising out of their constant striving for precedence.

2. ALARUMS AND EXCURSIONS.

Apart from the physical sufferings induced by the fast, these days of *Ramdhan* were days of unease at the *Wahhabi* capital. A cloud, vague but ominous, hung over the ruler and his people. The fast, unwelcome enough in all conscience, provided a respite for the monarch from the active prosecution of an enterprise, fraught with danger and uncertainty, to which he was committed by his word and condemned by the circumstances in which he found himself. For all the fortitude and stoicism with which he submitted to the rigours of the penance required of him he was consumed by an agony

[1] *H. of A.* i. 354-5.

of mind which he could ill conceal at moments of extreme physical exhaustion. He was at the parting of the ways and, though he had declared the course which he intended to pursue, he could always draw back from it until he had actually started. Once started he could not turn back. Meanwhile he concentrated his attention on the fast and refused to discuss his plans for the future. Even so is the ostrich, the feathered king of the desert, said to bury his head in the friendly sand in the presence of danger. Conscious of his strength and speed he seeks to evade the notice of the foe until the choice between fight and flight is forced on him.

Ibn Sa'ud was indeed at a turning-point of his career. The straight road led to Hail, where the traditional enemy of his house still ruled unchallenged with the substantial support of the Turks. The elimination of Ibn Rashid would probably break for ever the balance of power which made the position of the *Wahhabi* state so precarious in Central Arabia. And on that road Ibn Sa'ud could expect some measure of material support from the British Government, which, though in principle averse to any disturbance of the existing balance of power in the desert, sought some means of diverting *Wahhabi* attention from grievances against King Husain of the Hijaz and others, who happened to be our allies. Any substantial success against Ibn Rashid would also generally tend to weaken the Turkish position in Arabia and along the Hijaz railway. Thus the stage was set for Ibn Sa'ud by circumstances, while the very fact of such a con- spiracy of circumstances to urge him along a particular road made him uneasy and suspicious. The traditional enemy was not the real enemy and in any case could be dealt with to-morrow if not to-day in the ordinary Arab way. The real danger lay in a brood of vipers which the British Government was nursing to its bosom. It might do that with impunity to itself, but its friends would suffer. And Ibn Sa'ud felt that a rival in the desert was a minor menace in comparison with rivals on the coasts of the great sea, secure for ever in their reliance on British protection. Of the manner in which he dealt with those rivals in due course this is not the occasion to write. If he had been a free agent he would have preferred to direct his march against the Hijaz borders or against

Kuwait, and, if he had acted on such an impulse, it is unlikely that he would ever have become more than the ruler of *Wahhabi* Arabia. Fate directed his steps into the straight road and, though he moved along it at first slowly and almost unwillingly, he was definitely embarked from that moment on a career of conquest with infinite possibilities which none but the boldest would at that time have dared to envisage.

Meanwhile there was much to be planned and discussed in connection with the forthcoming campaign, which had in a sense been opened tentatively before the beginning of *Ramdhan*, when Turki, the young heir [1] to the *Wahhabi* throne, had ridden forth with a considerable body of *Ikhwan* to harry the Shammar frontier. About this time Sa'ud Ibn Rashid, doubtless alarmed by rumours of Ibn Sa'ud's intentions and glad of a reasonable excuse to get away from the headquarters of his Turkish allies at Madaïn Salih, where his position as an honoured guest was apparently more irksome than it sounded, had returned to his capital. His confidential agent, Rushaid Ibn Laila, had simultaneously arrived at Damascus from Constantinople with a welcome consignment of artillery and ammunition, with which he was about to set forth to rejoin his master. And the general restlessness of the Shammar was reflected in persistent rumours that Ibn Rashid was about to approach the British authorities at Baghdad with proposals for peace. King Husain had pressingly requested that any pourparlers of such character should be referred to him for negotiation, but so far as Ibn Rashid was concerned such rumours were probably without any foundation. On the other hand, however, some of his chief lieutenants were certainly inclined to sue for terms with a view to the relaxation of the blockade, from which considerable hardship had resulted both at Haïl and in the surrounding tribal territory in spite of occasional cases of leakage. Among others 'Aqab Ibn 'Ajil, having returned with his master from the Turkish camp, proceeded almost at once to Lina, whence he sent his brother, Majid, to Fahad Ibn Hadhdhal's camp. There he met Colonel Leachman,

---

[1] He died during the influenza epidemic of December, 1918, leaving his brother Sa'ud as heir apparent.

and with him arranged to proceed to Baghdad to discuss the terms of an arrangement for trading facilities with Zubair. At the same time a messenger from Ibn Rimal, one of the 'Abda chiefs, arrived at Riyadh, where in my presence he stated that, while Ibn Rashid was not privy to the matter, his master's [1] desire was to open up negotiations for peace. This statement was confirmed by the carefully worded contents of Ibn Rimal's letter, to which Ibn Sa'ud replied that, so long as Ibn Rashid maintained his alliance with the Turks, he had no alternative but to harass him to the utmost of his capacity. Should he, however, be desirous of peace and friendship, he had but to come forward and say so either to himself or to the British authorities. On the whole it is probable that these peace-feelers on the part of various Shammar chieftains were occasioned less by any genuine desire for peace than by the wish to secure supplies to pass on to Damascus and other places where very considerable profits were to be made at this time. Ibn Rimal's messenger, indeed, reported one important case of the evasion of the Euphrates blockade, the culprit being Dhari Ibn Tawala, who had been posted by me at Hafar to prevent smuggling into Shammar territory, but had moved down to Safwan and was doing a profitable business as a self-constituted clearing-house for goods destined for the enemy. On the occasion reported by the messenger a caravan of 500 camels had arrived at Ibn Rimal's camp near Hail laden with food and piece-goods received from the Zubair market on the recommendation of Dhari.

Such was the position at the inception of Turki's campaign which began with a concentration of six standards, perhaps 4000 strong,[2] at the wells of 'Ajba. Very early in the proceedings Faisal al Duwish, the redoubtable *Ikhwan* leader from 'Artawiya and Turki's chief of staff, had sent in a despatch to Ibn Sa'ud begging him to caution Turki against scattering his forces over too wide an area, and it was with instructions in this sense that Tami had been sent off in haste soon after our return from the Wadi. The danger was that Ibn Rashid

[1] *i.e.* Ibn Rimal.

[2] The *Bairaq* is nominally equivalent to 1000 men, but the strength of these units varies greatly.

might develop a counter-offensive or seize the opportunity
to raid the Qasim, while Turki was engaged in operations
against the scattered tribes in the desert, who had moved
across the Dahna from 'Ajba on receipt of news of the approach of the *Ikhwan*. Turki had followed them in the direction of the road from Haïl to Lina and, arriving at the
watering of Bashuk, found the place deserted and the wells
insufficient for the needs of his force. He was personally
for going on to the wells of Umm al Radhma,[1] a day's march
to the north-east, but Ibn Musaiyis, chief of the Mutair
contingent, had warned him that neither there nor at
Hidaqa to the eastward would he find sufficient water and,
after a heated argument, had prevailed on him to retire to
'Ajba. And there the brief campaign came to a premature
and inglorious end, for, whether acting on orders received
from Ibn Sa'ud or actuated by pique at his failure to find
the enemy, the young commander, accompanied by all his
regular citizen troops and the *Ikhwan* contingents from
Dahina and Furaithan, marched for Buraida, leaving the
Ghatghat and 'Artawiya contingents to follow with the
baggage. The offensive thus degenerated into a defensive
concentration in the Qasim, and the opening of the real
campaign was indefinitely postponed.

Meanwhile untoward developments on the Hijaz frontier
began to occasion fears of a widespread conflagration. Ibn
Sa'ud had replied evasively to an appeal for assistance from
Khalid Ibn Luwai, *Amir* of Khurma, who anticipated an
attack by the Sharifian forces. Not only had he counselled
him to be cautious in his actions, but he had himself taken
the precaution of diverting the whole of the Ghatghat
contingent of 'Ataiba *Ikhwan*, which had actually started off
in support of Khalid, to Turki's concentration. The Khurma
Wahhabis were thus isolated, and some ten days before the
beginning of *Ramdhan* their camp in Wadi Subai' was attacked
suddenly and without warning by a *Sharifian* force under
Sharif Hamza, which had come up unobserved and announced
their arrival with a salvo of artillery fire. Recovering from

---

[1] I have left the particulars as regards these places as they were given
me. Details, apparently more exact, will be found in the Basra, 1927,
sheet of the International Million Map—*vide* vi. and vii. by g and h.

their surprise the Subai' rose and fell upon the enemy, putting
them to flight with the loss of 28 men killed, one gun and two
machine-guns, while their own losses amounted to five men
killed.   Khalid's letter announcing this first actual clash
between the opposing elements, who had been vaguely
manœuvring for position since the previous December, left
us in no doubt of the seriousness of the situation.   There was
every danger that the *Ikhwan*, flushed with an initial victory,
might collect reinforcements and assume the offensive, in
which case the whole border from Tathlith northwards would
soon be aflame.   On the other hand it was not unlikely that
the Sharif, smarting under the ignominy of such a defeat,
would try to avenge it with larger forces, in which case Ibn
Sa'ud could scarcely hope to prevent all the *Ikhwan* elements
of Najd from flocking to the assistance of their brethren in
the faith.   There was nothing to do but to represent the
seriousness of the situation to the authorities at Baghdad
and to arrange with Ibn Sa'ud to restrain his subjects from
any forward action until the result of my representations
should be known.

For the moment the crisis was tided over in this way, but
it would take a fortnight for my message to reach Baghdad
and another fortnight for a reply to reach me, to say nothing
of the time to be spent in telegraphic communication between
Baghdad, Cairo and Mecca.   Meanwhile we had to possess
ourselves in patience, knowing that at any moment news
might come in of the renewal of the conflict.   And on the last
day of *Ramdhan* the dead stillness of the summer afternoon
was broken suddenly by the ominous bark of rifle-fire
announcing the arrival of messengers with good tidings after
the manner of Arabia.   And as the sounds came nearer I
observed a party of mounted men riding jauntily up to the
palace gate, where they dismounted and entered without
further ado, going straight to the presence of their monarch.
Thinking that the messengers must be from Turki, I dismissed
the matter from my mind and was a little nonplussed at the
manner of Ibn Sa'ud's greeting when I went to see him an
hour or two later.   ' It's no good,' said he, apparently
assuming that I had read his thoughts.   A Sharifian force,
said to have numbered three standards, under Sharif Zaid Ibn

Fawwaz, had attacked Khurma during the night about the
middle of *Ramdhan*, and a tremendous struggle had ensued,
in which both sides suffered severe casualties and the *Ikhwan*
gained a victory with two guns and two machine-guns to
grace it. The son of Zaid, the Sharifian commander, was
among the slain. Such was the ' *Bishara* ' [1] which signalised
the closing hours of the Great Fast. The fact that news of
a clash between the *Ikhwan* and the forces of the Hijaz was
treated as good news was in itself significant, and, when I
commented on this aspect of the matter to Ibn Sa'ud, he
replied quite simply and straightforwardly that news of an
Ikhwan victory at the expense of the Sharif was better than
news of a defeat. He was in fact in high good humour, and
discoursed at some length on the initial mistake the British
Government had made in negotiating with the Sharif.
' Some day,' he said, ' you will bitterly regret your mistaken
policy. I have no desire to interfere in the affairs of the
Hijaz, but you should know I have but to give the word and
a great host would flock to my banner from all parts—from
Bisha and Najran, from Ranya and Tathlith and elsewhere.
And not one of them but is convinced that death is better
than life, not one but lives to die for the great reward, and
every one of them convinced that to turn back or hesitate
is but to court the certainty of hell-fire.' The news had in
point of fact come not from Khurma itself but from one of
Ibn Sa'ud's officials, who was engaged in collecting taxes
from the 'Ataiba and Qahtan in the neighbourhood and had
fallen in with a refugee *'Atabi* from the Sharifian force. I
could only point out that this second attack had taken place
before the Sharif could have had time to receive any communication from the British authorities. I still counselled
patience, and I felt that the knowledge that the Khurma folk
could at need hold their own with such forces as the Sharif
might send against them went far to reconcile him to the
necessity of patience. He fully realised that an outburst of
hostilities between himself and his rival would be fatal to the
interests of all concerned, though there was little doubt that
Husain desired to provoke him to an open breach of the peace
in order to force the hand of Great Britain. ' If it were not,'

[1] ' Good news.'

he said to me one day, ' that an open breach between myself
and the Sharif would be a source of rejoicing to the Turks,
verily there is none I hate so much. And, as for 'Abdullah,
he is *khasis*—a poisonous fellow.' As circumstances were yet
to prove, his *obiter dicta* were never very wide of the mark.

During the afternoon of the day following the *'Id*, Ibrahim
al Junaifi came by arrangement to fetch me away to a picnic
in the Hauta garden, where I found Ibn Sa'ud and his party
squatting at ease on the rich grass in an orchard of peach-
trees. It was the first time I had issued out of the city walls
since my return from the South and my first experience of
Riyadh society returned to its normal ways after the fast.
The group consisted of Faisal Ibn Rashid, Ahmad Ibn
Thunaian, Ibn Sa'ud's brother 'Abdullah, the little princes
Muhaimid and Khalid, Faisal Ibn Hashr the *Qahtani* chief
and his little son, and some others. We sat and talked a while
round a large bowl of delicious grapes from the neighbouring
vine and then moved on to another garden, a somewhat
wretched grove called Qumaih, to inspect the royal herd of
milch-camels gathered in the courtyard of a ruined *Qasr*,
which had been built by the great Turki and subsequently
destroyed by Ibn Rashid.

Faisal Ibn Hashr, a warrior of note and a redoubtable
Wahhabi, who stood second in the councils of his master only
to the formidable Duwish, had often been present at my
interviews with Ibn Sa'ud during *Ramdhan* and had struck
me as a man endowed with no ordinary share of common-
sense, who allowed the facts of politics to temper the ideals
of religion. Be that as it may, it was generally in his company
that Ibn Sa'ud discoursed freely on various aspects of his
policy and administration, which were not easily intelligible
to the limited intelligence of the majority of his followers and
of such firebrands as Duwish. He had accompanied his
master, on whom he seemed to be in permanent attendance
—presumably because he could not safely be left to reside
and rule in his own tribal surroundings—to Basra in 1916 ;
and, when I ventured to twit him on his having visited such
a sink of moral iniquity, Ibn Sa'ud hastened to explain that
most of their time had been spent in close contact with their
English hosts and that they had seen but little of the local

Muslims. He then seized the opportunity of launching out into one of his favourite themes—the comparative merits of Christians and non-*Wahhabi Muslims*, lumped together in the category of *Mushrikin.* ' Why ! ' he said, ' if you English were to offer me of your daughters to wife I would accept her, making only the condition that any children resulting from the marriage should be *Muslims.* But I would not take of the daughters of the Sharif or of the people of Mecca or other *Muslims*, whom we reckon as *Mushrikin.* I would eat of meat slain by the Christians without question. Ay, but it is the *Mushrik,* he who associates others in worship with God, that is our abomination. As for Christians and Jews,' here he quoted a text from the *Quran,* ' they are " people of a book," though,' and here somewhat naïvely he permitted himself a delightful dash of inconsistency, ' I like not the Jews—they are contemptible by reason of their too great love of money.' Sincere as he was in his own religion, Ibn Sa'ud was fully convinced of the practical advantages of a British alliance, and it seemed to me in these days that anything like a cordial reaction on our part would result surely and steadily in the establishment of the toleration of Christians as a basic factor of the *Wahhabi* creed. In any case at this time such a confession of his own attitude in the presence of one of the outstanding leaders of the *Ikhwan* cause ·was not without significance.

On another occasion Ibn Sa'ud, who was feeling somewhat unwell as the result of a bilious attack which he proposed to treat with an emetic, was, when I arrived, engaged in discussing with Ibn Hashr the terms of settlement of a recent affray between the Murra and the Bani Hajir—the latter being akin to the Qahtan, as also are the Shammar. As I entered I found the *Wahhabi* monarch declaiming a chapter of the *Quran,* which he continued to the end—in a semi-musical chant lapsing occasionally into ordinary tones—after which he closed and reverently kissed the book before handing it with its cover of red cloth to Junaifi to put away. The chapter in question—whether he had selected it for Faisal's edification or not it would be difficult to say—was on the subject of Christians, and Ibn Sa'ud, by way of commentary and turning to me, remarked that he unlike Faisal was of the

stock of Isma'il—' cousins to you, for you are of the stock of
Ishaq.' The Turks, he said, were *Aulad Iblis*, being Tatars
by origin. And so we fell into a discussion of his administrative methods, that mixture of uncompromising severity and
unreasoning generosity which experience has shown to be the
ideal system in a *Badawin* country. During these days of
Turki's operations on the Shammar border Faisal was a tower
of strength to his master, sifting reports, official and unofficial,
from the front and advising on the proper course to pursue
and helping to dispel the impression which often gained
ground in ecclesiastical circles that Ibn Sa'ud's dalliance with
Great Britain was deflecting him from the straight path of
their cause. On one occasion, soon after the *'Id*, a visit
to the chief *Shaikh* and other *'Ulama* had given rise to a
discussion of the progress of the war and Ibn Sa'ud had announced the news of the Austrian defeat on the Piave, whereupon Sulaiman, the poet-priest of Riyadh, had uttered a
prayer that the news should prove true. Ibn Sa'ud had also
told them the story I had told him shortly before of the
Kaiser's claim to be a prophet of God—to which they had
fervently replied : ' May God cut him off ! ' ' As for the
English,' the ecclesiastics admitted, ' you may rely on their
word and they do not concern themselves with the beliefs of
others.' Thus in every way within his power Ibn Sa'ud, in
preparation for his coming campaign, was laying the foundations of a general acceptance of his basic policy of an alliance
with Britain. The picnic ended with prayers at sunset,
before which I discreetly withdrew to the Khizam garden,
where I amused myself watching a fox prowling about in the
lucerne beds outside the wall until it was time to return home.
And the following afternoon, after a barren discussion in the
morning with Ahmad Ibn Thunaian regarding the desirability
of setting up a council of representatives of the various
independent states of Arabia to consider and dispose of all
matters in dispute between any of them—the president
would be British, and Ahmad assumed as axiomatic that all
disputes would be decided in Ibn Sa'ud's favour—we foregathered again for a picnic in the Budai'a garden belonging
to the Imam 'Abdul Rahman. This was reputed to be one
of the best gardens in the whole oasis, though this year it had

a somewhat parched appearance and its date clusters were thin. The peach-trees, however, were loaded with fruit just ripening and the vine-trellis, covering an enormous area, was a lovely sight with its great stalactites of grapes hanging down in the deep shade of its tangled leaves. We sat in the shade of a large *Sidr* tree by the babbling stream of an irrigation runnel, eating fruit and discoursing unreservedly. The penance of *Ramdhan* had somewhat impaired the vigour of Ibn Sa'ud and Ahmad half-jokingly suggested that he should send down to Kuwait to bring up a supply of ' strengthening ' medicines. I expressed surprise at there being neither a sufficient supply of drugs nor a really competent doctor at the capital and volunteered to procure the latter if desired. ' Certainly,' said Ibn Sa'ud, ' I should like to have a good doctor—if possible a *Muslim*, though I would not object to an Englishman if a first-rate *Muslim* doctor were not procurable. It is a matter which I will discuss with you another time.' Unfortunately, as it proved, the subject was never renewed between us and the epidemic of Spanish ' Flu ' which invaded Central Arabia in the winter of that year found the royal family and the people in general defenceless. Dr. Harrison of the American Mission at Bahrain was hurriedly sent for, but arrived too late to save some of the chief victims of the fell disease.

At 5 p.m. on the following day—12th July—I was informed that Ibn Sa'ud had ridden out and that a pony was ready for me if I cared to follow him. So I mounted—it was a very uncomfortable saddle with stirrups depending from regular hawsers of very rough rope—and rode out by the north-east gate past the '*Id* prayer enclosure, in which I counted some twenty-five lines marked out by the feet of the worshippers, and past the *Badawin* tents in the Batha to the garden called 'Aud, by which we had waited on our first arrival at Riyadh until the signal was given for our entry into the city. The space to the east of the garden was full of *Badawin* tents, in one of the biggest of which—cleared for the occasion—Ibn Sa'ud was seated amid a large gathering. The little children of his brother Sa'd were there, and Fahad, when I greeted him, came forward a little timidly and put up his face for a kiss, which I duly gave him. Young Muhaimid was there also and

Ibrahim al Jumai'a, with whom of course I was not yet on speaking terms. In the midst of it arrived a courier from Bahrain, and they insisted on my reading out the contents of a batch of Reuter telegrams which I received. The Italian victory on the Piave was confirmed with some modification of its original completeness, and my audience was amused at the report that the Germans had taken to eating cats and dogs owing to their serious food situation. On one item contained in my mail-bag, an item more than ordinarily welcome, I was discreetly silent—a consignment of tobacco and cigars from the thoughtful British Political Agent at Bahrain.

That evening Ibn Sa'ud paid me a visit on my section of the palace roof and remained for more than two hours discussing the situation with which he was confronted. Since the 'Id, he said, he had been feeling far from well, not on account of any ailment but because of anxiety alone. He was beginning to be uneasy in his mind about ourselves and felt that our attitude towards him was no longer as cordial as it had been in the early days of my mission. And this change he attributed to a possible lessening of our own confidence in him. There was, he said, no unit in existence, Christian or *Muslim*, which had better reasons to hate the Turks than he. It was not only on religious grounds that he hated them, but because they consistently returned evil for good. In 1904, when they sent regular troops to assist Ibn Rashid against him, he had defeated them at Bukairiya but allowed them to depart unscathed to Basra and Madina. And again when he captured the Hasa in 1914 he had allowed the Turkish troops to depart with their arms. The capture of the Hasa had itself been forced upon him in self-defence, for the Turks had used their position there to squeeze him with economic weapons and he feared their return to those parts both because he was anxious for the future of his religion and because they would inevitably set themselves again to undermine the lives and livelihood of himself and his people. And, over and above all this, though he naturally followed the developments of the European war with the closest attention and was anxious about its outcome, he never doubted for a moment that the Gulf and 'Iraq would remain in British hands. He therefore had an obvious motive on purely selfish grounds for seeking to be on more than friendly terms with us.

I assured him that his loyalty had never been in question so far as we were concerned, but begged him to realise that his enemies never tired of pointing to his lack of achievement and of urging his incapacity either to control the smugglers in his territory or to gain any striking military success. Before my departure for the South I had mentioned to him an incident arising out of the blockade trouble at Kuwait during April. Two 'Aqailis, Qasim Ibn Rawwaf and Muhammad Ibn Dakhil, who had an interest in certain goods detained by the blockade officer, were alleged to have come down from Syria and to be at Zilfi or in its neighbourhood with the express intention of smuggling the goods through to the enemy. Ibn Sa'ud declared that he neither knew the persons in question nor had any news of their alleged movements, but promised to make enquiries. On my return he had informed me that both men were in Riyadh, and next day he had sent Ahmad Ibn Thunaian to me with a monster petition from the people of the Qasim declaring that the detained goods were the property of orphans and entirely innocent people. I had then declined to intervene on the ground that by so doing I would only be doing a disservice to Ibn Sa'ud, as the story was clearly too flimsy to be taken at face value. Ibn Sa'ud said he would not press the matter in deference to my representations, but suggested that we should interview the culprits together. This we duly did the following morning, and their case, as stated by themselves, was : firstly, that they were in Baghdad at the time of its occupation by the British ; secondly, that they had then proceeded to Basra with official British passes ; thirdly, that at Kuwait they had seen Shaikh Salim, who had advised them not to put their own names to the application for blockade passes—advice which they had taken unsuspectingly, while attaching themselves to the *Amir* of Zilfi's party ; and fourthly, that they were actually in Kuwait when the goods were detained but had been ordered by Shaikh Salim, when they appealed to him, to leave the town with the rest of the Najd people. I suggested that they had acted stupidly in having dealings with Shaikh Salim instead of going straight to the British blockade authorities, and now proposed that they should return to Kuwait under safe conduct from me to state their case. If their story was true their goods or the value thereof would be returned to them. And to this course they agreed, thus terminating an episode arising solely out of the machinations of Shaikh Salim, whose all-absorbing object was simply to bring discredit on Ibn Sa'ud.

In general he assured me that I was fully justified in the view I had represented that since the beginning of the year the Qasim blockade had been completely effective except for a single incident for which he was full of regret and in connection with which he was taking vigorous measures to lay the culprits by the heels to make an example of them by the simple process of execution. A party of *Badawin* had announced their intention of going to the Hijaz and had bought up seven camel-loads of piece-goods in the Qasim. Starting off on the Madina track they had turned off *via* Hayit and Huwaiyit into Ibn Rashid's country, since when nothing more had been heard of them. Ibn Sa'ud had now given orders in consequence of this incident that none should go from Najd to the Hijaz.

Our long interview on this occasion ended with a repetition of his assurances that he would attack Ibn Rashid in the near future, and I was able to point out to him that as I had, on my own responsibility and in full reliance on his word, placed certain funds at his disposal, he could scarcely expect any further favours or concessions until he had justified my confidence up to the hilt. Experience, I said, had made us a little sceptical of Arab undertakings, but we would not fail him if he proved that our scepticism in his case was without justification.

The following afternoon, when summoned by Junaifi to the presence, I found Ibn Sa'ud inveighing somewhat testily against a tendency, which apparently showed itself now and again in *Ikhwan* circles, of people not well versed in *Wahhabi* lore to give public vent to their own interpretations of the scriptures. He would have none of that sort of thing, he declared, to spoil the morals of his people, at whose disposal was ample opportunity of imbibing the truth from accredited teachers. What the occasion of this outburst was I never learned, but it ended with some disparaging talk about the Jews, who, he declared, were banned for ever by the Almighty from the privilege of forming a nation. By the tenets of *Wahhabism* all other sects of *Islam* were reckoned among the backsliders and toleration was extended to the Christians.

Later in the afternoon Junaifi and I joined the royal party at the Khizam garden. To my surprise and great pleasure the party included Muhammad Ibn Fahhad [1] of Saih, who had entertained me so charmingly during my visit to the Aflaj, and who had now come up on a visit to the capital. Ibn Sa'ud, who was in humorous vein, bantered him lightly about his cousins, the Sharifian family, as we sat as usual round a large bowl of grapes. The ruins among which we sat provoked some remark from me about the ubiquity of such sights in Arabia, whereupon Ibn Sa'ud, pointing to Faisal Ibn Rashid, said : ' He and his folk are responsible for all this damage—May God ruin the house of Rashid as they have ruined our homes ! ' As it drew near to sunset he called for the *Ward*, a selection of *Quranic* or *Traditional* readings usually read before the evening prayer, and I took my leave accompanied by Junaifi and 'Atallah. As we returned homewards *via* the Shamsiya garden we fell in with two Syrians—Sabri Effendi of Damascus and Musa Fir'un of Jerusalem—who had come down into Najd two years previously to buy camels for the Turks and had been arrested by Ibn Sa'ud at the request of the British authorities and detained ever since in open custody—free to roam about but not to leave Riyadh. Another of the party, a squat-built man with a game leg—Muhammad Taufiq Fir'un—had taken to dabbling in the tenets of the *Ikhwan*, and a fourth, 'Abdullah Sum'an, had definitely embraced the *Wahhabi* faith and become a *Mutawwa'*, spending all his time in the company of the Riyadh *'Ulama*. These two I did not see at all, but Sabri and Musa proved to be excellent company during the half-hour we spent together strolling quietly homeward. They seemed to be quite resigned to their enforced sojourn and inactivity at Riyadh and more or less content with their lot. Sabri was a large-limbed man of

---

[1] *H.A.* ii. 96-99.

extraordinarily fair complexion—obviously a Turk by origin
—while his companion was small, slim and dark, much interested by my account of the state of Jerusalem, where his
home was in the German Quarter, at my recent visit.

Entering the town we met the sleek Sultan Ibn Hasan of
Kuwait issuing from the door of his residence in the main
street. He failed to recognise me at first and afterwards
apologised profusely, saying : ' I thought you were some
Baduwi.' For in fact he had only seen me before this at
night on my roof, when I had discarded my head-dress. He
told me he was to start this same night for Buraida to prepare
the way for the pilgrims due to arrive shortly in the Qasim
from the coast. The idea of such a pilgrimage by land across
Arabia had originated with the British authorities in 'Iraq,
who were equally anxious that an 'Iraqi contingent should
go forth to do homage to the new *régime* in the Hijaz and that
it should not make any demand on our already fully occupied
shipping resources. A certain 'Abdul 'Aziz Ibn Hasan, father
of Sultan and formerly *Amir* of the overland *Hajj*, had applied
for an appointment in a similar capacity on this occasion,
and all that remained to do was to make the necessary
arrangements with Ibn Sa'ud. The idea was essentially
sound in the circumstances and Ibn Sa'ud, raising no objection in principle, only demurred mildly to the adoption of the
Kuwait route, on which, in view of the turbulent and unsatisfactory state of the 'Ajman and the so-called ' friendly '
Shammar elements, he could only accept full responsibility
from the Dahna westwards. He pressed for a diversion of
the intending pilgrims to the Bahrain-Riyadh route, in
respect of which he would willingly accept the fullest responsibility both for their safety and for all transport and other
arrangements. I informed the Baghdad authorities accordingly, adding my own opinion that, if the Kuwait route was
found to be definitely more convenient, Ibn Sa'ud's fullest
co-operation could confidently be relied upon. It was in
the early stages of the correspondence on this subject that
I had first met Sultan, who announced his intention of
settling down permanently in his old home at Buraida owing
to Shaikh Salim's intransigeant attitude towards all persons
of *Najdi* origin, and who always made a point of calling on

me after sunset when the rest of the world was securely at prayer. On the second occasion he brought me a small parcel of native tobacco, which was an acceptable reinforcement of my depleted stock, and earnest protestations of his desire that our acquaintance thus begun should ripen into eternal friendship. I always felt that his oft-proclaimed desire to be of service to me foreshadowed somehow or other a service which he desired of me, but our acquaintance ebbed and flowed through the months that followed without the slightest hint of what that service might be, and I certainly left Arabia without any consciousness of having in any way furthered his interests.

At my interview with Ibn Sa'ud the following day I found him issuing orders for the counting of the rounds of ammunition brought back by a *Badawin* party to which it had been served out for some purpose. For every missing round a fine of one *Riyal* was to be imposed unless it could be satisfactorily accounted for—this being his only check on the theft or undue waste of ammunition by those to whom it was issued, for excessive game-hunting and all *feux-de-joie* were strictly discountenanced in the *Wahhabi* state. During *Ramdhan* Ibn Sa'ud had received information from Ibn 'Askar, *Amir* of Sudair, that a party of Harb *Badawin* had arrived in his jurisdiction from the Hijaz with a caravan of twenty camels carrying 12,000 rounds of British small-arms ammunition, which they had received from the Sharif presumably for use in operations against the Hijaz railway. These *Badawin* were making for Kuwait to sell their spoil, but, in accordance with Ibn Sa'ud's instructions that no ammunition should be allowed to pass out of his territories, Ibn 'Askar had bought up the whole consignment. The Kuwait market was presumably the source from which the Persian tribesmen of the opposite coast drew their supplies. It was known at Baghdad that such supplies were reaching them, though it had generally been supposed that they came mainly from 'Iraq itself, where much ammunition had been abandoned on various battlefields to fall into the possession of the tribesmen. It was only gradually that we began to realise that a goodly portion of the ammunition supplied by us to the Sharif found its way into the same insatiable and often hostile market.

Indeed Ibn Sa'ud had in the manner here described purchased five such consignments of ammunition up to this time
—some 206,000 rounds in all—to replace a good deal of old
and perished (Turkish) ammunition which he had received
as a gift from us.

As I have already indicated in connection with the arrangements for the proposed pilgrimage across Ibn Sa'ud's territories, the Eastern Desert between Kuwait and the Dahna
was in a state of parlous insecurity. Dhari Ibn Tawala, who
had been withdrawn from my jurisdiction and allowed to
sojourn at Safwan under the shadow of 'Iraq, was making
substantial profits by facilitating the smuggling of goods to
the enemy. In one case he had allowed 500 camel-loads to
slip through to Ibn Rimal, and his absence from Hafar al
Batin, where I had posted him, had resulted in the 'Abda
being able to escape from the menace of Turki's concentration.
But the main responsibility for the general unrest in these
parts lay with Shaikh Salim, who lost no opportunity of
pin-pricking Ibn Sa'ud and, almost certainly, had an understanding on the subject with the Sharif. During the month of
Sha'ban an affray had occurred between the 'Alwa and
Buraih sections of the Mutair over a dispute about watering-
rights, and six of the former had been killed while the latter
had lost a number of camels. Salim represented to the
British Political Agent that certain chiefs of the Buraih, who
under the desert law would have to pay compensation for the
blood spilled in this affair, had come in offering to place their
section under his protection and to pay the *Zakat* taxes.
Salim, referring to an old arrangement dating from the time
of Mubarak, under which the Mutair were made liable to
Kuwait taxation when sojourning in that territory, enquired
innocently whether there was any objection to his acceding
to their request. Captain Loch, the Political Agent, scented
trouble and advised against such a course. And in due course
the matter came to me at Riyadh, where Ibn Sa'ud was
easily able to dispose of it once and for all. Two of the three
Buraih chiefs concerned—Tami al Quraifa and Mutlaq Ibn
Muhailib—were actually at Riyadh at this time in connection
with the settlement of the case under the normal desert
procedure, and were sent to me by Ibn Sa'ud to be cross-

examined. Speaking for themselves and the third *Shaikh*, Mishallah al Muraikhi, they categorically denied ever having applied to Salim, who, they added, was anxious to get them under his control both on financial and political grounds. Thus was another instance of Salim's clumsy diplomacy exposed, but it seemed that he was absolutely incorrigible, so strongly was he obsessed with the idea of doing harm to one who never deigned to consider him in the light of a rival and only complained of the exaggerated importance attached to him by the British authorities—presumably for ulterior motives, the real character of which would only manifest itself in post-war developments.

Salim was for the most part powerless to harm his greater neighbour, but he was by no means powerless to annoy him, for he had only to give asylum to raiding-parties launched by the Shammar or 'Ajman against caravans proceeding in the course of legitimate business to Najd and to procure the evasion of the Kuwait blockade cordon by less legitimate caravans, which he could represent as being franked through to the enemy by the *Wahhabi* authorities. Thus on one occasion, late in *Ramdhan* or early in the following month, Ibn Sa'ud had sent down a trusted retainer, 'Abdul 'Aziz Ibn Ruba'i, to conduct a large caravan from Kuwait to the Qasim and to see that no leakage of goods occurred. This caravan was raided by a party of the Aslam in Kuwait territory and lost some fifty loaded camels, while the same section had about the same time gathered a considerable haul of camels from the neighbourhood of 'Artawiya. In all it was said that some 200 camels had fallen into Aslam hands during these days, and it was alleged that they were all at Safwan loading up goods for the enemy under the sanction of Dhari Ibn Tawala, the protégé of a government which was straining every nerve to close all extraneous avenues of supply to the Turks. It seemed impossible, and it remained so till the end of the war, to scotch the machinations of some of our friends whose primary object was to enrich themselves by a very profitable trade and to throw the discredit of their operations on Ibn Sa'ud.

The picnic-life of Riyadh during the month following the great fast was a constant delight, and I saw it at its

best on 15th July when Ibn Sa'ud decided on an all-day
outing to the Batin palm-groves. He and his party had
ridden out in the early hours of the morning, but it was
not till about 8 a.m. that I mounted, in company with
Junaifi and Manawar, to follow them. I had taken the precaution of having my own saddle placed on the back of the
pony provided for me—a stallion of easy paces but otherwise
of no great merit—but contented myself with the native
bridling. This consists of a flimsy but tightly-fitting curb
attached to a very short rein which is normally touched only
to pull one's steed out of a gallop. The snaffle is a chain
nose-band attached to a rough halter and in most cases
seemed to be all that was needed.

We left the city by the Muraiqib gate, proceeding thence
through palm-groves and the ruins of the old city, built
by Dahham Ibn Da'as in the days of the rivalry between
Riyadh and Dar'iya. Thence cantering or picking our way
over the bare plain we entered the Batin channel and followed
it up to Ibn Sa'ud's own gardens, in one of which we found
the *Wahhabi* monarch having somewhat the worst of a
shooting-match—five shots each at a target about a hundred
yards distant—with one of the *Zigirt*. For a while thereafter
we sat imbibing coffee and incense in a mud-built bower.
We then moved off to an inner walled garden with a great
profusion of peach-trees, fig-trees, pomegranate-bushes and
vines, where, under the shade of a spreading fig-tree and a
thatched shelter, we lay on rugs by a runnel of sparkling
well-water, chatting and playing with the royal children—a
charming company consisting of Ibn Sa'ud's sons Muhammad
and Khalid; his brother Muhammad's sons, Khalid, about
eleven years old, and Sa'd, a charming child, amazingly
self-composed though badly disfigured by some disease of
the eye; Hamud, the eight-year-old son of Faisal Ibn
Rashid; and Faisal, Fahad and Sa'ud, the orphan children
of the hapless Sa'd. They played as any children might,
messing with the mud of the little runnel and flitting elf-like
about Ibn Sa'ud, who with his hand-fan flicked water at
them till they would rush off to other mischief and return
anon with a rich booty of unripe peaches.

Ibn Sa'ud and his party had already breakfasted before

To face page 34.

THE SOUTH WALL OF RIYÀDH.

our arrival. So Junaifi and I sat apart to a meal of dates and fresh butter, grapes and skim milk, after which we rejoined the party to share with them the contents of a huge tray of grapes and figs. The children then withdrew, and, after a while, leaving Junaifi and me where we were, Ibn Sa'ud retired for a siesta in the mud-bower where we had first found him. Having brought no tobacco I composed myself to sleep under the grateful shade, to be awakened by the movements of my companion as he roused himself for the midday prayer. I too rose and washed in the fresh runnel and wandered off in search of fruit, not however before the well-meaning and officious gardener had cleared and drawn my attention to a pleasant spot to pray in—' it is clean,' he said. Realising that he had no suspicion of the case in which I was, I cluded his kindly insistence and slipped off to a remote corner of the garden, where I was rewarded by finding a number of peaches ripening under the warm sun. Of these and grapes from the splendid trellises and a ripe pomegranate I made a substantial meal until it was time to rejoin Ibn Sa'ud, who after his midday rest had moved on to his other garden about a quarter mile up the channel. We found him and his party seated under a large fig-tree by a runnel issuing from a ten-fathom well, at which no fewer than ten camels were working simultaneously. The well in the other garden was worked by the great white asses of the Hasa, though it was Ibn Sa'ud's intention in due course to eliminate them in favour of camels.

Rushaid presided at the coffee-hearth and Ibrahim flitted about obsequiously, now coming forward to wave a cloth before his master to keep off non-existent flies as he sipped his coffee, now relieving him of an empty cup and retiring into the background. Some poet, long since come from Haïl —I did not discover his name—recited a poem or two for our delectation. Muhammad Ibn Fahhad led the conversation into irrigational channels in connection with the great possibilities of his own Aflaj district and Kharj. The advantages and feasibility of using machinery for the pumping of water from those natural reservoirs was ever present in the minds of Ibn Sa'ud and his father. Then the conversation turned into other channels—the war, the British and other constitutions and so forth, Sa'ud Ibn 'Abdul 'Aziz Ibn Sa'ud being particularly prominent. And so on until it was time for the afternoon prayer, when I disappeared for a solitary stroll in the garden. Immediately after prayers, about 4 p.m., dinner was served in a building in the first garden. The meal of seasoned rice mixed with sodden bread and surmounted by joints of delicious mutton was served on great trays raised on pedestals. I sat next to Ibn Sa'ud, with Faisal Ibn Rashid on his other side, at the topmost spread, and in spite of the uncouth hour did full justice to a sumptuous feast, having had nothing but fruit to eat all day. But I was not prepared for the next item on the programme—else had I eaten more moderately. For immediately afterwards the horses were brought round and the whole party mounted for the return journey to town. And one and all, regardless of their full stomachs, they tourneyed and jousted as they went ; and as they approached the town large crowds, mostly of women and children, gathered to see the cavalcade pass, greeting and blessing their prince as he went by mildly acknowledging their salutes.

Next day, as I sat talking with Ibn Sa'ud, a couple of rifle-shots suddenly rang out beyond the city to the north-ward—then more shots and still more ever approaching. We hastened to the lattice overlooking the space before the palace gate and in a few moments saw four *Dhalul*-riders trotting briskly up the street. ' These,' said Ibn Sa'ud, ' must be Subai' bringing news of a fight between them and a mixed band of Shammar and 'Ajman between the Hasa and Qatif. I heard a rumour of it this morning but did not think it worth telling you until the news was confirmed.' And so it proved to be. The four men came in as I sat with Ibn Sa'ud. One of them seemed to me a *Shaikh*, well-kempt and clean with a gay *Kafiya* of white, while the others were rough, burly individuals of the common *Badu* sort. Straight-way they saluted their master and began their simple tale in short sharp periods of inimitable eloquence. ' Look ye,' said Ibn Sa'ud, ' is it a *Badu* tale you bring me or God's own truth ? I want none of your false fancies.' ' *Wallah !* ' replied the *Shaikh*, ' if our tale is untrue we deserve no reward, for there is no profit in lies.' Their tale was roughly as follows :

The raiders, some hundred strong, were composed partly of
'Ajman—three sections were represented, namely the Salih
under Khumais Ibn Munaikhir, the Hadi under 'Id Ibn
Mutalaqqam, and the Safran under Kum'an Ibn Musai'id—
and partly of Aslam under the son of Salim Ibn Tawala, a
cousin of Dhari. It was this party which had raided and
captured fifty camels from 'Abdul 'Aziz Ibn Ruba'i's caravan
on the Kuwait road. Having sent back their booty to the
safety of Dhari's camp at Safwan they had worked down
the coast under the protection of the 'Awazim and their
Shaikh, Fahad Ibn Ma'attiqa nicknamed Ra'i al Fahma, and
had alighted suddenly at the tents of the Za'b—a section of
the Bani Hajir—near Qatif. The Za'b camels being away
grazing, they had passed on and swooped down without
warning on a Subai' encampment, capturing three herds [1] of
camels—about 150 animals in all. The outraged Subai' then
sought the assistance of the Za'b, whose *Shaikh*, 'Ajran Ibn
Faisal Ibn Sahub, immediately organised a pursuing party.
The combined force followed up and fell upon the raiders,
whom they defeated with a loss of five men—including Ibn
Khumaisa of the Sulaiman section of 'Ajman—and eleven
camels killed. They also recovered the raided herds and
took twenty of the enemy's *Dhaluls* in addition. Still
following hard on their tracks they found to their dismay
that the retreating enemy had claimed and been promised
the protection of the 'Awazim, who were too strong to attack.
Nevertheless the raiders had come in for rougher treatment
than they had reckoned with, and the affair was a notable
success for the defenders, among whom the Za'b appeared
to have borne the brunt of the day. The *Shaikh* who told
us the tale was himself of this section, being of the *Shaikhly*
house, Mandil Ibn Sahub by name. From my point of view
the situation was a serious one. I was supposed to be persuading Ibn Sa'ud of the advantages of inactivity, while the
Sharif attacked him on the west with perfect impunity so
far as we were concerned, and the 'Ajman and Aslam gangs,
propelled by the joint machinations of Dhari and Salim,
attacked him on the east. Over and above all this we were
giving asylum to the Shammar flying to our gates before the

[1] *Dhud*, pl. *Dhidan*.

advance of Turki, and there was murmuring in Najd where
Ibn Sa'ud's too great confidence in the good faith of the
perfidious British came in for ever-increasing criticism and
disparagement, as the evidences of our unwillingness or
inability to help him accumulated.   And I myself at times
found it difficult to rid myself of an undercurrent of suspicion
that the British authorities at Baghdad, playing second
fiddle to the Arab Bureau at Cairo, were trying unobtrusively
to damp down the fire that was already beginning to burn
fiercely in the furnaces of Najd.

I had scarcely finished my toilet the following morning
when I heard the voice of Ibn Sa'ud himself calling out to
me from the courtyard below. ' I bring you good news,' he
said, ' your baggage has arrived.'   I hastily thrust away my
pipe and tobacco and rose to greet him at the entrance :
' Your news is good indeed,' I said, ' and praise be to God !
I will not forget your guerdon.'   Seven months before I had
left this baggage behind me at Riyadh when I set out for the
Hijaz, and Colonel Cunliffe Owen had taken it back with him
to the coast, where it had eventually been dumped in one
of the cellars of the Agency at Kuwait.   I had written for it
to the Political Agent early in April only to be told that he
could find no trace of it.   Nearly two months later he had
found it in his cellars and taken steps to send it on.   Meanwhile I had had to travel to Wadi Dawasir and back without
films for my camera or tobacco for my pipe.   And since my
return I had written again and again in vain.   At last it had
arrived, and my joy knew no bounds.   I was restored to my
books, my tobacco and my films.   What matter if it had
taken 104 days for them to reach me ?

It was now beginning to be appreciably hotter at
Riyadh.   The summer winds had dropped as they do at
this season when the dates begin to mature and the melons
to become unwholesome, being over-ripe and tending to
produce an appreciable odour of staleness.   Ibn Sa'ud
attributed to these melons some days of unease which had
lately assailed his stomach and recommended me also to
discontinue eating them—advice which it was easy enough
to accept as other and equally delicious fruits became
available.   The afternoon temperatures ranged up to about

110° *Fahr.*, and life at Riyadh had become sufficiently familiar and stereotyped to make me long for the opening of the promised campaign and the life of movement amid new pastures which it would bring with it.

But so far no date was even approximately fixed and the days succeeded each other with their unvarying routine of interviews and picnics. Ahmad Ibn Thunaian continued to bore me with the jejune excursions into the realm of world-politics, for which his sojourn at Constantinople had equipped him to his own entire satisfaction. When he left Turkey before the outbreak of war his four brothers had remained behind and were still there, though he had had no news of them. Sa'ud, his elder brother, was, so far as he knew, leading the life of an ordinary citizen without employment. Faisal, next to him in years, had fought with distinction in the Balkan wars, being wounded and promoted to the rank of major—for all he knew he must either be dead or serving still against the Allies. The other two, 'Abdul Qadir and 'Abdul Rahman, were still but children.

At this time Ibn Sa'ud, who never tired of harping on the Sharifian problem, reckoned that there were some 500 *Najdis* serving with Sharif 'Abdullah in the neighbourhood of Madina and about 300 with Faisal. Some months previously the latter contingent had obtained permission to depart with their arms for which they paid. Nevertheless the British or Sharifian authorities had taken their arms from them at 'Aqaba, and it was only when Sharif Sharaf entered a strong protest against such action that a compromise was arrived at by which the cost of the rifles was returned to them. ' Remember,' said Ibn Sa'ud, ' we are fighting Ibn Rashid only for your sake, for we have no unsatisfied claims against him. On the contrary it is he who has claims against us for many a casualty in the house of Rashid. The real enemy of Najd, high and low, is the Sharif, and many members of my own household and many of the religious chiefs are displeased with me for allowing the *Ikhwan* to be attacked without striking back. I keep them quiet by telling them that all will be well. But the Sharif must be forbidden to attack my country. Fix the border between us and tell him not to transgress it.' I asked him what he would consider a reasonable boundary in relation to such recognisable landmarks as 'Ashaira, the Rakba plain and the Hadhn range. ' He can have all that,' he replied, ' and in fact everything from Marran westward. The Hadhn would be the most suitable boundary.' If only the Sharif could have brought himself in these days to accept a line joining Marran and Turaba by way of the Sha'ba channel, the history of Arabia would have been written on very different lines during the last ten years. But the Sharif's mind was set on a single object—the utter destruction of the *Wahhabi* state—and little he dreamed that it was towards the destruction of his own dynasty that he was inexorably working.

Meanwhile things seemed to be going all awry from the point of view of the achievement of my object in Arabia, and on 18th July the news from Kuwait contained a further shock for Ibn Sa'ud and myself. Salim's unceasing efforts to undo our blockade cordon had met with unexpected success. Our blockade policy had undergone a complete *volte-face*. In future there was to be no blockade *qua* blockade. Salim's past irregularities had been forgiven in return for his promise that they would not recur. He was made responsible to see that goods did not get into the enemy's hands. The people of Najd were to be allowed to buy without restriction, and the only check to be exercised hereafter was to be exercised in Bombay, whence exports would only be allowed in quantities calculated at intervals by the Political Agent at Kuwait on the basis of the normal requirements of the citizens and tribes of Kuwait and of the people of Najd—the latter being reported to him by 'Abdullah Nafisi, the agent of Ibn Sa'ud. It would have been difficult to devise a scheme better calculated to provide the Turks with their requirements, but the Government of India appeared to regard such leakage to the enemy as a minor matter in comparison with a breach with Salim, possibly involving a military occupation of Kuwait. At that port the removal of the blockade restrictions was hailed with joy and interpreted as a concession in part due to the unsatisfactory position in the French theatre of war. In Najd it was taken for granted that for some strange reason we expressly desired the Turks to get what they wanted in the way of supplies.

Haïl would live again and be able to face the coming *Wahhabi* attack with equanimity now that Ibn Sa'ud could no longer use the economic weapon in support of his armies. Ibn Sa'ud himself declined all further responsibility for the leakage of supplies to the enemy unless all goods intended for Najd were landed at Bahrain.

The following afternoon we all rode out to the Shamsiya garden and sat upon a raised mud-bank outside the wall lazily watching the long line of the royal milch-camels—some hundred of them of all sizes—troop slowly homeward from their pastures in the direction of the Makhruq hillock. All the time Ibn Sa'ud kept up a running comment on the animals as they went by—particularly noticing one great beast near the rear who, missing her calf, turned back in search until she saw the youngster following behind, whereupon the great hulk swung round again and resumed her homeward march. As we sat there two *Badawin* of the Subai' came up and a slave rushed forward to prevent them, but Ibn Sa'ud waved him off and called the two men forward. Thereupon one of them, making the most of a slight scratch on his scalp, began pouring out a tale of woe. Unwittingly— or so they said—they had trespassed with their flocks on the royal reserve at Khafs, whereupon they had been set upon, beaten and deprived of their sheep by the royal guards. ' Very well,' said Ibn Sa'ud, ' I will make it well for you— get you gone to your own folk.' So they rose and went forth, but in folly let their tongues wag, murmuring aloud as they went : ' Ah ! if it had not been for you we would have given them as good as we got—we would have trounced the interfering wretches.' This was altogether too much for Ibn Sa'ud. ' You dogs ! ' he roared angrily, ' beat them at once,' and ready staves were forthwith laid resoundingly across their retreating backs. Full of mercy for the contrite, the *Wahhabi* ruler knew that the very security of his realm depended on the repression of the *Badu*, and he was ever watchful to drop on the slightest hint of aggressiveness on their part. In this case there were eleven sheep in question, and the matter was ultimately settled by the release of eight, the other three being taken in settlement of a fine for trespass.

Next morning I was summoned to the presence in the

middle of breakfast to hear the official *Bishara*, which
confirmed the news of the second attack on Khurma about
the middle of *Ramdhan* with additional details. The Sharifian force was so numerous that ' *la yu'adduhum wa la
yahsibuhum ill' Allah*—only God could count and reckon
them.' Nevertheless the Subai' warriors, only 450 strong,
rose up and smote them ' with the help of the Lord,' routing
them and killing 115 of them and capturing 200 *Dhaluls*,
besides the guns and other equipment already reported.
Their own loss was only ten men ' martyred in the service of
the Lord,' including Sharif Muhsin Ibn Turki of the Khurma
notables. The letter which the messengers produced ended
with exultant pæans of praise at the handiwork of the
Almighty and with some very plain speaking on the failure
of Ibn Sa'ud to come to the assistance of his brethren so
threatened. ' And if it is the dross of the world's treasure
you seek that you come not to help us, then tell us so, Oh
'Abdul'Aziz, and we will excuse you. We have had no benefit
from our frequent sending of men to implore your assistance,
but, look you ! next time we will send forth our women to
raise Najd.' The captured guns were being sent to Ibn Sa'ud
in proof of the victory claimed, of which indeed no proof was
needed, incredible as it may seem that the well-equipped
Hashimite forces should twice within a month have suffered
such signal defeats at the hands of a handful of villagers and
Badawin. And with his letter the *Amir* of Khurma sent the
originals of three letters dated in the month of *Dhil Hijja*—
about ten months previously—in which Sharif 'Abdullah had
conveyed his ultimatum to the people of the settlement.

I had recently noticed an Indian in the town and, on
enquiry from Ibn Sa'ud, was told that a number of them had
recently arrived *en route* for Mecca, as they did every year.
Mostly they were of the *Darwish* type, making their way
laboriously by the cheapest way, mainly on foot and depending on the open-handed generosity of the *Wahhabi* court
for a brief respite from their terrible ordeal and for the
necessary provision of food and money for the last stage of
their journey. Another foreign visitor had come for a different purpose. He was a *Baghdadi* with a grievance, Shaikh
Tahir Lutfi Ibn Shaikh Isma'il by name, and his object was

to secure Ibn Sa'ud's intervention for the recovery of his
lands wrongfully lost and his recommendation for some comfortable post in the Government service wrongfully withheld.
He was a familiar type, sufficiently lettered to draft two
somewhat impertinent letters for Ibn Sa'ud to sign—instead
of doing so he handed them to me—and his present object
was to go on to Mecca to secure the additional support of the
Sharif for his double claim. Ibn Sa'ud, however, agreed with
me that it would be best to send him back to Bahrain, and
this decision was eventually confirmed after I had interviewed
the man some days later only to find that I had myself been
instrumental in creating the conditions he wished altered.
He had come to us in Basra as a refugee and been treated
with all consideration, including the grant of an allowance,
but when we had occupied Baghdad and enabled him to
resume peaceful possession of his property we had naturally
discontinued his charitable allowance. And that apparently
was the whole cause of his present grievance and annoyance.
He was a mischief-maker by profession and, finding himself
baulked of the object of his visit to Riyadh, would certainly
not miss the opportunity of speaking ill of the English into
the willing ears of the Riyadh fanatics. This was what
actually happened, and it came to Ibn Sa'ud's ears that he
was carrying on an active propaganda against us. Accordingly his departure to Bahrain was arranged for without
delay.

The Turkish officer, Qudsi Effendi, was still eating out his
soul in confinement in the great fort, and I begged Ibn Sa'ud
to let him have greater liberty if possible. ' What if he
escapes ? ' he asked. I expressed the opinion that that was
scarcely likely, and offered to entertain him myself and take
him for walks, whereupon Ibn Sa'ud instructed Junaifi to
make enquiries. I might have saved myself the trouble of
being so solicitous for his welfare—as a matter of fact he had
at my representation recently been given more comfortable
quarters and another prisoner, a Turkish deserter, as servant,
together with a sum of 40 *Riyals* for such luxuries as he might
require—as he met Juniafi's advances on my behalf in a
spirit of great hostility. ' He is a Christian,' he said, ' and
therefore an enemy. I have no wish to see him, though,

being a prisoner, I have no choice if you force me to do so.'
Junaifi was much impressed with him—a fine fellow, he said,
a *man*—and told me he had served ten years in the Yaman,
and had left a wife and family there when he set forth on
the mission on which he was captured. According to him
there was at this time some 8500 Turkish troops in the Yaman,
partly at Lahaj under Sa'id Pasha and partly at San'a under
Ghalib Pasha. The commanding officer in 'Asir was Muhiyaldin Pasha, who had 6000 men under him.

Next day Ibn Sa'ud's picnic was at the garden of Qirinain
to the west of the town, whither I rode out—as usual with
Junaifi and Manawar—to join him and where I was introduced to 'Abdul Rahman Ibn Suwailim, a tall spare man of
about fifty and a typical son of 'Aridh, who had been governor
of Qatif ever since the capture of that port from the Turks
and whose family had been closely identified with the service
of the Sa'ud dynasty ever since the Dar'iya days. Sa'ud al
'Arafa was again present, a well-built man of middle age with
an attractive manner of speech, with whom I became more
impressed as I got to know him better. He seldom spoke
to me directly, but generally spoke at me through Ibn Sa'ud,
asking acute questions about the war, about modern methods
and instruments of warfare and about agriculture and irrigation. I noticed that in such gatherings he always yielded
precedence to Faisal Ibn Rashid, who was presumably
treated as an honoured guest. Another important personality,
of whom I was able to take particular stock on this occasion
though I had often observed him before, was a *Qahtani* chief,
Ibn Sadhan, who regularly wore the white chaplet of the
Ikhwan and somewhat ostentatiously avoided sitting at the
common dish of fruit or other food whenever I was present.
Junaifi confided to me, however, that the man was a terrible
rogue and contented himself with an outward show of
religious virtue to stand well with his tribe. In his career of
raiding and robbery he was said to have accounted for 92
lives with his own hand, a number only surpassed by the
redoubtable Duwish, who at this time had 99 scalps to his
credit.

The conversation turning on the topic of fruit, Ibn Sa'ud
warned me against eating musk-melons on top of honey, for

the combination, he assured me, is deadly poison. The ass
is *haram* in *Islam*, neither its flesh nor its milk being lawful
food. As for horse-flesh the position is uncertain. Muhammad himself never ate of it but refused to declare it unlawful,
and it was left to Yazid or one of his successors to introduce
the fashion of eating it. As for the *Dhabb*, the horny-tailed
lizard, that also was never declared *haram* as it does not occur
in the Hijaz and was not known to the Prophet. Ibn Sa'ud
had eaten it in his youth, but had long abandoned the
practice, the *Jarbu'* being in similar case so far as he was
concerned. Doughty records that he never saw cats in Najd,
but they certainly exist at Riyadh though not in great
numbers. Ibn Sa'ud had formed the design of purchasing a
small garden adjoining the Qirinain with a view to converting
the combined area into a lucerne reserve—so great is the
demand and so inadequate the supply of fodder for the
animals congregating at the capital. The dates were now
just beginning to be eatable (21st July) in the initial unripe
stage called *Laun* ; from this they would develop into the
half-and-half stage known as *Bisr*, and the final stage for
fresh dates would be the *Ratab*.

Jabir the *Marri* was at Riyadh during these days, and on
one occasion I found him propped up against a pillar in the
palace hall, looking very forlorn and feeling very weak with
fever. This was my first meeting with him since he had been
so suddenly sent off by Ibrahim from the Wadi,[1] and, taking
him up to my room for a dose of quinine, I heard for the first
time the detailed story of Ibrahim's iniquity. ˙Mosquitoes
appeared to be non-existent at Riyadh—at any rate I saw
none during this summer season—but there were sand-flies
which, though not plentiful enough to be annoying, made it
necessary to cover up at nights when sleeping on the roof.
Moths occasionally visited the arc-lamp on the palace roof
which was hoisted on dark nights and lowered after Ibn
Sa'ud's *Quran*-reading. It was also visited by swarms of a
small cockchafer—about half an inch in length—among
which and other smaller insects the bats darted about with
great zeal. One day I developed a slight cold in the head,
which Ibn Sa'ud attributed to sleeping exposed to the moon.

[1] *H.A.* ii. p. 208.

' When I sleep in the open,' he said, ' I always wrap my head with a kerchief.'

After the evening prayer on most days Ibn Sa'ud would sit for some time listening to readings from the *Traditional* literature. The only collections of exegesis (*Tafsir*) admitted by the *Hanbali* school are those of Ibn Kathir in twelve volumes and of Al Baghawi in six volumes. On these occasions the passages most often resorted to were those explanatory of the circumstances in which various passages in the *Quran* were revealed, and also those describing the torments of hell—' to make men afraid of hell-fire,' added Ibn Sa'ud by way of explanation. The succession of persons whose exposition of the divine law is accepted is as follows : first the Prophet himself ; secondly his companions ; thirdly *Al Tabi'in* or the associates of the companions ; and lastly *Al Tabi'in al Tabi'in* or the associates of the associates of the companions. Ahmad Ibn Hanbal was of the last category —contact with the Prophet down to the third generation as it were being apparently regarded as being the last degree of remoteness from the fountain-head on which it was safe to rely for a true understanding of the scriptures. The faith remained, according to Ibn Sa'ud, unchanged for some three centuries after its revelation by Muhammad, but the thousand years that followed have been prolific in the dissemination of perversions and heresies which have been relegated to their proper place by the *Wahhabi* creed.

On 23rd July, having now eked out all but a month at the *Wahhabi* capital, I thought it time to stir Ibn Sa'ud's memory of his promise to begin his campaign immediately after the end of *Ramdhan*. ' I had every intention,' he replied, ' of opening the campaign after the fast and would have done so had it not been for the untoward occurrences at Khurma and in the 'Ajman area. These things made me fear a possible rising in the South as soon as I was safely in the North.' The answer seemed to me an excuse rather than a valid reason and I pressed the point. ' I am convinced,' I said, ' that you do intend to move, but it is very difficult for me to convince the authorities at Baghdad that that is so, when they see no sign of movement on your part.' ' Very well,' he replied, ' I give you my word to move in fifteen days' time

from now if you will guarantee that the Sharif will not attack
Khurma, that the 'Ajman will not act against me in the East,
and that the Shammar will not be pampered by the 'Iraq
authorities.' It was rather a large order in view of the
indecision prevalent in the counsels of Baghdad, but I caught
as at a straw—movement was essential. ' I guarantee you,'
I said, ' as regards the Sharif and the 'Ajman, and, if you find
my guarantee of no avail, you can tell me you want me no
longer at your court and I will go.' So it was agreed that a
move should be made northwards in fifteen days, and, as it
proved, Ibn Sa'ud was just two days better than his word.

Content with the promise I had wheedled out of my host
and wearied by the mental struggle, I gave up the idea of
my customary evening outing and retired early to my sleeping
roof, where I amused myself watching the roofs around me
starting to life as the sun sank westward. Every roof is
provided with screen-walls of some height to secure the
privacy of its occupants, and, as the lowering sun threw them
into shade, I saw women toiling up with great loads of matting
and bedding to spread for themselves and their lords. Then
they would descend again to fetch up their cooking utensils
and water-pots and even the family goats. The latter are
sent out every morning in great common flocks in charge of
professional herd-boys—invariably attended by a donkey
carrying their food and water for the day—and every evening
they return before sunset to be distributed to their proper
households, where they are promptly milked and penned up
for the night. In many cases the women worked at these
tasks carrying a babe nestling close under one arm, while the
other arm or the head was free for the burdens which had to
be brought up and arranged on the roof. In the richer
houses the work was of course done by slave women generally
decked out in gay colours—one I noticed in a rich smock of
gorgeous green—or servants. Occasionally a man or two
would come out on to the roof before sunset for a breath of
fresh air, but for the most part the women and children had
the scene to themselves until darkness descended on the town.

All of a sudden, as the sun sank behind the rugged rim of
Tuwaiq, the whole city would burst into discordant song as
countless *Mu'adhdhins* uttered the call to prayer from the

dumpy minarets—curious turrets with an irregular upward projection at one, usually the northern, corner. Immediately there follows a bustle of people—men only of course—in the streets, at first dawdling and later hurrying to the mosques. Then there is silence, broken only by the *Allahu Akbars* and *Amins* of the praying congregations, while on the roofs the women too go through all the motions and prostrations of the prayer, though always singly and silently. After prayers they go about their work or play, and on one occasion I saw a small boy playing with a very large, naked sword, with which suddenly and apparently for no reason he smote one of the bondwomen as she went about her tasks. He smote her hard, it seemed, and grinned with pleasure, and, as she rushed at him in protest, he smote her again and skedaddled down the stairs pursued by her vituperations. On a neighbouring roof I saw a woman taking leave of her lord as he rose to go down for the prayer—graceful were the gestures of her hands and arms as she appeared to entreat some favour of him, begging him perhaps to come back without delay to enjoy the dinner she would prepare against his coming. And so the darkness of night descended upon the great city, and I was summoned to my own dinner. On this occasion it was venison they served to me. One day during *Ramdhan* while I was with Ibn Sa'ud there came to us quite the strangest specimen of the human race which it has ever been my lot to set eyes on. A dwarf in stature and clad in a deerskin smock reaching right down to his feet, squeaking rather than speaking, to all appearances half-witted and apparently of rather more than middle age—it was a *Sulubi*, Muharraq by name, and a hunter by profession like all his kind. He had come in to get a rifle and a supply of ammunition in connection with an arrangement by which he was to go off to the Dahna to procure venison for the royal household. I seized the opportunity of begging him to bring in a few heads of the different species he might come across, and incidentally reminded Ibn Sa'ud about a young Oryx which he had told me some days previously he had secured for me —alas it had died, but he promised to get me another. Muharraq, accompanied by his son, had since completed his task, bringing in some thirty complete carcases, and it was of this meat that was placed before me that night. The process to which the gazelles are subjected after slaughter is very simple and effective. The animal is skinned, cut open and cleaned out, being then sprinkled with salt ' to drive away the smell.' The carcase is next hung up in the sun until it is dry and then seems to last, fit for consumption, almost any length of time. Before cooking it is carefully washed to free the meat of blood, sand and salt, while any portions which have gone bad are removed. When cooked it has a deep reddish colour, and is of a most excellent flavour. Such venison is called *Jalla*.

Ever and anon small incidents reminded me that I was indeed a stranger in a strange land. One morning Junaifi came to me with a tale of woe. One of the *Nawwab* or proctors, named Talashi, had approached him saying : ' Cleanse thy soul, oh Ibrahim ! ' On his replying that he was unaware of any special need of cleansing at the moment, the man had replied : ' Think a little, Ibrahim, and God will open the eyes of your soul.' ' Perhaps,' ventured Junaifi, ' you mean my frequenting the company of the *Inglizi* ? ' ' Precisely so,' was the answer, ' remember God and give him up.' Junaifi had boldly replied that this was a matter which did not concern his inquisitor, as I was a guest of Ibn Sa'ud, and that it was for his sake and for the furtherance of his policy that he frequented my society. He was in no way concerned with my faith nor I with his. A week later Talashi returned to the attack on different lines. ' I note,' he said, ' you do not attend the public prayers '—this was untrue— ' but more often pray at home—mend your ways ! ' Junaifi, with all the courage of the *Tamimi* stock, challenged him to prefer his complaint to Ibn Sa'ud, as he could not recognise his jurisdiction in the matter. And he himself reported the incident to his master by way of precaution against accidents. ' Never mind,' had been the reply, ' wait and see.' The following morning Junaifi had returned home after the dawn prayer when there was a knocking at his door. Looking over his roof parapet he observed Talashi with three other persons—a fellow-*Naib* called Shiddi, another man who was *Mu'adhdhin* of a neighbouring mosque, and Turki Ibn 'Abdullah Ibn Sa'ud, one of the *'Araif* branch of the royal family.

At first he declined to open, but as they stayed battering on
his door and making a great commotion he admitted them.
Talashi then accused him of not having been to the mosque
that morning and, insisting that it was so in spite of his
denials, declared that he must be punished. ' Well,' said
Junaifi, ' prefer your complaint to Ibn Sa'ud, you have no
jurisdiction to punish me or call me to account.' Whereupon
Talashi struck him hard across the neck and shoulder—he
was still in pain as he told me the story—with his longstaff.
Junaifi sprang at his assailant and, seizing him by the throat,
dealt him blow after blow upon his face and nose until the
others intervened and led the damaged proctor away. He
was not yet, however, at the end of his troubles, for shortly
afterwards he and the chief of the *Nawwab* were summoned
to the royal presence, and Ibn Sa'ud passed sentence that
the chief should belay his unruly subordinate until Junaifi
expressed himself satisfied. The chief *Naïb* declined the duty
imposed on him, which was accordingly entrusted to the
steward of the household, Hamad Ibn Faris, and in due
course Talashi was trounced to Junaifi's satisfaction and then
dismissed from the post he had abused. At the same time
Turki Ibn 'Abdullah received a warning in writing to mind
his own business in the future, remembering that he had no
part in the executive government of the country.

    Another cause of annoyance to me lay in the tendency,
against which I had always to be on the watch, of those in
attendance on me to discourage the visit of other friends
such as Jabir, Mitrak and the like. One day, meeting Jabir
in the street, I had invited him to join me at breakfast the
following morning. He had duly turned up, but Muhammad
Ibn Musallam, taking advantage of my being with Ibn Sa'ud
at the moment, had driven him away and then told me that
he had never appeared. The following day I discovered
quite accidentally from one of the *'Abid* that he had appeared
after all. This was more than I could bear and I expressed
my opinion very freely to Junaifi and Musallam when they
arrived with my breakfast. ' Look you,' I said, ' I know
Jabir is about and, as you turned him away yesterday, I
want him to breakfast with me to-day and, what is more, I
will not breakfast until he comes.' A frantic ' search ' for

Jabir was then ostentatiously organised, and every corner of the courtyard overlooked by my window was searched in vain. The searchers returned to report that he was nowhere to be found, so I left the breakfast to cool and a few minutes later was summoned, still fasting, to Ibn Sa'ud. As I sat at his window I saw Jabir walk into the palace and, when I returned to my room, I enquired if they had had any success in their search. ' Wallah ! ' said Ibn Musallam, ' we have searched everywhere but he is nowhere to be found.' ' No,' I replied, ' I have just seen him walk into the palace.' At that Junaifi remembered he had an urgent bit of work to attend to and slipped away, leaving Ibn Musallam to hear anything else I might have to say on the subject. He stayed but a few minutes and departed leaving the 'Abid to keep guard over the now cold dishes. At 1 p.m. they carefully covered up the dishes and crept away, while an hour later Ibn Musallam returned with a bowl of fruit. ' Shall I take down the breakfast ? ' he enquired. I replied that he could please himself as I proposed to eat nothing till Jabir appeared, and with his departure I lay down, hungry and disconsolate, for a nap, from which I was awakened at 3 p.m. by the return of the steward with Jabir in his train, who, having been carefully coached, swore by God that he had never been turned away the previous day, but had been absent from town as he was busy building a roof to his house and had also suffered somewhat from fever. I dismissed him with an invitation to dinner the same day, and broke my fast on grapes, unripe peaches and unriper dates.

During the afternoon when I was out for a stroll towards the ridge overlooking Manfuha with Manawar the conversation turned on Ibrahim, and I was surprised to hear that he had of late fallen somewhat in the estimation of the 'Abid, who, formerly his staunchest supporters, were now beginning to complain that he had been withholding part of the gratuities intended for them. The charge was probably without foundation, though their real grievance was possibly that he assessed amounts due to them on an unacceptable basis, for the 'Abid are proud folk and reckon themselves in every way the equals of the pure-bred Arab, to say nothing of the Bani Khadhir of mixed ancestry. Manawar went on to tell me of the life

of his royal master in camp in company with such bright
spirits as Tami and Nasir Ibn Sadhan, whom he would often
rag unmercifully, especially at meal-times, when he would
bid the *'Abid* carry them away before they had so much as
tasted the food before them. On one occasion Ibn Sa'ud
had taken Tami to task for the too great jauntiness of his
moustaches, and, receiving the pert reply with which he was
ever ready, had called for a pair of scissors and with his own
hand shorn him of his beauty. Tami, undaunted, claimed
monetary compensation, which he assessed at 40 *Riyals* with
a mantle thrown in.

Jabir came to dinner that night and Junaifi stayed away,
excusing himself on the score of his neck, still sore as the
result of Talashi's attentions. Jabir, on his last journey on
Ibn Sa'ud's service to the Hasa, had brought back his wife
with him and was now busy settling into their new house
outside the Dhuhairi gate by the cemetery. The expense
of the proceeding was, he explained, a serious matter for him
—the requisite timber came from the Batin, where good
Ithil-wood was available ; for thatch he drew on the palm-
fronds [1] of the Riyadh gardens ; and then there was the
additional cost of mortar [2] and water. Besides all this his
brother had taken a fancy to and deprived him of the *Bisht*
I had given him. And on all grounds there was a good case
for an additional present from me. There is no limit to the
greed of the *Badu*. Formerly he had another wife in the
Qasim, but he had divorced her long since for reasons of
economy, which also compelled him to treat the fever which
had latterly been much upon him with the cheap medicine
of an implicit trust in God, for, apart from the two quinine
tabloids I had given him some days before, he had used no
other.

Next day there were welcome signs of incipient preparations for the promised campaign. As I sat with Ibn Sa'ud
a score of newly-purchased camels were herded into the
Manakh below, where one by one they were branded with
the royal mark. The animal being couched and one leg
securely bound, one man would seize his head and bend the
great neck backwards towards the hump, holding on to the

---

[1] *Jarid* or *Khus*.   [2] *Liban*.

lower lip and cartilage of the nose in such a way as to appear
to be trying to distract the beast with as much harmless
pain as possible in that direction, while another man got
busy with the branding-irons on the left hind-quarter. A
sizzling sound and a spurt of smoke as the hot iron was
applied to the flesh would be followed by a violent lurch of
the animal which, with an agonising shriek, would in most
cases break loose and scamper away on three legs until caught
and brought back again for the completion of the operation,
which, in the case of Ibn Sa'ud's *Wasm*, involved four separate applications of the iron—one for each separate item of
the mark. ' What is your *Wasm* called ? ' I once asked Ibn
Sa'ud. ' Oh,' he replied, ' it is some uncouth name of ancient
times. Has anyone been telling you about it ? ' He would
say no more, and I vaguely remembered that Tami had once
jested about it. The name was certainly of phallic significa-
tion and the mark itself, doubtless descended from pagan
times, could scarcely have been of other origin—a rod
with two circles and a third circle surmounting the whole.
According to Ibn Sa'ud the branding of the human face
and all such practices as tattooing are forbidden by the
Islamic law.

For some time now he had been distinctly out of sorts—
the aftermath, as I imagined, of the rigours of *Ramdhan*
followed by the resumption of an ordinary diet, including a
liberal proportion of fruit. He himself, however, attributed
it to an unusually long spell of life at Riyadh, where the water
and air are polluted in comparison with desert conditions.
' Perhaps also,' he added, ' this is due to the close proximity
of the great cemetery. The depth of burials is about four feet
measured from the ground level to the bottom of the actual
inner groove [1] in which the corpse is placed and over which
palm-fronds are laid before the earth is filled in. Coffins are
haram, and to *Wahhabi* ideas the practice of burning, as
customary among the *Hindus*, is anathema. I urged that our
experts considered cremation the most hygienic method of
disposing of the dead and admitted that to a considerable
extent it is practised in Europe, while explaining that in all
such matters we enjoy a large measure of liberty, having no

[1] *Lahad.*

codes to restrict our practice. He readily agreed with me that
the Parsee method was the worst of all forms of sepulture.

In the afternoon we repaired to Ibn Sa'ud's favourite
resort—the bank outside the Shamsiya garden wall. I
had ridden a particularly pleasing grey pony and Ibn Sa'ud
was on his favourite mare—a splendid animal which carried
his weight superbly. It was a *Kuhaila* bred by the Shammar
Jarba' of the Jazira and had formerly belonged to Sa'ud al
Salih Ibn Subhan, from whom it was taken as he fled from
the battlefield of Jarrab and brought in by its *Baduwi* captor
as a gift to Ibn Sa'ud. ' Three Sa'uds,' said Ibn Sa'ud,
' distinguished themselves by flight that day—Sa'ud al
Subhan and Sa'ud Ibn Rashid himself, and the third,' he
went on merrily, ' was Sa'ud al 'Arafa, who is sitting there
by you.' The last-named was still at that time in the enemy's
camp, a potential pretender to the *Wahhabi* throne, but after
Jarrab he had made his submission and ever since he had
been a loyal supporter of his greater cousin. As we sat there
we watched once more the now familiar cortège of the royal
milch-camels wending their weary way homeward. A youngster dragged wearily after them, lagging in the rear until the
rearmost cow stopped to await him. The little one immediately proceeded to drink and, as he did so, another
camel stopped and walked back to contemplate the tableau.
' That one,' said Ibn Sa'ud, ' is the real mother and the other
only a foster-mother, for you should know that, when two
of our milch-camels calve about the same time, we slay one
of the young ones and leave the other to play child to both
mothers. It means a great saving in milk.' Ibn Sa'ud
reckoned that his burden and riding camels at this time
numbered about 1500 after the heavy losses incurred during
the year owing to the epidemic of mange which had ravaged
Najd, being brought back from the Hijaz by the animals
which had been sent thither with the *Najdi* pilgrimage of the
previous year. Practically all of them had come back affected,
and with the first heat of the present summer no fewer than
400 or 500 of his own animals had succumbed. The prices
at which he was now buying camels for the coming campaign
ranged from 100 to 160 *Riyals*.

As we sat there the attendants exercised the horses,

galloping over the plain and carrying out the evolutions of a
mimic battle—an unusually large number of animals being
out on this occasion, most of them looking exceedingly well
in motion, though a little grooming would have improved all
of them out of recognition. Later on Ibn Sa'ud and his
brother 'Abdullah had a shooting match at a rock target
about 18 inches high and six inches wide, set up at a distance
of 50 yards, but, out of ten shots apiece, only one shot by Ibn
Sa'ud just grazed the tip of the mark. Then Ibrahim al
Jumai'a, who had been very much to the fore handing
ammunition, etc., to the competitors, volunteered to outdo
them, whereupon amid yells of derision he made two of the
worst shots one could wish to see and Ibn Sa'ud deridingly
asked him whether he was aiming at the mark or the distant
ridge behind it. At length, the *Ward* being produced as a
preliminary to the sunset prayer, I mounted and cantered
homeward, re-entering the city from the east by a group of
Badawin booths from which the little children, naked or
clothed in dirty white smocks, ran out playfully to hold the
road against us. We cantered gently at them, whereupon
they dispersed whooping with joy and yelling greetings at us.
It was near the time of prayer, and the tents were tenanted
only by women, robed in red smocks with the typical stiff
black mask with large eyeholes, which contrasted strongly
with the town-woman's veil of soft clinging black muslin,
which they wind round the face and head, leaving one flap
loose to pull aside or across the face for concealment in case
of need. Continuing my way I turned aside in the hope of
seeing Jabir's new house, and meeting some boys, asked them
to direct me. ' Jabir the *Marri* ? ' they replied with alacrity;
' yes, indeed, the house he is building, it is over there ; come
and we will show you.' Jabir himself was away at prayer,
but I saw the house—a mere shell of clay walls still damp and
not more than a yard high. On entering the palace I found
Ibn Musallam and Balal, one of the *'Abid*, chewing melon
seeds, which are reckoned to possess certain aphrodisiacal
properties. Ibn Musallam was notorious even in Riyadh for
excessive sexual indulgence, and he had often enquired of
me whether I knew of any sovereign aid to his appetite.
' Yes,' I had replied untruthfully,' there are plenty, but you

should know that they are all concoctions of the drugs
forbidden by the laws of *Islam*.' At times one felt an irresist-
ible desire to waken these folk out of their sottish sensuality
by the very suggestion that the adoption of artificial aids
to enjoyment might jeopardise their prospects in the next
world.

On 29th July, nearly a month later than normal according
to all accounts, we had our first *Ratab* dates, and the afternoon's outing was to the Khizam *Qasr*, where among the
party I met Muhammad Ibn 'Abdullah Ibn Muhanna, the
last *Amir* of his line at Buraida, who rebelled against Ibn
Sa'ud and fled on being defeated, but subsequently made
submission and was now living in honourable retirement
at Riyadh. The family was no longer to be found in its
native city, most of its surviving members having migrated
to Suq al Shuyukh. And, as we sat there talking, an unpre-
possessing, hollow-cheeked individual in simple raiment
came forward and, sitting at Ibn Sa'ud's side, entertained
him to a long whispered conversation. He was Ibrahim, the
second-in-command of the *Nawwab*, a much-feared body of
some thirty or more sour-faced individuals whose chief was
'Abdul 'Aziz Ibn 'Abdul Latif, brother of the great *Shaikh*,
'Abdullah Ibn 'Abdul Wahhab. Faisal Ibn Rashid was much
interested when I mentioned that I had been reading
Doughty's account of Haïl forty years before when, as an
infant, he himself, now well over forty, may have been one
of the nameless children of Hamud referred to in the story.
' Was he the vaccinator,' he asked, ' of whom we used to
hear tell ? '

Next day some of the Khurma spoils arrived—a Turkish
7-pounder and an automatic rifle—with a letter from Khalid
Ibn Luwai describing the battle and a nominal roll of the
Sharifian forces found among the captured papers and giving
the total strength at 1689 men. According to Ibn Sa'ud,
who had just had a consultation with Shaikh 'Abdullah and
was somewhat peevish in consequence of his plain-speaking,
the Sharif's forces were reassembling at 'Ashaira, and a large
number of sympathisers were gathering round Khurma from
Bisha, Ranya and other neighbouring localities. He regarded
the situation as very serious, and all I could do was to beg

him to have patience as I was convinced that, in view of recent happenings, the British Government would not fail to restrain the Sharif from further aggression.

At this time a great deal of work was being done in connection with structural alterations in the palace. The courtyard between my quarters and the central block of the palace was apparently to be covered over to form a pillared hall, and the whole ground space was now dotted with incipient pillars in various stages of construction. For these rounded blocks of limestone were laid one on top of another with mud to cement them together up to the required height, the foundations penetrating the mud floor of the courtyard to the underlying rock. As the pillars and connecting walls rose beyond human height the mason climbed up on to them to continue the work, a boy below throwing up the rock slabs and great clumps of semi-liquid mud, half of which generally fell away before it reached the hands awaiting it above—a primitive and laborious process. The work of demolition kept pace with that of construction in equally primitive fashion and not without danger to casual passers-by in the *Manakh* below. The *'Abid's* quarters on the upper storey of the block in which I was housed were the first to come down. Great beams of *Ithil*-wood were placed against the wall slanting at an angle of 45° and were then subjected to human pressure, the rhythmic motion of the workmen causing the wall to sway and sway again until it cracked at the point of contact with the beams. But little more pressure and down it went with a mighty crash into the road below.

As I rode on after inspecting this operation I was suddenly hailed from behind : ' *Salam 'alaik, ya Philby !* ' and turned round to find the burly countenance of Mitrak grinning welcome at me. All this time he had been away from the capital on Ibn Sa'ud's service and had just arrived by way of the Qasim with the caravan of 'Abdul 'Aziz al Ruba'i, which had been raided by the Aslam and with which a mail intended for me had gone wandering about Arabia. On his outward journey he had traversed the desert with but one companion, and, having crossed the still fresh tracks of a large raiding-party travelling south, they had subsequently actually seen and had to use all their ingenuity and desert-craft to keep out of sight of another gang. The Mutair, he said, were spread out in the neighbourhood of the wells of Safa and 'Uwaina, while the Subai' were at Hafar al Ats, but the whole of the Eastern Desert was in a state of unrest. I was now able to make good to Mitrak the gift I had withheld from him on our return from the Wadi and he astonished me by not asking for more. He thanked me with a broad grin and asked me to coffee in his tent in the Batha—an invitation of which I availed myself the following evening. The vast array of *Badawin* tents,[1] which was said to be a regular feature of the beginning of the date season at Riyadh, in the Batha depression was a really imposing spectacle ; and it was with considerable difficulty that I eventually found Mitrak's abode—a very small booth, of which about two-thirds was reserved for the women, while the men's section was open on two sides. Its occupants were Mitrak himself, his wife and their two small children—a boy born about the time of Jarrab and a girl of two. On my arrival Mitrak was away, but an attendant of Qasim Ibn Rawwaf, to whom he had been attached on the journey back, was making coffee for two other visitors and I was made welcome. ' Will you ride to the Qasim,' he asked, ' with Ibn Sa'ud or go down to Kuwait ? ' ' I go with Ibn Sa'ud,' I said, ' you must consider me now a *Najdi*, for I will not leave this country.' ' *Inshallah*,' he replied piously, ' you will embrace the true faith.' Mitrak soon arrived with a few friends and we settled down to the coffee-drinking, eked out with a sort of tea made of *Hail*.[2] And the talk turned on incidents of the 'Ajman campaign of 1916, in which both Manawar and Mitrak had taken part, and on the prowess of the *Badu* women. One of Ibn Sa'ud's men, wounded in the fray, lay dying when a woman of the 'Ajman approached him carrying a pitcher of water. He begged for a drink to assuage his burning thirst. ' Give you water,' she shrieked at him, ' to save you from death that you may come again against our men ? Not a drop shall you have.' And with that she beat out the life that remained in him with a stick. A woman of the Hasa, however, proved the

---

[1] At this time the following tribes were represented : Shamir, Qahtan, Subai', Suhul and Dawasir.

[2] *Cardamum*.

equal of her *Badawin* sister. An *'Ajami* lay dying of his
wounds close to the brink of a well to which she came to
draw water. ' Help me away from this place,' he begged,
' I cannot move.' She approached him as if to help and,
loosening the cartridge belt from his body as if to ease his
pain, rolled the helpless man forward into the well and went
home glorying in the rifle and ammunition which she had
captured from a man. ' Such,' they said, ' are the women of
our country.' And I thought that Mitrak's wife might be
of the same stuff as I caught a glimpse of her silhouetted
against the setting sun as she strode out of the tent with her
baby girl—a firm-knit body clothed in no more than her
single smock of red. Young Fahhad, the hope of Mitrak's
house, played about the tent but refused to come to me or
even to shake hands, though on one occasion he playfully
thrust his little sister—stark naked and fearful—into our
midst. Mitrak pushed her back under the curtain, and I
noticed that at her next appearance she was clothed in a
diminutive red smock.

Taking my leave I came across Sa'id the *Qahtani*, a companion of the journey to Jidda, in a neighbouring group of
tents, and, after a few words of mutual greeting, passed on
into the town, where I noticed that the passers-by, mostly
Badu it is true, were more responsive in returning my
greetings than was usually the case. The previous evening
while riding out to the Shamsiya garden I had fallen in with
Sa'ud al 'Arafa and ridden in his company. With him was
his twelve-year-old son, Muhammad, whose mother was Ibn
Sa'ud's sister Nura, prancing about on a fiery steed which he
appeared to ride without effort. Sa'ud's eldest son, Sultan,
by another wife was about sixteen at this time and away at
the front with Turki. And he also had a daughter by Nura,
somewhat older than Muhammad. Sa'ud himself rode without
curb or stirrups—the Arabs thinking always of mounted
combat regard these as a positive danger in the event of a
rider becoming unhorsed—a beautiful mare of *Kuhaila* breed,
reputed to be one of the fastest animals in the country.
They always carry a cane riding, but never use it on their
mounts except when racing.

The heat was said to have been generally above the normal

during this summer, the hot-weather season being divided
into thirteen-day periods each connected with the rising of
some constellation. The *Rabi'* or spring season gives way
to the *Saif* or early summer with the rising of the Pleiades
(*Thuraiya*). At the intervals stated there follow *Tubaiya*,
the first *Jauza*, the second *Jauza*, then *Mirzim*, followed by
Kulaibain and then *Suhail* or Canopus. Thirteen days later
begins the season called *Safari* (pronounced *Sfiri*), which is
either synonymous with *Kharif* (autumn) or a transition
between *Qaidh* or late summer—which lasts from *Mirzim*
to *Suhail*—and the *Kharif*. The total length of the two
summers combined is 91 days, and we were at this time in
the section known as *Mirzim*.

As I returned home I noticed a man who from the pinkish
pallor of his skin I took to be a leper, but Manawar assured
me that this was not the case as the individual in question
had been like that from birth and was a member of the Imam
'Abdul Rahman's retinue, having always been in perfect
health and treated as quite normal. Perhaps he may have
been an Albino. Junaifi was awaiting me for dinner, and
soon after the meal the *Adhan* rang out and he rose to go to
prayers. ' You people pray too much,' I said ; ' will you have
to keep it up all the time you are in Paradise too ? ' ' No,'
he replied, ' there we have only to enjoy ourselves with food,
wine and women ; it is sufficient that we should observe the
hours of prayer in this world only.' ' After all,' he continued,
' there is the same bigotry in your religion too ; look at the
penance imposed on priests and monks and nuns—we have
nothing of that sort.' I pointed out that in our case it was
entirely a matter of personal choice.

Ibn Sa'ud, when I saw him next day, had the details of
another 'Ajman raid to report to me. Al Mutalaqqam and
some *Shaikhs* of the Safran had again raided an encampment
of the Subai' in the *Dira*, as they call the desert country
between Qatif and the Hasa, at a point about five days'
journey south of Kuwait. The Subai' had, however, pursued
them and gained a victory, capturing 30 and killing 11 camels,
and killing eight men, of whom three were well-known
Shaikhs—'Uwaiyidh Ibn Hadi and Dhumaid Ibn Juwai'a of
the Safran and Muhammad Ibn Mutalaqqam, nicknamed

Abu Haqta. They had also captured 31 rifles, and Ibn Sa'ud was in good humour at this second report of the ability of his own tribes to hold their own against the disadvantage of such surprise attacks. He attributed much of the prevailing unsatisfactory situation to the temporary absence of Sir Percy Cox from 'Iraq and hoped for some improvement in consequence of his return, which was due about this time and of which we momentarily expected information. ' If,' he said, ' you refuse to defend me from my enemies, I am free to defend myself without being accused of disloyalty to you. And, even if you let me down, be assured that I shall never dream of entering into hostilities with the British. That would be helping the Turks, whose success would mean my own undoing. But I'll tell you what I would do—I would take my dues from the Arabs.' In other words, he would consider himself free to attack the Sharif and the 'Ajman. He told me also that Ibn Dhuwaibi, one of the premier chiefs of the Harb, had just arrived at Riyadh to plead for his son, whom Turki had found in the Qasim buying camels for the Sharif's operations against Khurma and had placed under detention as hostage for the production of £16,000 paid to the Harb for this purpose. He proposed, however, to cancel Turki's order and direct the release of the *Shaikh's* son, but he would also prohibit the purchase of camels for the Sharif in his territories.

The first days of August were promisingly full of activity and there were signs that Ibn Sa'ud was really putting his house in order with a view to an early start. On the first of the month his administrative rearrangement of the southern districts was complete and Ibn 'Affaisan, hitherto governor of the Aflaj, set forth to take up the *Amirate* of Wadi Dawasir. He was accompanied by 'Abdul 'Aziz Ibn Duqaithir, who was to be his own successor in the former province, while 'Abdullah Ibn Mu'ammar, who had shown weakness in controlling the unruly elements of the Wadi during my visit there, was for the time being relegated to private life—his home being Sadus. Another sign of the coming move was a request by Junaifi for a ' loan ' on the ground that Ibn Sa'ud was not on this occasion making the usual advances to those who were to march with him. Whether this was true or not he knew

perfectly well that there could be no question of my lending
him money, and I gave expression to my very natural resent-
ment at his veiled begging for a gift. He was a queer
character,[1] likeable in many respects, though he had the
nervous, twitching manner of one who could not look his
conscience in the face. And many a time he had failed to
perform quite simple services for me, knowing that Ibn
Sa'ud's consent, which would have been forthcoming
without question, was necessary, but afraid to approach him
for that consent. For instance, I had asked him to get me
a list of the thirty or so villages constituting the Qatif area,
and he had readily promised to do so, but had never made any
attempt to fulfil his promise. Then came Ibrahim, whose
wife would expect him to make ample provision for her and
her family during his absence. He came with his accustomed
swagger, but sheepishly withal, explaining that, as I had left
only him out of grace in connection with the Wadi journey,
he had come to see if by now my anger had abated. At first
sight of him I had feared he might be come to announce that
he was to accompany me on the march again, and my relief
was great, but I declined to consider his request, adding that
I now knew the full details of the Jabir incident. He called
God to witness that he was unaware that I was particularly
interested in Jabir at the time, and I could only reply :
' Knowing God to be above you, how can you lie like that ? '
' May God strike off my neck,' he replied, ' if I lie.' I was
amazed that he should thus forswear himself, as indeed the
Arabs not seldom do, to one not of his own faith. Perjury
as between *Muslims* is a more serious offence, but there are
many that shrink not even from that. ' All I did,' he continued, maintaining his position, ' was in accordance with
Arab custom.' ' Yes,' I replied, ' in accordance with the
Arab custom of lies and deceit. So much I have learned by
now.' And seeing his case hopeless he rose with a laboured
swagger and marched out.

That same morning, 3rd August, I had looked out from
my roof on to the *Manakh*, which was full of ruckling, groaning
camels being loaded for the march, while in the midst of them

[1] He afterwards became (1925-6) the *Wahhabi* monarch's representative
in Egypt.

was planted the furled banner which would go before them. Half an hour later the cavalcade of nearly 400 animals carrying the tents, baggage and kitchen stuff was on the move, being due at Jubaila on the morrow, where they would await us. The day grew normally warm, but a heavy haze hung between earth and sky and dark clouds were about. A curious yellow light lay over the scene, and so noticeable was it that the Imam 'Abdul Rahman sent round to me to enquire whether the sun was eclipsed. It was only the 25th day of the lunar month (*Shawwal*), but I made a show of consulting the Nautical Almanac before pronouncing that there was no ground for nervousness. And my decision was apparently accepted as conclusive.

At long last dawned my last day at the *Wahhabi* capital, 4th August, the fourth anniversary of the outbreak of the Great War which was still convulsing the world. Here in the midst of Arabia we were far removed from the great turmoil, and I only felt a sense of relief that my too long sojourn at Riyadh was at an end. As a guest in the palace I had been well treated and been made exceedingly comfortable, while the opportunities I had had for developing and consolidating a friendship with Ibn Sa'ud, which was to last unimpaired through all the vicissitudes of the coming years, were beyond all price. But all along I experienced a feeling of restraint as of being a prisoner, which only free travel in the desert could dissipate. For 42 days on end I had resided at the capital, and in all that time I had only been out but four or five times to partake of coffee with other residents, who feared public opinion too much to invite me to their homes, though they were always cordial enough when they met me in public or had occasion to visit me in my quarters. I knew the city and its oasis as well as I could expect to do so, and I felt that I understood the strange society which inhabited them, for their lives were so standardised that there was little room for variety as between household and household. And I was glad that my sojourn was ended.

Nevertheless that last afternoon I went out for a long walk with the slave 'Atallah, to take farewell of the familiar scenes. The *Suq* was thronged with people buying and selling. Here one was selling a censer by auction, crying the last bid of

seventeen piastres ; there a *Baduwi* stood sentinel over a
bevy of white sheep while would-be customers inspected
them and went away and came again. Beyond them a couple
of women sat to one side vending the contents of a rag-basket
as it seemed—strips of tent cloth and the like. And the idle
sauntered to and fro as we passed down along the side of the
great mosque to the N.W. gate, where women were drawing
water from the narrow-mouthed masonry wells, of which
there are many sunk in the rock-platform on which the town
stands. By each well is a step of rock-slabs and a rough
stone trough for animals to drink from. Then beyond the
gate we had to struggle to make a path through the multi-
tudes of homecoming goats, among which there was but a
single sheep and the inevitable herd-boy on his donkey.
Ibn Sa'ud, restricting his household to the milk of camels
and kine, owned no milch goats or sheep, but his flocks were
entirely for the kitchen, to which was brought its daily quota.
Beyond the goats an old man trudged homeward, bending
under an enormous burden of firewood gathered in the desert
far away. We wandered then among the gardens, where
the butterflies flitted about over the sweet lucerne, in the
neighbourhood of Khizam, and there I sat awhile contemplating the scene while my companion went through his
ablutions and prayed towards the set sun. And as we
resumed our way returning homeward there came one running
after us crying : ' *Ya Philby !* ' It was old Nasir al Bishri,
one of the Harb *Rafiqs* and doyen of my companions on the
march to the Hijaz. After profuse and friendly greetings
he got down to business. ' Look you,' he said, ' I have just
taken a new wife and to-morrow I march with the *Shuyukh*,
and I have not wherewithal to make provision for her.' ' You
at your age '—he must have been sixty at least—' marrying
a wife ! ' ' Ay,' he replied, ' and she was a virgin withal,'
and he chuckled with satisfaction—the old sinner. I passed
on, suggesting that, if he wished to bring back some present
for his young wife from the *ghazu*, he might give me more of
the pleasure of his company during the march than he had
done since we last parted. And so we returned into the city
by way of the Hauta garden, and strolled homewards
deviously through side streets, in one of which a beggar

woman was crying aloud for alms before the house of Sa'ud al 'Arafa.

The city gates are closed every day after the evening prayer and on Fridays during the congregational service, but the palace gates are closed five times daily at the times of prayer, remaining closed from the evening till the dawn-prayer, during which hours they may not be opened on any account whatever, not even should Ibn Sa'ud himself be without demanding admittance. Such were his own orders, which none dared disobey, and such apparently the only precautions he deemed it necessary to observe against the incursion of possible foes. Inside the walls of the main courtyard are whitewashed with gypsum-lime to a height of about ten feet, the top line being surmounted with a frieze of delicate stepped pinnacles, which they call *Sharaf*, and believed to be of great antiquity. The bare brown clay above the frieze is roughly moulded in various designs—inverted *fleur-de-lys*, arches in low relief, leaves and the like, while pious texts are everywhere daubed upon the walls. Some of the doors too are highly decorated with confused patterns of red, yellow and blue spots, varied here and there with burned patches.

So night closed down upon us, all being ready for the morrow's march. During the morning Rushaid, who had eschewed my company for an inordinately long period, had surprised me by walking into my room. I upbraided him for his long neglect. ' *Wallah !* ' he pleaded, ' I haven't touched tobacco since I last visited you.' That in his view was punishment enough, and he brought me the good news that he and Manawar were to accompany me on the march. Junaifi soon joined us for breakfast, and I thought the occasion fitting for an exposition of the worries of past journeys, of which I hoped to avoid a repetition during the journey before us. The *'Abid*, who sat round us as we ate, could not restrain their laughter at some of the incidents I recalled to their memory, and Rushaid, with a great load off his mind owing to his approaching departure from the soul-restricting atmosphere of Riyadh, was in excellent fettle, promising everything without the slightest intention of performing anything that might cause him a moment's inconvenience.

Ibn Sa'ud, he told me, had been much amused at his recital of some of the incidents of the journey to the Wadi, and had called upon him again and again—once for the delectation of the lady Nura and his other sisters—to tell the story of a certain conversation in which he, Tami, Nasir Ibn Talaq and I had taken part. We were discussing religion, and Tami had clenched his argument by assuring me that hell would be my portion in the next world. Ibn Sa'ud was impressed at my not taking offence at a jest so terrible, for I had replied : ' That may be so, but I care not, for one thing I know—the first person I shall meet at hell's entrance will be you, Tami, and I shall find that you have been appointed by the devil to serve me eternally riding your *Dhalul* behind me in my endless journeys through the blazing fire.' There was nothing that he disliked so much as riding, as I rode, through the heat of the day. As I had surmised, Ibrahim had explained away my displeasure to his master on the ground that he had set his face against my visiting Hauta and Hariq on our return journey.

My last interview with Ibn Sa'ud had been a short one, as he was busy with other things. I found him with the child, Muhaimid, who was to have accompanied his father and thus have his first experience of a *ghazu*, but that plan had been abandoned as his little brother, Khuwailid, had screamed with distress at the thought of the parting. ' Do you teach your children to ride ? ' I asked. ' No,' he replied, ' we just put them on horseback at first with a slave riding pillion and then alone. Thus from an early age the child becomes accustomed to horses and develops into a natural horseman.' Riding and shooting are enjoined as the duty of all *Muslims* by the *Quran*, which says : ' Ride and shoot, but I prefer that ye shoot.' Swimming is ordained by the traditions, and most Arabs can swim. Ibn Sa'ud himself had learned to do so in the sea at Kuwait, but Arabs who have never seen the sea learn in the great *Jalibs* of their country and even dive into them.

A suggestion had been put forward at Bahrain that Ibn Sa'ud was interested in the question of reopening the 'Iraq shrines to *Shia'* pilgrimage on account of his *Shia'* subjects in the Hasa. His answer to my very tentative question on the subject was decisive : ' I would raise no objection,' he replied, ' if you demolished the whole lot of them, and I would demolish them myself if I had the chance.' When the opportunity presented itself years afterwards in another quarter he showed that these words had not been idly spoken, though circumstances compelled him to temper his convictions to the chill winds of political expediency. The straight-spoken iconoclast of 1918 was yet to experience the limita-tions imposed upon him by his own growing strength and by his sense of responsibility towards the great world of *Islam*, of which the *Wahhabi* sect might perhaps be regarded as the kernel or, at most, as a leaven destined to leaven the whole lump. But before such a consummation there must be much unravelling of the tangled skein of Islamic ethics and metaphysics. And the stoutest heart must quail before the great chasm that separates the faction of 'Ali from the rest of *Islam*. In August, 1918, there seemed little enough chance of any development which would place the *Wahhabis* in the forefront of orthodox *Islam*, and Ibn Sa'ud, whose *Shia'* subjects in the Hasa had nothing to complain of provided they avoided ostentation in the practice of their peculiar rites, was free to speak candidly and contemptuously of the great heresy which once cleft the fellowship of *Islam* in twain and may yet again play the leading *rôle* in a future crisis of the first magnitude.

CHAPTER II

NORTHWARD BOUND

1. The Upper Reaches of Wadi Hanifa

It was still dark when Manawar's gentle attempts to rouse
me from sleep with the strange address of '*Ya Mustafa*,[1] *ya
Mustafa* ! '—for in Arabia, as in eastern lands generally, it
is deemed unseemly to awaken the sleeper roughly—were
reinforced by the strident notes of a neighbouring *Muadhdhin*
in the early hours of 5th August, the day appointed for the
beginning of the campaign against Hail. It was barely 4.30
a.m., but I had scarcely begun to sip my morning cup of tea
when news was brought me that Ibn Sa'ud had started. I
lost but little time in dressing and completing my packing
by lamplight, and an hour later I was saying a final farewell
to the faithful steward, Muhammad Ibn Musallam, before
mounting in the palace courtyard.

A splendid '*Umaniya dhalul* [2] of excellent paces, though
a trifle nervous and difficult, especially in the neighbourhood of buildings, had been placed at my disposal. Rushaid
Akhu Hasana had now replaced Ibrahim as my guide,
philosopher and friend ; and my party for the nonce was
completed by Ibrahim al Junaifi, Manawar, a young cousin
of Rushaid called Haimid, and two drivers for the baggage
animals. Before the day was out I had occasion to complain
of the absence of a guide with local knowledge, and the
deficiency was immediately made good by the deputation
of Mitrak Ibn 'Amara, an old friend, to my party.

[1] ' Oh, elect one ! ' It may, however, have been an attempt to pronounce
my name with the prefix Mr.

[2] An Arabian camel-bridle, called *Khitāma*, consists of a single rope of
wool attached by a short chain to a ring in the head-stall, which consists
of a band of leather round the animal's nose held in position by a strip of
leather passing over and behind the ears. Round the neck is usually tied
a short strand of rope, called '*Aqal* or *Rasan*, which is used to tie up one
leg of the animal when halting for the night.

And so I left Riyadh—as it proved for the last time—after a continuous sojourn of 42 days since my return from the south; and right glad I was to shake the dust of the *Wahhabi* capital from my feet. Ibn Sa'ud had gone by the direct route [1] to Dar'iya; but I was minded to explore the whole length of Wadi Hanifa, and, on issuing from the city by the Dhuhairi gate, my small party followed the outer fringe of the palm groves in a southerly direction until we reached the Batin [2] after an hour's riding.

For a mile or more upstream, as we followed the winding bed of the *Wadi* in a north-westerly direction, we had the rich palm groves of this oasis-suburb on either hand, and ever and anon we passed by the black tents of *Badu*, arranged singly or in small groups in the midst of the sandy torrent bed. They were mostly of the Suhul and Qahtan, whose goats I noticed tethered by the neck to logs of wood or large stones, while the yearling kids frolicked with the naked *Badu* children, rushing at them in playful anger, butting at them and capering about. And, as we passed one group, a woman came forth from the gardens with a bundle of lucerne, whereat, leaving their games, the kids rushed upon her; she sat upon the sand and fed them.

The Batin palms come to an end at the point where the rich delta of Sha'ib Maidhar [3] joins the *Wadi*, with its profusion of garden plots of pumpkin, millet and cotton, guarded in former times of unrest by a watch tower, whose stone ruins are still seen on the crest of Hanifa's right bank. From here the valley rises perceptibly between ridges not more than 30 feet high, its whole breadth being some 300 yards, of which a third is occupied by the torrent strand. Here and there the latter is overspread with copses of dwarf-willow,[4] and is joined by unimportant *Sha'ibs* from either side.

Some three miles up from our entrance into the *Wadi* we came upon a body of *Badu* engaged in founding a new settlement on a long abandoned site. Water had already been reached at no great depth in a well they were engaged upon, and a few houses had been built. They were of the *Ikhwan*, but showed their ignorance of my identity by pressing us to

---

[1] *See H.A.* i. 108-110.   [2] *See H.A.* i. 368, 369.
[3] *See H.A.* i. 110.   [4] *Ghaf* (also dwarf-poplar).

delay our march and drink coffee with them. We made our excuses and passed on to find some old ruins of clay buildings and a derelict masonry well in a bay of the valley not far distant—another settlement of a glorious past[1]—and yet some more ruins of houses and wells close by at the mouth of Sha'ib Liban, here mingling with the *Wadi* after a long course through Tuwaiq.

Immediately after this we came to the still tenanted settlement of Quraishiya, lying some four miles up from the Batin. It consists of some hundred palm stems in all in two ragged groups, about which stood a few wretched hovels and a single *Qasr* of some pretension, the total population of which may be fifty souls. Here the banks on either side rose to some 70 feet, and the valley was choked with lofty deposits of silt through which the torrent bed cuts its way down steeply. Two miles further on we came to the confluence of the broad Sha'ib 'Ubair with the *Wadi*, and after some hesitation as to which was the Hanifa we turned up the latter due north towards the palm groves of 'Arqa,[2] visible ahead. For a mile or more before the oasis proper was reached we passed through its cornfields marked out in little rectangular plots in the valley silt. Here and there were a few wells for their irrigation.

The oasis of 'Arqa extends from side to side of the valley to a breadth of a quarter mile and for about half a mile upstream, the torrent bed cleaving through the midst of it. Retaining walls of masonry surmounted with clay contain the stream on either side, and the village proper lies on the right bank thereof. The village is of old and dilapidated appearance, but is walled and provided with a few watchtowers, while a few isolated houses are embedded in the dense palm groves of the left bank. At one of these, the house of the local *Amir*, we drew rein to ask for water, but were eagerly pressed to stay for coffee. Accepting the invitation we were entertained by the *Amir's* brother, 'Uthman Ibn 'Uthman, and an old man whose identity I did not discover. They pounded the coffee beans with a pestle of polished black stone,[3] such as is used, they said, at Haïl, in a solid mortar

---

[1] *See H.A.* ii. 8.   [2] See *H.A.* ii. 110.

[3] Possibly basalt, cf. *C.M.D.* ii. 359.

of greyish marble, about two feet square and a foot high, and decorated with simple lines. Twice they passed round the coffee, with a welcome course of fresh dates of a variety called *Dataïni* in between, and hospitably they pressed us to stay the night and break our fast with them on the morrow ; but, failing in this, they sped us on our way with the customary round of incense.

The population of 'Arqa may be 500 souls, claiming descent from Bani Hilal,[1] though it is commonly thought that there is a large admixture of 'Anaza blood in them. The coffee-parlour was far from large, but unusually cool and airy, its roof being supported by a single central pillar of stone plastered with gypsum and surmounted by a capital of the simplest character. Our hosts showed some little curiosity as to what I might be ; a stranger as they saw, but Junaifi would vouchsafe no more information than that I was an honoured guest of Ibn Sa'ud, while my statement that I came from a country a year's journey distant by camel-reckoning enlightened them not at all.

The ruins of Dar'iya lie at a distance of three miles upstream from 'Arqa in a north-westerly direction. Between these points the valley varies in width from 200 to 500 yards between buttressed sides rising to a height of from 70 to 100 feet. Three unimportant freshet-channels cut into it from the left bank, and just before Dar'iya is reached one passes the small palm grove and *Qasr* of Mukhtarra.

Here we came into view of the pinnacled ruins of the old *Wahhabi* capital,[2] and, lingering as we went to enjoy the scene, we passed along the channel between its retaining walls to the spot where we had camped for the night in the previous December. It was a gay and busy scene that now met our eyes, Ibn Sa'ud's cavalcade being spread out about the torrent bed and neighbouring palm groves. I was immediately invited to proceed to the house [3] of the local *Amir*, whither Ibn Sa'ud and his retinue had been bidden to dine. There was a goodly gathering in honour of the occasion and much talk, followed by the afternoon prayer. Then came dinner,

---

[1] A semi-mythical tribe, whose name is sometimes used to indicate great antiquity.
[2] *See H.A.* i. 110-113.   [3] In the hamlet of Al Dhahara.

a sumptuous banquet, and scarcely was this at an end when Ibn Sa'ud gave the order to march. At 4.30 p.m. the whole cavalcade was in motion, but the early part of that afternoon march on top of an enormous meal was far from comfortable, and I was thankful that the first five miles of our progress as far as Malqa was over country already traversed [1] by me.

It was already 6 p.m. when we reached Malqa and passed the farthest point of the *Wadi* reached by me before. Ibn Sa'ud, however, showed no sign of stopping, and on we went up the valley which was now half a mile wide between 100 feet slopes. A little above Malqa we passed the ruins of an abandoned farm of extensive cornfields, but an hour later it had become too dark to see either the features of the valley or my compass. I roughly judged our north-westerly direction by the Pole Star as we jumbled along in the dark, but it was not till nearly 9 p.m. that we reached the settlement of Jubaila and found to my joy that Ibn Sa'ud had halted for the night. We had marched some 28 miles in all by my reckoning, and had followed the Hanifa valley for 25 miles. We had already dined—by their reckoning, though I was again quite hungry after the march—so I lay down on the sand and was soon fast asleep.

At Jubaila,[2] one of the earliest settlements of the Bani Hanifa, who have given their name to the whole valley, Wadi Hanifa, hitherto a broad shallow trough between low bare downs, contracts its course to plunge sharply down the buttressed channel which I have already described. The village is therefore the key to an important strategic position between the settlements of 'Aridh and the uplands of Mahmal and Tuwaiq, and it is here that tradition places one of the decisive battles of early *Islamic* history, in which the companions of the Prophet, a handful of the true believers, met the forces of Musailama, the false [3] prophet of Huraimala. The victory of the true faith was purchased only at the cost of the lives of some seventy of the *Sahaba*, the only trustworthy repositories of the oral teachings of the master ; and it is believed in Najd that this serious loss of life among them was the direct cause of the immediate

---

[1] *See H.A.* i. 114.
[2] *See H.A.* i. 113, and ii. 145.   [3] *Al Kadhdhab*, the liar.

commitment to writing of the text of the *Quran*, dictated to scribes by the lips of the survivors of the small band who had had its verses from the lips of the Prophet himself. Be that as it may the graves of the companions who fell on that occasion are shown to this day close by the village in a deep deposit of river silt, which at the time of my visit had been partially eroded by the torrent, with the result that the sides of many tombs gaped open-mouthed into the valley. The surface of the silt deposit was not more than three or four feet above the graves ; and we must therefore suppose either that the burials are more recent than believed or that the silt had been deposited where it now is and practically at its present level before the battle of Jubaila. The latter alternative is certainly not impossible.

The village, now tenanted only by a few wretched inhabitants and for the most part in ruins, stands about a quarter mile from the cemetery of the Companions on the opposite, or left, bank of the channel. Here and there a patch of *Ithils* varies the drab monotony of the vast silt deposits which choke the valley. Several wells, including one of masonry lining in regular use, are to be found near the settlement, most of whose houses are but ruinous shells of clay from which the woodwork has been removed. Several are, however, still in a fair state of preservation, with gypsum-covered stone pillars still supporting their roofs, and in one I found a large double receptacle of clay covered with a fine brown plaster for the storage of dates—still stained with the juice of its former contents ; but the best preserved building of all was the mosque of typical *Wahhabi* architecture, with its roof supported by pointed arches [1] resting on pillars with simple capitals, reminding one of the familiar stepped pinnacle reversed. Many of the clay walls had in their lower half a strengthening of flat stone slabs set slantwise with a simple decorative effect.

In comparatively recent times Jubaila formed an appanage of the Ibn Mu'ammar princes of 'Ayaina, and it finally decayed and perished during the struggles of 'Abdullah and Sa'ud,[2] towards the end of the nineteenth century. The

---

[1] *Vide* Fig. 1.
[2] Partly also owing to water-failure.

country round about is as little imposing as anything I have ever seen, the bleak, featureless plateau of Tuwaiq spreading out on all sides in an endless monotone broken only by the low ridge of Hadhafa Salbukh to the north-east.

Ibn Sa'ud and his army were up and away some considerable time before I awoke to the sound of Mitrak's burly voice chiding the cook or the camels. But it was not till I had fully

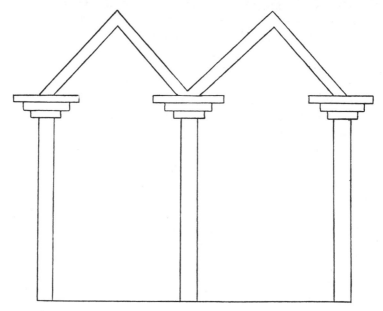

FIG. 1. ARCHES OF COLONNADE OF MOSQUE AT JUBAILA.

inspected the village and its surroundings that we too mounted and started up the valley. Our course was more or less westerly for about a mile and a half, when we reached the eastern extremity of 'Ayaina at a small group of houses close by a considerable clump of *Ithils*. At this point Sha'ib Maqraba, which has its beginning near 'Ammariya,[1] enters the *Wadi* from the south, while somewhat earlier we had passed the mouth of a freshet called Umm Sulaim entering from the north.

The once famous settlement of 'Ayaina, extending east and west along both sides of the torrent channel for about

[1] *See H.A.* i. 116.

two miles is now but the abomination of desolation. *Ithil* copses have usurped the spaces once reserved for flourishing palm plantations. The main town or *Hilla*, once the abode of the princes of the Ibn Mu'ammar dynasty, only differs from the lesser hamlets which dot the settlement here and there in covering a wider area with its ruins. Every now and then one may come across remnants of architecture— pillars with capitals such as those of Jubaila, pointed arches [1] and triangular ventilation holes disposed in decorative groups. Here and there are waterless wells of solid masonry and reservoirs cemented over. The banks of the torrent are faced with retaining walls of great solidity, which continue to keep its flood waters within their channel, though those who built them for their own protection have long since departed, and their habitations, guarded from the flood, have crumbled into dust. In some of these walls I noticed great blocks of masonry two feet long and half as much across.

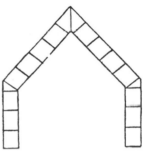

FIG. 1A. ARCH AT 'AYAINA.

The western end of the *Hilla* approaches a commanding conical eminence, perhaps a mound marking the site of an ancient village—so regular and smooth it is—of which tradition has it that it once stood in the midst of Ibn Mu'ammar's town. The ruling prince of those days one day ascended the hill in company with his daughter, who interrupted his exclamations of admiration of the scene before him with the curt criticism that the town would be better without the hill in its midst. Whereupon the order went forth to remove the eminence to a more convenient site, and there it is to this day to prove the truth of the story. Certain it is that 'Ayaina was in the past and until the rise of the Ibn Sa'ud dynasty of Dar'iya the seat of a great principality; the peer of Manfuha. Its decadence dates from the rejection of the opportunity placed within the reach of its lord by the prophet of *Wahhabism*,[2] and it was doubtless laid waste in

---

[1] *Vide* Fig. 1A.
[2] *See H.A.* i. pp. xvi, xvii.

the wars that followed with the barons of Dar'iya. Since those days it has never recovered, though it may yet revive as a new colony of *Ikhwan* settlers.

We passed out of the ruin-field of 'Ayaina by a regular avenue of well grown *Ithils* ending close to the last westward hamlet of the settlement. We now set our faces to the westward up the valley, which, from being about a mile broad at this point, widens to two and even three miles as it rises. On the right we noticed Sha'ib Haqar descending into the valley, rising, it is said, in a large cemented tank on the hillside, which, catching the rain water and drainage of the hill, still serves to irrigate a considerable patch of corn land amid the ruins. The next tributary of the *Wadi*, also on the right of our course, is Sha'ib 'Ayaina, which descends from the narrow tableland dividing Wadi Hanifa from the Sadus valley. Pelly [1] must have followed this ravine when marching from Sadus to 'Ayaina in 1865, and described the country as downs with the green stripped off. He found 'Ayaina deserted, though 'scarcely in ruins.'

Soon after leaving 'Ayaina behind us we crossed the Hanifa storm channel, which had hitherto been on our right, at its confluence with Sha'ib Zalaq coming in from the south. We now followed the downs forming the left bank of the valley, leaving the channel at some distance to our left, and did not cross it again until we arrived at Ibn Sa'ud's camp pitched in a wide circular basin formed by the confluence of two channels which constitute the sources of Wadi Hanifa. That on the left, Sha'ib Ghurur, comes out at this point from a great bay in the Tuwaiq uplands, whence it is joined by a lesser tributary, Sha'ib Bautha, and is of less importance than its rival, Wadi Haisiya, which may in fact be regarded as the true continuation of Hanifa upwards. The confluence of the two channels is known as Malaqi, whence, Ibn Sa'ud having for some obscure reason decided to stay here for the night, I was able to wander among the neighbouring ridges to get an idea of the country, which, to tell the truth, had little of interest to show. The soil in this neighbourhood was a distinctly reddish sand and the ridges about the valley were of limestone overlying sandstone. All around reigned

---

[1] Lieut.-Col. Lewis Pelly, Political Resident in the Persian Gulf.

a dull bleak monotony except only to the northwest, where the twin paps of Bakkain stood sentinel over the road leading between them over the ridge to Sadus.

It was for this point, some four miles distant, that I made next morning, following the channel of Wadi Haisiya, conspicuous with its long line of gum-bearing acacias,[1] of which they say that the foliage renews itself at the beginning of the autumn, though no rain falls at this season, providing camels with fresh fodder which enables them to go four or five days without water. The rest of the valley, about half a mile wide, was scantily clothed with desert scrub—'*Arta*, '*Arfaj* and '*Aushaz*.

From the summit of the western and higher peak of Bakkain, standing some 3200 feet above sea level and 200 feet above the valley at this point, Mitrak, Junaifi and I had a magnificent expansive view of the rolling plateaus and valleys of the Tuwaiq system while we consumed our breakfast of bread and water. To the northward, but two miles distant in a broad valley descending to the basin of Khafs,[2] lay the charming oasis of Sadus, easily discernible in all its detail though unfortunately too far out of our way to be visited. The palm groves appeared to extend along the storm channel for a length of about a mile with an average width of 200 or 300 yards ; at the extreme eastern end of the belt stood a *Qasr*, while two small hamlets stood at either side of the palms nearer the western end, the northernmost of the two being known as Ras, while the other, Hilla, was once famous for a remarkable obelisk of the Days of Ignorance, possibly a Christian monument ; this obelisk was still standing at the time of Pelly's visit and was sketched [3] by one of his party, but it has since been thrown down and broken to satisfy the bigotry of the *Wahhabi* community. The oasis contains a population of some 500 souls of Bani Tamin stock, while the lesser hamlets of Hizwa and Muharraqa, respectively 1½ and 3 miles lower down the valley, but invisible from my point of vantage, are said to house 300 souls apiece. Sadus was the ancestral home of my companion, Junaifi, but he had visited it but once in his life and showed no desire to

[1] *Talh.* [2] *See H.A.* i. 333.
[3] *See* Pelly's account of his ' Visit to the *Wahabee* capital.'

repeat the venture, remarking that its folk were as oxen (*Thiran*) in sturdiness and intellect.

Far off to the north east the coast of the 'Arma upland appeared dimly ; to the northwest, separated by a broad ridge from the Sadus valley, we could see the valley of Huraimala, which is another tributary of the Khafs basin. Southwestward we saw the break in the Tuwaiq escarpment marking the position of the Haisiya pass, and southward beyond the line of Wadi Haisiya and the Malaqi ridge extended the broad back of the Tuwaiq plateau to the dim distance.

As we sat here, unwilling to tear ourselves from the scene, I noticed a profusion of fossils scattered about the hillside, and before we descended to our camels waiting below I made a collection of them to bring home to the British Museum. They have since been examined and described,[1] proving to be of the Jurassic epoch.

Under Bakkain the valley spreads out somewhat indefinitely in a number of wide bays running up into the plateau wilderness, the most important of these being named Al Jiri. The actual torrent strand of Haisiya, however, follows the opposite or right bank of the valley, turning with it from a northwesterly to a southwesterly direction. A regular forest of *Talh* trees marks the confluence of Sha'ib Khamar from the west with the Haisiya, which, receiving further on a well-wooded affluent in Sha'ib Mazru'a, runs up into a bare, amazingly bare, narrow valley lined on either side by buttressed slopes rising to a height of 150 feet. At a distance of some seven miles we reached the Haisiya pass, marked by a spreading acacia, which may be regarded as the source of Wadi Hanifa. Our height above sea level was here about 3200 [2] feet, and our distance from the Batin about 46 miles. I had now seen the whole valley of Hanifa as far south as Yamama, a total of just over 100 miles, in the course of which it falls some 1900 feet. The scene at the watershed was not inspiring ; before us the land sloped down in a wide triangle formed by the diverging cliffs of the Tuwaiq escarpment, ending on either side in prominent headlands, Khashm

[1] *See H.A.* Appendix I.
[2] The heights given here are only approximate.

SHA'ĪB MAZRŪ'A.

To face page 78.

THE ROYAL CAMP-KITCHEN AT AL HISH.

To face page 79.

Kharsha to the south and Khashm Haisiya on the north ; between these extremities the base of the triangle was the bare ruddy sandstone shelf of Mirka, beyond which there is a sharp drop to the Butin valley below. The freshet of Sha'ib Hish meanders, at first steeply in a narrow deep bed and afterwards more gently in a broader strand, down the slope until, at the hither edge of the Mirka shelf, it spreads out in what was formerly a considerable and prosperous settlement and ultimately finds a way through the rocky barrier to the Butin valley. The remains of the Hish settlement lie some four miles distant from the watershed of Hanifa and consist of no more than scattered patches of dwarf palms and three wells, two of which are lined with masonry and in regular use, providing an ample supply of water at about two fathoms' depth. The colour of the water when first drawn is a slaty blue from the underlying shale, but it clears if allowed to set and is of excellent quality. The watering is reckoned to the Qahtan.

Here we found Ibn Sa'ud and his host encamped for the day on our arrival, and here, after the cooling southwesterly breeze which had favoured our march, we experienced one of those sudden changes common to the Arabian climate, and all that afternoon we had much ado to keep our tents steady in the teeth of a sirocco blowing as from a furnace. The temperature did not exceed 110°, which was fairly normal in comparison with Riyadh, but at midnight it was no less than 89° and at 5 a.m. next morning it stood as high as 78°.

The Haisiya pass presents no difficulty to camel traffic [1] and is probably the easiest of all the Tuwaiq passes—hence its selection for the pilgrim route, which we had in fact followed since leaving Riyadh and which now strikes down to Dhruma [2] and joins my westward track of the previous December at that point.

2. WESTERN MAHMAL

During the next two days, 8th and 9th August, we covered no more than 26 miles, our line of march striking through the district of Western Mahmal, a fertile tract lying athwart the

[1] It has since experienced motor traffic on a considerable scale.
[2] See *H.A.* i. 123.

upper reaches of the Butin or Dhruma valley, here known by
the name of Batin al Hawar. With a length of about 25
miles and an average width of not more than ten this district
extends from southeast to northwest between the *Nafud*
ridge of Turaif al Habil bounding it on the north and the
neighbourhood of Dhruma. Its eastern boundary is the
escarpment of Tuwaiq from Khashm Haisiya to the point
at which Sha'ib al Ats breaks through it on its eastward
course, while on the west lies a low sandstone ridge called
Safrat al Shams.

Ibn Sa'ud had as usual struck camp and marched off from
Hish long before I was awake, and my small party followed
at its leisure. It was only thus I could hope to inspect the
country in detail, but I had ever to listen to and override
proposals for night-marching. Rushaid and Junaifi had a
great dislike for marching during the heat of the day with
the temperature at 110° in the shade, but Mitrak was always
ready to do anything he was asked to.

A wide gap in the Mirka shelf gave me a good view to the
southward as far as Nafud Jau.[1] The pass of Ri' al Barqa
beyond Dhruma could be seen but not the latter settlement
itself, while the massive hill of Quraidan stood out a prominent
landmark during the whole of our journeying in this district,
which we actually entered by crossing the slender torrent-bed
of Sha'ib Ghadidda near a patch of dwarf palms. This
stream descends from the headland of Khashm Haisiya and
joins the Batin al Hawar at the farmstead of Nuqai'a recently
acquired by Ibn Sa'ud's eldest brother, Muhammad.

Shortly afterwards we descended from the shelf to the
valley level into the wide depression of Faïqa, beyond which,
apart from occasional ridges, the Mahmal plain is undisturbed
until the central ridge of 'Araidh is reached in its northern
section. Everywhere the withered appearance of the country
was eloquent of a shortage of rain during the past winter,
even the acacias along the line of the storm channel[2] being
dry.

To our right the endless *échelon* of headlands[3] stood out

---

[1] *See H.A.* i. 126. [2] Abal Safi.

[3] Kharsha, Haisiya, Muhaqqaba, Rumaidha, Turab and Husan in that
order from south to north.

'UWAINID.

from the escarpment of Tuwaiq and at intervals we crossed the dry torrent-beds, whose beginnings are in the bays between each pair of promontories. At the points of meeting of these streams and the main channel stood scattered granges consisting each of a single *Qasr* and a patch of corn-land such as might be cultivated by irrigation from a single well situated within the walls of the *Qasr*. Such farmsteads were Bulaida and Hujaila not far off on our left just before we reached the small palm-grove and hamlet of 'Uwainid on a *Sha'ib* of the same name.

The palm-grove, about 200 yards square, was surrounded by a clay wall with two *Qasrs* at the corners of its western side, while another similar building stood out from the enclosure on the east by a patch of *Ithils*. The population of this little settlement cannot exceed fifty persons, who belonged originally to the tribe of Harb and migrated hither from the district of Sirr. We found by experience that they were inhospitable folk, when we turned aside from our path in the hopes of refreshment. An old man was sitting on an earthen bench outside one of the buildings as we arrived, and shortly after there emerged a young man who immediately invited us to coffee and shouted to a boy within to prepare the parlour. He then informed us that he had no coffee utensils—I had to restrain the weary Junaifi from offering to assist him over this difficulty, for I did not wish to force him to the shameful confession that he had no coffee —and, after a short silence, volunteered the suggestion that we might find coffee ready in one of the other *Qasrs*. I assured him that we wanted nothing but a cup of water, and while this was being fetched we sat upon the bench outside chatting with the old man, who proved garrulous enough and inquisitive. Not being master of the house he begged us to stay in the hope, doubtless, that he would taste of our coffee ; but to the young man's relief we declined to do so, and resumed our march after a draught of water. The water here as also at Barra and apparently throughout the district has a slightly unpleasant mineral taste, the wells of this oasis being eight to ten fathoms in depth.

Ibn Sa'ud had pitched for the day beyond the northern extremity of Barra, which lies some two miles to the north-

west of 'Uwainid and may be regarded as the capital of the
district.   It lies along the broad bed of a torrent called Abu
Kitada, a tributary of Batin al Hawar rising on the escarpment of Tuwaiq and having a common watershed with Sha'ib
Huraimala.   The groves of the oasis extend for about a mile
along the torrent-bed from north-east to south-west, but are
liberally spaced and each has its own *Qasr*.   In the midst
of the oasis stands the imposing fortress of Qasr 'Ajlan,
forming a square of 60 yards, with stout well-built clay walls
surmounted by turrets, the upper part of the latter projecting
outwards and downwards after the manner of a lamp-shade.
Three roughly-arched openings without doors give admittance
to the castle from without.   Its lord is Ibn 'Ajlan, who, with
his following of a hundred souls, belongs by origin to the
Hudhail, a tribe of the Hijaz and originally a section of the
Mutair.   South of this stronghold lies the unwalled village
of Barra itself, a straggling group of habitations contained
within a space about 200 yards long and 100 broad.   It
has no *Suq*, and its main street, in which is the mosque,
is a branch of the torrent strand which enters and leaves the
village through a row of low arches supporting a wall that
blocks the street at either end.   The population, numbering
some 400 souls—another hundred tenant the scattered *Qasrs*
—is of Bani Khalid extraction, the local *Amir* being Ibn
Majid, who did me the honour of dining with me that night
and proved unusually communicative, though his chief
topic of conversation was the generosity to himself of Colonel
Hamilton,[1] who had been his guest the previous autumn.
He made it quite clear that similar generosity on my part
would not be amiss, and I trust I earned his eternal gratitude
by a present of ten dollars.   The village has no gates, but
some of the houses are surmounted by turrets of the kind
already described.   The wells are seven or eight fathoms
deep, but the water has the same unpleasant flavour as that
of 'Uwainid, except in one well standing well away from the
oasis to the north, from which drinking water is drawn.   I
noticed in this neighbourhood a gypsum deposit of inferior
quality, which is used by the local people to make *juss* or
lime by burning.

[1] Now Lord Belhaven and Stenton.

Ibn Majid had promised overnight to find an intelligent guide to attend me as far as Shaqra, but it was not until Junaifi visited him to remind him of his word that he produced a lad of most unpromising appearance, whom he seemed to be coaching in the names of places likely to be met with as he brought him along. The lad, Hamad Ibn Hazza' by name and of the 'Amir section of Subai', was not exactly eager to undertake the task, and pleaded for six dollars as payment instead of five ; I promised him seven if he turned out satisfactory, and by the end of the day I had inwardly determined to double his guerdon. He proved one of the best guides I had had and, though he seemed to know nothing whatever of the country outside his limited range, he knew the route from Riyadh to Shaqra and everything visible from it on either hand like a book. He was quaint withal : ' Have you date-palms in your country ? ' he asked. ' No,' I replied. ' Then doubtless it is rice your people cultivate ? ' ' No,' I replied, ' nor rice either, but only corn.' ' *Wallah !* '*Arab !* ' he exclaimed, meaning that we must be even as his own folk if it is only grain that we raise.

As we marched along from Barra we noted many scattered farmsteads about the countryside ; a newly-planted palm-grove in a walled enclosure close to the oasis on our track ; Qasr Sahak away to our right a mile distant ; the slender watch-tower of Burj Minhath and Qasr Husaniya further away to our left in front of the twin flat-topped knolls called Quwar[1] al Hawar over against the sandstone ridge. In front of us rose the conspicuous buttress of Dhaïna forming the southern extremity of the 'Araidh ridge, which soon hemmed us in against the upper course of Batin al Hawar. Away to our right lay the ridge of Umm al Hujair behind Sahak as we crossed the sandy bed of a cross torrent called Tharmaniya full of *Harmal* and *Salam* scrub, and soon after Sha'ib Qulailat, so called from numerous little mounds cropping out of the plain as we approached the ridge.

Here we re-entered the main caravan track from Riyadh to Shaqra, which passes to the south of Barra, and followed it along the slope which descends from the 'Araidh ridge to the Batin, beyond which, some five or six miles distant, I

[1] Pl. of *Qara*.

noted the hillock of Qarat al Shams on the sandstone ridge.
By it is a grange belonging to a man of Barra, and two miles
beyond it are the wells of Shumaisa in a ravine of that name,
but I failed to get any information about a place named
Dastiqar in Hunter's map.

In quick succession we crossed little freshet beds [1] descending into the valley. In the ridge itself stood the headland
of Khashm Suqur, so called from its resemblance to a falcon's
beak, and the watering of Qulaiyibat al Shawwaf, a shepherd
rendezvous attributed to a *Sharif* from the Hijaz. Further
on we encountered a small party of *Ikhwan* shepherds, male
and female, at the single unlined well of Umm al Shutun,
which has a supply of excellent water. The shepherds were
from the notorious settlement of Ghatghat, and were eager
to hear any news we might have as to the movements of the
contingent from that town—it was to join Ibn Sa'ud at
Shaqra. They did me the compliment of thinking that I was
a (Turkish) gunner in Ibn Sa'ud's employ, and we left them
unenlightened to proceed ourselves to a knoll on the ridge,
whence we could survey the country around us.

Our viewpoint commanded the whole district of Western
Mahmal from west to east and to its southern limit under
Quraidan. It lay practically on the water-parting between
the Batin al Hawar and a depression known as Umm Sidr,
which, starting from the junction of the Turaif Habil *Nafud*
and the Safrat al Shams, flows north-east along the southern
edge of the sands until it passes into and through the Tuwaiq
barrier under the name of Sha'ib al Ats. Not far from that
point lies the village of Thadiq, which was not visible, while
in the same direction but on the near side of the escarpment
we espied a lofty slender minaret or watch-tower rising out
of the houses and palm-groves of a considerable oasis—
Raghaba by name. It is probably the largest village in the
district, having, by repute, a population of some 800 persons,
belonging to the 'Arainat subsection of the 'Amir Subai'
living under the rule of 'Abdul 'Aziz Ibn Khuraiyif. The
oasis, about three-quarters of a mile long and 200 yards
broad, lies in the bed of a torrent descending from Khashm
Tarafiya in Tuwaiq.

[1] Sha'ib Thamam, Thaniyat al Raml and others.

Away to our left front, from Sha'ib al Ats northwards, stretched the grey cliff of Sudair, the northernmost district of Tuwaiq and the only settled district in Najd proper which I never managed to visit. Its main features are, however, well enough known, thanks mainly to the late Captain Shakespear, and it would seem from his accounts and from those of others who have seen parts of it, to be a particularly prosperous and well-favoured tract. Westward of the cliff, between it and the Turaif Habil sands, which form the eastern boundary of the district of Washm, lies the narrow but fertile strip of Hamada in which are several villages—Huraiyiq, with 600 souls, furthest south ; then Qasab, a mile to the north-west ; Furaithan, a settlement of *Ikhwan* from the Mutair tribe, twelve to fifteen miles further north ; and lastly Dahina, eight miles beyond—another *Ikhwan* settlement of mixed Mutair and 'Ataiba elements.

The land-level was 2900 feet [1] above the sea at our view-point, from which we now descended to continue our march across the Umm Sidr trough,[2] covered with camel-thorn and other dry scrub. We were soon climbing the deep pink sand billows of the *Nafud*, from whose summit we descried in the distance the palms of Tharmida, and a mile or so beyond the further edge of the sands, here scarcely two miles in width, we found Ibn Sa'ud encamped in a depression called Khubba Umm al Jadawal.

The temperature under the influence of a hot wind rose to 112° during the day, and the waters of the Mahmal district had produced a feeling of general unease and depression in the camp, whose slow onward progress was thus largely accounted for. Ibn Sa'ud was dosing himself with liver pills, but transacting business nevertheless with his usual energy. A newly-arrived mailbag from the coast had brought satisfactory news of representations made by His Majesty's Government to the Sharif and the *Wahhabi* monarch was in a good temper. We all spent the day preparing letters for the outgoing mail, with which would ride one Salih

---

[1] Only approximately.

[2] Sha'ib Abal Farawwah descends into it from the Safrat al Shams, while the next torrent from its slope, Sha'ib Abal Taiy, belongs to the Batin al Hawar system.

al 'Adhil, about to take up his appointment as Ibn Sa'ud's representative at Zubair. A native of Rass in the Qasim, he was one of the best men at the court, with a markedly Semitic countenance and brimful of good humour. He enjoyed moreover the distinction, rare in Najd, of being a Turkish *Pasha*.

3. The District of Washm

After the casual manner of the Arabs, Ibn Sa'ud had named Shaqra as the *rendezvous* of the various contingents which were expected to join his standard for the campaign against Haïl. The trysting-place was named, but no very definite date—hence a pause of ten days in our leisurely northward progress amid the settlements of Washm, one of the most important, though one of the smallest, of the districts of Central Arabia. Shaqra, its capital, ranks next after 'Anaiza and Buraida in commercial importance, having direct relations with the towns of the Persian Gulf coast ; half a dozen other settlements, almost worthy to be ranked as towns by the Arabian standard, provide a considerable *Badawin* population of the surrounding deserts with dates and grain in exchange for butter and wool ; while the barriers of sand, which completely encircle the district, afford both protection against enemies from every direction and grazing for the herds of the home tribes during their customary periods of concentration—be they for the annual fast or the seasonal marketing.

The great Dahna, which is itself but a continuation of the Northern *Nafud* of the Shammar country, throws a broad arm of sand round the northern extremity of the Tuwaiq plateau in a southerly direction, which, thrusting between Zilfi and 'Anaiza, protrudes three long fingers towards the south-east from the point at which it reaches the northern frontier of Washm. The most easterly and slenderest of these is separated from the cliff of Sudair by the Hamada tract, and is known by the names of Nafud Sharqi, Nafud Shaqra and Turaif al Habil in its various sections, which form as it were the eastern boundary of the district. The latter, comprising an oval tract of sand-rock soil sloping from a western cliff to the foot of the eastern sand-strip and seared into valleys by the flow of torrents, is enclosed on the west by the broad band of Nafud Qunaifida, which almost touches the sands of Turaif al Habil on the south.

Thus situated Washm forms a self-contained basin with no drainage outlet, and its agricultural prosperity is certainly due to the fact that such rain as falls within its limits is held up by the sand barrier at the foot of its valleys with no alternative but to sink into their sandy soil. A certain amount of salinity is thus engendered, and on it thrive the date-palms of the district. Cereals too are raised to a considerable extent both in the oases and especially in the broad valley—called Al Butin—which divides the sloping sandstone plateau and its valleys from the eastern *Nafud*. This depression runs the whole length of the district from north to south and contains two large groups of farmsteads, Qusur Sunaidi opposite Shaqra and Qusur Dayil over against Marrat, to say nothing of the large oasis of Tharmida. All the other oasis settlements nestle in the bosom of wedge-shaped valleys traversing the district in a generally west to east direction between ridges of the sandstone wilderness.

Resuming our march on the morning of 10th August we first passed through the abandoned corn patches of Umm al Jadawal, which with the two *Qasrs* standing in their midst are said to have fallen into decay for two reasons. The insecurity resulting from the struggles of Ibn Rashid to maintain his position against the growing power of Ibn Sa'ud in the opening years of the present century compelled men to look elsewhere for a livelihood. At the same time a boom in the pearl trade afforded a suitable opening for many in Arabia who little knew who might reap the fruits of their agricultural labour. And so from many a district troubled with the alarums and excursions of the rival claimants to supremacy in Najd, numbers flocked to the oyster beds of the Persian Gulf, and it was not till the Great War itself made pearls for the time being of little account that the claims of agriculture could make themselves felt once more. ' Back to the land ' is the motto on which Ibn Sa'ud has based the *Wahhabi* revival of the *Ikhwan* movement, and it may well be that by now the ' Mother of canals ' [1] has ceased to be barren.

Following up the Butin depression we now came to an extensive area of cornland dotted with eight fort-like farm-houses of identical appearance—each about 25 yards square with projecting rectangular bastions but little higher than the walls of the buildings. In each of these *Qasrs* is a well with a channel conducting its water to the fields outside, which are divided up by low earth borders into diminutive beds about 10 yards square. These farmsteads are collec-tively known as Qusur Dayil, and belong, as the name sug-gests, to the Dayil subsection of the Wudda'in Dawasir, who form part of the population of the neighbouring village of Marrat. At this season—between the harvest and the next sowing—the farmsteads were, according to custom, entirely deserted, and I was told that the local practice was to leave the land fallow for long periods—for five and even as much as ten years at a time—in order to profit by the greatly increased fertility of the soil resulting from this treatment.

About a mile to the west of the Dayil granges and in a broad circular bay of the sandstone wilderness lay the oasis of Marrat commanded by the lofty flat-topped hummock of Qara Kumait. The summit of the latter, comprising a thick stratum of limestone and flint over the ruddy underlying sandstone, towers some 200 feet above the oasis and affords a splendid view of the country for miles around. To the west the view is blocked by the sands of Nafud Qunaifida, while immediately below lies the oasis of Marrat extending east and west for about a mile with an average breadth of a quarter mile. To the north lies the oasis of Tharmida, and beyond it eastward the *Nafud* ; beyond this again the Hamada plain with its villages backed by the imposing arc of the Sudair and Tuwaiq escarpments with their sheer cliffs and frowning headlands. The gradation of colour from the ruddy brown of the sandstone plateau of Washm and the pure light pink of the *Nafud* to the purple haze of lofty Sudair and the darker shadows of the Tuwaiq gorges was a scene not easily to be forgotten.

---

[1] Literal meaning of Umm al Jadawal, so called from the numerous irrigation ducts spreading out from its few wells.

The village of Marrat,[1] which lies at the west end of the
oasis, is protected by a turreted wall along its north and east
sides, each about 300 paces long, but opens directly on the
other sides on to an extensive palm-grove round which the wall
is continued in a wide semicircle.   Admittance is gained to it
by a single gate in the north wall, and its only outstanding
building is the mosque on its south side with a lofty square
minaret and a portico of eight pointed
arches, four of which had been walled up
with bricks.   The turrets of the outer
walls are of the ' lamp-shade ' pattern
common to all this part of the country.

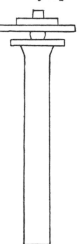

Junaifi and Manawar having preceded
us to announce our coming, we were met
on arrival at the gate by one who greeted
us with unwonted warmth and introduced himself as a cousin of Ibrahim Ibn
Jumai'a.   He then conducted us through
the gate, which was of mud bricks and
common woodwork, by a labyrinthine
way past the mosque to the house of
the local *Amir*, where we couched our
camels.   Our guide now explained that
the *Amir*, Ibrahim Ibn Dayil, who had
succeeded to his post on the death of his
father the previous year, was away at

FIG. 2. CAPITAL IN
PARLOUR OF IBRAHIM
IBN DAYIL'S HOUSE
AT MARRAT.

Tharmida on a visit to Ibn Sa'ud.   We therefore proceeded
on foot to the house of the head of the Qahtan [2] community, Khalid Ibn Da'aij, who also happened to be
away, and here we were entertained to coffee by a relative
of the absent host.   The room was on the upper storey
of the house, and its bare mud walls were without other
ornament than a dado of common whitewash up to a
height of about six feet, picked out at the top in a stepped
pinnacle pattern.   The roof of palm-trunk beams and *Ithil*-
wood rafters was supported by a single central pillar [3] of

---

[1] The wells of Marrat, 10 fathoms deep, contain excellent water, clear
and sweet, and reputed to be the best in Washm.
[2] The population of Marrat is about 1000 souls, mainly Dawasir and
Qahtan by origin, with a few Bani Khadhir families.
[3] *Vide* Fig. 2.

mud and masonry with a covering of gypsum lime, and a skylight above the coffee-hearth provided an exit for the smoke.

We had not been here long when we were summoned away to the house of the other *Amir*, where on arrival we were ushered upstairs into a large chamber whose wall decorations proclaimed its owner a man of taste. The monotone of the clay walls was broken by six bands of gypsum frieze of varying width at varying intervals, each band being adorned with a different pattern.[1] The effect of the whole was certainly extremely pleasing to eyes wearied by the drab void of *Wahhabi* art, and the simple crudity of a design relying for effect on endless variations of the only available theme— circles and triangles, pothooks and petals and stepped pinnacles and the like—was a welcome indication of a social atmosphere to some extent emancipated from the purely material outlook which governs the society of the *Wahhabi* capital and its surroundings. In Shaqra we were to find this tendency developed in a yet greater degree, and in the Qasim we were to find it culminating in as near an approach to art as modern desert Arabia is capable of. A rough and very primitive sketch of a steamer, independent of the main design, betrayed perhaps the origin of our host's inspiration ; he may perchance have been of those whom fortune treated kindly at the pearl-fisheries.

Fresh dates of two [2] varieties were placed before us for our refreshment, and these were followed by a large dish of *Marasi'*, the constituents of which were thin pancakes soaked in *Saman* and thickly besprinkled with shredded onions. Manawar, who had excused himself from accompanying me to the top of Qara Kumait on the ground of a bad headache, surprised me by eating inordinately of the savoury fare regardless of the march yet before him under a noonday sun. By this time, I think, every one of my companions had suffered badly from headaches owing to my refusal to march at night, while I had not experienced the slightest inconvenience ; I can only attribute the sufferings of the Arabs in this respect partly to the fact that, so far as possible, they normally avoid travelling during the heat of

---

[1] *Vide* Fig. 3.   [2] *Dakhaini* and *Makwizi*.

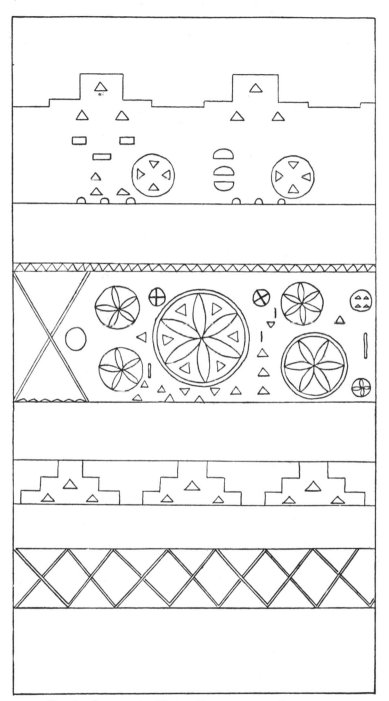

FIG. 3. SECTION OF MURAL DECORATION IN PARLOUR OF
AMIR OF MARRAT.

the day, partly to the lack of restraint when food is placed before them, and also partly to the fact that they would wear their white *kafiyas* [1] rather than the thicker mottled red variety which I always found an unfailing protection against the sun. During our stay at Shaqra I presented each of my following with a red kerchief, which they accepted gratefully but generally reserved for high days and holidays.

A short march of about three miles northward now brought us to Tharmida, where we found Ibn Sa'ud's camp pitched on the east side of the town, close to the ruins of an extensive fort built during the Turkish occupation of the middle of last century by Khurshid Pasha. During the occupation of the *Wahhabi* country by Ibn Rashid, Tharmida was one of his main strongholds, and the Turkish fort was duly occupied by his garrison. It was reduced to its present state of ruin by Ibn Sa'ud to requite the people of Tharmida for their loyal acceptance and support of his rival's rule. The broken outer wall, marked at intervals by tumbled turrets, is no longer capable of defence, and the interior of the fort has been converted into cornfields.

The oasis of Tharmida, a solid rectangular block of palms a mile long and half a mile wide, lies roughly north and south in the Butin valley, with the *Nafud* sands half a mile away on the east and the sandstone slope rising immediately from its palm-groves westward. Round the whole oasis runs a wall dotted at intervals with turrets, and the town itself lies within its circuit in a bulge of the oasis at its north-eastern extremity. A market-place of fifteen to twenty shops is the only feature of an otherwise scattered and straggling settlement of unimposing buildings and meandering streets, whose population of 3000 souls belongs for the most part to the 'Anaqir section of Bani Tamim, with some admixture of negro, Bani Khadhir and miscellaneous elements. An open space separates the town from the fort ; two gates in the outer wall give access to the latter from south and east, and the graveyard lies outside the former. Half a dozen

---

[1] The word *Kafiya* is seldom heard in desert Arabia, where the ordinary term for the head-kerchief is *Qatra*. In Washm apparently only the white variety is called *Qatra* and the red *Shamagh*, which is of two qualities, the better (or *Khariq*) at this time costing 2 *Riyals* and the inferior (or *Ibn Nasrullah*) 1½.

THARMIDA.

To face page 92.

detached palm-groves stand away from the main block of the oasis under the edge of the *Nafud*, and the valley is dotted with a few isolated *Qasrs* and wells—many of the latter in ruins—in the midst of cornfields. The water, which lies at a depth of from six to eight fathoms, is brackish.

The local *Amir*, 'Abdul Rahman al 'Anqari, combines with his executive functions those of chief priest, and is held in high esteem by Ibn Sa'ud. Among the latter's visitors at his camp here, come thus far to welcome him, was the brother of the *Amir* of 'Anaiza, who surprised me by sending a message through Rushaid saying that, while he could not afford to be seen visiting me, he would be grateful for a few cigarettes ! I stifled my first inclination to resent the impertinence of such a demand, and sent him a box of cigarettes in the hope—to be realised beyond all my expectations—that he would repay me with hospitality at 'Anaiza.

Some few miles northward of Tharmida in the Butin valley lies a group of farmsteads [1] which, together with a similar group higher up over against Shaqra, is known as Qusur Sunaidi. Towards the first group runs down from the western summit of the sandstone wilderness one of the wedge-shaped valleys to which I have referred, the valley of Sha'ib Musamma, on which lie the oasis and village of Wuthaithiya. This was the first stage of our march on leaving Tharmida on the morning of 11th August—our general direction being slightly north of west and the distance covered some six miles. A well-marked track led us from the northern extremity of the oasis and imperceptibly up the land-slope to its summit beyond a shallow depression called Abal Sulaim.[2] From here across the depression we looked forward to a line of flat-topped hillocks arranged like a chain of forts covering the approach to Wuthaithiya from eastward, the direction in which lies its overlord of former times and present rival.

About a century and a half ago the people of the village paid tribute to Tharmida in the shape of a saddle of camel

---

[1] This group contains some thirty *Qasrs* close under the edge of the *Nafud*.

[2] This drains down to Qusur Sunaidi and Raudha Abal Samari beyond them.

every Friday, the weekly slaughter-day then, as it is still, in most Arabian villages. So every Friday the corporation of the suzerain town despatched a slave with an ass to bring back the tribute of its lieges, and every Friday the slave duly returned with the meat. But there arose at this time one, whose name is not preserved, to counsel rebellion, and on the ensuing Friday the ass returned to Tharmida alone with its burden of meat. And the meat was the carcase of the slave carved into two portions and packed into the saddle-bags. The expedition organised to avenge this insult resulted in a fierce encounter among the hillocks which now confronted us, and the troops of Tharmida were routed with heavy loss. Thus did Wuthaithiya win its independence— now of course merged in a common subservience to the house of Sa'ud—and the incident is graphically celebrated in a ballad composed at the time by a local bard called Humaidan, respectfully admired by the descendants of his fellow-citizens as a ' master of all the sciences.' [1] The poem was recited to the evident appreciation of all present as we sat round sipping coffee in the house of the local *Amir* that day. Line by line a local poet declaimed the story, often prefacing a verse with such remarks as ' I forget how it goes on,' and ' What comes next ? ' while the audience in chorus anticipated him by murmuring the last rhyme of each couplet. It was always at such times that one could feel the great past behind the Arab race—at times when the froth of a new religious patter became forgotten in the stirrings of the old primitive paganism, which produced a literature worthy to rank with the great creations of humanity. I confess to having always experienced some difficulty in following such recitations— the wealth of language and literary or historical allusion was such that only with great effort could one follow the meaning, much less appreciate the beauty of their ballads—except in a very general way—and in my travels I never had the time to make the necessary effort. Yet there are but few among the Arabs who have not an extensive repertory of song and poem—the former, alas ! ruined always by the execrable rendering of their harsh, discordant voices.

Round about the flat-topped hillocks lay a number of

---

[1] *Dhabitan kull al 'ulum*—note the pronunciation of the *Tanwin*.

WUTHAITHIYA—AQUEDUCT ACROSS SHA'IB MUSAMMA.

To face page 95.

isolated walled palm-groves and an extensive area of corn-lands studded with wells. Half a mile beyond to the north-west lay the main block of the oasis astride the torrent strand of Sha'ib Musamma, across which water is brought from the northern to the southern palm-groves along an earthen aqueduct raised some four feet above the bed of the valley on masonry pillars. Behind the oasis runs the dark line of the Furugh ridge, rising to a prominent headland some miles to the north-westward.

Both the main blocks of the oasis and a few detached groves close outside them are surrounded by solid clay walls some ten feet high and dominated by turrets. The village itself lies at the north-east corner of the oasis, and is extra-ordinarily picturesque. On the only gateway of the settle-ment, whose irregular circuit wall enhances its beauty, stands a tall watch-tower, while within rises the mosque minaret yet taller and tapering gracefully. The upper storeys of the houses adjoin each other to form a solid block under which run the tunnelled streets and the ground floor chambers, which according to a custom largely prevailing in Washm are almost exclusively relegated to the use of the household cattle—sheep and goats—when they come home each evening from the pastures. I may here mention once and for all that the fleeces of Washm are both white and black, with neither colour noticeably predominating.

Couching our camels in an open space immediately within the gate we sought the hospitality of the *Amir*, 'Abdul 'Aziz Ibn Sa'd of the Sa'd subsection of Bani Tamim, which with the Zamil subsection of the same tribe forms the population of the village—some 600 souls. The *Amir* was away in his palm-groves when we arrived, but soon appeared to greet us, while one by one the villagers dropped in to the ringing summons of pestle and mortar. The room, on the upper floor of course, was of no great dimensions, and its walls were plastered with limewash of greyish hue with a faint lattice pattern. The roof was supported by two pillars with simple capitals,[1] while the women's quarters were separated from the guest-room by an *Ithil*-wood door and an earthen lattice of triangular ventilation holes, at which

[1] *Vide* Fig. 4.

many bright eyes could be seen peeping at the new-come
guests. Within the door of the women's apartments, which
was open at our arrival, stood a fixed earthen screen to secure
the necessary privacy for the folk within. Coffee and dates
followed by incense sped us on our way, and we found on
reaching our camels that their needs had not been forgotten
—green stalks of millet being their portion.

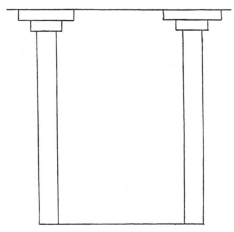

FIG. 4.   CAPITALS OF PILLARS IN PARLOUR OF AMIR OF
WUTHAITHIYA.

A march of two miles over rough stony ground brought
us to the Furugh headland, where we found ourselves at one
corner of an isosceles triangle, the further side of which was
the Qaraïn ridge with its headland roughly north-west of us.
The base of the triangle lay between the two headlands
roughly along the summit of the slope, while at its apex lay
the oasis of Qaraïn. Descending the slope towards the latter
we followed and eventually crossed the rocky ravine bed of
Sha'ib Mahriqa ; and, after a march of four miles from the
Furugh headland, reached the northern edge of the Qaraïn
oasis, which runs down the valley in a south-easterly direction
for a distance of about two miles with an average width of a
quarter mile. The main block of the oasis, at the northern
end, contains two small hamlets about half a mile apart :
Al Waqf,[1] a long narrow and straggling settlement on the

[1] About 500 × 50 yards.

left bank of the rocky torrent-bed of Sha'ib 'Anbari, without other wall than the continuous edge of its houses ; and Al Ghusla, also a straggling unwalled collection of dwellings with a large open space before it. The latter hamlet can scarcely contain more than 200 souls, mostly of 'Anaqir origin, whose leader is 'Abdullah Ibn Sallum : while Al Waqf is somewhat larger, having a population of some 300 souls of the Luhaba subsection of Bani Tamim [1] living under the guidance of 'Abdul Rahman al Salih. The streets of this hamlet, like those of Wuthaithiya, are as burrows under the solid mass of upper storeys, and its mosque is a strongly-built fort-like edifice with the usual portico and a lofty minaret.

It was not, as a matter of fact, until some days later that I visited this oasis from Shaqra, from which it is separated by a broad ridge of sandstone upland. The room in which the *Amir* entertained us to coffee was small, dismal, and grimed with smoke, but it had one unusual feature—a series of diminutive casements opening on to the palm-groves behind, and each fitted with wooden windows swinging open on a pivot by a simple but ingenious device. As we rode away I noticed a young lady of the village with moon-like face and braided locks gazing out upon us from her upper casement.

Some part of the oasis is girt around by a dilapidated wall, and the outlying groves lower down the valley towards the Butin are for the most part straggling and unprosperous. Besides the palms there is a considerable amount of *Ithil*, and at the extremity of the settlement there was a fine well of uncemented masonry choked with sand—its measurements being ten yards long and three broad. About a mile down-stream of this point to the north-eastward lies the second group of Qusur Sunaidi farmsteads, about ten of them in all. Shaqra lies about two miles from this point up its valley and about three miles from the western extremity of the Qarain oasis beyond a saddle of the sandstone ridge to the north-west.

It was midday when we rode into Ibn Sa'ud's camp spread out over the valley eastward of the main city gate, and our sojourn at Shaqra lasted some six days. This period marked

---

[1] There are also some Subai' families here.

the first definite stage in the development of the Haïl campaign since the nucleus of Ibn Sa'ud's army marched forth from Riyadh. It may therefore be convenient to pause at this point of my narrative for a brief survey of the political and military situation in so far as it affected Ibn Sa'ud and his plans for the future.

The horizon on either side of the Arabian peninsula was already dark with storm-clouds at the beginning of August when Ibn Sa'ud left Riyadh to redeem his promise of a campaign against Ibn Rashid. Such a campaign had the full approval and active support of the British Government, not so much, perhaps, for any striking results expected from it as from a desire to divert the attention of the *Wahhabi* monarch from his western and eastern borders. From the former came from time to time ominous rumours of *Sharifian* preparations to renew the attack on Khurma, where the Hijaz forces had twice already been decisively beaten. On the east lay the traditional enemy, the 'Ajman tribe, based on the borders of 'Iraq and Kuwait, whither it had fled for refuge from the wrath of Ibn Sa'ud.

Haïl, as an ally of the Turks, was the common enemy but not particularly obnoxious to Ibn Sa'ud, who hoped, it is true, to annex it to his dominions some day, but was content to bide his time. It was notorious that he would far rather have marched against the 'Ajman—to avenge himself on them for the death of his brother Sa'd—and they had quite recently provoked a fresh outburst of his anger by raiding a Subai' encampment in the Hasa. He would far rather too have marched against the Sharif to crush his pretensions before they should mature. In both directions, however, his way was barred by the British authorities, at whose instigation he was thus marching north, seeking a safety-valve for his long pent-up energies and emotions.

The Turkish commandant and governor [1] of 'Asir, whose garrison, amazing as it may seem, still held out after nearly four years of war and even maintained its communications with the General Staff at Constantinople, lost little time in trying to derive profit from the Khurma trouble. The tribes of Bisha and Tathlith were roused to go to the rescue of

[1] Muhiyaldin Pasha.

their fellows in faith, the Subai', and about this time Ibn Sa'ud received a letter obviously written by a clerk on the governor's staff but signed or sealed by four representative *Shaikhs* of the 'Asir tribes.[1] The letter professed the undying loyalty of its signatories to the Turkish Empire, under whose rule 'Asir was peaceful and prosperous. The destruction of *Islam*, it declared, was the aim of the Allies, and it was Ibn Sa'ud's plain duty to assist in the defence of the true faith. This communication was considered of sufficient importance to be submitted to *Shaikh* 'Abdullah Ibn 'Abdul Wahhab, the High Priest, who indulged in some frank criticism of Ibn Sa'ud's policy. Either, he said, the British are powerless to restrain the vagaries of the Sharif and the 'Ajman or else they can and won't—in either case it was Ibn Sa'ud's duty to take his own steps to prevent the infringement of his frontiers. But Ibn Sa'ud was too wise in his generation to be tempted into a popular policy.

Madina was at this time still undergoing a desultory siege by the *Amir* 'Ali,[2] eldest son of King Husain ; and Ibn Dhuwaibi, one of the leading chiefs of the Harb tribe, had recently arrived from that quarter with the latest news and gossip. He had heard the salute of 47 guns fired in honour of the Turkish *Sultan*, Muhammad Rashad, lately deceased, and had attended the prayers said for his soul. The trains, he reported, were running regularly between Madina and Tabuk, and the troops were well supplied with provisions. Nevertheless the *Amir* 'Ali had sent a message to the redoubtable Fakhri Pasha inviting him to surrender on a guarantee of honourable treatment by the King. The reply was dictated in public audience : ' Oh madman 'Ali,' it ran, ' do you not know that I am an officer of the *Daula* and held in high esteem ? Why then should I surrender that which is entrusted to my charge ? But you, who claim to be a descendant of the Prophet, whose tomb is in my keeping, why do you not come up and fight, trusting in your ancestor's power to help you ? '

[1] Mu'ammar, Qahtan and Shahran.

[2] He succeeded to the throne of the Hijaz in October, 1924, on the abdication of his father, and himself abdicated in December, 1925, on the conquest of the Hijaz by Ibn Sa'ud.

Ibn Rashid, who had been practically compelled to spend
a considerable period during the summer with the Turkish
force at Al Hajr on the Hijaz Railway, was now back at
Haïl ; and intercepted letters addressed by him to the Turks
gave clear indications of a growing estrangement between
the latter and their only Arab ally. The *Amir* 'Abdullah,[1]
who was at this time reported to be at 'Ashaira with a
Sharifian army destined to renew the attack on Khurma,
took advantage of this state of affairs to send Ibn Rashid
an offer of peace and friendship. Ibn Sa'ud naturally interpreted this action as intended to be hostile to himself ; and,
on the very day of his departure from Riyadh, this interpretation was amply confirmed by the contents of letters
addressed by the *Amir* 'Abdullah to two 'Ataiba *Shaikhs*,
Dhawi Ibn Fuhaid and Hadhdhal Ibn Hadhdhal, and duly
forwarded by their recipients to Ibn Sa'ud. These letters
announced the conclusion of peace between the Sharif and
Ibn Rashid ; an impending meeting between the two parties
to ' settle the affairs of north and south ' ; 'Abdullah's own
appointment to command the Khurma expeditionary force
and the concentration of the latter at Marran. They were
not without offensive allusions to Ibn Sa'ud, and closed with
directions for the 'Ataiba to rally round the *Sharifian*
standard without delay. To make matters worse, 'Abdullah's
agents had arrived in the Qasim to buy camels for the projected campaign—they were soon sent about their business.

Such was the position of affairs at the outset of the Haïl
campaign—a regular Gilbertian situation it would have
seemed to any detached observer not vitally concerned with
the momentous issues involved. For me, situated as I was
in the middle of Arabia at a distance of 12 to 15 days' journey
from any source of accurate information, with the task of
preventing Ibn Sa'ud from attacking those of his neighbours
—the Sharif, the 'Ajman and Kuwait—who were in alliance
with us, and inducing him to attack the hostile Shammar,
it was serious enough. On the east side the *Shaikh* of
Kuwait, always hostile to Ibn Sa'ud, and the 'Ajman—to
say nothing of Dhari Ibn Tawala—were conniving at the
supply of provisions and other necessaries to Haïl, whence a

[1] He became *Amir* of Trans-Jordan in April 1921.

large caravan had recently gone on to Damascus. On the same side the 'Ajman lost no reasonable opportunity of raiding into Ibn Sa'ud's territory. In the west the *Amir* 'Abdullah was negotiating a treaty of peace and friendship with Ibn Rashid, while his brothers were vigorously prosecuting the war against the latter's ally, the Turks. Moreover, on his own showing he was making all preparations for an attack on Najd, and the arms and ammunition for use to this end were supplied [1] by the British.

From this moment onwards every mail from the coast was eagerly scrutinised for news of further developments, and the political barometer fluctuated violently almost from day to day—now giving ground for hope and again plunging us into the depths of despair. Except the *Amir* Faisal,[2] who was busily engaged in prosecuting the war against the Turks in the north, our Arab friends and allies had, one and all, forgotten that they were but pawns in the game of the Great War and had begun to scramble for petty advantages in the general ferment of their peninsula. They were beginning to get out of hand, and there wanted but little to precipitate open hostilities between Ibn Sa'ud and the Sharif. Fortunately, His Majesty's Government intervened just in time with a serious warning both to the Sharif and to Ibn Sa'ud that the inception of any movement calculated to cause a breach of the peace between the two would meet with their severe reprobation. This warning was accompanied by a fair offer to mediate, as soon as the Great War should be over, on all points in dispute between the two parties. Ibn Sa'ud accepted this act of intervention with enthusiasm, and it only remained for the Sharif to withdraw his son, 'Abdullah, out of reach of temptation. The next step would have been the fixation of a temporary line of demarcation between the two zones, and I suggested that the line [3] should run— without prejudice to the settlement to be undertaken after the war—east of Marran and Turaba, leaving these two

[1] Not for this purpose, of course.

[2] King of Syria, 1919-20, and King of Mesopotamia ('Iraq) since August, 1921.

[3] This line represented the actual position of the rival claimants at the time, *e.g.* Turaba was held on behalf of the Sharif, and Khurma was in the hands of the *Wahhabis*.

places and everything west of the line to the Hijaz and Khurma and everything east of the line to Ibn Sa'ud.

This message was received by me at our camp at Al Hish, and for the moment the barometer indicated a period of settled conditions. After days of conflict with his own soul Ibn Sa'ud definitely confirmed his orders for a concentration in force at Shaqra, and every day of our sojourn at the capital of Washm was marked by the arrival of some contingent or other from far or near. Meanwhile Ibn Sa'ud's intelligence agents were able to report the failure of 'Abdullah's efforts to recruit *Badawin* elements for his attack on Khurma, and, while everyone was convinced that the peace offer to Ibn Rashid from the same quarter was little likely to succeed, only one thing was needed to create enthusiasm for the Haïl campaign—the very fact that the Sharif was straining every nerve to win Ibn Rashid over to his side.

Accordingly, on 15th August, Ibn Sa'ud took counsel with his assembled army to explain his policy and his plan of campaign. Faisal Ibn Duwish, chief of the 'Artawiya contingent, acted as spokesman for the *Wahhabi* contingents as a whole, and the case was argued out between him and his sovereign before the assembled multitude. Nothing, declared Faisal, was being done to help their brethren at Khurma threatened with another attack by the *Sharifian* forces ; nothing was being done to counter the 'Ajman activities in the east. ' All we want,' he continued, ' is to be allowed to attack the foes of the faith. Give but the word and we will follow you to death against the Sharif or the 'Ajman.' There was clearly some uneasiness in the minds of the *Ikhwan* lest this project of a campaign against the Shammar, *Wahhabis* like themselves, might be but the outcome of traffic with the infidel and designed to serve some recondite political aim with which they had no sympathy. The danger to their brethren from sources known to be supported by British influence or money was all they could see, and they chafed at the thought that perchance they might be lending themselves to the service of a cause not their own.

Ibn Sa'ud's method of meeting the arguments of his followers was characteristic. ' Look ye,' he said, ' you people are my army in that I have no army but my God and you. In the days of your ignorance, when you were but robbers and brigands, you were my army and, now that you have taken to the faith and settled in villages, you are still the army on which I rely. Think not that I am unmindful of what is necessary, and as for the Sharif, think no more of him. Either the English will stop him from attacking Khurma again or—and I give you my word on that—I will march against him ; but remember that that is no affair of yours. All I need do is to send a member of my family or a slave and the whole south will rise against the Sharif. And as for the Shammar [1] and the 'Ajman, you know not what you are talking about when you say that the English are supporting them. Why, the English say to me : ' You are very foolish ' ; and they are right, for I have the means withal to strike the Shammar at their heart and yet I dally. Of what account would Dhari and the 'Ajman be if I held Haïl ? If only I would make myself master of the Shammar capital the English would leave all the desert tribes to my rule, and we should have no more trouble from those who sit on the borders of our land.'

The *Wahhabi* monarch then unfolded his plans for a sustained campaign against Ibn Rashid and, having thus laid his cards on the table, invited the High Priest of Washm—no other than Muhammad Ibn 'Abdul Wahhab, brother of *Shaikh* 'Abdullah—and other *'Ulama* present to declare their opinions as to who was the real enemy of the moment. With one voice they assured the assembled multitude that no other than Ibn Rashid was the arch-enemy, and the *Ikhwan*, as they do when under the stress of strong emotion, fell to weeping and declaring through their tears that, if only they had been taken into their sovereign's confidence earlier, they would have come forward to a man without any foreboding.

At this point Ibn Sa'ud, well content with the success of his lecture, closed the proceedings with specific instructions for the guidance of his followers. His plan of campaign was now matured, and he would actually set out for Haïl from the Qasim on the 5th day of *Dhil Hijja*—almost a full month hence. ' Get you gone, therefore, every man to his home

[1] *i.e.* the following of Dhari Ibn Tawala, who was supporting the 'Ajman.

and make ready for war and, having set your houses in order, join me at Buraida at the new moon, and God, in his mercy, will give us victory. But, mind ye, I want no half-hearted response to my call ; let every settlement send forth its full quota ready for a long and arduous struggle. I will provide you with food and arms and, please God, we shall so harass Ibn Rashid and his people that they will surrender their stronghold.'

And so the *Ikhwan* contingents melted away in the course of the next few days. The campaign was originally to have started on the 1st day of *Ramdhan* or over two months before and was now to be postponed for another month. I was disappointed at the result, but well enough accustomed to the dilatory ways of the Arabs to conceal my chagrin with congratulations to Ibn Sa'ud on his adroit handling of a difficult situation. I held obstinately to my faith in Ibn Sa'ud and to my conviction that he would in due course move, but I feared that something might happen within the next month to postpone still further the day—at any moment 'Abdullah might strike at Khurma.

Meanwhile I had, while at Shaqra, many opportunities of realising that, whatever might be said for the proposed Haïl campaign on grounds of higher policy, it was rather the Sharif and his pretensions that occupied the thoughts of the upper classes. It must be remembered that in the more advanced sections of Arabian society—in the Qasim and Washm and the Hasa—there still lingered deep down in the hearts of men a fellow-feeling for the Turks in their religious aspect, in their *rôle* of defenders of the *Muslim* faith. Genuine *Wahhabis* as they were, the merchants of the districts named had been too much in contact with the world to value uncompromising bigotry, and in the Turks they found an ample and sufficient refuge for their oriental pride in the rough-and-tumble of commercial life in a predominantly Western atmosphere, a great and established power professing the same faith as themselves without compelling on the part of its subjects the austerity of conduct imposed upon them by the conditions obtaining in their homelands. They would regret the passing of the Turk, and resented *Muslim* activity directed towards that end. Their hearts condemned the

Sharif as a traitor to the common cause of the East, but, as Ibn Sa'ud was professedly in the same camp—without, however, any likelihood of contributing materially to the downfall of the Turks—their tongues condemned the pretensions of King Husain to rule Arabia. The duplicity of their arguments was perfectly natural in the circumstances and transparent ; it was not even meant to deceive.

The first morning of my sojourn at Shaqra I awoke to be informed that Ibn Sa'ud had sallied forth from the camp for a round of visits to the notables of the city, and had left word that I should follow at my convenience if so minded. The camp, consisting of some 40 or 50 tents, spread out over the valley at a distance of about a quarter mile east of the main gate of the city. I accordingly strolled across the intervening sandy space through a cemetery, whose graves, contrary to *Wahhabi* practice, were marked, head and foot, with rough sandstone slabs set on end, about two feet in height. It was explained to me that this cemetery was no longer in use and belonged to a period anterior to the birth of the new faith, but immediately within the gate in a considerable open space, whose further side was bounded by a semicircle of dwelling-houses, I noticed another cemetery of the same type, and came to the conclusion that in all probability Shaqra had not advanced to the extreme of bigotry prevailing in the southern districts.

As we passed a shanty of rough palm branches occupied by the mercenary camel-graziers of the town, my companion, Ibrahim al Junaifi, hailed a local notable who happened to be there on business or pleasure and introduced him to me. This was one 'Abdul Rahman Ibn Sulaiman al Jammaz al Shuwaimi, who without further ado conducted us through a main thoroughfare, whose houses were adorned with thresholds and lintels of sandstone, and up a side street to his own house. His coffee-parlour, in which we awaited news of Ibn Sa'ud's actual whereabouts—for according to custom he had spent the morning in going from house to house to greet his loyal subjects—was comfortably furnished with sumptuous cushions and rugs. A cemented coffee-hearth with its usual accompaniment of pots and utensils occupied one corner of a room, whose walls were covered with a spotless white gypsum plaster richly decorated with circles, triangles and other symmetrical designs. Several openings, furnished with decorated wooden shutters, led out from one side of the parlour on to a sort of roof-garden or open-air coffee-parlour, dedicated apparently for use during the long evenings of a summer *Ramdhan*, when our pious host and his friends, having subdued the rigours of the fast by slumber, would foregather to eke out the hours of darkness in desultory conversation over the coffee-cups.

My contemplation of the room was interrupted by the entry of a distinguished-looking person, whose fine raiment, particularly the *'Aqal* of gold thread upon his head, suggested that he might even be a member of the royal family. It was not till later that I discovered him to be the governor of the Shaqra district, Muhammad Ibn Sa'ud by name, though in no way connected with the house of Sa'ud, being a member of the 'Isa [1] section of Bani Zaid of the tribe of Tamim. The new-comer was unusually affable. ' Are you not he,' he asked, ' who went from Riyadh last year to the Sharif ? ' My answer in the affirmative provoked him to candid speech. ' How can the Sharif call himself " King of the Arabs " ? Did not Shakespear visit Najd and see Shaqra and all these provinces ? Did not Hamilton do the same ? And now here are you. Do not the English realise that these are the Arab countries and that their ruler is Ibn Sa'ud ? Why, at the beginning of his revolt the Sharif sent me several letters, but I simply handed them over to Ibn Sa'ud.' We talked much of the trade of Shaqra. I expressed astonishment at the fact that caravans with goods intended for Riyadh should fetch so long a circuit *via* Shaqra from Kuwait. This was, he explained, only a survival of pre-war times, when the natural trade route from Bahrain *via* the Hasa to Riyadh was rendered insecure by the Turkish occupation of the eastern province. Merchants therefore preferred to plunge straight into the desert from Kuwait, and Shaqra had become an important distributing centre for the south. Its leading merchants have agents or branches all over the country, in the Hasa, at Duwadami, at Sha'ra and elsewhere. Ibn Sa'ud hoped to restore trade in due course to the shorter and more

---

[1] The Shuwaimi family belongs to the same section.

natural Bahrain route, but had been too busy with other matters since the outbreak of war to do anything in this direction.

Junaifi, who had gone forth to seek out Ibn Sa'ud, now returned to summon us to the house of one 'Abdullah al Subai'i,[1] the local tax-collector. His coffee-parlour, where we found Ibn Sa'ud with a large gathering, differed little from that which I have already described, except that the colour-scheme of the walls was of a dark greyish hue in place of white, while the decoration was less elaborate and

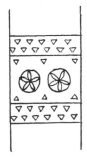

FIG. 5. DECORATIVE BAND round pillar supporting roof of parlour in house of 'Abdullah al Subai'i at Shaqra.

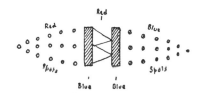

FIG. 5A. DECORATIVE PAINTING ON DOOR-TIMBER AT BURAIDA (?).

consisted of a series of friezes separated by bands without decoration. The eternal circle and triangle provided the motive of the friezes. A simple gypsum-plastered pillar with a plain capital and a thin band of the usual decorative design [2] supported the roof, in which over the fire-place a trap-door, worked by rope and pulley, was fixed to let out the smoke and keep out the rain as required. High up on the walls a number of openings provided with shutters appeared to be meant for ventilation or the reverse. Shaqra houses appeared to me for the most part to cater more generously for light and air than those of Riyadh.

Faisal Ibn Duwish, the redoubtable *Ikhwan* leader of 'Artawiya, whom I now saw for the first time since I was first introduced to him in the previous December, was of the party; as also Faisal Ibn Hashr, who, however, appeared to be for some reason in disgrace and was once or twice

[1] Of the Subai' tribe by origin as his name implies.   [2] *Vide* Fig. 5.

sharply chid by Ibn Sa'ud, who himself seemed from all appearances to be suffering from an attack of liver or spleen. Sa'ud al 'Arafa was there and Faisal Ibn Rashid and other members of the royal family, including Ibn Sa'ud's brother, Sa'ud.

The climate of Shaqra, which seemed to me more bracing than that of Riyadh, came in for some pettish criticism by Ibn Sa'ud, whose internal unease was probably due to the local water which, though clear and pleasant to the taste, is reputed to have disturbing qualities. On the whole, however, the wells of Shaqra, ten fathoms deep to water on an average, are the best in Washm, though falling far short of the Hassi water of the *Wahhabi* capital. As a matter of fact the weather at this period was by no means pleasant. Varying winds, short bursts of cyclonic conditions, dust storms, cloudy skies, and temperatures reaching a maximum of 110° *Fahr.* on several days—such was our lot. August 14th actually brought a fitful attempt at rain—the first since May 6th—and it seemed to me that we were perhaps experiencing the outside edge of the monsoon. This season, during which some rain is usually expected, is known as *Kharif.*[1] Worst of all—the late evening and early morning temperatures were seldom below 80°, while on several occasions the thermometer gave readings of over 90°.

The following day Ibn Sa'ud again held his court in the Subai'i house, and the conversation turned on the burning topic of the hour—the Sharif. Sa'ud al 'Arafa maintained— dangerous ground for one whose own claim to the *Wahhabi* throne on the ground of hereditary right was at least equally indisputable—that Husain, being of the 'Abadila clan which owed its present position to the Turks, had less claim to the Hijaz throne than his relatives of clan Dhawi Zaid, the descendants of 'Abdul Muttalib and therefore the main branch of the Prophet's family. He contended also that the Ashraf, being of much-mixed blood through their negress, Circassian, Turkish and other mothers, could not claim to be pure Arabs like the people of Najd. How then could Husain claim to

[1] According to local reckoning we were just entering or about to enter the *Suhail* period—Canopus rising at dawn—which is in fact reckoned as the last period of summer or is perhaps included in the *Safari*, which is sometimes treated as identical with *Kharif*. See Chapter I. p. 60.

be King of the Arabs or we support him ? He spoke at great
length and with much fervour, but his arguments seemed to
lead nowhere, and all I could do was to explain that, while
the British were in no way responsible for the Sharif's
assumption of the title of ' King of the Arabs,' they were
powerless to prevent him calling himself what he liked.
Our recognition of his kingship of the Hijaz, I continued,
was due to the fact that, when the Sultan of Turkey declared
against us and proclaimed a *Jihad*, we were forced for the
satisfaction of the millions of our Indian *Muslim* subjects to
find a recognised *Muslim* leader to raise the standard of
revolt in our favour against the Turks.

Ibn Sa'ud, intervening, declared that he coveted no title
nor any territory outside the boundaries of his birthright in
Najd. As for Mecca he had no desire whatever to be its
master—all that interested him therein was the House of
God, and that only in that it was incumbent upon him as a
devout *Muslim* to visit it once in his life for a period of ten
days at the outside. The forts and palaces, erected by his
ancestors at Mecca, Madina and Taïf, merely reminded him
of an episode in the past history of Najd, and he had no desire
to reoccupy them. He turned abruptly to another subject—
an obvious source of uneasiness to many of his people—his
alliance with the British. ' Why, they are not of our faith,
forsooth, but they are people of a Book and therefore entitled
to toleration. In any case the obligation of *Jihad* is condi-
tioned by the ability to carry it out, and that is from God.'
He fully realised his inability to carry any such venture to a
successful issue, and therefore considered himself absolved
by God from attempting it.   On the contrary he had himself
frequently sought British assistance against the real enemy
of the true faith, the Turks, and we had steadily refused it
until we ourselves were in need of his help. Such an exposition of his views in the presence of the notables of Shaqra
and such leaders of the *Ikhwan* as Ibn Duwish and Ibn
Hashr was all to the good. It paved the way for the prosecution of his campaign against Haïl and, above all, it made for
better public feeling towards myself as the representative of
Great Britain, whose motive in pressing for an attack on Ibn
Rashid was the subject of constant speculation and suspicion.

And so, in spite of a constant fear that any day might bring news of the renewal of Sharifian attacks on Khurma, the days of my sojourn at Shaqra passed pleasantly enough. My only expedition into the surrounding country was the visit to Qaraïn, which I have already described. I was, however, fully occupied in making myself thoroughly acquainted with the details of the town and oasis of Shaqra, and scarcely had time to grudge our camels their enjoyment of the neighbouring *Nafud* [1] pastures, from which they came in every third day to water. At this season two days seemed to be about as much as they could do comfortably without drinking. Camels let out to graze are said to be *'Azib*, while those in the spring pastures are said to be *Jazi*,[2] *i.e.* at the *Jazu*.

One night my curiosity was aroused on hearing a pro- clamation in the camp—a phenomenon associated in my mind only with the perils of lonely camps in the wilderness. It seemed strange that such a thing should occur amid the ample security of Ibn Sa'ud's tents, but rumours had been abroad of a projected raiding expedition by Ibn Rashid, and I thought perhaps that an alarm was being given. Enquiries, however, elicited the information that some *Baduwi*, taking advantage of the gathering of the *Ikhwan* contingents from far and wide, was merely advertising a reward of 30 dollars to any person who might give him information leading to the recovery of three camels stolen or strayed during the previous year. My tents were situated not far from the spacious black-hair *Madhif* or guest-tent, which with several tents near it served to shelter the leaders of the various *Ikhwan* contingents and their attendants—contingents from 'Artawiya, Mubaïdh, Dahina, Furaithan, Ghatghat and the rest of them. The white chaplet of the brotherhood was much in evidence during these days and, so far as I was able to judge, the gathering of the clans must have amounted to about 600 men-at-arms. One inconvenience arising out of my propinquity to the *Ikhwan* contingents was that their target-practice tended to disturb my peace of mind. In

---

[1] Nafud Qunaifida, where the favourite *Nussi* grass is abundant.

[2] Doughty uses the term *Jazzin* of camels at the spring pastures, but I failed to get confirmation of the word. Possibly a mistake for *Jázi*.

season and out of season, though not without regard to
economy—for ammunition was a valuable commodity and
Ibn Sa'ud sternly discouraged all waste—they would do
their musketry courses at a cliff beyond my tent and about
100 yards wide of it.   I calculated that at the range of about
800 yards it would not be unreasonable for an occasional
shot to find my tent instead of the cliff.   In the circumstances
I raised a protest against the practice, at any rate while I
was at home.   It stopped with occasional lapses intended
doubtless to annoy, and it was not till the royal chamberlain
intervened with considerable vigour that a more suitable
target was selected.   Modern rifles and ammunition were
plentiful enough in these days, but Ibn Sa'ud was not blind
to the necessity of the exercise of some control over traffic
in a commodity which might some day constitute a danger
to the state.   The lavish supply of munitions to the Sharifian
forces by the British authorities and the reckless distribution
of them to all and sundry by 'Ali and 'Abdullah had by this
time given rise to a brisk trade in rifles and ammunition
throughout Central Arabia.   *Shaikhs* of Mutair, Harb and
'Ataiba gathered their clansmen and their camels in the hope
of sharing in the bounty of the Sharifian princes, to whom
they swore undying loyalty.   But no sooner had they received
an appropriate number of rifles and boxes of ammunition—
to say nothing of bags of gold—than they loaded up their
beasts and returned to their pastures, to take no part in their
patrons' operations except perhaps to return a second or
even a third time to replenish the stocks of ammunition
exhausted by sales in the markets of Najd.   The principle
adopted by Ibn Sa'ud was that, while it was to his general
advantage that every man capable of bearing arms should
be armed with a serviceable weapon, it was not to his advantage to supply rifles.   He therefore made no attempt to
control their circulation ; but with ammunition it was a
different matter.   Raiding within his territories or without
his sanction being forbidden, he regarded it as the duty of
the state to provide ammunition for operations undertaken
with its sanction or at its bidding, while at the same time he
fully realised the urgent need of keeping private supplies of
ammunition down to a minimum.   His officials throughout

Najd had, therefore, orders and full discretion to buy up all such supplies immediately on their arrival at reasonable fixed prices, and, although there were inevitably cases of smuggling and private disposal of such wares at higher prices, the quantity of ammunition so purchased on state account was astonishing.   One day, while I was sitting with Ibn Sa'ud discussing affairs in the great single-pole Cawnpore tent which he had received as a present from Dhari Ibn Tawala, to whom it had been given by the British authorities at Basra, the Treasurer, Muhammad Ibn Shilhub, brought in for his master's inspection and approval a number of belts of Turkish machine-gun ammunition, part of a store purchased by a *Kuwaiti* dealer in the Hijaz.   Later on, during the course of a short sojourn in the Qasim, some 600,000 rounds [1] of S.A.A. were similarly purchased, and Ibn Sa'ud himself reckoned that the number of rifles from the Hijaz which had been brought into his territories and privately disposed of was between 7000 and 8000.   The price of munitions was effectively kept down to a reasonable level by stringent measures adopted to prevent their export from Najd to the Persian market.

Apart from Ibn Sa'ud's own reception-tent, the encampment consisted for the most part of white bell-tents or small Indian tents of various patterns.   The great guest-tent, to which *Shaikhs* and other notable persons were conducted on arrival, was, as already mentioned, a great *Badawin* tabernacle of black hair, before which was planted the furled standard of the true faith surmounted by a shining metal ball and spike.   The meals of notable guests were served in a separate white tent from a different kitchen to that which supplied the meals of Ibn Sa'ud and myself.   The food was always simple—rice, meat and soup or gravy [2]—but of excellent quality, and, besides my suite, visitors occasionally dropped in to share my meals.   Among the most welcome was Jabir [3] the *Marri*, as satanic as ever and none the worse for some strenuous riding [4] during the preceding twelve days

---

[1] *See* Chapter I. p. 31.   [2] *Marq.*

[3] He died, to my great regret, during the influenza epidemic of December, 1918.

[4] He had been from Riyadh to Hufuf and back and on to Shaqra.

SHAQRA—A LANE ON WEST SIDE OF THE OASIS.

To face page 113.

in his master's service. Another was Mansur Ibn Rumaih of Buraida, one of three brothers who play an important part in the trade in camels between Arabia and its borderlands and were at this time busily engaged in buying transport animals for the Sharifian armies. In addition to such occasional visitors my small party had become more or less permanently augmented by three Indians, who, having arrived at Riyadh on their long and dreary journey to the Mecca pilgrimage, had taken advantage of Ibn Sa'ud's march to accompany it northwards in the hope of finding in the Qasim a party bound for the Hijaz, to which they could attach themselves in the hope of getting food enough to keep themselves alive and an occasional ride to relieve their long weariness. Treated with scant courtesy by the servants and camp-followers of Ibn Sa'ud, they drifted one by one into my little camp, where, viewed with suspicion by my suite as potential thieves, they at any rate got food enough and rides on the baggage animals of my train. One was a native of Delhi, Ahmad by name, a simple insignificant body typical of the worn-out peasantry of the Ambala division ; the second was a tall, lean Bengali with the scantiest knowledge of Urdu and none of Arabic ; while the third was a swashbuckling *Baluchi*, hailing from Gwadar and speaking several languages, including Urdu, Persian and Arabic, fluently. At 'Anaiza they drifted away from my party almost without being noticed, and who shall say whether they ever got to the goal of their ambition or fell by the wayside, as so many do ? And no wonder, seeing that they start without provision for the way from distant homes, trusting to be enabled by the charity of their fellow-men to perform an arduous penance, enjoined upon his followers by a prophet who could never in his wildest dreams have anticipated that the faith he preached would indeed take root in the uttermost parts of two continents.

During these days of my sojourn at the capital of Washm I had ample opportunities, during the intervals of leisure between my foregatherings with Ibn Sa'ud and the local notables for the transaction of official business or the discussion of politics, to study the town and its environs. The oasis is situated with a river frontage, as it were, of about

P.A.W.   H

1500 yards on the left bank of a *Wadi*, which, descending from the sandstone plateau in an easterly direction under the name of Sha'ib 'Ashara, is joined at the south-eastern corner of the oasis by the torrent-bed of Wadi Ghadir coming from the south and, changing its name to Wadi Shaqra, runs northward in a valley varying from a mile to half a mile in width until at some distance north of the town it splays out in a broad delta into the Butin at the point where stand the granges of Qusur Sunaidi. Half a dozen detached walled palm-groves dot the northern part of the valley, while about two-thirds of the main block of the oasis consists of a dense plantation of flourishing palms closely investing the more or less dilapidated western wall of the town itself, which is lozenge-shaped and occupies the eastern and northern sections of the oasis. A retaining wall along the torrent-bed protects the settlement from attack by the floods which on occasion sweep down the valley, while, standing back from it a short distance, a thick mud wall, 15 feet high and provided at intervals of about 100 paces with turrets, extends along the whole frontage from the south-west corner to the northern extremity to serve a similar purpose against human foes. This wall must at some time have been carried round the complete circuit of the settlement, but the extension of cultivation in a westerly direction, the encroachment of sand on the same side and human neglect have contributed to the denuding of the western flank of the oasis of its defences ; and even the inner wall separating the town from the palm-groves has fallen into such a state of disrepair that an enemy, having once gained a footing in the palm-groves, would have little difficulty in effecting an entry into the town. The imposing river-wall is therefore of little practical use for the purpose to which doubtless it owed its erection.

The town itself, contained by the circuit wall on its east and north sides and by the remnants of the broken-down inner wall already mentioned on the west, runs up to an apex on the south, from which point to the extreme north point is a distance of 700 yards. Its greatest width is 450 yards. Its population may be reckoned at between 7000 and 8000 souls, consisting partly of cultivators and partly of merchant princes and petty traders. The last-named conduct their business of retail sale to the *Badawin* and other customers in a small roughly triangular *Suq* occupying a central position in the town and containing some 40 or 50 shops overshadowed by the unostentatious pile of the great mosque, which forms its north-east side. From here a broad street runs in a northerly direction until it meets a cross-thoroughfare connecting the *Sudairi* or main gate at the north-east corner of the town with the western gate in the north-west quarter. Neither of these, the only proper gates of the town, is of any architectural merit, while a northern entrance is no more than a breach in the wall giving access to a small open space in which there were generally a few *Badawin* tents. A similar but larger open space occupies a considerable area immediately within the *Sudairi* gate, while a large space at the southern extremity of the town is also free of buildings and is separated by the town wall, which here makes a sharp angle, from the large modern cemetery immediately outside. The houses in the central part of the town in the neighbourhood of the *Suq* are of poor appearance and closely packed together, their upper storeys completely covering the streets below with only occasional breaks to admit light thereto. The rabbit-warren arrangement of this part is in strong contrast with the southern or aristocratic quarter, where the great merchants live in well-built mansions, in the ground-floor rooms of which they transact their wholesale business and store the consignments of piece goods and other commodities which they receive at intervals from the coast. The upper storeys contain their living rooms, those of the family being of course entirely separate from the rooms in which the master of the house receives visitors or accommodates guests.

The palm-groves are irrigated in the rainy season by the admission of flood water into the circuit of the oasis through channels for which arched sluices, capable of being closed by boards or brushwood, are provided in the outer wall. Such irrigation gives the palms the annual soaking which their roots require, but perennial irrigation is also carried on for the benefit of the palms and of the important subsidiary crops of fruit, vegetable and corn by means of great wells of the *Jalib* type. Donkeys and kine and camels are used here

to draw up the water, the first-named being in great pre-
ponderance over the others. The largest well I actually saw
was one of eight wheels—a great oblong cavity well limned
inside with masonry blocks from top to bottom, 20 feet long
and 10 feet broad with a depth of 10 fathoms ; it was being
worked by a team of eight donkeys ascending and descending
the inclined plane which, in this case, was only on one side
of the well. Besides the palms the oasis of Shaqra is characterised by a rich undergrowth of fruit trees, among which
the citron is particularly prominent. Vines do not appear
to be very successful here and the grapes are of inferior
quality, but figs are plentiful. Among vegetables the pumpkin was most conspicuous, while there were considerable
stretches of millet and lucerne cultivation—the wheat and
barley having of course been long since harvested. Fresh
dates now began to appear regularly with my meals, but the
season was said to be very backward in comparison with
the normal, and the great bunches of fruit on the trees were
still for the most part green. There is no grazing in the
Shaqra valley for camels, which have to go out to the surrounding *Nafuds* or to be stall-fed with the highly-prized
Nussi grass brought therefrom ; but the local goats and sheep
find a precarious subsistence in the immediate neighbourhood
of the oasis, where the most plentiful plants are the *Harmal*
and *Dha'a* grass. Every evening the flocks are driven into
the city by the hireling shepherds, and the owners there take
charge of their animals and drive them off to the ground-
floor chambers of their houses, where, having been milked,
they spend the night.

One evening while watching this process of the driving
in and distribution of the sheep and goats—it was astonishing
how easily each owner picked out and rounded up his own
belongings—I observed a number of boys absorbed in a
curious game, which I can only describe as a primitive
ancestor of golf. It is called *Al Bir* or ' the well ' (the hole
we might well translate it) and is said to be a common
amusement of all northern Najd from Washm to Haïl. A
small piece of wood about six inches long is placed over the
edge of a shallow hole scooped out of the ground so that
about half of it rests on the ground and the remaining half

SHAQRA—A TYPICAL DRAW-WELL WITH COWS AT WORK.

To face page 116.

is in the air. The player with an ordinary stick or cane strikes the unsupported end of the wood so as to make it leap into the air, and then with another stroke of the cane sends it hurtling through the air as far as possible from the hole. His object is then to guide the piece of wood back to the hole by striking one end of it so as to make it bounce in the required direction. The player who succeeds in getting his wood home (presumably in the least number of strokes, though on this point I did not make very precise enquiries) is adjudged the winner.

Another game I saw during these days was called *Hadraq* or *Hadraj*, and is apparently of *Hijazi* origin and in Najd confined to the slaves. Eight or nine small cavities having been scooped out of the ground in some sort of order, a pebble or pellet of camel-dung is placed in each. A handful of pebbles or pellets is then sprinkled by the player over the area covered by the holes. He then proceeds to remove the contents of the hole having the greatest number of balls from the scene, and taking up the contents of the hole having the next greatest number, sprinkles them over the whole area. These two moves are continued until the total number of balls remaining does not exceed the total number of holes and no hole holds more than two balls. Having reached this point he has to distribute his balls in accordance with rules, which I did not altogether succeed in grasping and which seemed quite complicated, in such manner that the surviving balls should lie in holes adjacent to each other and not be separated from each other by empty holes.

Shaqra, like the rest of Washm, formed part of Ibn Rashid's dominions during the last decade and a half of last century, but it was always an unwilling dependency and somewhat of a thorn in that ruler's side. It was for this reason that 'Abdul 'Aziz Ibn Rashid strengthened the fortifications of Tharmida and used that town as his military base in the province rather than the capital. In the autumn of 1903,[1] a year after Ibn Sa'ud had recovered Riyadh and the southern provinces, Ibn Rashid made an attempt to recapture Dilam in the Kharj district, but was forced to retire ; and Ibn Sa'ud, pursuing his disorganised and

[1] *Vide H.A.* ii. 42.

disheartened forces, had no difficulty in occupying the whole
of the Washm province without opposition in the spring of
1904. Ibn Rashid in the same year returned to the charge
and ' besieged ' Shaqra from the position he had taken up
amid the *Qasrs* of Sunaidi, but the governor, Ibn Suwailim
of Riyadh, was successful in defending it against repeated
attacks for a month and, in due course, the occupation of
the Sudair province (also without opposition) in the summer
of 1904 by Ibn Sa'ud and his subsequent occupation of the
greater part of the Qasim in the same year, finally relieved
Washm of all further danger. Since then its history has been
uneventful.

Our last day at Shaqra was Friday, 16th August, when
the slaves and retainers of Ibn Sa'ud turned out for the
midday prayer in the great mosque in all their best finery
of purple or flame-coloured *Zabuns*.[1] I gazed with admiration at the splendid cavalcade as it rode across the valley
towards the *Sudairi* gate and made sure that Ibrahim Ibn
Jumai'a, whom I now very seldom saw, was somewhere in
their midst outshining the dandiest of them in some splendid
raiment. For some reason I could never reconcile this
harmless indulgence in fine clothing with my conception of
Arab virility—which, it must be confessed, is largely the
result of indigence—and, turning to Mitrak who was at my
side, burly, pock-marked and with simple travel-stained
garments, I asked him if he would ever wear such finery if
he could. ' Most certainly—*bil hail*,' was the disappointing
reply. And one has, indeed, only to see the effect of contact
with luxury and civilisation on the Arabs of the Syrian
borderland to realise that the simplicity of Arabia—the rock
on which the *Wahhabi* movement is so firmly established—
is a delusion which the long-delayed but inevitable advance
of modern luxury must surely dissipate. A century ago
Wahhabi militancy had, after the first flush of its far-flung
victories, to reckon with a great Oriental power which it
had ventured to challenge ; it was then thrust back into its
desert wastes, crushed but by no means dead, and a century
of hardship under primitive conditions has rekindled the
flame that had seemed extinguished for ever. ' The old

[1] Also called *Jaukha*.

Wahhabi power,' wrote S. M. Zwemer [1] as recently as 1912,
' is now broken for ever and Najd is getting into touch with
the world through commerce.' The old *Wahhabi* power was,
as a matter of fact, just beginning to find its feet again.
The *Ikhwan* settlement of 'Artawiya was actually founded
in that very year, and twelve years later a *Wahhabi Sultan*
was again master of Mecca. And now there is no Oriental
power concerned or able to intervene in the interests of
Islam, but the *Wahhabi* power is of its own choosing face to
face with an enemy far more insidious than the Great Turk
of old, and Najd is for the first time in touch with the world
not through commerce alone but in the political sphere. If
'Abdul 'Aziz Ibn Sa'ud and his successors can steer their ship
safely amid the shoals and rocks of world-politics and maintain among its uncouth crew amid the temptations to which
it will now be exposed the discipline which has characterised
the early stages of the new *Wahhabi* movement, an Arabian
Empire—and who would be bold enough to predict the
precise limits to which it may extend ?—may yet fill the
place till recently occupied by Turkey in the forefront of the
Islamic powers.

But to resume my narrative—the morning of 17th August
saw the camp struck and Ibn Sa'ud off at an early hour on
the short march to Wushaiqir, our next halt. I had impressed
upon Rushaid and Ibrahim al Junaifi that I must have a
competent guide at all costs, but when I came out of my tent
ready to start, the latter was absent—presumably enjoying
a final cup of coffee with some friend in the town—while the
former was endeavouring to cover an obvious delinquency—
failure to find a guide—by feverish activity over the loading
of the camels. I mounted without a word and set forth
accompanied by Mitrak and Manawar, leaving all explanations till afterwards.

From the south-east corner of the oasis I struck away from
the Wushaiqir track in a south-westerly direction over the
bare sandstone downs to some high ground about a mile
distant, from which I had a good view over a dreary scene.
The ruddy rocky desert plateau extended for some miles to
the west as far as eye could see ; to the north-east the whole

[1] *Arabia—the Cradle of Islam,* 4th edition, 1912, p. 151.

oasis of Shaqra lay in full view backed by the orange sands
of the *Nafud*, beyond which rose the grim purple barrier of
the Sudair cliffs ; while to the north-west at some distance
we could discern the white tents of the new-pitched camp
beyond the palms of Al Fara'a. Moving down the slope in
the latter direction we passed from the bare rock to a level
stretch of loam with a light covering of sand and grasses.
Crossing the channels of Wadi Ghadir (about 30 yards broad
at this point) and Sha'ib 'Ashara, we found ourselves again
on rocky ground about a mile south of the elevated wedge
which separates Shaqra from the northern settlements. We
soon struck the main road along the low cliff-face of this
wedge, passing at about a quarter mile to our left a single
Qasr in a small patch of cultivation bordered along the road
by a rough brushwood fence. At this point the wedge-shaped
valley of Wushaiqir appeared before us in all its extent
between two low cliffs converging gradually from the west
towards the northern extremity of the Butin, beyond which
in the *Nafud* rose three knolls of pink sand collectively known
as Rumhain. We were, as it were, at one extremity of the
broad end of the wedge, and a wide sandy plain lay between
us and the two oases. Having marched about half a mile
across this we came to a tall tapering turret at the corner of
a dilapidated wall, which before it was destroyed—apparently
under orders from Ibn Sa'ud—enclosed a considerable patch
of corn cultivation without habitations. Another half mile
or less brought us to the only gate of Fara'a, a walled village
somewhat dilapidated and straggling but picturesque. From
the gate a single street burrows through a densely-packed
mass of houses to the further end of the village and thence
curves round back to the gate, forming a complete loop and
leaving just enough room between ground level and the roof
of the tunnel for a *dhalul*-rider to pass through without
dismounting.

The population of the village may be about 400 souls of
the Nawasir subsection of Bani Tamim under Musa'id Ibn
Faïz, the local *Amir*. The palm-groves, in the midst of which
it lies, extend about three-quarters of a mile in length with
a width of less than half a mile, and are of a somewhat
straggling character. The wells have a depth of six to seven

WUSHAIQIR—ENTRANCE TO HAMLET OF AL FARA'A.

To face page 120.

fathoms, some of them having excellent sweet water, while others are quite brackish.

Half a mile north of Fara'a lies the more prosperous oasis of Wushaiqir, where the water is sweet and abundant, while the palm-groves form a dense circular block about half a mile in diameter, in the midst of which lies the village, invisible to one approaching from this direction. Ibn Sa'ud's camp was pitched in the open space separating the two oases, my tent being in a newly-planted *Ithil* grove close under the circuit wall of the northern settlement. Wushaiqir is said to be the oldest settlement of Washm, and is proud of its antiquity, claiming an uninterrupted existence of 400 years, dating from a period when the present capital was a mere desert watering known as Shaqra Wushaiqir. A less creditable episode in its history was its long and eventually unsuccessful struggle against the early champions of the *Wahhabi* creed. Its population at the present time cannot be less than 2500 souls of mixed origin, largely drawn from the Wuhaba section of Bani Tamim, to which belong the local *Amir*, Ibrahim al Kharashi, and his brother 'Uthman. The village itself, situated towards the western side of the oasis, where the palm-groves are less dense than in other parts, is of irregular form and entirely unwalled—the oasis on the other hand is completely surrounded by a circuit wall —but covers a considerable area. The streets are crooked and winding but the houses are lofty and of solid construction, while the rabbit-warren effect typical of the Washm villages is but little in evidence. The *Suq* is roughly lozenge-shaped and not unlike that of Shaqra, though more spacious, and contains about thirty shops or rather more. The people and particularly the more youthful folk seemed to be entirely devoid of the bigotry and mock-piety characteristic of most *Najdi* settlements, and quite embarrassed me during a visit of inspection I made on the evening of our arrival to the village and oasis by an exhibition of cordiality and inquisitiveness to which I was quite unaccustomed. My camera attracted a good deal of attention, while some of my self-appointed cicerones had formed part of the Washm contingent at the Shauki camp during the spring and, having there seen me, seemed to take a special delight in giving me all the information they could about their native village.

The oasis is flanked on the north by a low cliff similar to that at Shaqra, whence I had an excellent view of the settlement and its surroundings. No fewer than six torrent-beds,[1] descending from the tilted plateau to west and south, mingle their strands in the Wushaiqir valley on their way to the bushy tract of Raudha Rumhain lying against the *Nafud* sands at the head of the Butin. At Fara'a and more parti-cularly at Wushaiqir the abundant sub-soil water supply is tapped by numerous wells, some of which are of considerable dimensions. One of these was the largest I had yet encoun-tered, a deep pit [2] of seven fathoms to water level—in the dry season the water level descends to as much as fourteen fathoms, they say, though the supply is never exhausted—surmounted by a ponderous wooden structure fitted with no fewer than sixteen wheels, eight on each side, worked by a mixed team of cows,[3] donkeys and camels. The kine were the sturdiest I had seen in all Najd and the donkey population of the village is very considerable, to judge by the number I saw out grazing in the valley. The palm-groves are finer here than anywhere in Washm, but the undergrowth of fruit-trees is less striking than at Shaqra. I also saw considerable areas under millet, little and great,[4] and large patches of pumpkins.

A number of visitors, too late for the gathering of the clans at Shaqra, came to pay their respects to their sovereign at Wushaiqir. Among them were several leading *Shaikhs* of the 'Ataiba—Ibn 'Uqaiyan, Manahi Ibn Haidhal and Ibn 'Amaidi,[5] the two last-named being the individuals who had gone to King Husain the previous December to claim redress

[1] They all run roughly from west to east, Wa'ra being the most northerly, Khalif the most southerly, and Mudhlim occupying a central position. Between the first and the last is Shubarim (? Shuraimi). Besides these the 'Udhaij and Sudais are tributaries of Wa'ra from the north.

[2] Known as Al Sudais—it was said that four extra wheels (two on each side) could be fitted to the structure on occasion—making a total of twenty wheels in all. Another well I saw had twelve wheels, six on each side.

[3] Cows are here more commonly used for well-traction than donkeys or camels.

[4] *Dukhn*, little millet ; *Dhurra*, great millet.

[5] ? Humaidi.

against the *Ikhwan* of Ghatghat[1]—and *Shaikh* Muhammad, the son of *Shaikh* 'Abdullah Ibn 'Abdul Wahhab, the chief ecclesiastical dignitary of Najd. This young man had just arrived with his following from a tax-gathering expedition in the Sha'ra district and was very affectionately received by Ibn Sa'ud. His followers trooped into the tent to salute their ruler with the customary kiss on the left side of his nose and immediately withdrew, while Muhammad remained to give the news of the district whence he had come. He seemed to me to be a young man of no more than twenty-five, but Ibn Sa'ud told me that he was not far short of forty, his beardless immature physiognomy betokening not so much youth as a deficiency of intellect, for it was commonly said that, destined by birth to the primacy of Najd, he had but an imperfect understanding of the principles of *Wahhabism*, and was regularly accompanied by an *'Alim* to instruct him in lore of which one day he would be expected to be the chief repository.

Another—and to me most welcome—arrival was Dr. 'Abdullah Sa'id, whom I had not seen since December and who had just arrived from the Hasa to accompany Ibn Sa'ud for the rest of his tour. I noticed that he spoke French less fluently than before, but he was as friendly as ever, and for the rest of my time in Arabia we saw a great deal of each other. He was the bearer of the unwelcome news that a recent 'Ajman raid on a Subai' encampment at Hafar al Ats, which had resulted in 300 camels being carried off, was the work of the Safran and Salih sections, whose headquarters were at Shuwaibda on the Mesopotamian border under British protection. Rumours had also come in of another raid by the 'Ajman[2] in the neighbourhood of Juda in the Hasa, but Ibn Sa'ud, having at this time high hopes of a settlement all round by British intervention both with the refractory 'Ajman and with King Husain, did not take these matters very seriously, though he deputed one of his trusted lieutenants, 'Abdul Rahman Ibn Mu'ammar, to tour the raided districts, collect the necessary statistics of losses and repair to Basra to arrange a settlement through the British authorities.

[1] *H.A.* i. 313; the quarrel was composed by Ibn Sa'ud under the usual tribal arrangement for the payment of blood-money at 800 dollars per man killed.

[2] Led by Sultan Ibn Hithlain and one of the Mutalaqqam family.

It had been arranged that the march should be resumed early next morning (18th August), but for some reason the orders issued overnight had been cancelled and Ibn Sa'ud, having nothing better to do, took it into his head to pay me a visit in my camp at an inconveniently early hour. I was in fact still abed and my tent strewn with pipes and other odious apparatus, so I sent out a message that, as I was engaged on my toilet, I couldn't see him for a few minutes. Without ceremony he sat in our larger reception or meal tent until I was ready, and then insisted on sending for his own frugal breakfast to share with 'Abdullah and myself. It consisted of fresh dates, little hard and slightly sweetened flour cakes called *Kulaija*, dry milk sherds or *'Iqt* and camel's milk. A mail had just arrived from Kuwait with good news —how very good we little guessed—of developments on the western front, but nothing of local import, and we frittered away the whole morning in desultory talk. It was then broken to me gently by 'Abdullah that a night march was contemplated, and during the afternoon I observed throughout the camp active preparations to that end. At 5 p.m. the whole plain was filled with camels and men shouting, loading up and running about. In their midst was planted the furled banner and close by it sat Ibn Sa'ud and his chief attendants drinking a last cup of coffee and transacting final details of business. Of a sudden the standard-bearer at a word from his master rose and mounted, the flag unfurled was handed up to him and he set forth. Indescribable confusion ensued as party after party set out in his wake, and before long the whole *Qaum* was on the move, its line of march passing to the east of Fara'a. A few stragglers only remained, and among them a camel which had but a few moments before given birth to a calf and was being assisted to get rid of the after-birth by means of a large stone attached to it. The calf had been removed and, I believe, slaughtered, and the miserable mother was couched as she was, saddled and loaded, it being explained to me that the after-birth would come away during the march.

I now mounted and followed the bed of Sha'ib Wa'ra, leaving the Fara'a oasis to the left or east and marching from its south-western corner in a south-westerly direction up the slope of the plateau. We now followed the Mudhlim torrent-bed while the *Qaum* followed up the Khalif, a longer but easier route. A camel had already fallen by the way exhausted, and was being cut up for its meat and skin. The marching host was a splendid sight as it straggled over the plateau down which, as we ascended, we had a good view over Wushaiqir to the Rumhain peaks in the *Nafud* and to a low escarped ridge called Lautal to the north. The ravine of the Mudhlim deepened steadily in a great gloomy crevice 30 yards across and of considerable depth, the elevation of the first distinct ridge of the plateau being about 3000 feet above sea-level and rather more than 200 feet above the oasis behind us. From this point a bare plateau rose steadily before us with a surface of marl curiously marked with patches of bright mauve colour overlying the sandstone. The well-marked track ran up midway between the Mudhlim and Shubarim ravines until it struck a tributary of the latter called Sha'ib Ausa', a shallow rocky depression about 30 yards wide. The whole region was exceedingly dry and the vegetation almost without a sign of life, the preceding winter and spring having been entirely rainless. Following the Ausa' we came out upon a wide crater-like depression on the summit of the plateau, about 3200 feet above sea-level, which being the source of the Mudhlim is known as Fara'at al Mudhlim. It was surrounded by low broken ridges in which here and there appeared patches of black rock. It was now dark and my companions, who had been provided with new untrained *dhaluls*, were already far behind while the baggage had gone round with the *Qaum*. For better or worse I decided to halt for the night, and having despatched Nasir, a newly-recruited guide, to go in search of the baggage, lay down to rest on the hard rock-slabs of a small conical hummock called Mabda. It was not till 9 p.m. that the baggage camels turned up and we had dinner. According to Nasir, who seemed intelligent enough, the Washm plateau extends twenty miles northward from this point and ends at the junction of the Shaqra and Batra *Nafuds*, whose combined sands run up north or north-east towards Zilfi. Batra is the local name of the northern extremity of Nafud Qunaifida.

We were up betimes next morning and soon on the move
down the short western slope of the plateau. Washm had
passed from our sight and before us lay a boundless sea of
sand, ridge upon ridge of orange light in the dawn. In five
minutes we reached the edge of a narrow sandy valley called
Farq, separating the Washm rock plateau from the sands, and
soon struck into the tracks of the *Qaum*, which had passed
overnight. In rather more than an hour we reached the foot
of the Batra *Nafud* at a green patch of *Sharr* bushes known
as Khal al Sharr and reputed to have been formerly a very
conspicuous *Raudha* resembling a palm oasis until the new
Ikhwan settlers of Furaithan came and cut down every
tree of decent size to provide themselves with beams and
rafters.

4. AL SIRR

We now stood at the threshold of a small district rejoicing
in the picturesque name of Al Sirr, which appears to mean
' the murmuring,' [1] and to be due to the exiguous perennial
streams rising in a number of springs near the surface. This
is the generally accepted interpretation of the name, though
Ibn Sa'ud himself was inclined to connect it with *Surra*—the
navel or centre, *i.e.* of Najd. Before arriving at the district
properly so called, however, we had to negotiate a broad
band of *Nafud* sands some twenty-seven miles in width and
interrupted only by a thin tongue of plain forming the northern extremity of the broad Maruta plain separating Nafud
Qunaifida from Nafud Dalqan, which latter is but the
southern continuation of Nafud al Sirr just as the Batra, on
which we were about to enter, is the northern continuation
of the former. Both these *Nafud* strips join at no great
distance to the north of our line of march, and reinforced by
the Shaqra *Nafud* thrust up a solid barrier of sand between
the Qasim and Zilfi. Nasir, however, informed me that the
thin tongue of plain parts the two *Nafud* strips up to their
northern extremities which end in the *Safra* north-east of
Buraida, and that at the northern extremity of the plain is
the small settlement or well of 'Ain Ibn Fuhaid. This infor-

[1] *Musarsar.*

mation would not seem to be exact,[1] though it indicates an
interesting fact, namely, the uninterrupted continuity of the
Mustawi valley of the north and the Maruta plain of the south.

The width of the Batra strip along our line of march, a
well-beaten track having been left for our guidance by the
Qaum, was about four miles. Its surface consisted of alternate
ridges and depressions with exposures of clay in the bottom
of some of the latter, and a difference in elevation of from
fifty to a hundred feet. The plentiful dry *'Arfaj* bushes threw
a greyish sheen over the billowy downs, while patches of
green *Adhir* lent variety to the scene. The *Shih* bushes and
Thamam grasses were withered with the drought, but the
dry boughs of the useful *'Arta* were putting forth tendrils of
light green. For the most part the way was easy enough,
but occasionally the slope up to the ridges was quite steep
enough for the camels. One of these animals had strayed
from the *Qaum* during the night march and was wandering
about disconsolately with its saddle-frame hanging under its
belly, while its load of choice *Khalas* dates of the Hasa had
been deposited by the roadside. These we appropriated
for our own use, and the camel we took charge of until we got
into camp, to the great relief of a search-party of three men
whom I met about a mile out of camp cursing the unkind
fate which had robbed them of their siesta and sent them
forth to find a stray camel which might by this time be anywhere in that vast desert. They were deeply grateful for the
good news I brought and turned back with me to the tents.
The leader of the party was riding a *Hurra dhalul* from
Northern Arabia, another an animal of the *Dar'iya* breed from
the Manasir tribe, and the third an *'Umaniya* like myself.
The high rolling downs in the centre of this sand strip were,
according to my aneroid, about 2950 feet above sea-level, and
are known by the separate name of Jau Ibn Matruq. Rounding a shoulder of them we came suddenly upon a grand view
of the narrow plain close before us and the rolling sand
billows of Nafud al Sirr beyond.

The valley or plain separating the two sand strips is about
four miles across, and much encroached upon by tongues of
sand from either side. About two miles south of our course

[1] This route is now (1928) regularly used by motor-cars and Nāsir's
information is thus corroborated.

it was almost blocked from side to side by a detached sand
dune about two miles long called 'Afariya, while the Sirr
sands protruded eastwards almost to the line of our track
before falling back again in a semicircular bay to its main
north and south direction. The surface is generally of loam
covered with a thin sprinkling of coarse sand-grit, and in
places with dry grass. Our course lay W.N.W. slanting
across the plain on a well-marked track, and we came upon
a small party of *Badawin* on trek. They were five men with
a dozen animals carrying their goods and chattels, including
two women riding in the fantastic panniers called *Qin*. I
saluted them and received a cordial greeting in return, but
it was to Nasir they addressed themselves for news, and it
turned out that they were 'Ataiba *Ikhwan* from the settlement of Sajir south of Al Sirr. As we approached the line of
the greater *Nafud* the plain became more sandy with patches
of gravel and shingle and occasional low ridges of black
cinder-like rock such as I remembered to have seen in the
same plain further south. In one spot we passed a considerable patch of ruinous cairns, which looked to be possibly the
remnants of some former settlement, and in due course we
came to a tract of raised rocky ground called Hajra, in the
midst of which we found Ibn Sa'ud's host encamped and for
the most part endeavouring to make good the hours of sleep
they had lost during the night. The tents were pitched in
a shallow sandy depression of triangular shape and about
200 yards from base to apex, the base being formed by the
Hajra rock ridge, about 50 feet high, and the other two sides
by the *Nafud*. The whole area was thickly covered with
newly-sprouting *'Arta* and dry *Dha'a* grass, while the black
rock, which seems to rest on a sandstone foundation, is
certainly of volcanic origin, consisting partly of shining
sharp-edged blocks of a basaltic nature and partly of brownish
slaggy masses. The black streaks across the plain already
noticed would appear to be of the same volcanic character.

My baggage animals having not yet arrived, I went to the
tent of 'Abdullah Sa'id for coffee, tea and breakfast, and
there I found Muhammad Ibn Sulaiman,[1] one of Ibn Sa'ud's

---

[1] He died in 1919 or 1920, and was succeeded in his secretarial post by
his brother, 'Abdullah.

secretaries, and, of all people, Ibrahim Ibn Jumai'a, doubtless attracted by the prospect of a smoke. It was the first
time I had foregathered with the latter since leaving Riyadh,
and we conducted ourselves each towards the other with
the distant frigidity required by the circumstances, but I
realised that so far as possible I must see 'Abdullah in my
tent rather than in his to avoid awkward meetings with
mutual friends, with whom I definitely preferred not to be
on visiting terms.

Ibn Sa'ud again intended to march through the night and,
as I did not propose to imitate his example, I started off
well before the *Qaum* at 4 p.m. with the idea of getting as
far as possible on the way before dark and then camping
wherever we might be. The outer slope of the *Nafud* was
steep, and this sand-barrier throughout its whole width
proved to be as heavy and difficult as any I had yet met with.
It was a continuous switchback up over low ridges and down
into shallow hollows, without any striking feature and with
none of the lofty dunes of pure sand which relieve the monotony of the Dahna. Here and there were shallow troughs
with clay bottoms, and at frequent intervals we passed herds
of camels, mostly of black or dark colour, belonging to the
Sajir *Ikhwan* grazing on the plentiful though dry herbage
which covered the downs. We had but recently had our
evening meal, but I noticed that almost every man of the
advance party preceding the *Qaum* made a bee-line for the
camels on such occasions and filled himself with milk. The
Arab, like his camel, has an unlimited capacity for taking
nourishment against the lean days when he has to do
without food.

In the midst of the *Nafud* there is a sort of glade which
to the unwary is a pitfall. It seems to provide as far as one
can see an easy passage, but it is said to end in a veritable
maze of impossible sand heaps, among which one may
wander for hours without finding a way out. This spot is
known as Al Maghda—the losing place—and the road to Sirr,
ignoring it, strikes up a difficult-looking slope to the right,
beyond which the going becomes again tolerably easy. A
few drops of rain encouraged us to hope for a shower, but
we were disappointed, winding our way now along the foot

of some sand ridge [1] and now along the edge of a shallow depression. A narrow causeway leads the track between two fairly extensive depressions known as Hawijan, that on our right being of considerable depth, but exhibiting none of the characteristics of the horseshoe *Falj* pits of the Great North *Nafud* beyond Jabal Shammar. Towards sunset we crossed a shallow depression called Khubbat 'Awwad, in which Ibn Sa'ud's herd of milch-camels [2] were grazing on their leisurely progress to the next camping-place. From this depression we ascended the steep slope of a great cross ridge running north and south called Arqab al Buqara, on the summit of which, 3000 feet above sea-level according to my aneroid, we decided to camp for the night as the sun had already set and it was rapidly darkening, the western sky being lit up for only a few moments by a glorious blaze of pink and purple shades.

The *Qaum* was at this moment almost on our heels, and we drew aside to watch it pass, headed by the solid phalanx of the royal escort, which, having passed about half a mile beyond us, halted for a brief space for the evening prayer and a cup of coffee before resuming its march. We heard next day that it had strayed from the track in the darkness and had got involved in a maze of sandhills to the southward before striking into the Sirr plain.[3] The ridge on which we had camped is reckoned the *Mansifa* or half-way mark of the Sirr *Nafud*. Dr. 'Abdullah, somewhat to his annoyance I fancy, had by now been attached definitely to my party, and we celebrated the occasion by a heated argument as to the respective merits of day and night marching. He expressed a strong preference for the latter on the ground of its greater coolness, but my obstinacy on the point was perhaps less a source of grievance with him than my habit of having all my meals with my little suite. It was certainly a curiously-assorted party—a fact which struck me more particularly that evening as I sat apart on a low hummock surveying the desolation of rolling sand billows which filled the scene on every side around the little camp and the small group of the

---

[1] Some of these ridges have distinctive names, *e.g.* Umm Suwaik, Umm 'Aïdh, etc.

[2] *Mish.*   [3] At Qusur Ibn Sakran.

faithful performing the rites of the sunset prayer. Junaifi played the *Imam* and 'Abdullah took his place somewhat sheepishly in the line behind him next to Rushaid, who divided his attentions impartially between his God, his camels, and his dinner cooking on the unattended fire. Before dinner we had the excitement of a snake-hunt, a small viper eluding all efforts to kill it and taking refuge under a bush which was duly set on fire.

The going was rather better the following day than it had been up to this point and, starting off at about six o'clock, we negotiated the same sort of succession of ridges and low depressions. One of the latter, Jau Daramiya, was broad and clay-bottomed, beyond which we came to a steep and difficult slope called Mutaqqa, a spot celebrated for the frequency of accidents occurring on it. One of the *Qaum* camels had indeed come to grief on it and still lay there as if dead with its load upon its back. Mitrak, having freed the unfortunate beast of its burden, found it none the worse for its fall, and just at that moment two men of the *Qaum* appeared hastening along a track somewhat to our left, which the *Qaum* had followed by mistake, in search of the lost animal. Soon after this we got a fleeting glimpse of the *Safra* or rock wilderness beyond the *Nafud*, and, passing a depression called Khubba Sakrana, topped the last ridge of the *Nafud* 2880 feet above sea-level.

Far and wide before us extended the plain of Al Sirr, and I climbed up to a little hummock close to the track to take in the details of the expansive view. From this elevated position the plain below looked flat, though in point of fact it rises very gradually from the foot of the *Nafud* towards the western horizon, which is closed in as far as one could see to north and south by the rim of the *Safra*. I could see no feature by which to connect the scene before me with the country I had passed through further south during the previous December, but it seemed to me that the Sirr plain cannot but be a northerly continuation of the Ardh uplands. The slope of the land is eastwards in the main with a northerly tilt from a point somewhat to the south of my position, where the *Nafud* projects into the plain westward. South of this bulge, I was told, lies a bare plain called Sinad, which

I take to be the northern extremity of the Hadba Qidhla plain east of the Ardh district.

The southern part of the Sirr district, which I was unable to visit, contains two settlements, namely, Qusur Ibn Sakran in the plain a few miles away from the edge of the *Nafud*, and Sajir, hidden from view in a fold of the *Safra* eastward of a prominent ridge called Fuqm Sajir. The latter settlement, said to contain some 40 *Qasrs* and approximately 400 inhabitants, lay at a distance of 10 miles south-west of my position and is, as already mentioned, an *Ikhwan* settlement of 'Ataiba elements. Qusur Ibn Sakran is a somewhat smaller settlement of some 200 inhabitants, and consists of a small palm plantation and village together with three scattered *Qasrs* in the midst of cornfields. Further northwards lay the numerous petty oasis settlements which constitute the Sirr district properly so-called, and will be described in detail hereafter in the order in which I visited them. The only other feature of the scene that calls for remark is a pair of conical hillocks, one of them with an almost flat table-top, called Wushai'ain, which break the otherwise monotonous surface of the plain.

Having had my fill of the view and given our baggage animals time to come up to us, I resumed my march down the final gentle slope of the *Nafud* in a north-westerly direction. The edge of the plain,[1] into which we now passed, was in the main sandy with patches of gravel-strewn loam and occasional outcrops of white chalk and gypsum. About a mile to our left stood a single *Qasr* called Hujailana, and the surface gradually changed from sand to gravel. Having thus marched about three miles we came to a spring of water known as 'Ain al Qannur, from which a gentle trickle of clear, cold water, said to be unwholesome and liable to cause fever, flows in a channel partly subterranean and partly open to the oasis of Junaitha about a mile distant to the north-west. The subterranean portion of this channel is of the *Kariz* type with shafts five feet long and two feet broad sunk through the limestone soil at intervals to the water-level (ten feet below the surface at the head of the channel

[1] This strip between the sands of the *Nafud* and the plain proper is about two miles in width and called Al Adh'ad.

PERENNIAL CHANNEL OF 'AIN AL QANNŪR.

To face page 132.

and gradually decreasing as the water approaches the surface). Two sections of the channel are open, forming a stream about two feet wide with high banks of silt thrown up on either side during the periodical cleaning of the bed. The settlement of Junaitha, so-called—though the name for some reason gives offence to the inhabitants of the village, who prefer to call it 'Ain al Qannur after the spring—after the grandmother of 'Ali Ibn Qannur of the Hutaim tribe, who discovered the spring and founded the village, is a solid block of houses, forming roughly a square of about 100 paces each way, without a separate circuit wall, though it has a sort of gate on the west side. One or two of the houses are comparatively large and well built with ' lamp-shade ' turrets, and the population of some 400 souls is mainly of Hutaim origin. The head-man or *Amir* was at this time Nasir, the son of the above-mentioned 'Ali. The stream we had followed passes beyond the village to irrigate a small palm-grove on its north side and another newly-planted grove about a quarter mile to the west, beyond which it spends itself in watering a considerable tract of cornland, which also receives on occasion the flood of a torrent called Sha'ib 'Artawi descending from the *Safra* slope to the north-west.

We now followed this torrent-bed upwards past a ruined *Qasr* and a number of ruined wells on its right bank. Formerly cultivated, this patch has become strongly impregnated with salt—apparently washed down by the torrent—and has consequently been abandoned, though it is still sown occasionally when a heavy fall of rain has washed some of the salt out of the soil. A mile further up the channel we came to the large single *Qasr* of 'Artawi, also on the right bank, at which we found Ibn Sa'ud and his host encamped for the day. Here there are four wells in the immediate vicinity of the *Qasr* with plentiful though inferior water at a depth of only five or six feet from the surface, while a single well [1] of excellent water at a similar depth lay about half a mile to the south-west. Sand-grouse and rock-pigeon were plentiful in this neighbourhood.

I found Ibn Sa'ud suffering from an attack of biliousness

[1] This well is called *Al Marwa*, *i.e.* the place of drawing water.

which he attributed to a draught of *Marisi* (*Iqt* dissolved in water) he had taken during the night march, while 'Abdullah and Junaifi, having had more than they liked of the sun, were making sly efforts to detach themselves from my party. At any rate they had pitched their tent at some distance from mine and I saw no more of them for the rest of the day. Rushaid, obviously glad to be free of the rivalry of Junaifi, told me that the latter had called him an infidel because on some occasion recently he had neglected the call to prayer until he had finished pitching my tent.

By 4.30 in the afternoon the *Qaum* was again astir, but by now it was tacitly recognised that there was no obligation on my part to conform with its movements. I accordingly left Rushaid to pack up and go direct to the village of Tarafiya, where I proposed to spend the night, and, taking Mitrak and Nasir with me, started off on a tour of the Sirr settlements. The Junaitha tract lies in the lowest part of the plain, separated from the main body of the settlements by a low ridge through which Sha'ib 'Artawi cuts its way. Ascending this channel I found its upper reaches thickly covered with *Tarfa* bushes and grasses—its width being about 30 yards with low cliffs on either side. Just beyond the point at which it cuts through the ridge I came to a diminutive palm-patch called Taubi with a solitary watch-tower, whose sole occupant came forward to greet us and hear the news of the world. The palms of this grove number about a hundred and stand in the torrent-bed itself without other protection against the force of the flood than a light barrier of palm branches. We were now south-west of Qasr 'Artawi, while not far distant southward of us—perhaps two or three miles —in a depression fed by a torrent from the *Safra* slope lay the considerable oasis—the largest in Sirr—of Faidha, consisting of half a dozen fairly large palm-groves, a patch of *Ithils* and a walled village of mud-huts inhabited by some 400 souls of the Nawafila subsection of a tribe called Bani Husain, which is said to be either of Ashraf or Tamim origin. Eastward of Faidha lies the single *Qasr* of a small settlement called Bughaili with half a dozen palms and some cornfields.

North of the 'Artawi channel at this point runs a transverse ridge at right angles to the ridge already mentioned. It is

To face page 135.

THE OASIS OF 'AYAINA.

of gypseous composition, and beyond it, following the track from Faidha to the northern settlements, we entered upon a wide flat plain white with extensive salt deposits and dotted with straggling oases as far as one could see. The salt grains sparkled like diamonds in the sunlight as we rode across the soft and treacherous surface of the plain—without Nasir, whose *dhalul* suddenly sat down with him and absolutely refused to move in spite of all his efforts to stir her into action, including throwing dust into her mouth. He had to walk to Tarafiya, where he arrived much exhausted, and a search party was sent from the village to bring in the beast during the night. The ridges here are in the main of limestone with patches of a reddish rock coated with salt and a good deal of gypsum.

Marching north-west we came after about a mile to the end of the first patch of *Sabkha*, beyond which lay a sand tract with plentiful *'Arfaj* and *Alanda* scrub. Crossing a small sandy *Sha'ib* running from west to east (a tributary of the 'Artawi) we passed through the centre of a miserable straggling plantation of palms extending for about half a mile across our path and called Damthi. The only buildings in it were a watch-tower and a single *Qasr*, but neither was tenanted, the palms belonging to residents of Faidha. A mile beyond this we came to a charming little oasis called 'Ayaina, whose palms, watered by a running stream, are dominated by its only building, a small square *Qasr* with turrets set on an eminence of the ridge dividing this section of the district from the Junaitha depression. At somewhat less than half a mile to the east of the ridge are two almost moribund, exceedingly briny springs about 100 yards apart. The water in them lies about two feet below ground level, flows but feebly and is impeded by slimy weed growth. *Kariz* channels issuing from each merge their contents in a single open channel at a distance of about 100 yards from the springs, and a thin line of palms lines both banks of the channel, which shortly widens out into a sort of pool or reservoir, from the east end of which the stream continues through a breach in the ridge in which is a thick mass of palms. Having passed through the ridge the stream turns north to water the circular palm-grove of Rishiya,

about half a mile north of 'Ayaina. The former, having a
diameter of about a quarter mile, has a single *Qasr* and two
watch-towers, and both settlements belong to the people of
Faidha. It is amazing that palms should be able to derive
nourishment from water so salt, whose brine forms a thick
crust along the banks of the stream. Continuing in a north-
westerly direction we crossed a second low transverse ridge
into the Tarafiya basin and turned west to visit the spring
which feeds the long straggling oasis of that name. 'Ain
Tarafiya is an unattractive weed-covered pool six yards long
and two yards broad, whose banks are piled high with the
salty mud of which it is cleansed from time to time. From
its eastern end issues a clear but sluggish stream a foot deep
and a yard wide flowing between banks piled with mud on
either side to a height of 15 or 20 feet. About a mile to the
west lies the tiny settlement of Al 'Amir, with a thin strip
of palms about a quarter mile long and but four or five houses,
of which the population may be thirty souls. The first palms of
the Tarafiya oasis begin about a quarter mile to the north-east
of the spring and extend on both sides of the stream about
four abreast for about a quarter mile, ending in a thicker
grove, to the east of which at a distance of a few hundred
yards stands the village. The latter consists of some dozen
Qasr-like habitations built close together so as to form a
solid block of houses whose outer walls serve for the purpose
of defence against attack. Its population of a hundred souls
is of mixed character, including a number of negroes, one
of whom is the *Amir* of the village, Huwaidi by name. He
invited us to partake of coffee in his house, and extended his
hospitality to our jaded mounts, which spent the night
contentedly munching the fodder he provided. The *Amir's*
reception-room was a plain rectangular chamber with
unadorned clay walls and innocent of carpets or other
luxuries ; it was, however, comparatively well ventilated
by rows of small apertures, square and triangular, close
under the roof, while a large irregular breach in the wall
above the hearth let out the smoke engendered by the
operation of coffee-making. Rather more than a dozen of
the villagers joined us and we spent the evening pleasantly
enough drinking two rounds of coffee and inhaling incense

before our return to the tents. They told me that the springs of the Sirr district are reputed to have been in existence for more than three centuries ; from time to time during that period they had been lost and rediscovered and lost again, but the existing springs went back as far as their own memories and those of their fathers. 'Ain al Qannur was the first to be rediscovered in recent times, followed by the Tarafiya source and later by that at Suwaina—thus had the district attracted its present population. At Tarafiya there are also wells,[1] three fathoms to water, in a little *Sha'ib* to the north-west, which is said to have been the original site of the hamlet before the spring was discovered ; its bed is covered with *Ithil* and *Tarfa*, and occasionally carries a small torrent stream. The original inhabitants were Bani Tamim, who, being attacked by raiders and driven out, migrated to a tract known as Asyah,[2] northward of Wadi Rima, where they founded the settlement of Tarafiya,[3] which I visited some time afterwards. For the rest the conversation turned on the always absorbing topic of religion. My folk had in accordance with their custom combined [4] the sunset and evening prayers at sunset, and our hosts, when it was time to say their evening prayers, enquired whether my people would join them or would content themselves with the abbreviated [5] service permitted to travellers. After some discussion it was agreed that, as they had already combined their evening devotions with those of sunset, they should do neither, and that therefore the question of the justifiability of a shortened form of evening prayer was one of purely academic interest. But the point was not yielded without vigorous discussion, in which the humble villagers displayed the keenest interest. During the day the wind had been very variable, and the temperature in the early afternoon had reached 111° *Fahr.*, the sky at that time being over-clouded and having a regular monsoon look about it. Sunset brought a dead calm, and as we retired to our well-earned rest the atmosphere was brilliantly clear and cold under a moonlit sky.

---

[1] The water is all briny and undrinkable, but there is a *Marwa* or drinking-water well about a mile to the S.W.

[2] Plural of *Saih*.   [3] *See* Chapter III. p. 322.   [4] *Ijma'*.   [5] *Taqsir*.

Soon after resuming our march at an early hour the following morning we came to the tail of a thin stream, which we followed up through patches of millet and corn stubble to the diminutive oasis of Huwaiyina. A double row of straggling palms on either side of the channel led us to a prosperous little patch of cultivation, in which, by the side of a small palm-grove, lay beds of lucerne, pumpkins and beans, over which two watch-towers and a ruined *Qasr* kept their vigil. The oasis belongs to the people of Tarafiya, and its soil is brittle with incrustations of brine. In all there are about 200 palms, and the banks of the stream are covered with reeds. About a quarter mile beyond the cultivation is the source, about five feet below ground level and piled high around with brine-saturated soil ; the surface of the stream, which is sluggish and about two feet deep, is covered with noisome weed for a distance of twenty yards.

From here we traversed a clearing of *Hamdh*-covered waste to a wretched little plantation of a hundred straggling palms lying along the sides of a moribund channel about 400 yards in length flowing—if indeed it flowed at all— northwards. This was Simra, another property of the Tarafiya people, who have built a single watch-tower amid the palms. About a mile to the westward I saw an isolated *Qasr* amid a patch of grain cultivation presumably watered by another spring.

We now proceeded over a strip of desert bounded by a low ridge to the east and gently sloping upwards to the west. Here and there were evidences of abandoned wells—perhaps trial shafts sunk in the search for springs—and on our left ran what looked to be a buried stream channel ending in a small patch of newly-planted palms.

About two and a half miles to the northward of Tarafiya we came to the comparatively large oasis of Raushaniya, consisting of a circular palm-grove about four acres in extent, watered by lift from a well or spring, and of a palm strip about half a mile in length along the banks of a running stream emanating from a source about half a mile to the south. In each of these sections were a couple of watch-towers and a *Qasr*. This plantation belongs to the people of the Suwaina settlement, which now lay before us in a north-easterly direction.

We directed our course to the springs which feed the channels that make Suwaina in many respects the most prosperous of the Sirr settlements. There are two of them, half a mile apart, with roughly-constructed *Kariz* channels converging from them to a point 300 or 400 yards distant, whence an open stream flows to the oasis through a tract of briny loam overlying limestone. The more northerly of the two sources, which alone I inspected, lies in a shaft ten feet deep and six feet in diameter, whose upper parts were limned with masonry blocks. The channel issuing from it into a shafted tunnel was about two feet wide and the shafts themselves were each about two yards across where they projected from the ground level. Some few hundred yards lower down the channel runs through a narrow avenue of palms, which spreads out into a grove just in front of the village itself. About a mile and a half towards the north-west lies a small oasis called Shahama and comprising about a hundred straggling palms, a watch-tower and a *Qasr* in the bed of a *Sha'ib* of the same name.

Apart from half a dozen low square protective towers amid the palms and a single detached mansion outside the only gate of the village on its east side, Suwaina (or 'Ain al Suwaina as it is generally called), forms a compact square of clay habitations about a hundred yards on a side. The turrets on the building occupying the south-west corner made an exceedingly picturesque scene. The population, some 300 souls, are of the Bani Tamim, to which belongs the local *Amir*, 'Abdul Karim Ibn Subaihi.

Beyond the village a strip of palms with a single watch-tower in their midst stretches some 200 yards along the stream, which comes to an end about a quarter mile further on in a patch of 35 palms and a considerable walled area of flourishing millet and cornland, in which the stubble of last harvest still remained. Outside this walled tract is more cultivable land dependent on such water as there may from time to time be spared from the stream and partly on the spill of the Shahama *Sha'ib*, which drains down to a tract known as Wuthailan. In this torrent-bed we were tempted to make a brief halt by the appearance of half a dozen gazelles, but Mitrak was too tardy with his preparations, and as soon as he was ready for business his quarry, having stood gazing at us for some minutes, bounded away over the brown plain. At this point the *Sha'ib* ran between a thirty-foot ridge of the *Safra* and a fifteen-foot cliff of alluvial loam, the scene being littered with glittering fragments of gypsum, of which, according to Nasir, a quantity had not long before been gathered and carried away by a Moor [1] who had visited these parts.

Our course for the next two miles generally followed the *Sha'ib*, whose meanderings we avoided by crossing and recrossing its sandy ever-broadening channel, until we came to a group of unlined wells [2] on the right bank. These are about six feet deep and contain sweet water, constituting the drinking supply of Wuthailan, only a quarter mile distant, which we soon reached. The settlement consists of a picturesque turreted *Qasr* with a few subsidiary buildings on the slope of a limestone ridge—the same ridge that had lain to eastward of our track from Damthi onwards. The *Qasr* is of limestone masonry and mud, and has an ancient dilapidated appearance and two square-built turrets. Its population is some thirty souls under one 'Amir of the Bani Zaid, originally hailing from Shaqra. A number of unlined wells of brackish water, a patch of *Ithils*, a walled grove of newly-planted palms and an extensive area of open cornland in the track of the torrent, though partly irrigated from wells, completed the scene. The whole lies in a wide circular depression of loamy soil surrounded by a low rim slightly raised above the general level—into it the torrent pours its superfluous waters and there, having no exit, they sink into the ground. In years of favourable rainfall a considerable area outside the actual basin is capable of producing corn, but, the small population of the settlement being unable to cope with the area over which they have the first claim, strangers are allowed by custom to intrude, and I was told that in 1917 a considerable acreage was sown by enterprising cultivators from Mudhnib, who carried away 2000 *Sa's* of grain.

[1] *Maghrabi.*   [2] *Marwa, Muraiwiyat.*

Striking across the basin, which is about two miles across and ends eastward close under the *Nafud* sands, we ascended the *Safra* slope and shortly afterwards entered upon and followed a depression called Al Jiri. It slopes down to the north-west with low ridges of limestone on either side, and is of sandy composition with scanty dry vegetation. The *Nafud* now lay back about three miles to our right, while to our left westwards there was the seemingly boundless *Safra* wilderness—perhaps twenty miles or more in extent and reaching to Nafud Shuqaiyija, whose northward continuation we were to see at 'Anaiza.

Two miles further on the rocky bed of Sha'ib Abu 'Ashaira strikes into the Jiri from the west, and we followed its course past occasional bushes of *Talh* over slabs of rock crusted with a whitish substance—perhaps salt crystals. This ended in a *Raudha* called Qa'iyir, about a mile in diameter and thickly covered with *Tarfa* brushwood. We were now again close under the edge of the *Nafud*—not half a mile distant— and at the end of the Abu 'Ashaira channel, which has no exit from the depression. We exchanged greetings with a party of *Ikhwan* bound for Sajir, and in the midst of a patch of *Tarfa* came upon a single unlined well [1] of sweet water at a depth of six feet. In it a weary grass-cutter was bathing while his heavily-loaded ass stood patiently by. We were not tempted to drink.

A large sand ridge [2] called Salhamiya stood on the edge of the *Nafud* about three miles from the point at which we left the *Raudha*, while at the same distance to the westward a *Rijm* on a ridge of the *Safra* showed us the line of the direct track from Tarafiya to Murabba', from which we had strayed in our desire to explore the various localities I have described. Our track now led through a pass called Jidariya between the limestone cliffs of a ridge of the same name and over a narrow boulder-strewn passage into Raudha Jidariya, a circular depression, half a mile across, of sandy loam with *Tarfa* scrub. It absorbs such drainage as it receives, having no exit, and was not long since a favourite *manzil* or campingplace of 'Ubaid Ibn Lughaimish, a *Shaikh* of the Bani 'Abdullah section of the Mutair, who with his following have

---

[1] *Qulaiyib.*   [2] *Zubara.*

now settled down as *Ikhwan* in the new colony of Furaithan.[1]
Passing out of the depression we came to a ridge of low crags
of reddish colour like rock-salt, in a projection of which
Nasir pointed out the graves of some wayfarers who had met
a violent death at the hands of highway robbers years before
when this spot had an unenviable reputation as a danger-zone.
Before us lay a rough bare tract of undulating desolation,
our track taking advantage of occasional shallow depressions
until we came to a low ridge from which, with the orange line
of the *Nafud* a mile away to our right, we looked out over
a vast plain of shingle-strewn loam. Far off in the midst of it
we could see the scattered palm and *Ithil* patches of Murabba',
in front of which danced a dust-devil [2] as perfect in form as
any I ever remember having seen—a long spiral column
wriggling, for all the world like some monster serpent, up
to a height of some 400 or 500 feet and then gathering up its
tail under it from the ground before disappearing from view
as suddenly as it had appeared. This phenomenon seemed to
occur simultaneously with a sudden change of wind from
north-west to south-west.

In half an hour we reached and camped for our midday
siesta at the main section of the settlement, a single large
Qasr of considerable age to all appearances by the edge of
a four-acre grove of heavily-laden palms [3] with a patch of
green young millet beyond and a considerable area of stubble
fields of the current year's harvest. A mile away to the
north-east lay a solitary *Qasr* in the midst of cornland ; half
a mile to north-north-east was an *Ithil* patch, while somewhat
south of east and only a quarter mile away was another
solitary *Qasr* guarding a grove of young palms and an *Ithil*
plantation. Such is the settlement of Murabba', all sections
of which lie in the shallow bed of a torrent descending from
the *Safra* on the west towards the *Nafud*, in front of which
a low sand-covered hillock stands out from the plain. The
water of the settlement is derived from wells about six feet

[1] In the Hamada—the wells of Faruthi lie 3 miles to the north of it.

[2] The ordinary shapeless dust-devil is called *'Ajjaj*, but a spiral column
like this is known as *Ma'asir*.

[3] The dates were not yet ripe here and hung in huge bunches of green
and yellow from the palms.

deep in the torrent-bed, and is for the most part of inferior quality, but there is a *Marwa* about 200 yards north-east of the main section which has good drinking water. The population cannot exceed forty souls in all, and are Buwahil [1] of Tamim origin. Most of the families settled here came originally from Mudhnib, but a blind old man of seventy, who came over to our tents to gossip, said that he came from the small oasis of Umm al Barud [2] in the Sinad plain. Close by our camp I noticed a small cemetery, apparently old and no longer used, as the modern graveyard was some distance away according to Nasir; in it were half a dozen graves marked out by stones and oriented north and south [3]— possibly a relic of the time before the *Wahhabi* faith had taken root in these parts.

The Murabba' settlement may be regarded as the last outpost of the Sirr district northwards, though by some it is considered as belonging to Mudhnib. I did not definitely ascertain with which it is included for administrative purposes and the point is perhaps of little practical importance. It can provide the central exchequer with but little in the way of revenue. Be that as it may, the desert to the north of it with its torrent-beds coursing eastward to the edge of the *Nafud* may safely be regarded as forming part of the Mudhnib district, into which we now therefore passed, leaving the land of murmuring waters behind us. By the route we had followed the distance from Tarafiya to Murabba' was about nineteen miles.

5. AL MUDHNIB

During our midday halt at Murabba' the steady north-west wind of the morning suddenly gave way to cyclonic gusts alternately from the north-west and south-west. Great drifts of sand swept across the wilderness before them, but by 3.30 p.m., when we resumed our march, the wind came steadily and moderately from the south-west and west, bringing up clouds on to the horizon.

[1] Captain Shakespear noted that they were Nawasir, which is possibly a kindred section, though I could get no information on the point.

[2] About 15 miles south of Sajir.

[3] The usual *Muslim* arrangement is of course that the body should be turned on to its right side with the face towards Mecca.

Beyond the left or north bank of the *Sha'ib* lay an extensive stretch of *Safra*, stony and gently undulating with the distant *Nafud* along its eastern border. Half a mile from camp we crossed the torrent strand of Sha'ib Asqul, twenty yards across and running down eastward to sink into the *Nafud* barrier ; its banks were low and of crumbled limestone *débris*. Beyond it Sha'ib Rayadan, a tributary of the Asqul, thrust its sandy bed of a hundred yards' width across our track, and the desert beyond glittered with flakes of gypsum scattered over a shingly surface. A large herd of *Ikhwan* camels was grazing afar off under the edge of the *Nafud*, which here, according to Nasir, is of considerably greater width than along the line by which we had crossed it. Towards its eastern extremity is a wide circular depression, about two miles in diameter, called Saiyada—the scene of a memorable conflict of the past between the Buraih and 'Alwa sections of the Mutair, one of which was caught by the other and annihilated in this desert Sedan.

A mile beyond the Rayadan channel we came to Sha'ib al Zar', which from this point runs east to the *Nafud*, coming from the north-west, in which direction we followed its course upward through a patch of vegetation—mainly *'Arta* and *Adhir al Safra*, a species of plant similar to but of a brighter green than the *Adhir* found in the *Nafud*—known as Raudhat al Zar'. A considerable part of this *Raudha* had been cleared for cultivation, of which it bore ample evidence in the stubble patches left from the recent harvest. The ground is divided up into diminutive rectangular plots, and is entirely dependent on rain and torrents, being cultivated by folk from Mudhnib. There may have been some thirty acres of cultivation in all, individual holdings being separated from each other by shallow trenches a foot wide and two inches deep. We were now on the main track, whose direction was marked by a line of cairns on the ridge to our right and, shortly after passing out of the *Raudha*, we had our first view of the dense palm-groves of Mudhnib nestling under the lea of the *Nafud*, which now lay about a mile to the east. Before us stretched an immense undulating plain of extraordinary nakedness. Across the track runs Sha'ib Tubailan, splaying out as it descends into a considerable depression called Namasiya occupying a great bay in the receding flank of the *Nafud*. This depression constitutes a *Hima* or grazing reserve of the people of Mudhnib, and is guarded against trespassers by two or three slender towers at intervals in its midst. Hither from time to time parties of grass-cutters come to cut and carry away the various herbs [1] which grow in great profusion.

Beyond the Tubailan the surface of the wilderness becomes exceedingly rough with large slabs of limestone either embedded in the soil or scattered loose upon its face. Beyond this the plain again becomes smoother and strewn with grit and sand with occasional excrescences of rock. Our destination was now in full view, so I sent Mitrak and Manawar to warn the *Amir* of our arrival, while with Nasir as my guide I struck off the beaten track over a rough rocky surface to a distant cairn from which, as I expected, I had a splendid view of Mudhnib and its subsidiary settlements. To get there we had some very rough going to negotiate and crossed Sha'ib Nasr and another smaller torrent, both of which carry down their waters when in flood into the great depression in which lie the settlements.

Soon after we reached the cairn the sun sank below the horizon in a short-lived blaze of flaming streaks, producing no effect on the *Nafud* sands, which retained their dull orange colour of the day. Nasir, having performed his ablutions with the remnant of water in my water-bottle, but deprecating the offer of my *Aba* to spread upon the rocky surface of our eminence on the ground that the hillside was (ceremonially) clean, set about his prayers while I turned to examine the scene before me. Our *dhaluls*, disliking the hardness of their couching place, took it into their heads to rise and move off, whereupon Nasir, quitting his devotions, gave chase to them and, having brought them back, resumed his interrupted prayers. I always felt at such times that there was something very admirable in the simple informality of *Wahhabi* ritual, which ever takes account before everything else of the practical needs of everyday life.

While we were still surveying the scene three persons,

---

[1] Most notable among these grasses are (1) the *Nifal*, a sort of wild lucerne ; (2) the *Haradh*, called *Shamatri* in Syria ; and (3) the *Qahawiyat*, and others.

apparently of some standing and indeed, according to Nasir, cousins of the *Amir* of the district, came up to enquire whether we had seen anything of some strayed camels of theirs. Nasir himself, who belonged to the Nawasir [1] section of the Tamim, claimed a distant relationship with the *Amir*, who was of the same section.

The northern end of the Namasiya depression almost impinges on the edge of the Mudhnib basin, which from this point is separated from the *Nafud* by a broad sandstone ridge called Al Khartam, whose outward or western flank runs nearly due north apparently to the neighbourhood of Wadi Rima. The *Nafud* itself falls back in a north-easterly direction and before long decreases apparently to a width of some three or four miles only, being bounded on the east by the plain of Al Mustawi. A narrow strip of plain is also said to separate the western fringe of the *Nafud* from the Khartam ridge, which increases in width as it proceeds northwards and is in parts streaked with strips of overlying sand.

The Mudhnib district forms a vast basin flanked on the east by the Khartam ridge and completely surrounded on the other sides by the rim of the *Safra* desert, on an eminence of which we stood and from which descend the numerous torrent strands which, finding no escape from the depression, give life to its fertile alluvial soil. Of these the Nasr, already mentioned, flows from south to north through the Qufaifa plantations ; further westward Sha'ib Qufaifa itself descending from the *Safra* through the plantations of Thulaima, Hisha and Naba'a waters the Qufaifa groves and part of the Mudhnib tract itself ; Sha'ib 'Alaiya, coming from the west through a settlement of the same name, runs into Sha'ib Mudhnib, which supplies the main part of the Mudhnib oasis itself after irrigating in its upper reaches westward the territories of Al Qa' and 'Aqaila. All these channels end against the foot of the Khartam ridge and overflow into a considerable area of good cornland to the northward known as Al Sufala.

[1] The Nawasir, according to Nasir, are to be found at Fara'a (of Washm), Mudhnib, Ghat, Raudha, Hauta, and Tuwaim (the last four localities being in the Sudair province).

THE FORTRESS-MANSION OF *AMIR* OF MUDHNIB AT QUFAIFA.

To face page 147.

Darkness having now overtaken us we descended from our point of vantage into the basin, at whose edge we cut across the *Rimdh*-covered bed of Sha'ib Qufaifa to the well-built and very picturesque *Qasr* of the *Amir* at the edge of the Qufaifa plantations. Our tents had been pitched close by the *Qasr* near a fine masonry-lined well which was still in process of construction, the shaft having already been sunk to a depth of several fathoms without reaching the water level. The water of the Mudhnib tract generally is spoiled by a mineral and slightly brackish taste, the depth to it being on the average from eight to ten fathoms, but the *Marwa* of the whole district is a single seven-fathom well situated in and known as Qufaifa, in the palm-grove behind the *Amir's* mansion.

We were by now tired after our long march—the actual distance from Murabba' to Qufaifa being about six miles by the road—and I was not sorry to hear that our host, Fahad Ibn 'Abdul Karim al 'Aqaili, was of a mind to take advantage of the night to follow Ibn Sa'ud, who had departed for 'Anaiza about 4 p.m. after the *'Asr* prayer and dinner. The *Amir* had, however, announced his intention of giving us dinner before he departed, and it was not long before we were summoned to the *Qasr*. We were received at the entrance by Fahad himself, who conducted us into his coffee-parlour, a hall of spacious dimensions—forty feet long, eighteen feet broad and about twenty-five feet high—with solid masonry walls faced with clay and sumptuously furnished with carpets and cushions. The hearth was at the further end from the doorway, and the long wall on the inner side was interrupted by three large apertures a few feet above the ground level, each furnished with an elaborately decorated wooden door. Here we rested awhile drinking several rounds of coffee and exchanging greetings with our host, who frequently expressed his delight at receiving as a guest one so honoured by Ibn Sa'ud himself. He suddenly disappeared, only to reappear with the summons of a hospitable host on his lips. ' *Iqlatu*,' he said, ' come forward,' and we followed him upstairs to a room on the first floor, where we were soon busy at a sumptuous repast of boiled mutton and rice, delicately salted. We did it ample justice, for it was the first real meal we had had that day, and after it we descended again to the great parlour, where a considerable company was gathered to drink coffee with us. In it I noticed quite a number of *Ikhwan*, distinguished from their fellows by the white fillet head-band. Coffee passed round several times, and the slave insisted on my having a fourth cup, though I had thought it polite to say ' enough ' after the third. The heat of the room was rapidly becoming unbearable, and I was bathed in perspiration. In such circumstances it was difficult to keep up the flow of ordinary conversation, and I soon took advantage of my knowledge that my host was contemplating a night journey to make my apologies and withdraw. Fahad was without doubt a man distinguished above the average—a man of enlightened and progressive views who had had some experience of the outer world. He remembered Shakespear's visit to him very well, but had no recollection of Leachman, who certainly visited Mudhnib before the war during his journey down to Riyadh. Incidentally Fahad is, like so many of the leading men of Najd, connected with Ibn Sa'ud by marriage, his mother being the aunt of one of the numerous ladies who have enjoyed the fleeting honour of marriage with the *Wahhabi* ruler. On my return to my tent I sent Rushaid with a good *Aba* for the *Amir's* acceptance, but he returned it with a message that it would be contrary to the rules of hospitality for him to accept a present from a guest. I fancy that he really meant it, for he had a wide reputation for lavish hospitality. He coupled his message with a desire that I should take coffee again with him before his departure, but, as I purposed to attempt an observation before going to bed, I pleaded fatigue as an excuse, and shortly before midnight I saw him and his following mount and ride away by the light of the full moon. That night I was very glad of my bed, for all the consciousness that before dawn I should have to be up again to follow in the impetuous wake of the *Bairaq*, which I had not seen since the camp at Qasr 'Artawi.

As a matter of fact Rushaid very considerately refrained from waking me until the sun was well up, and a start was further delayed by the unexpected appearance of breakfast —a light but very welcome meal of rice seasoned with onions and fresh dates. The *Qasr*, which I now saw for the first time by daylight, appeared as a great square building, whose regularity was, however, interrupted by projections of the turrets at the four corners. The tops of three of the turrets were crenelated, while the fourth at the S.E. corner of the building, much lower than the other three and of the peculiar broken appearance typical of the minarets of the real *Wahhabi* country, seemed to serve the double purpose of a turret and a minaret to the *Amir's* private mosque. There are two other *Qasrs* in the Qufaifa tract, which comprises some twelve to fifteen acres of palms divided up into four or five walled groves with a rich undergrowth of fruit-trees.

I had made up my mind to make a detailed inspection of all the settlements constituting the Mudhnib district, and by 6 a.m., having distributed bounty to the servants of the hospitable *Amir*, we had started out on what proved to be a long and tiring day's journey. For about a mile we followed the channel of Sha'ib Qufaifa upwards over a surface of shingle, crossing and recrossing the torrent-bed on several occasions, and then diverged from it towards a watch-tower at the extremity of the Naba'a oasis consisting of a few scattered *Qasrs* and four or five palm-groves in or along the bed of the *Sha'ib*. Beyond these lay a tiny, half-ruined hamlet of nine or ten houses in a gap between two groves with a few square mud-huts scattered about here and there. This plantation belongs to the people of Mudhnib, whose tenants, resident on the estate, may number about a hundred souls. As everywhere else in the district camels are almost exclusively used for well traction. The groves are straggling, but their interstices are filled up with considerable patches of lucerne and millet. I also saw some beds of pumpkins and other vegetables. The length of the oasis is about half a mile from south-west to north-east and it lies about a mile south-west of Qufaifa. Beyond it we re-entered the channel of Sha'ib Qufaifa, whose sandy rock-strewn bed was about 200 yards wide between limestone cliffs twenty feet high. About a mile away to the south in a small tributary ravine lay the small settlement of Hisha, a quarter mile in length and lying east and west, with its palms and two or three small *Qasrs*.

Continuing up Sha'ib Qufaifa south-westward we came to

a fairly dense and extensive oasis called Thulaima, situated on the right bank in a recess of the *Safra*. It is almost completely surrounded by a mud wall built on courses of limestone masonry along the edge of the torrent-bed. The palms of the eastern portion of the plantation seemed to be very poor owing, it was explained, to the poverty of the owners, who had been unable to engage labour during the fertilisation season and could not afford to buy camels for irrigation. The western part was more prosperous and had a considerable area of millet, lucerne and corn stubble. At the south-west corner are a cemetery and a derelict hamlet of ten houses, whose total population cannot exceed fifty persons.

Turning to the north-west across the edge of the undulatiug *Safra* we came after a mile to the oasis of Al Qa', whose population of fifty souls inhabit seven or eight scattered houses along the edge of a palm patch about a hundred yards in average width with heavily laden but not densely planted palms, varied by *Ithil* and the inevitable millet and lucerne. The settlement is completed by a single detached grove with one house towards Sha'ib 'Alaiya, which we soon reached at the western extremity of the 'Alaiya oasis. The channel here has a rock bottom with a small well hewn out of it to a depth of two fathoms, close by which were a couple of *Badawin* tents. The oasis extends down the channel to its confluence with Sha'ib Mudhnib, along which the palms straggle on for a short distance. Besides scattered habitations amid the palms there are two small hamlets of ten houses each, the lower one of the two being situate just below the junction of the two streams on the right bank. The resident population does not exceed a hundred souls.

An open space of about 200 yards separates 'Alaiya from the next oasis, 'Aqaila, a prosperous and well-tended plantation of considerable density and the personal property of the *Amir*. It lies south-west and north-east, extending about half a mile from the edge of Sha'ib Mudhnib. The central grove, some twenty acres in extent, is surrounded by a low crenelated wall and contains three well-built *Qasrs*, one of which, standing at the edge of the grove, was as fine a specimen of a fortress-mansion as I had seen anywhere. It had

THE TOWN OF MUDHNIB—EAST FRONTAGE.

To face page 151.

the same well-kept appearance as the *Amir's* residence at
Qufaifa, but was very much larger and of more irregular
form with a fringe of crenelations round the lofty wall,
whose sides were perforated with ventilation holes of the
usual triangular shape arranged with decorative effect. To
the west of the main grove lay three smaller detached groves
on the higher ground towards Majmaj, while towards 'Alaiya
along the *Sha'ib* were a few small groves. The *Amir's*
tenants [1] resident on this property, including some members
of his own family, constitute a population of a hundred souls,
and a similar number dwell in the Qufaifa plantation.

We now struck across the *Safra* to the little village of
Majmaj, only a quarter mile distant to the north and standing
at the western extremity of the larger of two palm-groves
which constitute the oasis. These are watered by a channel
fed from a well in the smaller grove about 400 yards from
the village, which has a population of about a hundred souls
resident in a score of houses, including one more pretentious
than the rest at the western extremity. As we stood by the
channel—I was engaged in changing a roll of films—there
came up to us one of the *Ikhwan* with rifle slung over his
shoulder and the white fillet of his profession on his head.
Nasir, always nervous of a stray accusation of backsliding,
though personally and in solitude more than cordial to me,
hastily suggested that we should move on. But I was
temporarily immobilised by the operation I had in hand,
and our visitor, having exchanged salutations with us, stood
by without further attempt at conversation. ' Whence come
you ? ' asked Nasir, by way of distracting the fellow's
attention from me. ' *Min quraiyib*—not from far,' he replied,
without any apparent desire to continue the conversation.
' Are you of the *Ikhwan* ? ' tried Nasir once more. ' If God
will,' he replied, and without another word turned his back
on us and was gone. A few moments later as we rode past
the village an old man came out, and after greetings gaily
shouted out to me : ' And who may you be and what is it
you write ? '

We passed on over a bare loam plain, and crossing the

---

[1] Tenants are known as *'Ammal* (workmen), and besides them there are
a number of household slaves.

rocky bed of Sha'ib Mudhnib came to a small isolated and apparently nameless patch of palms, close by which but in the open we saw a man lying asleep prone on his stomach with the hot sun beating upon his ill-protected spine. Mitrak woke him with a shout, and he got up and resumed his way.

From Majmaj we marched eastward for about a mile and entered the main oasis of Mudhnib at the suburb-hamlet of Sharuqiya, a settlement of some thirty mean mud-hovels and a population of 200 tenants engaged in the cultivation of the southern block of palms extending for about a mile southward of the village towards Qufaifa. On our left the dense and extensive palm-groves called Rafi'a extended northward to the edge of the Mudhnib *Sha'ib* and eastward to within half a mile of the Khartam ridge. The gap between these two tracts, about a quarter mile in width, was filled up with well-irrigated cornland, through which we passed to skirt the eastern edge of the Rafi'a groves, in which were a number of scattered *Qasrs*. In the space between us and the Khartam ridge were a few isolated groves, and the tail of Sha'ib Qufaifa, which irrigates both Sharuqiya and Rafi'a, seems to sweep through it to merge with the eastern extremity. of Sha'ib Mudhnib.

The northern edge of the Rafi'a tract lies along the right bank of this main artery, across which lay the picturesque town partly screened from view by a few straggling patches of palms. The *Sha'ib* just above the town divides into several branches, one of which is that already mentioned running between the town and Rafi'a ; another passes to the north of the former to irrigate extensive groves on that side ; while a central branch passes along the eastern front of the town, which curves inwards in a wide and picturesque semi-circle. It was on this side that we entered, passing through a maze of streets until we came out again on the further side by the western gate.

The town of Mudhnib is unwalled and largely in a state of decay—half the houses seemed to be in ruins and unin-habited. It forms a rough oblong half a mile long from north to south and perhaps 200 or 300 yards across, the western front being, like the eastern, curved inwards in a semicircle facing the northern branch of the *Sha'ib*. To north and west

A VIEW OF MUDHNIB FROM THE NORTH.

To face page 152.

A STREET IN MUDHNIB.

To face page 153.

of the town lie a number of straggling groves and a considerable area of cornland, while outside the west gate begins a
dense strip of palms, which with an average width of 200
yards runs due west for about a mile to the encircling *Safra*
rim. The existence of this gate on the west side would seem
to show that at one time the settlement was enclosed within
a wall—perhaps no more than the continuous barrier of
houses round the outside ; and, even on the east side, where
an entrance may be effected at any of a dozen points, the
regular approach is through a particular gap which may
formerly have been adorned with a gate when the line of
houses on this side was less interrupted by ruinous breaches
than it now is. A slender tapering minaret is a prominent
feature of the view on this side. On the north side there is
a sort of gateway which leads out into the groves on that
side and to the Sufala depression, the houses here presenting
a continuous barrier as also immediately round the western
gate. Both these gates are but rough structures of clay
roofed over with rafters supporting a covering of palm
branches matted together with mud. There is no *Suq* in the
place, and it is said that there is not even a single shop,
while the population cannot exceed 2000 souls. Mudhnib
has clearly been in the past more prosperous than it now is,
but I was unable to discover any specific explanation of its
decay beyond the fact that its inhabitants had succumbed
to *Dha'f*, an expressive word indicating not only material
poverty but a state of spiritual and moral degeneration
which robs its victims of the will to overcome the difficulties
of their situation. And yet from what I had seen of the
district as a whole it seemed to me that it enjoyed potential
advantages, which the energy of men like the *Amir* might
yet, under the *ægis* of the peace which Ibn Sa'ud has brought
to his dominions with the *Wahhabi* revival, turn to good
account.

A narrow strip of *Safra* half a mile north of the town
separated us from the Sufala valley or depression, which we
soon entered on resuming our north-westerly course along
the high road to the Qasim. Wells and scattered *Qasrs*
dotted the valley at intervals, and we passed large areas of
stubble and fallow. The wells are six fathoms deep, but at

this season, between harvests, had been dismantled of their gear and stood out in the scene like gaunt skeletons. The soil is a light fertile loam with a northward slope, and comes to an end about a mile and a half north of Mudhnib at a gentle upward incline of the *Safra*, from which the spill of the combined torrents of the district is turned back to sink into the soil. Some distance further on we came to an *Ithil* patch in a depression fed by Shai'b Raudha, along whose banks there is more cornland irrigated from wells with scattered *Qasrs* here and there, singly or in groups. This channel striking against the foot of the Khartam ridge is deflected northwards down a broad plain which, after receiving the drainage of the narrow Sha'ib 'Ataiyiq, passes by a narrow and deep ravine cleaving the *Safra* barrier into a vast salt-pan extending for some miles along the edge of the Khartam ridge with a width varying from a mile to half a mile. From north to south the length of this salt-pan, Mamlaha 'Aushaziya as it is called from the oasis of 'Aushaziya, whose distant palms now came into view, is not less than six or seven miles. Its northern extremity receives the spill of a branch [1] of the great Wadi Rima itself, and it thus forms a self-contained basin having the appearance of a vast frozen lake covered with snow. In fact it consists of a solid block of pure white salt, hard and firm, overlying to a depth of a foot or eighteen inches an undersoil of black slime, which after floods becomes treacherous to those who walk upon it unwarily. They say that in good seasons the flood waters sweeping into this depression from every direction overlie the salt crust to a depth of several feet until gradually absorbed. From this salt-pan the people of Sirr, Mudhnib and 'Aushaziya draw their supplies, having a prescriptive right to carry away as much as they please without payment. The Turkish system of salt monopolies has not penetrated into the deserts of Najd, and Arabian salt, plentiful as it is, is scarcely likely ever to compete in the markets of the world, for the cost of carriage to the coast would be prohibitive. The Mamlaha supply is probably inexhaustible, but it is more particularly the northern part of the pan over against 'Aushaziya that is drawn upon as having the best salt. Even so, excellent as

[1] Called Al Zuqaibiya.

THE SALT-LAKE OF 'AUSHAZĪYA.

To face page 154.

it seemed to me in quality with the additional attraction of its unblemished whiteness, this salt is locally reckoned as being of inferior quality to that of Shiqqa near Qara'a in the Buraida district, and, so far as I was able to note, the bazars of 'Anaiza and Buraida exposed only the pinkish-brown product of the Shiqqa pan—also a lake-like deposit —for sale to their customers.

Continuing our march we came to Sha'ib Abu Khishba at a point where there is a small patch of untended palms, whence the channel, thickly covered with *Tarfa* scrub, runs north for about a mile into the southern end of the Mamlaha. Along the further bank extends an area of cornland protected by a four-foot retaining wall against encroachment by the torrent. This cultivation is undertaken by Mudhnib folk, and the neighbourhood of the torrent affords good grazing for camels. Beyond it we came to Sha'ib Muwaih, another affluent of the salt-pan, a thirty-yard channel running over a bed of limestone rock, and after proceeding across the undulating *Safra* for half a mile we came to another torrent channel, whose south or right bank is locally reckoned the dividing line between the Mudhnib district and the province of Qasim. This is Sha'ib Dhabba, which runs down across the *Safra* eastwards towards the *Mamlaha* and has a width of half a mile. It takes its name from a straggling patch of un-tended [1] palms in its bed two miles up-stream without any *Qasr* or other habitation, while only a quarter mile from our track, also up-stream, lay a group of four *Qasrs* called Qusur Fadhl amid a tract of cornland deserted by its owners except at the seasons of sowing and reaping. On our right the edge of the salt-pan approached to within half a mile of the main road. We had travelled about eight miles since leaving Mudhnib, and the rest of that day's journey must be reserved for the next chapter, in which I shall recount my experiences in the famous province of Qasim.

[1] *Hamlan.*

CHAPTER III

AL QASIM

1. The 'Aushaziya District

BEYOND the channel of Sha'ib Dhabba we had still about three and a half miles to march across a rolling down of loam varied by patches of limestone rock before reaching the settlement of 'Aushaziya. A low conical hillock close by the edge of the *Mamlaha* marked the spot where the excavation of salt is most usually practised, while beyond the snowy expanse the Khartam ridge seemed to be cleft diagonally by a broad expanse of *Nafud* sand. From a distance it was difficult to determine whether this sand strip really penetrated through the rock or whether, as seemed more probable, it merely overlay the ridge. If the latter, was it wind-borne sand from the *Nafud* beyond or was it the product of that rock-disintegration which is presumably the genesis of all the *Nafuds* of Arabia ? It was tempting to think that in the Khartam ridge with its unusual arrangement of substantial sand streaks across its rocky mass we had before us a living specimen of a *Nafud* in the making.

The road crosses the channel of Sha'ib Abu Tulaiha, an affluent of course of the *Mamlaha,* near a single solidly-constructed well with masonry lining called Umm al Shaqq with a fathom of clear but mineral-tasting water at a depth of four fathoms. The well is roughly circular with a diameter of twelve feet and surrounded by a patch of cornland guarded by a slender tapering watch-tower of masonry and clay with a doorway only two feet high. The well-gear having been dismantled in accordance with local custom, the water was approachable through a gently inclined shaft ending in a low opening in the masonry of the well just above water-level. A single nameless *Qasr* stood amid cornland a mile and a half to the west, and the well stood, according

to my aneroid, about 2300 feet above sea-level. I reckoned
the *Mamlaha* opposite this point to be some thirty or forty
feet lower and probably the lowest point in all the tract
between the southern extremity of Sirr and Wadi Rima.

As we proceeded the ground seemed to develop a strongly
saline character and exhibited a considerable variety of the
plants reckoned by the Arabs as belonging to the *Hamdh* [1]
family. We now passed through a dip in a ridge of discoloured, blackish limestone and crossed the bed of Sha'ib
Mishari flowing into the salt-pan by the conical hillock
already mentioned, which was now only a quarter mile to our
right. The torrent channel ran over slabs of limestone with
a solid white incrustation between banks varying in height
from four to ten feet. Up-stream in a bulge of the channel
lay a corn patch with two *Qasrs* most inappropriately named
Raudhat al Janna—the garden of Paradise. The Arab is
sometimes not without a sense of humour, but he could
scarcely have chosen a more benighted spot to taunt with
such a name. A small torrent channel of the same name joins
the lower reaches of the Mishari. Another discoloured limestone ridge brought us close up to 'Aushaziya, to reach which
we had to cross two shallow artificial runnels [2] designed to
conduct rain-water into the cultivated area and finally the
torrent-bed of Sha'ib Qusaibi, by whose left bank we came
upon an exiguous running stream emanating from a spring.
We then couched our camels at the door of a single *Qasr*
standing at the western extremity of the most easterly palm-
grove of 'Aushaziya. Here we came upon a flock of about
600 sheep in charge of three shepherds watering at the stream,
and it turned out that the flock was the private property of
Ibn Sa'ud and making its way direct to Buraida. The owner
of the *Qasr*, an unpretentious building seventy paces long and
fifty broad, had unfortunately gone to 'Anaiza, as we soon
learned from a small crowd of idlers who gathered round us,
and our hopes of refreshment seemed likely to be disappointed
until a small boy of ten appeared on the scene. Being the
son of the owner and hearing that, having ridden all day,

---

[1] *e.g. Shinan, 'Ajairiman, Arad, Suwwad,* and *Rimdh.*

[2] Such runnels are called *Masila* (pl. *Masail*), or in the diminutive
Musaiyil.

we were weary, he invited us to enter and conducted us into one of the most squalid parlours I had experienced, a small chamber twelve feet by seven leading out of a small and very dirty porch at the entrance of the building. We were glad enough to rest here while coffee was being prepared. The walls were begrimed with smoke, whose only exit was a rough hole in the roof at the end of the room furthest from the hearth, but we were not to be left alone, as the shepherds, scenting coffee, soon joined us, while a dozen of the local folk, all of them mere boys and not over fifteen, sauntered in to see the stranger who had so suddenly appeared in their midst. They were most friendly, however, and gave me much information about the salt-pan which I have already recorded, adding that all the water of 'Aushaziya was so briny and undrinkable that they had to go no less than five miles to the north—probably to one of the wells in the Zuqaibiya depression—to fetch drinking water. They were indeed at the moment so short of water that they had to draw on our supply for a second brew of coffee. After a while the son of the house, a charming child with exquisite manners and not unconscious of the dignity conferred upon him by the temporary *rôle* of host, came in with a palm-mat and a bowl of fresh dates, off which and the coffee—poured out only to the guests—we made a hearty meal. We learned that the owner of the *Qasr* was named 'Ali al Tarudi.

The stream already noticed emanates from a spring about a quarter mile due west of the *Qasr* bubbling up in a shaft twelve feet deep with a palm-tree growing in it. From this a sluggish trickle enters a channel, three feet wide at the bottom and five feet across the top, hewn out of the limestone. Opposite the *Qasr* the water-level is flush with the surface, and a few hundred yards further on the stream enters the eastern palm-grove, whence it eventually trickles down to the salt-pan.

The oasis consists of a solid central block of palms extending with an average width of 300 yards for half a mile northwards from within a hundred yards of the spring. This block lies in two separate sections on either side of the broad track to Buraida, from which the 'Anaiza track diverges westward just beyond the extremity of the oasis.

The eastern palm block at which we had halted extends about a quarter mile from west to east down to the border of the salt-pan. Finally there is a third palm block about a quarter mile south-west of the spring. Apart from the usual scattered *Qasrs* there is a small unwalled hamlet on the east side of the southern section of the central block. The population comprises about 150 souls of a Bani Khalid subsection called Tarudi,[1] the chief man of which is one 'Abdullah al Tarudi. The settlement is said to be of great antiquity, though I observed nothing to justify such a claim, and is administratively dependent on 'Anaiza. The dates here are mainly of a variety called *'Abud*, large, mellow and brown when ripe, and very sweet ; another variety found here is the *Makhtumiya*, characteristic of the Sirr district. There is considerable subsidiary cultivation of millet, lucerne, pumpkins and wheat, particularly in the central block, where the palms are somewhat straggling. The height of the spring was given by the aneroid as 2340 feet.

About a mile due north of the spring lies a projection of the Khartam ridge marking the northern extremity of the *Mamlaha*, beyond which extends the Zuqaibiya depression expanding steadily northward and forming a wide valley between the Khartam and the *Sufra*. Its northern extremity impinges on Wadi Rima, from which it is partially cut off by a narrow transverse sand-strip called Itaiyima, about four miles long and only a quarter mile broad. This forms as it were the base of a triangle from which the Zuqaibiya runs southward almost to an apex at the northern end of the salt-pan. This depression is a grazing reserve belonging to the people of 'Anaiza, and is dotted with *Qasrs*—said to be no fewer than twenty, though I myself only saw half a dozen of them in the distance during our afternoon march. In effect it constitutes a sort of diversion or escape of Wadi Rima when overcharged with flood water ; unlike its southern counterpart, Wadi Dawasir, the Rima is said to come down in spate five or six times in an ordinary year, while in seasons of heavy rainfall it has been known to maintain a steady flow

---

[1] I also heard the name of this section given as Matrudi, said to have been formerly a well-known and prosperous though now somewhat decayed family of 'Anaiza.

without intermission for as long a period as forty or fifty days.

The Buraida road runs roughly north-west, and we turned off from it in a westerly direction soon after passing the village. Our course lay over a vast bare expanse of gently undulating desert, and as we crossed a shallow depression called Al Qurai, an affluent of the Qusaibi, I noticed, looking back, a small patch of palms—said to be untended—called Ghuwaitir lying back in a crack of the Khartam ridge near the south end of the Zuqaibiya depression, which, from the high ground on which we were, could be seen in all its length as far as the barrier of the Itaiyima sand-ridge. The slope of the *Safra* was eastward. About two miles out from 'Aushaziya we dropped by a short steep descent down a marked forty-foot escarpment into the depression of Sha'ib Makwaza, in which a quarter mile up-stream is a *Mishash* or petty watering. We soon joined the direct track leading from Mudhnib to 'Anaiza without touching 'Aushaziya, while somewhat further to the west lay a still shorter route [1] which the *Bairaq* had followed. Our track veered gradually to a north-westerly direction at right angles to the axes of a series of ridges which with intervening valleys constituted the *Safra*. Crossing the rocky bed of Sha'ib Ma'aidhar, an affluent of the Zuqaibiya, we rose imperceptibly but steadily to a ridge where my aneroid recorded 2640 feet. Beyond the shallow trough of Wadi 'Amaran, which runs northward into Wadi Rima, we topped a ridge affording a view of the sands of Nafud Shuqaiyija beyond 'Anaiza and also, afar off to the north, of the Buraida *Nafud*. The view was extensive but desolate in the extreme, with nothing to suggest that close at hand lay one of the great cities of Arabia, but the summit of the very next ridge looked out on a very different scene. As far as we could see to the westward there rolled a sea of billowing sand, and at our feet in a deep depression between those sands and the abrupt escarpment in which the *Safra* suddenly terminated lay a vast oasis. It was at last 'Anaiza, but the sun was already low and the scene was

---

[1] It was apparently by this route that Shakespear travelled, but I could get no information about Sha'ib Ladha which he mentions, unless it be identical with Sha'ib Wudai, which the route in question follows to the point where it enters the 'Anaiza basin south-east of the outlying palm-grove of Juhaimiya.

partially veiled from our eyes by a thick haze. In any case we were too weary to pause, and without further ado descended the rough but gentle track down the face of the escarpment to the level of the depression. Then, making what haste we could, we urged our weary mounts towards the camp, where my tent was pitched about a quarter mile outside the southern gate of the great circuit wall which encircles oasis and town. I was not spared an interview with Ibn Sa'ud, but fortunately it was a brief one, and after it I abandoned myself in utter weariness to the luxury of complete rest, leaving the writing up of notes and other irksome accompaniments of travel to the morrow, happily conscious that the camp would remain where it was for at least a few days. We had travelled about seven miles from 'Aushaziya and nearly thirty miles in all during the day. We had, moreover, been steadily on the move for nearly a week without any kind of respite, and such travel can be exceedingly fatiguing, especially in the month of August.

2. First Impressions of 'Anaiza

The following morning—it was 23rd August—I woke up to find myself in a new world as it were. Accustomed to independence amid the inhospitable and uncouth bigotry of Najd, I planned as I awoke to do a little sight-seeing before entering the town to pay my respects to the *Amir* and other persons who would expect to be visited. But early as it was, a little past 6 a.m., I found my plans forestalled by the *Amir* himself, whose messenger was already awaiting to bid me to breakfast. I had reckoned without my hosts, and was destined that day to see but little of 'Anaiza beyond the interior of its hospitable houses. And, much as I had already heard of the difference between 'Anaiza and the rest of Najd, of the open-handed hospitality of its people and of its complete freedom from any kind of religious or sectarian bigotry, I must admit that my actual experiences astonished and bewildered me. It seemed to me that I had stepped suddenly out of barbarism into a highly civilised and even cultured society, where the stranger within the gates, far from being an object of aversion and suspicion, was regarded as the common guest of the community to be entertained—somewhat mercilessly and regardless of his own feelings—by every household that claimed to count in the local scheme of things. I was fortunate to have seen and experienced almost every province of Najd before coming to the Qasim and to have tasted the bitter in full measure before the sweet—doubly fortunate in that, though Buraida was yet to remind me that its sister-city was altogether exceptional, my last memories of Central Arabia are intimately associated with the days of my sojourn in this gem among Arabian cities.

Having had my morning tea, with which they brought me figs and peaches and fresh dates, I accompanied the *Amir's* messenger, 'Abdullah Ibn Rashid by name, to the southern gate, whence, proceeding along lanes between walled palm-groves whose palms, as I was told, bore this year an exceptional burden of fruit, we reached the town, unwalled and straggling. A maze of crooked picturesque streets, arched over here and there by the upper storeys of the houses on either side, brought us to the *Majlis*, an irregular nearly lozenge-shaped open space with the great mosque on our left adorned with a lofty curiously-tapering minaret and a lower square tower at another corner. Here the *Amir* is wont to sit in public assembly to transact municipal or judicial business after the public prayers ; on all sides are shops, and in every direction radiate the crooked alleys of the great *Suq*, one of these streets extending hence through the whole length of the town to its eastern extremity. At the time of Doughty's sojourn at 'Anaiza the *Amir's* house abutted on the *Majlis*, but we struck up one of the side streets to reach the residence of the present governor. The doors of most houses were provided either with regular knockers [1] or curious double chains [2] about six inches in length hanging from metal rings fixed in the woodwork. At length reaching the house we sought we passed through the ordinary coffee-parlour, in which is the hearth and which appears to be used only during the heat of the day and in winter, to an open court surrounded by lofty walls where coffee, prepared indoors, is customarily served during the summer when it is cool enough in the mornings and

---

[1] *Mataqqa.*   [2] *Silsila* or *Marsan.*

A LANE IN 'ANAIZA.

To face page 162.

evenings to sit out of doors. This arrangement appears to
be a regular feature of 'Anaiza, and is a great improvement
on the Najd custom of sitting at all times in rooms heated
to suffocation, but the great height of the surrounding walls
—the houses frequently being built up to three and even
four storeys—deprives one of the benefit of any wind that
may be stirring.

'Abdul 'Aziz Ibn 'Abdullah al Sulaim, a charming old man
of about sixty, tall and slim of figure, with a pleasing gentle
expression about his thin, almost wizened countenance,
received us on behalf of his nephew, 'Abdullah Ibn Khalid al
Sulaim, to whom about a year previously he had of his own
free will resigned the office of *Amir* with all its cares and
worries. 'Abdullah himself soon appeared, a man of about
35 or 40 with a neat black beard and cheery, prosperous face,
and the company was joined by other visitors, whose general
appearance betokened them as persons of distinction. The
conversation naturally turned on my predecessors at 'Anaiza.
Abdul 'Aziz had been away on a foray with Ibn Sa'ud at the
time of Shakespear's visit, when Salih Ibn Zamil was acting
in his absence as *Amir*, destined like his guest to fall at the
battle of Jarrab less than a year afterwards. But 'Abdul 'Aziz
had not forgotten having as a boy of ten or thereabouts seen
Doughty, of whose still being alive they were much interested
to hear. Such an one they thought must indeed have made
his mark perhaps in some high diplomatic post. Of Charles
Hüber the recollection was still fresh, and of his death in the
Hijaz at the hands of his Arab escort. Since his day, they
said, foreigners could only appeal to the Arab through their
purses, for he had been very lavish. It was in July, 1884, that
he met his end and was buried in the little cemetery at Jidda,
the French Government acknowledging his services to the
cause of humanity by a granite monument set up at the
expense of the state over his grave and inscribed with an
epitaph which few have better deserved : *Mort pour la
science.* One of the company, an old man close upon eighty,
white-bearded and very deaf, who, I afterwards learned, was
named Yahaya Ibn Dhukair, professed to remember further
back than Doughty another European traveller, but I was
unable to discover his identity. Of the treatment experienced

by Doughty at 'Anaiza the passage of long years had
acquitted their consciences ; it was true that he had been
expelled from the city for a while to Malqa in Wadi Rima,
but it had so happened that his arrival had coincided with
the beginning of a smallpox epidemic, and they could not
stand against the insistent demands of the local prelates and
divines for the removal of the obvious cause or occasion of
the scourge.[1] They had, however, subsequently made amends
to him by further hospitality. The Khunaini house in which
he lodged still exists, but alas ! in ruins, though the Doughty
legend persists enshrined in local history.

So we talked on until 'Abdul 'Aziz, rising abruptly, claimed
the right of continuing my entertainment and led me off to
his house, a lofty four-storeyed building adjoining a magnificent garden visible through the open windows of a
passage along which we made our way to an open court,
where we reclined on benches. At 'Abdullah's reception we
had sat upon carpets with cushions to lean against. A low
wall separated us here from the garden, but, after the usual
rounds of coffee, we were ushered into a private [2] parlour of
diminutive size on the ground-floor where, for the first time
in my experience of Najd, cigarettes were passed round
to myself and others of the company who smoked, the
coffee-man rolling and lighting the cigarette before handing
it to me.

After a short interval of such indulgence we trooped back
to the *Amir's* house for breakfast, an immense mat of palm
leaves being spread upon the floor covered with countless
dishes of seasoned rice, vegetables and fruits to which we did
ample justice. No sooner was this meal disposed of than
Muhammad Ibn Sulaiman, Ibn Sa'ud's secretary, and a
resident of 'Anaiza, claimed our company at coffee in his
house. A long narrow passage, adorned to a height of about
five feet with a dado of plain gypsum picked out in stepped
pinnacles [3] along the top, led us to a small open court
adjoining the coffee-parlour. The clay walls of the latter
were covered to a height of fifteen feet with white gypsum

---

[1] Doughty mentions the epidemic, attributing it to a different cause,
vide C.M.D. ii. 348.

[2] *Mukhtasir.*   [3] *Vide* Fig. 6.

plaster tastefully picked out in simple decorative designs and
the chamber was sumptuously furnished—far more sumptuously than the rooms of the *Amir* and his uncle—with rich
carpets and cushions.

The day was now well advanced and I was allowed to
return to camp for a few hours' rest—not, however, without
having committed myself to a number of social engagements
for the latter part of the day. My first host in the late afternoon was 'Abdul Rahman Ibn 'Abdul 'Aziz Ibn Zamil, a
direct descendant of the great Zamil of Doughty's day, the
man whose administration of 'Anaiza in the troublous times

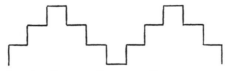

FIG. 6.   STEPPED PINNACLE DECORATION
along top of dado in house of Muhammad al Sulaiman at 'Anaiza.

of half a century ago has become invested with a legendary
halo. His grandson was a youth of about twenty-five with
a somewhat pale weak face and an incipient beard, only
dimly reminiscent of the great man himself, whom Doughty
described as ' a small-grown man with a pleasant weerish
visage and great understanding eyes.'   A good-looking,
clean-shaven cousin somewhat older than himself and named
Sulaim helped 'Abdul Rahman to entertain us in the somewhat stifling atmosphere of his cosy little parlour.   I had
brought my pipe with me and smoked without embarrassment while others indulged in cigarettes—in public only is
smoking not tolerated at 'Anaiza, otherwise it is considered
neither unclean nor unlawful.

Leaving Zamil's house, which is at the western extremity
of the town and had the appearance of being of comparatively
recent construction—I noted that visitors arriving at the
door and knocking always addressed its owner as Zamil,
his honourable and historic surname—we made our way
through the *Suq* to the house of Sulaiman al Dhukair, where
in addition to coffee we were served with a somewhat sickly
concoction of sherbet. The Dhukair family, like many of
the 'Anaiza families, has spread far and wide from its

homeland, and at this time was represented at Basra, 'Amara and Bahrain, the chief branch of the house being at the last-named place in charge of Yahaya's brother, Muqbil. I had had while at 'Amara during the early months of 1917 a good deal to do with Hamad Ibn Muhammad al Dhukair, and it was on account of my friendship with this cousin of his that Sulaiman, who was of the company at the *Amir's* house during the morning, had invited me to coffee on the morrow. Owing to a mistake on the part of Rushaid we thought the invitation was for the same afternoon, and were on the way to his house when we met our host in the *Suq*, obviously unconscious of the appointment we were hastening to keep. The mistake was clearly ours, but he insisted on accompanying us to his house, and there entertaining us and vowing that, had the mistake been his, he would according to local custom have had to give a public dinner in our honour to expiate such a breach of etiquette. We assured him that he was blameless, but as we left about the time of the evening prayer he insisted that on the morrow we should do him the honour of keeping the original appointment. The niece of Muqbil was at this time one of the four wives of Ibn Sa'ud, to whom she had about six months previously borne a daughter. She had after her marriage remained among her own people at 'Anaiza, and so had not seen her husband for a considerable time, and this was the first time that the latter had set eyes on his small daughter.

I now returned to camp and set out to the not distant sand-peak of Dulaima to get a good view of my surroundings. Even there I was not to be left alone, as a grey-bearded old man, Ibrahim al Qadhi, came puffing up the slope to see what I was doing. He asked me many questions on the subject of photography, and was as delighted as a child when I allowed him to take my camera in his hands and look through the view-finder. Then as abruptly as he had come he rose and left me, and, a messenger having come from Ibn Sa'ud with letters from Kuwait, I returned to camp, where I scarcely had time to glance hastily through my correspondence when 'Abdullah Ibn Rashid appeared to summon me to dinner at the *Amir's* house. The meal was served in a

room on the first floor overlooking the court in which we had
had coffee, and consisted of rice, vegetables and mutton
excellently cooked and the usual variety of fruit. Immediately it was over we rose, took our leave and returned
to camp thinking that at last the day's round of entertain-
ments was over. But this was not the case, and after the
evening prayer I again repaired to the town to be the guest
of Fahad Ibn 'Abdullah al Bassam, a charming but slightly
senile old man who obviously enjoyed the luxurious appoint-
ments of his mansion, one of the best in the city. He told
me that he had often seen Doughty drinking coffee in that
very room in the days of his father, 'Abdullah. Doughty,
indeed, refers [1] to a young man of the household, but his
reference must have been to an elder brother, for Fahad in
those days was, he says, a small boy of eight or nine, and
used to be commissioned by the womenfolk to watch and
mark the exact part of the common dish from which Doughty
ate—that portion, with a reasonable margin on either side,
was apparently reserved for the household cats, and the
remainder only eaten by the women. With much ceremony
he produced a box of Egyptian cigarettes for me alone, while
Dr. 'Abdullah was handed the ordinary kind in local use—
much to his disgust. Fahad, moreover, insisted on my retaining the box, which I handed over to the care of Rushaid
and, of course, never saw again.

The day was at last at an end, and I was glad to retire to
rest. According to local reckoning it was the first day of the
Kharif or cool autumn season, ushered in by the rising of
Suhail [2] at dawn. In effect there had been a marked fall in
the temperature, and the highest point reached during the
day was under 97°. At 6 a.m. the following morning it was
as low as 64°.

The hospitality of 'Anaiza is not only lavish but well
ordered. The burden of entertaining us—apart from coffee-
drinking—had fallen during the first day of our sojourn on
the *Amir* himself, who had provided both breakfast and
dinner, and was now quit of his obligations towards us.
His uncle, 'Abdul 'Aziz, arranged for our breakfast on the
second day, and as I had been able to slip away before it for

[1] *C.M.D.* ii. 350.   [2] *Canopus*; cf. pp. 60 and 108.

a ride, I was on arrival at my host's house in a state to appreciate the feast he had had prepared. There was rice and chicken, fried eggs and tomatoes stuffed with mince, lady's fingers, figs, peaches and dates of three kinds—all the fruit being from the adjoining garden in which, having washed down the meal with cow's buttermilk, we enjoyed a stroll in the cool shade of the rich foliage. In a little summer-house or bower of palm branches we found the *Amir* and young 'Abdul Rahman al Zamil, with whom we discussed agriculture. As I have already remarked, the date crop of this year was an exceptionally heavy one, and the *Amir* told me of a single palm in his garden reckoned to have a burden of 100 *Sa's* (between 250 and 300 *kilos*) valued at 40 *Riyals*. It is the practice here for townsfolk who are not owners of palms not to purchase their date requirements in the *Suq*, but to buy the crop of one or more trees as they stand, and during the season to help themselves at will to the fresh fruit. The system seems to work satisfactorily, for 'Anaiza boasts of a high standard of commercial probity.

We were bidden to coffee by one Salih al Fadhl,[1] a most delightful old gentleman whom I had already met at Riyadh. He was then on a visit to beg Ibn Sa'ud's intervention in favour of his son and nephew, who had been thrown into prison at Jidda by King Husain for no other ostensible reason than that Salih himself was at the time at Madina, where indeed he had resided for several years before the war, having married a lady of that city who had no desire to abandon the amenities of life to be found there under the Turkish *régime* for exile, as it appeared to her, in the deserts of Arabia. Salih had lost no time, after realising the predicament in which his son and nephew were, in returning to 'Anaiza, but in spite of the intervention of the British authorities at Jidda, King Husain could not be induced to release the young men till after the armistice. Salih was on their account in great distress at this time, though his *Medinite* wife had accompanied him, and by her domestic accomplishments had made

[1] In 1919 Salih migrated to Karachi to take charge of an important branch of his family's business in that city, where a few years later he was gathered to his fathers full of years and honour. The family is also represented at Bombay, and is held in high honour in the Hijaz under the new *Wahhabi régime*.

her husband's table the envy of the housewives of Qasim. Of its surpassing excellence I had an opportunity of judging that same evening when Salih insisted on our dining with him. A raised metal tray placed in the middle of a large mat bore a noble pile of rice and mutton exquisitely seasoned with delicate spices, and around it was spread a profusion of little dishes of minces and stuffed vegetables alternating with plates of delicious fruit—the choicest figs and peaches and a great variety of dates. Coffee followed the meal, and afterwards I accompanied Dr. 'Abdullah on a semi-professional visit to a half-paralysed aged relative of our host, the invalid's left side being completely atrophied as the result, according to 'Abdullah, of syphilis contracted long since in the course of a visit to Basra—one of the rare cases of this disease which came to my notice during the year I spent in Najd.

I was fortunately left sufficiently free during the day to see something of the great oasis, of which I managed to make a complete circuit. It lies in a great sandy basin bordered on the east by the escarpment of the *Safra* and on the other sides by a wide semicircle of the *Nafud*, beginning with the lofty peaks of 'Ayaida near Khashm Wudai in the south and passing through Dulaima,[1] a similar peak in the midst of high ridges, to the west of the oasis, where it sags to a lower level until it reaches the high sand peaks to the north of the settlement. On the south side the oasis is fed by the torrent channel of Sha'ib Wudai, which enters the depression between the *Nafud* and the escarpment under a headland known as Khashm Wudai—this appears to be the only affluent of the basin, but a good deal of rain-water also descends the steep slope of the escarpment, whose westerly inclination from the *Safra* summit is of no great extent. North of the Wudai headland, two other promontories project slightly from the line of the escarpment into the basin, namely, Khashm Sallum and Khashm Rafi', on each of which stands a circular watch-tower of solid construction, being made of masonry and cement and having no opening except a narrow window just

---

[1] About a quarter mile and one mile south of Dulaima and in the *Nafud* lay respectively the well of Kahlan and the single palm, *Qasrs* and cornland of Nuqailiya.

below the level of the roof to which access was ordinarily gained in case of need by rope and grappling iron. The latter standing at a point opposite the centre of the oasis commands a splendid view of it and of the town in its midst, which I was able to survey also from the lofty sand peak of Musabbih beyond its northern extremity and the peak of Dulaima, already mentioned, towards the south-west.

Almost the whole of the oasis lies within the circuit of an oval wall some twelve to fifteen feet in height with a shark's-tooth fringe along its summit and of enormous circumference. The wall is extremely dilapidated—the result of neglect—in many places as it was in Doughty's time, and though Doughty calculated that the breaches could be rapidly repaired in case of need, it scarcely seemed to me that the oasis could stand against a sudden attack, such as is characteristic of Arab warfare. Those I questioned on the subject attributed the neglect of the walls to a long period of security in the recent past, but the explanation did not seem to be very satisfactory in the case of a settlement which in the course of a century or less has experienced so many vicissitudes of fortune as 'Anaiza.

During the long period of anarchy which followed the overthrow of the *Wahhabi* power by Ibrahim Pasha in 1818 and ended only with the final accession of Faisal to the throne of Riyadh about three decades later, 'Anaiza appears to have maintained a semblance of independence under a loose Turkish control, and was for some years kept in subjection by the army of Khurshid Pasha, whose sojourn at the gates of the oasis was at any rate long enough to justify the erection of masonry barracks, whose ruins and those of a clay *Qasr* (just within the gate), still known as Qasr Kharshit, litter a considerable area outside the eastern gate. Then again during Faisal's reign, about 1862, 'Anaiza lay between two fires during the incipient struggles of Ibn Rashid and the *Wahhabis* of which Palgrave makes mention, and being invested for fourteen months as closely as Arab methods permit, closed its gates against Ibn Rashid and had no difficulty in resisting his attacks, producing as it did and does all the food its population required within the circuit of the wall. But circumstances had changed thirty years or more later when

'Anaiza,[1] like the rest of the Qasim and the whole of Najd, was occupied by Ibn Rashid until the present *Wahhabi* ruler recovered the whole province in 1906. Ibn Sa'ud at this time always spoke enthusiastically of the loyalty of the people and leading families of 'Anaiza to himself. and I myself never observed the slightest indication of any straining at the leash. It must be remembered, of course, that his policy is eminently conciliatory ; no one knows better than he how to employ force when necessary in the face of recalcitrancy, but the secret of his success lies in the fact that he can cure the wounds of fire and sword by generosity to his foes and tolerance. The people of 'Anaiza are not such as to bear lightly any infringement of their traditional independence, but with them business is ever the first consideration, and they are not slow to realise the advantages of subjection to a tolerant ruler over a spurious independence always at the mercy of warring neighbours. And so there was at this time and has been since no question of disloyalty at 'Anaiza, which has, however, of recent years been the prey of anxiety on account of the existence of strained relations between Ibn Sa'ud and the rulers of Kuwait, the supply-base of commercial Qasim. Yet Ibn Sa'ud can scarcely be expected to tolerate easily an arrangement which results in the appropriation by the state of Kuwait of the customs dues on merchandise destined for the Qasim, to which he has a legitimate claim. It will be good news for the merchants of Qasim when the long-overdue customs convention between Kuwait and Najd is negotiated, signed and ratified, and British statesmanship would not do ill to hasten a just settlement of a thorny problem.

Ibn Sa'ud is wise in his generation, and one may wonder whether he is ever assailed by twinges of conscience in consequence of his toleration in the Qasim—and in the Hasa—of a laxity which could not be permitted elsewhere without detriment to the very foundations of his system. He has since ridden the storm skilfully enough at Haïl, and is now at grips with the supreme test of his political sagacity in the

[1] Yahaya Ibn Sulaim was then *Amir*, and it is said at 'Anaiza that the *Rashidite* occupation of the town only lasted from 1308 to 1322 A.H. (*i.e.* 1890-1904). In any case the city remained under the general domination of Ibn Rashid.

Hijaz, where his frail barque has launched out from the shelter of Arabian creeks amid the perilous currents of *Islam's* uncertain sea. But these things were yet to be, and the difficulties of the future were but vaguely foreshadowed by rare and fitful breezes whose passage over the calm surface of home waters remained almost unremarked except by the vigilant eyes of the man at the helm, who saw but shrank not from the perils of the adventure on which he had embarked. For success he must have the confidence of his crew, and to secure and retain that he must accustom them to bold manœuvres, at which not understanding they might murmur, to their own eventual discomfiture. So it was in his dealings with the Qasim, which not a few attributed to nervousness of possible discontent in that province, but Ibn Sa'ud was looking far ahead and, as occasion offered, he taught his uncouth subjects certain essential lessons in statecraft, not least of which was that, as subjects free in the fullest sense to criticise and advise, it was no part of their business to assume the prerogative of government. Such an occasion had recently presented itself. A party of *Qusman*,[1] half a score of them, had set forth on a journey and, having halted for a midday siesta, were quietly enjoying their cigarettes when half a dozen *Ikhwan* passed by. Incensed at the atrocious conduct of the Qasim folk the representatives of God's elect took it upon themselves to upbraid them for their backsliding into the ways of the infidel. Such a taunt is not lightly borne by people who, for all their enlightenment, are convinced adherents of the one true faith, and the *Qusman* in wrath fell upon their accusers and slew them. The relatives of the ' martyred ' men appealed to Caesar, only to be sharply reminded that their dead kinsfolk had been guilty of the heinous sin of trenching upon the royal prerogative of judgment and to be sent about their business without the monetary compensation they sought from the offenders. Hamad, the Barra guide, who told me the story, suggested that the issue might have been different had the accused been from elsewhere than the favoured province, but I held my peace, dimly conscious perhaps that Ibn Sa'ud regarded the *Wahhabi* movement as a means towards an

[1] Pl. of *Qasimi*, inhabitant of the Qasim.

end envisaged already but not formulated even in his inmost thoughts.

The main gates giving access to the oasis are three in number, respectively at the north and south extremes of the circuit wall and at about the middle point of the eastern front. Besides these a postern gives admittance to the enclosure close by the south-west corner, where stands a solid circular watch-tower or *Sangar* on an eminence of sand, while two gates in the western wall lead out on to the roads towards Khabra. A line bisecting the walled area from the north gate to that on the south divides the oasis into two parts of distinctive character, that on the west up to the edge of the *Nafud* forming a dense tract of magnificent palm-groves of considerable thickness, while to the east the ground is more open with scattered palm patches and extensive areas of cornland, vegetable gardens, lucerne fields and the like. Cultivation has also been extended outside the eastern [1] wall on a considerable scale, while to the south are the isolated palm-groves of Juhaimiya and Khuraijiya, embedded in a tract of low dunes between the southern extremity of the oasis and the high *Nafud*. The former consists of a *Qasr* and a fairly dense group of high palms, while the latter comprises a small patch of palms with a good sprinkling of fruit-trees (fig and peach), to say nothing of its melon and vegetable patches. This garden also boasts the best drinking water of the whole oasis and is easily accessible, being only about a quarter mile outside the south gate. My tents were pitched half-way between the two points. Another detached garden is Muzaira', lying in a sandy depression north of the oasis between the *Safra* and the Musabbih and Huliban sand-peaks —the highest points in the 'Anaiza enclave and commanding a wide view of the surrounding country as far as the palms of Wadi Rima. Other extensions of cultivation of comparatively recent times had grouped themselves round the north and north-west confines of the circuit wall, lower subsidiary walls being built out from the main wall to contain

---

[1] *i.e.* the walled palm grove of Huwaita at the S.E. corner of the oasis with a patch of cultivation called Mughaira to S. of it ; the Shuqaira well with some cultivation outside *Darwaza Sharqiya* or east gate ; beyond this, northward, the palm-groves of Sallumiya ; the cultivation-patch and well of 'Uwaisa at the N.E. corner.

such excrescences in the case of new palm areas, while vegetable and melon patches centring round new-dug wells outside the oasis were vouchsafed no better protection than brushwood or palm-branch fences. Many of these extended areas contain single *Qasrs* for the accommodation of tenants, but the only group of buildings worthy of the title of hamlet outside the main wall was Sufaila, about 200 yards outside the north gate.

As seen from the *Sangar* of Khashm Rafi' the city of 'Anaiza seems to occupy a central position in the oasis with a tendency to bulge southwards, for it is on the southern side that lie the two oases of Dhulai'a and Umm al Himar— the former a long straggling group of buildings extending from the edge of the town in a south-easterly direction and containing perhaps a population of 1000 souls, while the latter with but 200 inhabitants nestles snugly in the thick forest of palms impinging on the south-west corner of the city. About 300 or 400 yards due east of the main town area lies the small hamlet of Shu'aibi with 100 souls in an open patch of fields, while a large hamlet of some 500 inhabitants, Malah by name, extends as a suburb for some distance along the north road. Dhabat, a smaller hamlet of 300 souls, lies about a quarter mile outside the town to the north-east. These groups and an apparently nameless collection of buildings near the south gate complete with the main town itself what may be regarded as the city of 'Anaiza. Further afield and outside the north gate on the left of the Buraida road is Sufaila, already noticed, with its 100 inhabitants, while Janah, with no more than 200 souls, lies buried within the thick belt of palms near the north-western corner of the circuit wall. This hamlet, for all its seeming lack of prosperity at the present time, claims to have been the original settlement of 'Anaiza.

The population of the 'Anaiza oasis, including the main town, the suburbs and the scattered *Qasrs*, cannot well have been less than 15,000 souls at this time. The main town was fully inhabited and its habitations closely packed together, and there were probably not fewer than 1000 shops all told in the main and various subsidiary *Suqs*. The chief characteristic of the city was a lack of symmetry which made it

very difficult to find one's way about or to get any exact
idea of its topography and lay-out. Its only outstanding
feature was the tall tapering minaret of the great mosque—
there were at least a dozen other minarets of similar architecture but of less height scattered about the town and
suburbs—which stood out prominently in the scene from
every point of view. And finally there was the great cemetery
lying astride the main north road beyond the suburb of
Malah and occupying a considerable area. In its older parts
the head and foot stones of the graves were noticeably larger
than is customary under *Wahhabi* conditions—rough-hewn,
oblong sandstone slabs about two or two and a half feet
high—while the more recent graves exhibited a tendency to
follow the precepts of the new dispensation. In these cases
the stones, of the same material, did not exceed a foot in
height.

3. THE ROAD TO BURAIDA

Ibn Sa'ud had only tarried a single night at 'Anaiza and
left for Buraida early in the morning of the second day.
But he had considerately suggested that I might prefer to
remain a day or two to see something of a place and community of which I had heard so much. I gladly availed
myself of his permission, and it was not till the morning of
26th August that, having had two full days in the delightful
social atmosphere of 'Anaiza, I was once more in the saddle
to rejoin the *Wahhabi* monarch. Buraida lies at a distance
of some fifteen miles almost due north of its sister-city. The
intervening country is a tract of rolling sand dunes of true
Nafud type, through which the important valley of Wadi
Rima, rising in the lava-waste of the Khaibar mountains
some four hundred miles distant, struggles for a passage only
to find itself in the end blocked by the great sand barrier of
the Dahna. The central belt of the Qasim province owes
its agricultural reputation mainly to the fact that the floods
of the *Wadi* reach thus far in years of plenteous rainfall, but
have never been known in living memory to proceed further
eastward. In the *Wadi* itself the subsoil water-level is
always close up to the surface, though both at 'Anaiza and
at Buraida the depth of wells is comparatively considerable.

The main road to Buraida leaves 'Anaiza by its north gate, but there is ample scope for variation of the monotony of travel between the two places. And it was in fact not the main road that we selected for my first journey. Camped as we were at the south-western extremity of the oasis, we marched along the Malqa road which skirts the western fringe of the palm-groves and is crossed at an early stage by the main road to Rass. The latter issues from a patch of *Ithils* on the edge of the oasis and runs westward over the dunes of Nafud Shuqaiyija, while our course was about north-west. The higher sand masses were absolutely bare and at the mercy of the winds, but the lower-lying parts had a goodly covering of *Adhir* and *Rimdh* bushes. One of these may be the ' canker weed,' [1] to which Doughty refers as being unwholesome food for camels—probably the former, though it is in fact eaten by the camels of Buraida. Mitrak, who was with me and was, from the *Badawin* point of view, an acknowledged authority on camel lore, declared that the *Adhir* is never eaten by grazing camels except in the Dahna, where the young sprouts of springtime are not disdained. As for the *Rimdh* it is eaten sparingly as a regular part of the camel's diet. On my arrival at 'Anaiza I had collected a supply of this plant from a neighbouring patch of luxuriant growth to feed my *Dhalul*, whose regular fodder had not arrived. Mitrak had chid me for my rash proceeding on the ground that *Rimdh* when too well grown was apt to disagree with the camel's anatomy, but so far as I could observe my *Dhalul* suffered no inconvenience, though she ate of it greedily until she had had enough of its saltiness.

Far off to the west the solitary hill of Saq showed up prominently over the waste of sand and, after we had marched about a mile and a half, the palms of Malqa appeared ahead of us. Another mile of marching brought us to a patch of ruins ; some *Qasr* of former times now level with the ground and known as 'Amara. One Salih, whom I had picked up to act as guide before starting and who rode pillion [2] behind me, could throw but little light on the history of these ruins, among which I found a number of sherds and fragments of gypsum cement. According to him 'Amara flourished before

---

[1] *C.M.D.* 332.   [2] *Radif.*

the birth of 'Anaiza, and might be attributed to the vague era of the Bani Hilal, to which are relegated in popular esteem all antiquities of which there is no more precise tradition.

The locality lies on the edge of a short valley-depression known as Sha'ib Malqa, which starts about a quarter mile westward of this point and runs down between sand ridges north-eastward into Wadi Rima. In it about half a mile up-stream lay the single well and small patch of cultivation of Jalib Mansur, where the depth to water is said to be five fathoms. Beyond that, at the head of the depression, lay Wahalan, a large patch of *Ithils* with a single well in its midst. Malqa itself lay close by us to the eastward and we reached it a few minutes later. First there was a patch of cultivation about 200 yards square, divided up into fields of wheat stubble and growing millet and adorned with numerous *Ithils*. Beyond it lay a rectangular grove of palms, some 200 by 100 yards in area, with several turret-like buildings at its western end. This grove belongs to the Bassam family, but appeared to be more or less derelict, and the palms bore little or no crop of fruit. The buildings and palms were surrounded by a dilapidated wall with a shark's-tooth fringe—altogether a pathetic memorial of some days of Doughty's sojourn in Arabia, for it was to this spot that he was sent in the interests of his own safety on the occasion of the murmuring that followed the smallpox outbreak.

A low ridge of sand separates Malqa from the single *Qasr* of Al Quai',[1] standing in an *Ithil* grove by the side of a garden patch of melons and vegetables, which extends about a quarter mile along the sandy edge of the *Sha'ib*. A small and unprosperous grove of some thirty palms lay a short way off to the north with some fields of wheat stubble. And the tale of the place is complete with the mention of some three or four wells with water at about four fathoms.

We were now rapidly approaching the confluence of the Malqa depression with Wadi Rima, which from this point of view appeared to be a huge oasis of serried palms—a magnificent though deceptive scene, for closer inspection was to show the raggedness and wretchedness of the numerous

---

[1] Pronounced Al Juai'.

groves which the Wadi, as the whole area is called, comprises. The mouth of Sha'ib Malqa was about half a mile across, and subtended almost across its whole width by the palm-grove of 'Aiyariya, a settlement consisting of a single *Qasr*, four or five wells about four fathoms deep, the palms and a large field of well-grown millet, which a youth was lazily defending from the depredations of birds by periodical crackings of a sort of whip.

Wadi Rima at this point runs about west and east, and appeared to be not more than half a mile wide. A palm plantation called Athamir lay along our right flank as we now marched up the valley over a surface of sandy loam disfigured with a white saline efflorescence. Here and there, as we marched, I noticed new plantations of palms. The salty *Sabkha* surface being penetrated to a depth of some three feet, the shafts are pushed down two or three feet further through an underlying stratum of gypseous appearance until the brackish subsoil water is tapped. The young plants are then embedded in the mixture of brine, water and mud at the bottom, and there they take root and apparently prosper until, as palms of somewhat miserable appearance, they come to the age of bearing.

At the western extremity of the Athamir palms—wretched, straggling, undersized stems with small branches of dates and fragments of a broken-down wall to protect them here and there—I found a well of briny water dug down to a depth of four fathoms, but without any lining of any kind. About a mile away to the westward stood the small grange of Qusair Ibn Jabr with its surrounding patch of vegetable and wheat cultivation, beyond which the course of the *Wadi* is lost to view as it bends round to the south-west.

We now had the whole of the Wadi oasis, so-called, down-stream of us, and turned eastward to visit some of its component parts. To our left lay the dunes of the Buraida district, whose southern boundary is the left bank of the *Wadi*. The oasis of the latter is accounted to the 'Anaiza district, whose sand masses—Nafud Shuqaiyija—skirt the right bank. Our course ran along an irregular torrent channel somewhat nearer the left bank than the right, and we came soon after leaving the Athamir grove to that of Nuzai'a,

which was a straggling plantation with thicker groups of
palms at its eastern extremity. Soon afterwards the valley
broadened to about a mile, and we cut across a north-easterly
bend of it back to the right bank, where, after passing between
denser plantations than those hitherto encountered, we came
to a halt at the small hamlet of Janah, a settlement almost
entirely inhabited by slave cultivators. Its population
may have been some 250 souls of the slave population of
'Anaiza, whose free citizens hold all the proprietary rights
in the Wadi plantations. Hence we passed through a
considerable area of vegetable gardens into the palm-tract
of Al Muskh, straggling along the right bank of the valley,
which between this plantation and a long tongue of
palms forming the eastern extremity of Nuzai'a is bare of
cultivation.

Returning across this open space to the left bank we
reached a fairly dense palm-grove, about 400 yards long and
200 broad, known as 'Ain al Mabrak, though it did not seem
to be blessed with a spring as its name suggests. We did,
however, not far beyond it, come to a nameless spring
apparently only recently discovered, by which stood a small
hut in the midst of a few palms and vegetable patches.
This spring consisted of a well, square-cut and about three
feet long and broad, whose top lay sunk some four feet below
the surface of the valley and which was filled almost to the
brim with exceedingly foul and stinking water with a scum
of yellowish-green slime. A channel in process of excavation
had by now almost reached the top of the well, whence the
water would flow into it as it welled up to the brink, but the
occupant of the hut informed me that, before any irrigation
could be attempted, an effort would have to be made to locate
the real head of the spring, which was thought to lie not in
the well already mentioned, but some 200 yards further back
at the edge of the *Nafud*. It would be necessary to open up
the real source to secure a strong flow.

Resuming our march down the valley in a north-easterly
direction and passing a single well and hut close to the right
bank we came next to a palm-grove named Al Thaila near
the opposite bank with a mud tower at its edge. And
immediately beyond it we visited the spring of 'Ain Suhai-

bani,[1] an excellent specimen of the work of local husbandry under favourable conditions. A rectangular cistern, some six feet by four and two feet deep, was full of clear, slightly greenish water, which could be seen bubbling up through two minute holes in the floor. No attempt had been made to line its sides with masonry, but its brink was strengthened all round with a lining of *Ithil* timber, through which by an aperture on the north side a sluggish flow of water passes into a well-made *Kariz* channel. The sides and bottom of the latter were of masonry and the channel was roofed over, being about a foot wide, with stone slabs of considerable size

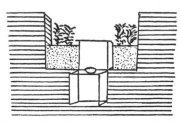

FIG. 7.   Diagram showing arrangement of Ain Suhaibani
spring and channel.

at regular intervals. The cistern itself was situated at the head of a broad trench dug out to a depth of five feet below ground level, and the *Kariz* ran down the centre of this trench, being raised some three feet above the top level of the cistern. The spaces between the raised *Kariz* channel and the banks of the trench on either side had been filled in with loam soil in which palms had been planted—they were now about ten years old—at regular intervals, and had so prospered that their summits now showed about two feet above the top of the trench. In the interstices between the palms grew melons and pumpkins. The water, which though clear is briny and very unpleasant to the taste, was but a few inches deep in the channel and flowed so sluggishly that its movement was scarcely perceptible. It eventually reaches and irrigates part of the Thaila palms.

While we were engaged in examining the spring we attracted the notice of a group of women sitting in a hut near by. Clad in scarlet smocks, whose bright hues were dimmed

[1] *Vide* Fig. 7.

THE SPRING OF 'AIN SUHAIBĀNĪ IN WĀDĪ RIMA.

To face page 180.

by dirt, and veiled in black muslin like the women of 'Aridh, they came out and, standing at a safe distance, shrilly enquired our object in examining their spring. And Mitrak replied jestingly that our purpose was to purchase the concern if it took our fancy. Scarlet appeared to be the favoured colour of women in these parts, though I noticed here and there the black smocks of the south and more rarely garments of a bluish colour. The better classes in the Qasim, according to Dr. 'Abdullah, generally prefer garments of sober black or dark blue.

About 200 yards eastward of 'Ain Suhaibani was another spring, 'Ain Junaini, precisely similar to it in every respect except that its cistern was a good deal larger, being fifteen feet long, five broad and three deep. The water also was clearer and devoid of the usual scum, and for about 200 yards the channel leading from the spring was bare of palms. At that point the palms begin and the stream flows on to irrigate the grove of Al Jaraya, which is an easterly continuation of the Thaila plantation hugging the edge of the *Nafud*. The masonry of this *Kariz* seemed also to be stronger and more solid than that of the other. Neither channel greatly exceeds a quarter mile in length.

Close by on the north-east lay the spring or rather well of 'Ain Ibn Suhaim—an excellent masonry shaft descending to the water-level three fathoms below and measuring fifteen feet by six. In its bottom lay a three-feet depth of greenish-yellow water covered over with a nauseous slime, from under which the water oozes sluggishly into a narrow open channel so completely overgrown with palms of from fifteen to twenty years of age that the stream itself was invisible. It ends eventually in a further continuation of the palm strips already mentioned known as Al Maliha. Round the well were a few wretched huts, while to our right beyond an open clearing and in the midst of the valley lay the prosperous palm-groves known as Thulth Abu 'Ali, with a small hamlet of that name inhabited by some 300 negroes.

To the north-eastern extremity of this plantation we came in due course after passing the derelict channel and ' dead ' cistern of 'Ain Ibn Sulaiman on the way. This pit had a diameter of some fifteen feet, but its stagnant water lay at a depth of three fathoms considerably below the aperture by which it formerly entered the channel. Near it were two small huts and a straggling palm-grove. The Abu 'Ali plantation, lying on the main road from 'Anaiza to Buraida, was the most compact and prosperous of all the Wadi plantations, of which it was also the furthest down-stream, excepting only a small straggling patch of palms called 'Adaïn in the middle of the valley eastward of the main road and the plantation of Al Jasar, which is the last and most easterly continuation of the *Nafud*-edge groves already mentioned.

The main road after passing close by the Abu 'Ali hamlet strikes across the valley and passes through the midst of the Jasar tract, which derives its name from a causeway of dilapidated masonry by which the road crosses the main torrent channel of the valley. This keeps close in to the left bank throughout the oasis tract and is of insignificant width, and it may be to this channel rather than to the *Wadi* as a whole that Doughty referred as being barely a stone's cast [1] across. Wadi Rima in these parts never seemed to me less than a quarter mile wide, and here and there it was certainly as much as a mile across. Perhaps Doughty did not realise that the whole depression between the two *Nafud* tracts formed the valley of the 'river,' whose source he himself had discovered far away to the west. In any case I found it somewhat difficult to satisfy myself with any certainty as to the exact route followed by Doughty across Wadi Rima. The oozy trickle of water which he found flowing under his feet may have been the channel of 'Ain Ibn Suhaim or that of 'Ain Ibn Sulaiman, now no longer in action. And he may then have passed across either to Abu 'Ali or to Al Janah—I cannot certainly determine which. It is of course more than probable that the agricultural topography of the valley has somewhat altered since his time. Two of the channels I have mentioned were certainly not in existence then, and the death and birth of springs in this country of sand must play a constant part in moulding the activities of the local cultivator.

Al Jasar, lying astride the exit of the main road, extends for about a mile along the course of the torrent channel and

[1] *C.M.D.* ii. 332.

is approached from westward over an open space scored by the channels of numerous streams, some still flowing but most of them dead long since. High piles of silt cleared from these channels in the tedious attempt to keep them alive indicate their courses from the springs that gave or give them birth. There are, I think, about five of these. The first two furthest west, known together as Al Sinani and situated about fifty yards apart, contained clear water to a depth of two feet at the bottom of rectangular well-pits about four fathoms deep and twenty feet by ten in superficial extent. From each a sluggish flow of water passed into a channel, and the two channels converged at no great distance to irrigate the up-stream section of the Jasar groves. So far as I could ascertain one of these channels if not actually dead was practically moribund and contributed little if any water to the common stream. About a hundred yards further east lay another pair of spring cisterns—Umm Al Jarbub—of which one was certainly dead, and whose channels met at a point some twenty yards from the most easterly to form a single stream. Here again the springs lay in unlined well-pits of the kind already described, though I should note further that all four of these pits have a thin dressing of masonry round their upper parts. The last of the five springs, close by the main road, is 'Ain al Jasar—a narrow well-shaft descending to the level of the water, which flows in a piped channel under the road to irrigate the eastern or lower section of the groves by way of the torrent-bed.

We had now diligently ' done ' the Wadi oasis and were weary. There was little enough in it to warrant the high praise bestowed by the prosperous citizens of 'Anaiza on their outlying colony, and I could find no justification in the wretched straggling patches of the oasis for the suggestion that the Wadi was richer in palms than the dense groves of the city. The crop of the one cannot possibly compare with that of the other, even if it be true—which I doubt—that the number of palms is greater. Above all, the soil of the *Wadi* is of poor quality and full of salt. But, be that as it may, we were weary and gladly seized the opportunity of halting awhile in the company of a small group of negroes engaged in clearing silt from the last channel on our course.

Very hospitably they offered us a share of the inferior fresh dates and coffee which constituted their midday meal, and very welcome was their humble entertainment. And as they entertained us they spoke of conditions in the *Wadi*. Nothing that I had seen—the torrent-bed was but a shallow depression not more than forty yards across—suggested the passage of considerable floods at not infrequent intervals down the great valley. And yet the local report of the frequency of such floods cannot be lightly dismissed, even though it be necessary to discount exaggerated accounts which are natural enough in a folk to whom water means life and who rejoice with a great rejoicing when water comes. Wadi Rima certainly differs from its great southern counterpart, Wadi Dawasir, both in experiencing the passage of actual floods and in the high level of its subsoil moisture. They are alike in being bounded by sand dunes on either side, but the southern sands are white while the sands of the Qasim are reddish and pink. After crossing the road the right bank of the valley changes from *Nafud* sand to sandstone, where the northern extremity of the *Safra* wilderness running up from behind Al Sirr and Mudhnib abuts on the *Wadi* and parts the Zuqaibiya depression from the main channel. The point of bifurcation is prominently marked by the long, isolated and markedly pink sand barrier of 'Itaiyima.[1]

Having had our fill of dates and coffee we bade our negro hosts farewell and rose out of the valley on to the Buraida *Nafud*, from the top of whose first ridge we looked out before us on a rolling sea of sand billows, for the most part of monotonous aspect and moderate elevation, but varied here and there by loftier, wind-swept crests and peaks. The road was a well-beaten trail in the sand winding gently round the shoulders of the ridges and undulating with easy gradients, while the sand slopes were sparsely covered with the usual vegetation of *Adhir* and *Rimdh*. About a mile on we came to a ridge which by local reckoning is considered the half-way mark between the two towns, the Wadi itself—presumably the Abu 'Ali hamlet—being the first and Al Khadhar the second of the three stages into which the journey naturally falls.

[1] *See* p. 159.

Marching thus over the rolling *Nafud* for some two or three
miles we reached a saddle between two higher ridges to be
confronted by a scene of extraordinary beauty.   One behind
another the yellow sand-waves stretched back to the purple
horizon of a sandstone wilderness [1] far off behind Buraida,
and in the intervening folds of sand there appeared patches
of deep contrasting black—groves of palms or *Ithils*.   Nearest
to us and most conspicuous as it lay silhouetted against a
setting of sand dunes at our feet was the oasis of Al Khadhar
with its palms of deep dark green, while further off a lofty

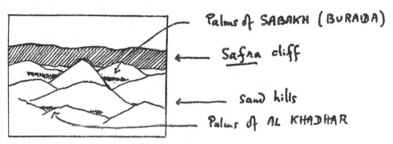

Palms of SABAKH (BURAIDA)

Safra cliff

Sand hills

Palms of AL KHADHAR

FIG. 8.   Rough Diagram showing appearance of Nafud looking
towards Buraida from south.

pyramid of sand broke the long dark line which was the
oasis of Buraida.   Of the city itself we could see nothing, nor
indeed were we destined to see anything of it until we were
almost within a stone's cast of its great walls.   To see
Buraida from afar one must approach it from the north.

It did not take us long now to reach Al Khadhar, whose
oasis lies wholly to the left of the road in a firm bottom of
whitish gypsum soil of an inferior quality, unsuitable, they
said, for use as cement or plaster.   The first palm-grove was
a goodly patch, about 200 yards long and 100 broad and
densely packed with stems, to say nothing of a rich undergrowth of vegetables and lucerne.   About it were scattered
some six or seven mud huts of unpretentious appearance,
and beyond it was a good sprinkling of *Ithils*, well grown and
tipped with the russet flowering which I had noticed in Wadi
Dawasir.   But here apparently the flower does not mature
sufficiently to be used for the making of dyes, though,
according to Tami, further north at Haïl some use is made of

[1] *Vide* Fig. 8.

it.   Further on was another patch of palms, small and
straggling but with much *Ithil*, a prosperous tree in these
parts, and found everywhere in any fold of the sandhills and
even planted freely on the ridge crests to serve as defences
against the blowing sand.   The depression of Al Khadhar
is of roughly oval shape and receives the drainage of the
neighbouring slopes and the valleys between them.   Its
resident population can scarcely exceed thirty souls in all.

A quarter mile beyond we entered the similar oval, white-
soiled depression of Khabb al 'Uqaiyan with the usual *Ithil*
patches and two small groves of palms.   Next we traversed
the bottom of Khabb al 'Aushaz to ascend the ridge beyond
—generally speaking these sand ridges seemed to lie south-
west by north-east [1]—from whose summit we descried the
oasis of Rawaq, about half a mile away to the right on the
direct road to Mudhnib, which now rapidly converged on
our course.

We soon found ourselves in a valley bottom between two
sand ridges half a mile apart and marching north-west on the
first groves of the Buraida oasis, known as Al Sabakh.   At
its edge were two or three little hamlets, passing one of
which close by we followed a sandy corridor, some hundred
yards wide, between the palm belt on the one side and the
rounded slope of a sand ridge on the other which curves
gently round to the town, of whose wall we now had our first,
though only a partial view.   And so, glad to be at the end
of a short march strenuously and profitably employed, we
reached at last the south-eastern corner of the town wall and
soon after entered Buraida by the Bab al Qasr—the Fort
Gate.

4. BURAIDA

' And from hence appeared a dream-like spectacle !—a
great clay town built in this waste sand with enclosing walls
and towers and streets and houses ! and there beside a
bluish dark wood of ethel trees upon high dunes !   This is
Boreyda ! and that square minaret, in the town, is of their
great mesjid.   I saw, as it were, Jerusalem in the desert !
[as we look down from the mount of Olives].' [2]

[1] Others lay north-west and south-east.
[2] *Arabia Deserta*, vol. ii. p. 314.

"A DREAM-LIKE SPECTACLE"—THE EAST WALL AND GREAT FORT OF BURAIDA.

To face page 186.

Thus wrote Doughty of his first view—from the north-west
—of a great city whose beauty has altered as little as the
churlish disposition of its citizens. In it he suffered the extreme of tribulation, before which even his stout spirit must
have quailed ; and from it, having escaped the death that
lurked for him at every corner, he was driven forth on the
third day to the hospitality of rival 'Anaiza, where his memory
is cherished to this day to its own glory. At Buraida they
speak not of Khalil, and if, in the presence of strangers from
afar, their conscience sometimes reminds them of that episode
in their history, they mention it not and ' fain would blush,
if blush they could, for shame.' Yet neither remorse nor
enlightenment born of travel will ever wean the citizen of
Buraida, when at home, from the bigotry in which his city
has grown great among the cities of Arabia. Abroad he is
not less genial or hospitable than the rest of them, and it is
difficult to account for the blight that settles on his soul
within the precincts of his native town. It is just a fact of
which every European visitor to Buraida has had experience
—myself perhaps least of all for being there in the train of
Ibn Sa'ud. You may travel where you will with a native
of Buraida in perfect friendliness and companionship, but
the moment you enter the gates of the city the friendship is
at an end until your sojourn is done and you set forth once
more together on your travels as if nothing had happened.
Colonel Hamilton had quite recently had experience of this
strange phenomenon. On his arrival at Buraida the companions of his journey, including a number of prominent
citizens of Shaqra who were to continue their journey with
him southwards, completely vanished from his ken and did
not reappear, I was told, until the southward march had
begun. It is a problem of psychology to which there appears
to be no solution.

Turning into the city by the Bab al Qasr we were conducted
across the open camping-ground called Jarada and past the
great castle to the governor's house, which, as I afterwards
discovered, had been evacuated by the *Amir* for my benefit.
This was not his private family residence, which was elsewhere
in the town, but comprised as it were his chambers, in which
he transacted the official and ceremonial work of his im-

portant office. Outside the building and fronting the *Qasr*
a long earthen bench ran the whole length of the wall, in
the centre of which was a portion divided off from the rest
by low arm-rests to serve as a chair of state, on which the
Amir sat in the cool of the mornings and evenings in public
assembly, dispensing justice or merely chatting with visitors.
I had scarcely entered into occupation of the cosy, carpeted
upper room, which was to be my home in Buraida, when the
governor himself, Fahad Ibn Mu'ammar, paid me a formal
visit of ceremony to assure himself of the comfort of his
guest. The conversation, as always on such occasions, was
entirely formal, but left me with the impression of a person
of some distinction, somewhat crabbed to be sure and of
crafty mien—perhaps on account of a cataract in one eye—
but nevertheless in appearance as in public repute a leader
in the great cause of which he was so devoted a servant, and
for which some years later he was to lay down his life on the
battlefield.[1]   It certainly seemed to me that Barclay
Raunkiaer, who visited Buraida in 1912 and was not made
particularly welcome there, allowed personal prejudice to
colour his picture of the man—in any case he painted him
in somewhat unnecessarily lurid colours. He was always
more than polite, sometimes even cordial, to me, and among
his own folk he was of a mild disposition. One afternoon I
overlooked from my window the proceedings of one of his
courts of justice, the disputant parties being two *Badawin*,
one of whom had sold the other for 70 dollars a camel which
had died the following day. After listening with all patience
to an argument which became ever louder and more acri-
monious Fahad gave a divided verdict condemning the seller
to refund 30 dollars as partial consolation to the disappointed
purchaser.

His departure left me free to bathe, change my clothes
and breakfast at leisure, and I was glad enough of the excuse
which such occupations reasonably provided to decline an
invitation to visit Ibn Sa'ud during the afternoon. It was
indeed he who visited me a little later in my own rooms to
speak of the progress of his dispositions for the coming

---

[1] He was killed while leading a cavalry charge during the final campaign
against Haïl in 1921.

campaign. And, after his departure, I was visited by *Shaikh* Ahmad Ibn Jabir,[1] the eldest son of the late ruler of Kuwait and nephew of the actual *Shaikh*, Salim Ibn Mubarak. He had been some days at Buraida on the way with a small party of Kuwait pilgrims to perform the great pilgrimage at Mecca. He had his own reasons to be none too friendly with the uncle who had for the nonce usurped his right to rule Kuwait, and Salim was uncompromisingly committed to hostility with Ibn Sa'ud, which eventually ended in war.[2] It is not, therefore, improbable that conversations on this occasion between Ibn Sa'ud and Ahmad laid the foundations of a friendly understanding which took definite shape some years later on the demise of Salim, though Kuwait would seem to be doomed to lose its old position as the trade entrance of Eastern and Central Arabia if it insists on its present policy of political isolation from its hinterland. The *Hajj* party from Kuwait was nominally under the command of Sultan [3] Ibn 'Abdul 'Aziz Ibn Hasan, who, for reasons best known to himself, insisted on treating me as an old friend ; while the possibility of political vagaries on the part of Ahmad had been duly guarded against by the attachment of Salim's private secretary, one 'Abdul 'Aziz, to his personal suite.

I naturally saw a good deal of these people during the days which intervened before their departure for Mecca, but the relations of Ibn Sa'ud and Salim were so strained at this period that I judged it wise to restrict myself to the conversation of formal friendliness, leaving Ibn Sa'ud · himself to tackle in his own way with Ahmad the problem of the betterment of political relations between the two states. Encouraged *sub rosa* by Salim the 'Ajman tribe had latterly been getting badly out of hand and raids by it as far afield as Hafar al Ats and Juda had been reported. Such activities,

[1] Mubarak Ibn Subah was succeeded in 1915 by his eldest son, Jabir, who died a year later in suspicious circumstances and was succeeded by his brother, Salim. The latter died in 1921 and was succeeded by Jabir's son, Ahmad, who still rules.

[2] A *Wahhabi* attack on Jahra in 1921 necessitated the despatch of British aeroplanes to protect Kuwait from further trouble and, in due course, the fixing of the boundary between the Kuwait principality and the *Wahhabi* territory through the good offices of Great Britain.

[3] *See* p. 30.

coupled with the ever-present Sharifian threat on the west, constituted for Ibn Sa'ud a serious military menace, but all my appeals to Basra for action to suppress the intrigues of Salim met with but lukewarm support. On the other hand I was able at this time to communicate to Ibn Sa'ud—much to his satisfaction—the news that the British Government had expressed its formal approval of the guarantees I had given him at Riyadh [1] before he began his march northward.

Tami was my last visitor on this my first day at Buraida, where he was at this time living with his married daughter in a house on the northern edge of the Jarada near the small north-eastern gate, or rather postern, of the town. I saw a good deal of him during the first few days of my sojourn, frequently visiting him at his home where, at various times, I met mutual friends. Rushaid was a regular visitor, but the unedifying conversation of Tami's parlour generally singled him out as its butt, and as often as not ended in his retreating abruptly before a ribald bombardment of facetious references to his alleged impotence. He did not mind how much he was chaffed about his stupidity, but the attack on his physical qualities was more than he could stand, and I have already [2] recorded how some years later he had his revenge on his tormentors. Tami's little grandson, Mutlaq (Mutailij) Ibn Hamud, was generally present at these parties—a child of barely two years and of the greatest charm as Arab children often are—and, after an initial bout of shyness, made great friends with me. As often as not he would nestle up against my side, gazing with his great eyes at his ribald elders, and doze off into the sleep of the innocent.

As the days passed by I began to realise that the social expectations raised by my experiences at 'Anaiza were doomed to disappointment. The fanatical and narrow-minded exclusiveness of Buraida society was as that of Riyadh, and even the fact of my frequent visits to Tami's house began after a while to affect the normal popularity of that harbour of mirth. His friends, he said, were welcome to keep away, but he himself would not be branded as a fool for driving away a past and, possibly, future benefactor whose gifts had been and would be worth receiving. Never-

[1] See p. 47.   [2] See p. 10.

theless, after the first few days, the general atmosphere of
public disapproval proved too much even for him, and it was
only at rare intervals thereafter that he visited me. And
in the end he fell between two stools, for he was branded as
a friend of the infidel and failed to secure the present, whose
prospect made him bold and boastful in the beginning.

On one occasion I was visited under cover of night by a
member of a family well known to me at Baghdad. This
was Mansur Ibn Rumaih, one of a trio of brothers long
prosperously engaged in the Arabian camel-trade and trading
indifferently with ourselves or the Turks wherever a good
market offered for their stock. I had already met him down
at Shaqra, and he was now desirous of obtaining my good
offices in connection with a visit he contemplated making
to 'Iraq. But the furtive nature of his visit had aroused my
displeasure, and I had taken steps to let him know indirectly
that I could not further the business of anyone who could
not bring himself to receive me in his house. Doctor
'Abdullah some days later visited him in his palm-grove on
the outskirts of the city and approached me on the subject of
his request for assistance in the matter of his visit to Baghdad,
but I would not accept as adequate the excuse that Mansur
was afraid of public opinion and insisted that, if he desired
my assistance in any matter, he must extend to me the
hospitality which I had a right to expect from a house so
intimately connected with the British authorities in Mesopotamia. In the end he swallowed his scruples sufficiently
to invite me to a garden-party in his palm-grounds to meet
Turki and other distinguished guests—Ibn Sa'ud himself
was away on a three-day visit to 'Anaiza. His garden of
some ten or twelve acres lay just outside the south-western
gate of the city, and had been purchased by him for 4000
Riyals only the previous year—almost immediately afterwards he had received and refused an offer of 5000 *Riyals* for
it—since when he had spent as much again in redeeming it
from the state of desolation into which it had been allowed to
fall by its former owners. About half of the area was occupied
by a plantation of palms of from ten to twenty years' growth
with a rich undergrowth of lucerne and millet, while the
remaining half was more or less bare. Amid the palms was

a fair-sized bower or summer-house of palm fronds, in which, reclining on carpets and cushions, was the assembled company of Mansur's guests—Turki himself and his brother Sa'ud, Faisal Ibn Rashid, Salman al 'Arafa, and Fahad, the eldest son of 'Abdullah Ibn Jiluwi, whom I had not previously met, though our paths had crossed at the wells of Abu Jifan the previous November. The refreshments consisted of dates— Buraida seemed to be astonishingly deficient in the fruits so plentiful elsewhere—and coffee, and the conversation turned on horses, rifles and war. So long as Ibn Sa'ud was himself at Buraida, Turki seemed to efface himself completely and, though I occasionally saw him afar off in the lower seats of his father's public audiences which I frequently attended during these days, it was in vain that I sought for and pressed Dr. 'Abdullah to arrange for a meeting with him. Apparently court etiquette discouraged, if it did not actually forbid, him to receive me in his residence while his father was in the place. Thus it was that, though I arrived at Buraida on 25th August, it was not till 31st August—the day of Ibn Sa'ud's departure for 'Anaiza—that I was able to call on him by arrangement. I found him in residence in a house near the southern end of the town, though it was too dark—the reception-room being very dimly illuminated —for me to see much of the surroundings in which he lived. On that occasion Faisal Ibn Rashid was the only other guest, though the room was filled with Turki's own attendants.[1] He received me with shy effusiveness and insisted on my occupying part of the small becushioned area intended only for himself. Then, much to my embarrassment, he absolutely insisted—and would take no refusal—on my taking the first cup of warm sweetened milk which was the first item of the refreshments served round. The ice being thus broken by my submissive acceptance of this great mark of honour, the ceremonial of audiences re-established itself between us and he was served first with coffee and incense thereafter. In such cases the practice of hosts varied—my negro host, the *Amir* of Tarafiya, for instance, took his cup as a matter of course before me on the occasion of my visit to him, and Fahad Ibn Mu'ammar, the governor of Buraida, was in-

[1] As heir-apparent he had his own retinue of *Zigirt*.

variably served first and made no bones about it—and the
main requisite in a well-bred guest was to deprecate the
honour of first service and to judge for himself when to yield
if pressed.

On that occasion Turki, having heard of my riding out
during the afternoon, asked me why I had not joined his
own party which was out further to the east. In the hope
of more social enjoyment in the future I replied frankly that
it was because I had not been invited to do so. ' Do so in
future,' he replied hospitably, ' and ride with me whenever
you like. *Saiyir*,' [1] he continued, ' go and visit people—don't
sit alone at home.' Perhaps he scarcely realised how difficult
it was to follow his advice and how often I had tried to visit
him in vain. I asked him if he was kept busy. ' Only when my
father is away,' he replied, ' and then I have plenty of work,
but it all stops when he returns.' It seemed to be a curious
arrangement that, never being consulted about or kept in
touch with affairs, he should become immediately and fully
responsible for their conduct whenever Ibn Sa'ud was absent.
I had once asked the latter whether Turki took after him in
the matter of sleeping little and waking at will. ' I have
never tested him,' he replied simply. Turki's mother was
of the house of Mandil,[2] a Bani Khalid family, and had long
since been divorced—the story of the incident being a somewhat curious one. On a visit to the Hasa many years after
his heir's birth Ibn Sa'ud had married a girl of the Mandil
family, and it was not till some time after the marriage that
he discovered she was a sister of Turki's mother, a daughter
of the same mother by a different husband. It being unlawful to marry two sisters, the mistake could only be rectified
by the divorcing of the first wife—presumably with retro-
spective effect. The sister was still on the active list of Ibn
Sa'ud's conjugal establishment, the chief lady of which was
the great and beautiful Jauhara [3] Bint Musa'id. A third
wife at this time was the Dhukair lady already referred to
as resident at 'Anaiza, and, so far as I could ascertain, the
fourth place was vacant—Bint Sudairi, the widow of Sa'd,

[1] Visit.
[2] The Mandil family of Zubair and Basra is of Dawasir origin.
[3] She succumbed to the influenza epidemic at the end of 1918.

and the *Badawin* wife married in the spring of this year having both been divorced.

A nervous manner made Turki somewhat difficult to converse with, and he was not by any means free yet of the callowness of youth and inexperience, but he was undoubtedly a noble lad—a thoroughbred. He explained the failure of his recent campaign as being due to the unwieldy size of his force, which could not get further than Bashuk owing to the insufficiency of reliable wells to the northward. But he was eagerly looking forward to the opportunities of fighting presented by the forthcoming campaign. Some day, he said, he hoped to visit Baghdad and Egypt to see something of the great world, of which he knew nothing beyond its terrible and devastating methods of warfare. He himself generally rode bareback and without stirrups—and he was a magnificent horseman—but the use of saddles and stirrups was becoming commoner in Arabia, and many, like Ibn Sa'ud himself and Faisal Ibn Rashid—who being present admitted the soft impeachment—had become so accustomed to them that they could no longer ride in the traditional Arab way.

Turning to Sa'ud, who was of the party at Mansur's garden, I remarked that it was a long time since I had last seen or conversed with him. ' And it will be as long before you see him again,' Turki broke in, ' for he has recently married a girl he loves fondly.' ' How can you endure,' asked Salman, ' to be tied to one wife for life ? Our system is indeed better than yours, for, if we will, we can put away a wife if she please not the first night.' So we chatted pleasantly enough under the palm-frond bower until the sinking sun warned me of the uncrossable gulf between my hosts and myself. I rose and took my leave, for they would pray where they were, and Mansur accompanied me to the end of his garden plot under the *Nafud*, explaining the while that, having often enjoyed the hospitality of Europeans, he was only too pleased to entertain me, though he was afraid of the tongues of his fellow-citizens. I exhorted him to fear not and passed out of his garden close by two wells, where camels toiled up and down the *Majarr* causing the wheels to shriek and groan. In a field near by a group of women was busy cutting lucerne.

As I ascended the steep sandy bank of the *Nafud* I enjoyed
some glorious views of the great city and its fortress over
and through the palm forest, in which were some stems of
prodigious height, reaching almost to the level of the summit
of the sand ridge. Near the watch-tower on the latter I
found that a considerable area of the *Ithil* forest had recently
been cut down to the roots, and so I enjoyed an uninterrupted
view of the town panorama against a background of the
setting sun, while the still air vibrated with the raucous
clamour of the many *Muadhdhins* proclaiming the call to
prayer from the tapering minarets. The *Adhan* was in
general far more musical than that of Riyadh, though it
could not compare with the trilling melody of the borderlands,
whose influence was, however, discernible in the almost
theatrical staging of the ordinary prayers in some of the
mosques. The *Imam* of the little oratory attached to the
Amir's house, whose operations I had frequent opportunities
of watching, was for instance a case in point. Having first
done duty as *Muadhdhin* in the high-pitched affected accents
of Syria—*Hé 'ale'l salét, etc.*—he would descend to take the
service, conducting it in impassioned tones and producing
every possible permutation and combination of expression.
'*Allahu akbar*' he would start, fully pronouncing both words ;
then '*Allahu* —— ' with a passionate emphasis on the first
word while completely suppressing the second ; and then
again ' —— *akbar*,' reversing the process, and finally '*Allahu
akbar*' in the tones of ordinary conversation. And in the
Surat al Fatiha he faithfully reproduced the nasal accent of
the North. The first call was from the stout minaret of the
great mosque, and, as it was caught up by the neighbouring
minarets, those who loitered among the gardens or at the
foot of the *Nafud* hastily turned their steps citywards to
spend the best moments of the day at prayer in their stuffy
cloisters. Mirwij made his solitary devotions on the sand
by my side and we sat on awhile until the rapidly darkening
twilight warned us to get home. Like his fellow-slaves,
'Aïdh and Surur—the latter now promoted to be assistant
to Husain, the master-gunner—Mirwij had until the previous
year been in the service of Ibn Rashid at Haïl. They had
then absconded—economic pressure had undoubtedly made

life somewhat burdensome at the Shammar capital—to seek
service with Ibn Sa'ud, under whose *régime* the life of slaves
was full of homely comfort and genuine happiness. Mirwij
had at one time spent five or six years with the Ibn Razi
subsection of Aslam under *Shaikh* Dha'ar Ibn Razi and had
acquired a fair knowledge of the Shammar country.

My sojourn at Buraida lasted some seventeen days, and
if I saw but little of its crabbed society, I missed but little of
its topographical detail, external or internal. The city,
which covers an area of about 180 [1] acres, is entirely surrounded by a wall two feet thick, from fifteen to twenty feet
high and surmounted by a fringe of stepped pinnacles. As
Doughty has pointed out, it rides upon its ridge, whose axis,
like that of the *Nafud* waves [2] immediately to westward, lies
N.W. by S.E. The summit of the ridge, whose underlying
rock is overlain by a thin sprinkling of sand, carries the east
wall—an almost straight length of about 1200 yards oriented
in accord with the axis of the ridge—from which the city
spreads downwards to west and south almost to the bottom
of the trough between its own ridge and the outermost wave
of the *Nafud*. The trough itself from a point opposite to the
northern extremity of the city wall to the extreme end of the
Sabakh groves to southward contains an almost unbroken
line of palms of varying width and density. And the circuit
wall conforms to the outline of this palm belt and the slopes
of the ridge to north, west and south. On the east side the
ridge slopes abruptly to a shallow gypseous depression in
which lies a group of wells called Saqa'a—the source of the
city's supply of drinking water, which had a disagreeable
mineral taste and an anti-digestive tendency which seemed
to convert one's food into lead—and a grove of *Ithil* trees,
near the south-eastern corner of the city. The wells here
varied from six to eight fathoms in depth, and nowhere, so
far as I could ascertain, in the Buraida district was water
found so near the surface as six feet, which Palgrave gives as
the greatest depth to water he found anywhere in the Qasim.
A new well recently excavated in the Jarada space reached

---

[1] Considered as an oblong 1210 yards long and 725 broad.

[2] The *Nafud* ridges nearer the *Wadi* lay nearly due east and west, perhaps
rather E.S.E. by W.N.W.

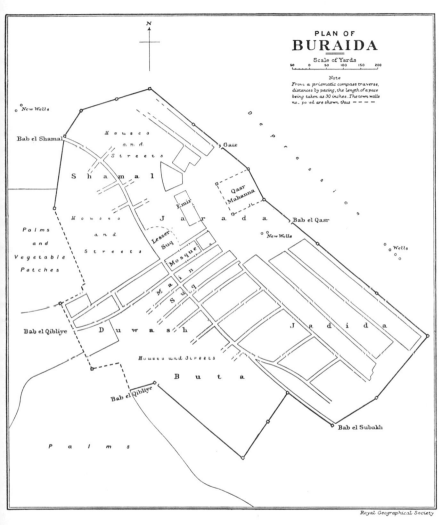

PLAN OF
BURAIDA

Scale of Yards

50   0   50   100   150   200

Note
From a prismatic compass traverse,
distances by pacing, the length of a pace
being taken as 30 inches. The town walls
no. po ed are shown thus — — — —

N

New Wells

Bab el Shamal

Houses
and
Streets

Shamal

Houses   J   a   r   a   d   a
and
Streets

Palms
and
Vegetable
Patches

Lesser
Suq
Mosque

Main
Suq

D   u   w   a   s   h

Gate

Qasr
Mahanna

Emir

Bab el Qasr

New Wells

Wells

J   a   d   i   d   a

Bab el Qibliye

Houses and Streets

B   u   t   a

Bab el Qibliye

Bab el Subakh

P   a   l   m   s

Royal Geographical Society

PLAN OF BURAIDA.

To face page 196.

water at twelve fathoms, and another I saw in the course of excavation near the south gate, in which water had not yet been reached though it was thought the workmen would not have to go deeper than nine fathoms.

In all there are four main gates roughly at the four cardinal points, of which those on the north and east sides are the most important—the latter being used for southward and eastward traffic, while caravans coming from and going to Jabal Shammar or the Hijaz use the former. The western gate or *Bab al Qibliya* gives access only to the palm-groves and the *Nafud* ridge, while the southern portal or *Bab al Sabakh* is also of only suburban significance. A second gate, also giving access only to the palm-groves and also known as *Bab al Qibliya*, has established itself between the two last named, while there is an unimportant postern in the east wall north of the main gate or *Bab al Qasr*. The great fortress known as Qasr Muhanna stands in a commanding position between the two eastern gates, a length of the main east wall forming its own eastern flank. Roughly a square of a hundred yards it projects westwards from the wall into a considerable semicircular clearing—traces of former house foundations clearly indicate that the troubles of past governors have preached the wisdom of having a clear field of fire round the official residence. This open space and the buildings immediately surrounding its semicircular fringe comprise the so-called Jarada quarter. South of this are the quarters known as Jadida (to south-east), Buta (to south-west), and Duwash (to west round the *Bab al Qibliya*), though one does not hear these names at all frequently, if ever, on the lips of men. The Jarada quarter, being the ordinary camping-ground, is however often named, as also the quarter known as Al Shamal, the northern quarter, which occupies the whole space north and west of the Jarada and north of the *Suqs*, which form a quarter of their own in the heart of the city. The main thoroughfare of the city leads from the north gate to the lesser *Suq*, probably the original *Suq* of a less prosperous time—an oval camping-ground surrounded by shops which continue for some distance northward up the main street. These shops are for the most part occupied by the smiths, who seemed to be eternally busy hammering out the rough pots and pans which represent the metal-work of the city. Live-stock, mostly camels, were apparently sold in the Jarada quarter, where on one day of my stay I saw a large concourse of Arabs and their animals, the latter being sold by auction. As each bid was made and called by the auctioneer and recalled and called again, the particular victim in the ring would make frantic efforts to escape, but without any visible effect on the crowd of eager buyers or watchers. The bidding was so leisurely that in the case of one animal the sum offered rose from 70 to only 80 dollars by one dollar steps during a quarter of an hour. The patience of the auctioneer was quite amazing. Immediately to the south of this *Suq*, and occupying a very central position in an angle formed by the crossing of the main north-south street already mentioned and a broad thoroughfare connecting the east and west gates, stands the great mosque, a spacious building measuring 100 yards from east to west— its axis is perhaps rather E.N.E. by W.S.W.—and a little less than forty yards in width. According to some accounts this mosque, comparatively recently built, occupied the site of the original castle of the 'Alaiyan governors of Buraida, known as Qasr Hujailan, where Doughty abode two days as the guest of ' Jeyber.' In any case the ' square minaret ' which Doughty mentions could not have been the minaret as it now is—tapering to a slender point from a broad circular base—and it is clear that some changes have taken place in the buildings of Buraida since those days. On the whole, after hearing various accounts of the matter, I came to the conclusion that Doughty's ' *Qasr* Hujailan ' probably stood on the site of and possibly formed part of the subsequent extension commonly known as *Qasr* Muhanna or Hasan's [1] *Qasr*, which now in its own turn forms but the kernel of the great *Qasr*, which had been considerably extended in area by 'Abdul 'Aziz Ibn Rashid and was undergoing much structural improvement and rearrangement at the time of my visit. The only entrance to the *Qasr* was the main door in the middle of the south side. From this a dark corridor, about 50 feet long, 10 broad, and 15 high, leads under the living-rooms above to an inner entrance to the courtyard,

---

[1] After Hasan Al Muhanna, a former *Amir* of Buraida.

INTERIOR OF GREAT FORT OF BURAIDA WITH NEW MOSQUE UNDER CONSTRUCTION.   To face page 199.

from which one ascends by a stairway to the great *majlis* or public reception-room on the first floor. To the right, as one faced north, was the old *majlis* constructed by Ibn Rashid, while about two-thirds of the length of the south wall had been taken up for Ibn Sa'ud's new reception-room or rather suite of public or semi-public apartments. The new *majlis* was 44 feet in length, 22 feet broad, and about 18 feet high ; adjoining it was a retiring-room of the same width but only ten feet long, with a spacious bathroom beyond it and perhaps other apartments, the whole suite being continued inwards by a broad pillared veranda from which one looked out on the old *Qasr* Hasan, occupying the north-west corner of the courtyard, and the new buildings—a mosque and private apartments for Ibn Sa'ud himself—which were in course of construction in the north-eastern section. The roofs of the various sections of the *Qasr* were surrounded by walls almost six feet high with the usual stepped pinnacle crenelations, and the whole fortress was dominated by a lofty central tower on which during these days they hoisted the familiar arc-lamp which had been brought along from Riyadh, together with other household paraphernalia, including a number of female slaves. This last item I had on the authority of one of the slaves in attendance on me, but though the suggestion clearly was that these women served as concubines—the only evidence of recognised concubinage under the *Wahhabi* code which came to my notice—I never felt sure that the information was reliable, and have often thought that these female slaves were brought up to the Qasim as a gift to Ibn Sa'ud's wife at 'Anaiza. Unmarried slave-women are, nevertheless, ' *halal* ' or lawful under the code of *Islam*, and children borne by them are recognised as the offspring of their father—Ibn Sa'ud had, I believe, one daughter by concubinage at Riyadh. One of the girls brought up to the Qasim was said to be of quite tender years and another was subsequently given over to Ibn Nasban in wedlock. At the *Wahhabi* capital slave-women are allowed a considerable amount of freedom in the matter of seeing the men and women of their own kind, but here at Buraida, with so many spouseless slaves in the train of the army, they were kept in strict seclusion.

Immediately south of the great mosque [1] runs the grass-market, the eastern end of which leads into the Jarada space and in which at all times might be seen large numbers of women selling lucerne or desert-grasses—*Nussi* and the like. From this street as also from the parallel street on the north side of the mosque two doorways gave admission into the latter's open courtyard—occupying about a half of the whole space and leaving the remainder for the pillared and roofed *Liwan*. Another door there was on the narrow east side of the mosque, and yet another—for the private use of the governor and, of course, of Ibn Sa'ud and his family when in residence—on the west side near the shallow outward bulge of the *Qibla* niche. Beyond the grass-market southwards lay the main *Suq*, consisting of a broad primary street lying north and south with about a hundred shops on each side and numerous side streets, each of which seemed to be devoted to a single class of goods. The main street on the other hand had a more mixed assortment of wares on sale in its shops—rock-salt in great reddish-brown blocks, cardamum and other spices, coffee, onions, dates, melons and pumpkins. Another part of the main street was devoted to the sale of saddle-bags, coffee-mortars of sandstone, cloths of various kinds, guns (one of these, a wretched old specimen, I saw exchange hands at three dollars) and meat. The main meat-market, in which camel-meat seemed to be dominant, was in one of the side streets. The crowd of buyers presented an animated scene in the mornings, when it was often almost impossible to move without jostling human beings or sheep or lines of camels bringing in fodder or firewood. I estimated that there must be at least 800 shops in all in the two *Suqs* with their various branches, and there may well have been more.

Apart from the great open space of the Jarada the whole area of the city seemed to be very fully occupied with buildings, though it was only recently that the southern section had been engaging the attention of the local masons. This area was, however, rapidly filling up, and at this period it seemed that the building profession was

---

[1] There were about a dozen mosques in the city, all of which had circular minarets tapering from a broad base to a slender top.

having a good time. The earth for mortar-making was, I
was told, brought from a depression some distance away in
the northern *Safra*, which also supplied the quarries from
which the required building material was brought. Buraida
was in every way a better-built city than 'Anaiza—indeed
one might almost have thought that its construction had
developed in accordance with a well-thought-out plan. It
was also larger, and, making every allowance for the fact
that its buildings were more spacious and better spaced than
those of its rival, I came to the conclusion that the population
of the city could not well be less than 20,000 souls. Its
component elements were said to be Shammar, Bani Khalid,
'Ataiba, Subai' and the inevitable Tamim (Al Wuhaba
section), to say nothing of the mixed stock of Bani Khadhir.[1]
The prevalent religious outlook was *Wahhabi* and distinctly
fanatical, but the fanaticism seemed to be of a different
quality from that of the desert—a town-bred fanaticism
with well-developed outward features and little depth or
sincerity.

Before leaving Baghdad for Arabia nearly a year before
I had been commissioned by an old friend, Sulaiman al
Dakhil, to carry a letter and a sum of £10 in gold for a relative
of his named 'Abdul Rahman al Dakhil. In the meantime
the latter had received letters informing him of the trust committed to me, and the very day after my arrival at Buraida
one of the clerks in attendance on Ibn Sa'ud came to me
saying that 'Abdul Rahman, being unable to leave his shop,
had asked him to get the letter and money from me. Realising that the real reason was not truly stated, I replied that
I could only hand over the money in person and, accordingly,
'Abdul Rahman visited me the same afternoon. I received
him with befitting coldness, and the young cub—he was
barely out of his teens—beat a hasty retreat, not without
taking the pains to count out the golden coins for himself.
I never saw him again.

But I did make the acquaintance of another resident of
Buraida who sent a message through Rushaid that he would

[1] To this belonged a large proportion of the household officers and
attendants such as Ibrahim al Jumai'a, Rushaid, Shilhub even, and more
surprisingly still Ibn Suwaidan, the confidential clerk, whose features were
of the pure *Najdi* type, 'Uwaid and Ibn Nasban.

like to renew an acquaintance begun at Basra and was
anxious to invite me to his house. I had no recollection of
his name—'Abbas al Fallaji—and was quite satisfied that I
had never set eyes on him before, when, one morning as I
came in from a visit to the *Suq*, Rushaid unctuously introduced a man with whom he was conversing in our courtyard :
' This is 'Abbas.' I passed on with no more than a formal
salutation, and when my visitor a few minutes later followed
me to my room, he had to admit that in fact he had never
met me before. ' But once,' he said in self-defence, ' I saw
Captain Wilson.[1] And also I remember meeting the great
Cokas at Baghdad, but that was long ago in the days of
Sultan 'Abdul Hamid.' Not the noblest of 'Abbas' idiosyn-
crasies was the obsession that he was personally acquainted
with everyone of note within the ken of his little world, and,
after all, it was not difficult for an Arab to confuse the names
of Sir Percy Cox and Sir William Willcocks, the great irrigation expert, with whom he had had a chance encounter.
By reputation a man of low degree and indifferent character,
'Abbas was of Shammar origin and had transferred his
residence from Haïl to Buraida some twelve years previously
—for some reason about which he preferred not to talk.
Why he wanted to receive me in his house I could not fathom,
but when I suggested that the afternoons were generally free
so far as I was concerned, he immediately replied that he
himself was seldom in except at night. Obvious though the
reason was for this suggestion of a nocturnal visit, I found
myself one night a few days later wending my way after the
evening prayer towards the southern part of the city, where
'Abbas had purchased a house for the sum of 1000 *Riyals*.
The hall-door, like most of the doors in the better class of
houses, was of massive timber with a central crossbar studded
with heavy nails, the knocker being a plain metal ring of
about an inch and a half in diameter. Immediately within
the door was a small bare hall, to the left of which was the
entrance to the coffee-parlour, as good a room from the architectural point of view as I saw during the whole of my
sojourn in Najd. The walls of masonry were about eighteen

---

[1] Captain (now Sir Arnold) A. T. Wilson, Deputy Chief Political Officer
of the Mesopotamian force.

inches thick, with three doorways—other than the entrance
—giving access to various parts of the house, and were
covered with a plain brown clay plaster. They rose to a
height of about 25 feet including a sort of clerestory gallery,
supported on pillars (ten in all) and running round the whole
circuit of the chamber, whose length and width were 25 and
15 feet respectively. There was no attempt at mural decoration other than a *Wasm* [1] mark in white paint at one end of
the room and a single *fleur-de-lys* pattern over the coffee-
hearth at the other, but here and there were faint traces of
triangular mouldings in very low-relief. The roof of *Ithil*
rafters laid upon palm-trunk beams was supported by the
pillars already mentioned, which terminate in plain rectangular capitals picked out with a very faint design of a
triangular moulding. A low wall surmounted by a line of
stepped pinnacles concealed the galleries from observation
from below.

Such was the reception-room of 'Abbas, who modestly
admitted that there were perhaps three or four other houses
at Buraida as good as his, and told me that it was not more
than ten years old. We sat round on carpets with a profusion
of cushions made of the best Manchester fabrics, and I was
greatly impressed that one of so little apparent merit should
be so luxuriously installed. 'Everything I have,' said he,
'I owe to Ibn Sa'ud,' and I concluded that perhaps the
Wahhabi monarch had found ways and means of making use
of his humble and apparently unworthy subject, to whom I
was at any rate grateful for the opportunity he gave me of
seeing and examining at leisure the interior of one of the
better houses of the leading city of Central Arabia. On one
occasion I was praising the elegance and comfort of the
Qasim houses in general, when Ibn Sa'ud, partially agreeing,
warned me against supposing that all the rooms of the houses
were on the same scale as the public reception-rooms. In
general other rooms were bare, and no house was provided
with proper bathrooms—one had to bathe in the open or use
a living-room temporarily for the purpose. Consequently
neither the men nor the women of the Qasim bathed over

[1] This was painted on a pilaster in low-relief continuing downwards
the central clerestory pillar at the end of tho room.

much, but at Riyadh the practice was much commoner. Buraida was famous for its masons, and the improvements being carried out at this time in the palace at Riyadh were under the supervision of a Buraida man specially engaged for the purpose.

As at Riyadh, the roof of my quarters commanded a fair view of the neighbouring house-tops, on which at sunset and in the early mornings I often saw the women of the city at their ordinary vocations. It was specially at sunset, when all the men of the population were certain to be at prayer in the mosques, that the rank and fashion of Buraida's female society paraded on the roofs, the women taking courage to move about unveiled and exposing the glory of their braided locks. I saw perhaps but half a dozen of the better class of women thus—and they all unconscious of my interest—and none of them struck me as justifying the boast of Qasim in the beauty of its daughters. One lady I observed, whose apparel [1] was far from new or fine, as being particularly devout and regular with her ablutions and prayers, but for the most part the women did not seem to observe strictly the prescribed hours of prayer, particularly in the mornings, when they often prayed long after the sun was up. One evening I was forced to an ignominious retreat behind the cover of my walls when two young ladies on a not distant roof not only showed no signs of bashfulness on discovering me gazing out upon the scene, but displayed a lively interest in me and my appearance.

One day—it was Friday, when it was Ibn Sa'ud's custom to distribute alms to the poor and needy—I noticed at least 200 women of the poorer sort, clad in dingy black smocks and muslin veils, seated in lines along the outer wall of the *Qasr* and the walls of the houses round the edge of the Jarada and taking advantage of their very slender shade at noonday or early afternoon. There they sat in all patience waiting for the dollar or fraction of it that might be their weekly portion, and thence later in the day I saw them all trooping back over the open space. As they went, I saw a slender spiral of dust ascending from a sand-eddy on the ground to a height of 100 feet and moving slowly and gracefully along,

---

[1] The commonest colours were red and a dirty indigo.

whereat from many of the women arose pious exclamations
to avert such consequences as might be portended by such
a phenomenon. ' There is no God but God,' they said, and
' I ask pardon of God.'

On another occasion—it happened to be the day on which
Ibn Sa'ud went off for his short visit to 'Anaiza—I sallied
out for a walk with Mitrak and Mirwij as was often my
custom. Having no special objective in view, I struck at
random through a maze of side streets which brought us to
the fringe of the *Suq*. Here in a side street was established
a line of women selling miscellaneous wares—one had a
basket of saffron petals, two others sold a coarse white sugar,
while yet another had before her a basket full of odds and
ends—scraps of cloth, cotton, etc. Japanese matches were in
general vogue here—the ' Lion Brand,' made in Japan for
the Parsee (Bombay) firm of Bhimoiwala, and the ' Rex '
being most in evidence, whereas at Taïf I had found the
products of Austria and at Riyadh the matches of Austria
and Sweden. Rifle ammunition, which cost a dollar for 17
and 15 cartridges at Shaqra and Riyadh respectively, was
comparatively cheap at 20 per *Riyal*, the chief purveyors
thereof being Harb tribesmen, who got it for nothing from
the Sharif. We passed on into the fodder market, which
was doing great business from the piled-up stacks of green
stuff and desert-grasses. And so continuing past the shops
I noticed little groups of shopkeepers and clients who looked
up at us with a cold hostile gaze. I stared back at them with
a steady glare—feeling somewhat hostile at the thought
that much of their wealth was achieved by traffic in the
products of the infidel—and they lowered their eyes. Apart
from the pots and pans already referred to, the manufactures
of Buraida related mostly to the leather and kindred indus-
tries, comprising camel saddles and camel furniture of all
kinds, saddle-bags, head-ropes, sandals, leather gun-cases,
scabbards, cartridge belts, etc. And so we passed out of the
city by the south-west gate into the prosperous gardens
beyond, where the ground was spread with a rich carpet of
lucerne or variegated with pumpkin trailers. Here and
there too were small groups of cotton plants—with smaller
leaves than in the south and less rank in growth—whose bolls

were just bursting to expose the white fluff within. For the most part cotton is grown in this district as a border plant in unimportant quantities. Patches of green millet varied the peaceful prosperous scene, through which flowed bubbling runnels of well-water in every direction. And in one place I came across a little reservoir formed by the obstruction of a well channel with a small dam of masonry, through a hole in which flowed the water with a pleasant bubbling as of mountain brooks, while beyond it two channels flowing at right angles to each other crossed—the one passing over the other on a short aqueduct of stone slabs.

Everywhere the palms towered above us, lofty and dense, with their great clusters of fruit, in great part not yet ripe. Here and there were rude bowers of palm branches for the labourers to rest in from their daily toil. And so, as we wandered, we came to the further extremity of a large garden which we had entered by an open pathway. Our further progress was obstructed by a long low wall of earth, still wet, at one end of which a small group of men were still at work on it. To avoid a tedious *détour*, I cleared it with a bound, and my companions having done the same after a moment's hesitation, we became suddenly aware of the owner of the garden shouting at us angrily. ' What are ye doing coming through my garden ? There is no way through it and our womenfolk are about [this was untrue]. Fie upon you ! ' As usual in such circumstances I tried to avoid a scene by continuing on my way without paying any heed to the blustering of the fellow, who was certainly not near enough to have recognised me ; but the underlying cur in him got the better of Mitrak, who in spite of my orders dawdled along at some distance behind me shouting out abuse at the other party. This infuriated the owner, who advanced with renewed vituperations, while Mitrak stood his ground defiantly and Mirwij turned back to support him. My hand was thus forced, and I had to go back to exert my authority on my companions, who very unwillingly broke away from the prospect of a scuffle, but at the same time I had the satisfaction of noticing a look of wonder and astonishment spread over the owner's face as he recognised me and turned away without further parley. He could go, I shouted after

him, to Ibn Sa'ud if he had any complaint to make instead
of wasting his anger on the dogs that accompanied me.
With that I turned on Mitrak and dismissed him forthwith.
He went off sulking, and when I got home I was astonished
at being asked by Dr. 'Abdullah what had happened.
Mitrak had gone straight off to the *Amir* to report that I had
sent him to lay a formal complaint against the offending
owner, who had been sent for and was about to be committed
to prison on the ground that he had insulted me and actually
laid hands on Mitrak. I was thus only just in time to prevent
a miscarriage of justice, and it was Mitrak who spent the day
in solitary confinement in the kitchen, unutterably shocked
at my having publicly denounced the whole of his pretty
tale as a pack of lies. I had, however, distributed bounty
in respect of the last march the previous day, and he lost
little that he really valued.

During my peregrinations of the morning I had seen Sa'd
al Yumaini in the *Suq* and noticed that he had quite deliberately turned his back on me as if he was expecting
somebody from the opposite direction. Equally deliberately
I walked up to and confronted him with a greeting, whereupon
his manner immediately changed, and he replied with effusive
friendliness though there were witnesses of the scene. He
declared, perhaps truly, that he had paid me a visit the
previous night when I was out, and at all times I was convinced of his essential friendliness, though his fear of public
opinion was enhanced by the ever-present danger that his
enemies might report on his conduct to an extremely bigoted
old father of whom he stood greatly in awe. Besides, Sa'd,
whose first experience of active service had been at Bukairiya
in 1904 when Ibn Sa'ud defeated Ibn Rashid and his Turkish
allies, had at one time himself been a wearer of the white
chaplet, though he had since repented of such energy and
taken to the seductive weed in secret. At this time he was in
especial attendance on the young princes Faisal [1] and Fahad,[2]
the former being slightly the elder and, according to Sa'd,
a boy of much charm and gentle withal ; while Fahad was
a regular little spitfire, ever spoiling for a fight, and even at

[1] Now Viceroy of Mecca ; he visited Europe in 1919, and again in 1926.
[2] He died during the influenza epidemic of December, 1918.

the tender age of twelve exhibiting tendencies towards bigotry. Quite recently he had drawn his sword on one of his attendants, wounding him on the arm and cutting his mantle, but had been driven by shame to make amends with an apology and a new cloak.

The same afternoon—Ibn Sa'ud having departed and no work or other activity being in prospect—I had indulged in a siesta rather earlier than usual and had slept till late in the afternoon, when Muhammad Ibn Shilhub came up to inform me that, having come to fetch me to Turki's *majlis* soon after the midday prayer, he had found me asleep and left me to my slumbers. In reply to my protest that all my efforts to see something of the society of the place were ending in failure and disappointment, he promptly invited me to breakfast with him on the morrow and agreed with me that Rushaid was a broken reed. He certainly had the kindest of hearts and quite a sense of humour. ' You must excuse,' he said, ' the boorish simplicity of my household, for, if you would know the truth, my wife, though very beautiful, is a terrible shrew and so unpleasing to me that for two days I have not been near her.' The woman, who was the widow or perhaps discarded wife of a member of the great Ibn Sharida family, had possibly been offered to Ibn Sa'ud, who had, however, passed her on to his treasurer, and it was only fear of displeasing his sovereign that was at this time preventing the latter from putting her away. She had furthermore borne him a son—still an infant—but the unfortunate Shilhub was saddled with her former husband's progeny—a grown-up son and others. Such is their domestic bliss at times. Yet he confessed that now and again, when he was far away from this lady, he actually found himself thinking fondly of her, though when with her he was never in any doubt that he hated her. She had nevertheless a great reputation for cooking *Marquq*, and I was welcome to try it if I would.

Therefore on the morrow, when Hamdani fetched me, I accompanied him to Shilhub's house beyond the main *Suq* in a side street leading towards the S.W. gate. We gained admission by a door of solid *Ithil* timber studded with large iron rivets and adorned with a chain knocker in place of the usual small metal ring of this city—the solid knockers of

'Anaiza were apparently unknown at Buraida. The coffee-parlour, though well furnished with rugs and cushions, was distinctly dingy with its bare walls of undecorated clay plaster. A central pillar of masonry coated with white gypsum supported the roof and a similar pillar was embedded in the wall, which was probably a later addition to a larger room supported by a row of pillars. Among the guests bidden to meet me was one Sa'ud, an under clerk on the royal clerical establishment, and 'Abdullah Ibn Nasban, who came in for a good deal of light banter and ribaldry by reason of having wedded [1] afresh the previous night. Breakfast was served in a small outer hall and very excellent it was, though the lady's *Marquq* was a disappointing mess of sodden bread flavoured with shredded onions and a rich sauce. In addition there was a great dish of rice with mutton and venison, to say nothing of fowls, hard-boiled eggs and egg-fruit boiled in halves. And I felt justified in telling my host as I took my leave that, with a spouse capable of preparing a meal so delicious, he had not really much to complain of. I have already commented on the paucity of fruit at Buraida, though I personally had little to complain of in this direction, for Muhammad al Sulaiman, who had accompanied Ibn Sa'ud back to 'Anaiza, taking with him certain presents from me for his younger children, was kind enough to send me two kerosene tins full of fruit from the 'Anaiza gardens. I therefore had a full supply of peaches, figs and pomegranates —to say nothing of dates—for some days, but it was by no means an unmixed blessing. The flies began to resort to my quarters in distressing numbers, and they were the horrid drowsy flies of summer—a positive plague of them—which were too lazy to do anything but drown themselves in my tea or even drinking-water when not disturbing my siesta by crawling over my face.

Fahad Ibn Mu'ammar had kindly placed his stable at my disposal, and one afternoon I rode out on a fine grey stallion of his with Manawar and Mirwij along the Haïl road, which leads almost due north over a grit plain to the *Safra* [2]

---

[1] *See* p. 199.

[2] This *Safra* comprised a series of steppes starting from distinct cliffs on their west sides and running down in gentle slopes eastward. Three such steppes were visible from my point of view.

wilderness, through which it strikes along a shallow valley in a north-westerly direction. From a cairn on the nearest point of the latter I had a splendid view of the whole Buraida area, the central tower of the great fort being due south and the plain being dotted with the dark lines of the numerous oases around the city. The *Nafud* appears to subtend the *Safra* boundary in a spacious semicircle, the space so enclosed being an extensive plain broken at intervals by sand-ridges of lower elevation and of whiter sand than the *Nafud* itself. For the rest its surface was partly of grit on the *Safra* side and occasionally of clay. The drainage of the *Safra* area runs down the Haïl road and other channels southward to irrigate the cultivation of the district, the best general view of which is certainly to be obtained from this point on the Haïl road, though the view of the city and its immediate surroundings from the watch-tower on the first *Nafud* ridge was perhaps more attractive, and a good view was also to be had from various points on the ridge of Wahtan (taking its name from a large palm patch and dilapidated hamlet close by) to the eastward. A low sand-ridge separates this little oasis from the next one eastward called Khudhaira —a small hamlet and a good grove of palms—and behind that again a sand ridge, on which is a watch-tower [1] with a commanding view of the surrounding country, conceals the small oasis patch of Khabb al Qabr.[2] To the north of the city at no great distance lay the ruin-field of Shamas, reputed to be the original site of the first settlement of Buraida. Its remnants seemed to be of comparatively recent date— mere mounds of crumbled clay with traces of stone-work— but, search as I might, even with the unwitting assistance of Manawar and Mirwij, who performed great feats of excavation in an unsuccessful effort to rout out a *Jarbu'* from its hole, I could find not the slightest trace of anything interesting except a number of land shells and a single fragment of coarse pottery. To westward of it under the edge of the *Nafud* lay the palm grounds of Matrahi, and through Shamas, past its ruined watch-tower, runs the road to Qusaiba and other settlements of north-western Qasim.

[1] The central tower of the fort was slightly north of west from this point.
[2] Other palm-groves or hamlets in this neighbourhood were named to me as 'Ukairsha, Sumair and Rafi'a.

Ibn Sa'ud returned from 'Anaiza on 3rd September with his imposing cavalcade of 25 cavalry and 44 cameleers mounted on 22 camels. The first day he had spent as the guest of the old ex-*Amir*, 'Abdul 'Aziz ; the second with Salih al Fadhl ; and the third and last at the house of Muhammad Ibn Sulaiman al Shubaili, a wealthy merchant with very extensive properties at Basra. And thus, having as it were distributed his favours equally among the leading families of 'Anaiza, he returned to the rival city with a clear conscience to face the rapidly-approaching campaign. I found him somewhat querulous. He had hoped for a great improvement of the situation in the East as the result of Sir Percy Cox's return to 'Iraq, but, apart from a very slight though satisfactory modification of the Kuwait blockade arrangements, no effort had been made to unravel the 'Ajman tangle, and it was clear that the Basra authorities were in general not in agreement with me as to the desirability of placating Ibn Sa'ud. He now put forward the redoubtable Faisal al Duwish himself to explain the effect on his fellow-tribesmen of the Mutair of being forbidden to indulge in counter-raids, though he admitted that occasionally they disregarded the embargo as the Buraih had recently done at Riqaï, where they had captured forty camels laden with coffee, rice and arms *en route* to Haïl. Moreover, we did not know yet in Arabia that Sir Percy Cox had merely returned to Baghdad *en route* to Tehran, where he was to be the British Minister. I could only urge that the capture of Haïl was the only solution of Ibn Sa'ud's difficulties, and he was sufficiently conscious of that fact to have fixed a date for the concentration of his forces at Buraida. He had originally fixed on Mudhnib as the centre of the concentration, and Turki was to go down in due course to bring up the force which Ibn Sa'ud would accompany for the initial stages only, but he had since modified his plans and the *Hilal* or new moon of the coming month (*Dhil Hijja*) was definitely to see the opening of the campaign, and, though Ibn Sa'ud was a little nervous on financial grounds lest the duration of the operations should exceed his capacity to maintain them, I knew that I had sufficient latitude in this direction to help him when his need of help was proved.

A day or two before this a messenger from Dhari Ibn Tawala had arrived with letters for me. At first he had been turned away from my door by my too officious attendants, but he managed to find an opportunity of presenting himself before me. Dhari's letter was disingenuous in the extreme, being a long plea that I should use my influence with the Basra authorities to restore his monthly allowance of Rs. 3000 in lieu of the reduced subsidy of Rs. 1000 which he had been receiving since my recommendation that he should receive nothing at all. He made no attempt to explain away his desertion of his post at Hafar, and he had taken the precaution of sending his message by the hand of a half-wit—Hadran by name—in order that I should not be able to ascertain the details of his iniquities. My reply was made verbally through the same channel, but I know not whether Hadran ever had the courage to report the failure of his mission to his master. I expressed quite candidly my opinion of Dhari's betrayal of his trust, and added that I could have no communication with him until he resumed his post at Hafar and came in person to see me. Hadran begged me not to misjudge his noble master, and pleaded hard at least to have the message in writing. All was in vain, and he departed broken-hearted when I rejected his final appeal for a little present for himself.

The situation on the Hijaz frontier was at this time more or less quiescent, though the latest news indicated the presence of the *Amir* Shakir at Marran with a hostile concentration of regular troops and *Badawin* auxiliaries. He had, however, seriously alienated a considerable part of the latter by the issue of orders for the forcible collection of *Zakat* from Ibn Humaidi, an 'Ataiba chief who had paid taxes and owed allegiance to Ibn Sa'ud. The effect was immediate, for Ibn Humaidi summoned the whole of his following and marched with it to join the defenders of Khurma, who had also received considerable reinforcements from the southern valleys. An *'Atabi*, who arrived at Buraida soon after our arrival, created something of a sensation by the light he threw on the ambitions of the Sharif. 'If you surrender the whole of Najd to him,' he said, 'he will not relent ; if you give up to him all your women and

children and your men, yet will he not relent ; it is your
religion that he is bent on crushing.' For an ordinary
Baduwi it was an astonishingly accurate estimate of the
position, but it was after all common knowledge in Arabia,
and even the Buqum, formerly loyal adherents of the
Sharifian cause, had begun to have qualms about the justification of these attacks on their neighbours—Arabs like
themselves—and Ibn Sa'ud had recent information that their
house was divided against itself with the result of disturbances
and trouble at Turaba. Ibn Sa'ud was at this time seriously
concerned to secure from me a reasonable definition of
British policy in the event of complications arising out of
the Khurma situation. I could only tell him that the British
Government appeared to have accepted the Cairo contention
that Khurma lay within the territories of the Sharif, in which
case they could not logically object to any action the latter
might take to establish his authority there. But I added
that I had made further representations with a view to the
reconsideration of the whole matter. He was entirely frank
with me and warned me that he could and would accept no
responsibility for any action the people of Khurma might
take in the event of the attack being renewed.

However these matters might be, preparations were now
well forward for the march against Haïl, the secret of which
had been tolerably well kept, for, though everyone knew
vaguely what was coming, even Turki had no exact knowledge
of his father's plans until 5th September, when orders were
issued to bring in the royal camels from Tarafiya where they
were grazing. That evening, as I sat on the western sand
ridge with Manawar, we saw a number of cavaliers practising
the evolutions of warfare, one of whom, observing us, came
and joined us after his jousting. This was Sulaiman, more
commonly known by his nickname of Ra'i al Qauda, a slave
whose reputation as a warrior had travelled far and wide
through the desert country and whose name was a terror to
the *Badu*. In various combats he had had nine horses killed
under him, and it was clear from his enthusiastic manner
that he was looking forward to fresh opportunities of distinction. But why, they asked each other, had the gates of
Buraida not yet been shut ? Usually for three days before

the start of a *ghazu* the gates would remain shut lest traitors from within should go forth with news of the coming operations.   And during this period anyone found lurking suspiciously in the neighbourhood of the city would be arrested, while on one occasion a year or two before, of which they spoke, a spy from Haïl had actually ridden straight into Ibn Sa'ud's *Gom* during a night march, having apparently failed to see the ' pillar of fire '—or masked lantern which replaced the *Bairaq* after dark—which went before it.   It was not till 8th September that, the secret being well out and everything ready for the army to start on the morrow, I found the subsidiary gates locked and bolted, while the main gates were under guard.   From that moment no unauthorised person was allowed to leave the city, but it would surely have required but little intelligence in the enemy to realise what was in the air.   The various *Ikhwan* contingents were camped all over the Qasim in the various *Khabbs* to lessen the difficulties of grazing and watering.   And, though Ibn Sa'ud had men out all over the district roping in loiterers or suspicious persons, I felt that Ibn Rashid and the *Shammar* in general had full warning of the storm about to burst on them.

During these few days—since my first casual meeting with him—I saw a good deal of Ra'i al Qauda, who had volunteered to train a pony which Ibn Sa'ud had presented to me quite recently.   I found him to be quite an extraordinary person with a passion for horses second only to his passion for fighting.   He had started life—so far as his memory went —in the service of some *Shaikh* of the Harb and had passed, by capture in a foray, into the service of the 'Ataiba, whence he had come by gift into the possession of Ibn Sa'ud.   He appeared to be absolutely devoid of intellect—except in the matter of horses and war, in which he was a genius—and his slowness of comprehension was greatly accentuated by a partial deafness.   His knowledge of Arabic was also quite defective.   Nevertheless he was the first to congratulate me on the choice I had made out of three horses brought up from the Hasa by Ibn Sa'ud's orders for my benefit, and to assure me that I had secured as fine an animal as could be found in Arabia.   As a matter of fact the necessity of making

a choice had somewhat embarrassed me. There was no
possible doubt as to which was the best of the three animals,
but he happened to be but a yearling—I think exactly fifteen
months old at this time—and therefore of no immediate
use to me for riding purposes. The other two were older
animals, and I chose the best and least serviceable of the
three in the hope that I might have a reasonable excuse for
leaving him behind when I should depart. Meanwhile Ra'i
al Qauda exercised him—I thought with excessive zeal and
vigour considering his tender age—and in the end the animal
followed me to Basra, where he entered upon a somewhat
chequered career until, my own almost equally chequered
career coming to an end in Trans-Jordan during 1924,
circumstances compelled me to sell him into bondage in
Egypt. There he fell into the best of hands,[1] and, when I
saw him again in 1927 on the race-course at Alexandria—the
first time I had ever seen him race, and that in what was
probably the last race of his career—I heard again the words
of Ra'i al Qauda, but this time on European lips, and I heard
him praised in terms that absolutely astonished me. He
was said to be the best Arab that ever came to Egypt, where
he had headed the first class of his kind for three seasons
and, in spite of a tenderness in one leg which was a serious
handicap to him and invariably interfered with his training,
had had a good record in actual racing.[2] He was indeed a
beautiful animal and full worthy of the princely treatment
now being accorded to him in his old age. His months of
infancy had also been spent in luxury, for, when he came to
me, he had never tasted barley—the ordinary horse-food of
Arabia. He had indeed, as the old man who brought him
up to the Qasim told me, been brought up entirely on camel's
milk and dates, and was only just beginning to nibble at hay
and lucerne. His name was Marzuq, but he was subsequently
renamed in Mesopotamia from his colouring—he was a

[1] Mr. A. L. Benachi, the well-known owner of race-horses, of Alexandria.

[2] In addition to about half a dozen races won in Mesopotamia between
1919 and 1923, his Egyptian record is as follows : 26 races ; 9 firsts, 3 seconds,
and 4 thirds. The following passage occurred in an article in the *Egyptian
Gazette* of January 26, 1928 : "How many of the good old type like
Romany or *Amir* present themselves here for sale to-day ?—the answer is
not two in a blue moon."

flea-bitten grey—and for the rest of his life remained under the name of Rummani (often mistransliterated in other ways).

According to Ibn Sa'ud the Arabian horse trade had at this time definitely entered upon a period of decline, from which there appeared to be little hope of recovery. This state of affairs owed its origin to the substantial diminution of the number of horses available in Arabia during the period of anarchy, which preceded Ibn Sa'ud's accession to his ancestral throne, and of war, which had accompanied the establishment of his authority. A great number of horses had been killed during those troublous times and local demands absorbed all the products of the Arabian studs. This process had possibly driven the Bombay horse-dealers to seek elsewhere for their requirements, and for some years now the prices obtainable in the Indian market had not been such as to encourage export. At any rate Ibn Sa'ud had only made a profit of Rs. 1000 on ten horses he had recently sent to Bombay, and was inclined to think it scarcely worth while to worry any further about the matter. Indeed the knell of horse-breeding in Arabia may have sounded with the advent of the high-velocity rifle and the motor-car, and the maintenance of studs will perhaps remain only as the hobby of the wealthy. For in Arabia, as in England and elsewhere, it is scarcely likely that the decline in the practical utility of the horse will circumscribe its popularity on the national playing-fields. It was always, as they put it, to ' play ' that they rode out in the afternoons, and often I joined young Turki and his companions in their recreation, which consisted mainly of galloping exercises. Turki claimed to have the fastest animal in these parts, a glorious mare of the *Wadhna Kuhaila* breed, but Salman al 'Arafa was not far behind with a chestnut stallion, which had recently won a long-distance race in which the *Wadhna* mare had not competed. And on one of these occasions, when I saw Faisal Ibn Rashid riding with stirrups so small that it seemed impossible for him to disengage his foot in the event of a fall, I was shown a yearling colt, also of *Wadhna* provenance, which was expected to turn out exceedingly well. These afternoon joustings, in which even Faisal and Fahad, perhaps twelve or thirteen years old at this time and delicate-looking creatures, took part, lasted generally half an hour or more and ended in an outdoor session until the sunset prayer, before which I was always careful to take my leave. Water was the only refreshment served round, and I noticed once, when I had called for some, that the servant served young Sa'ud and others before coming to me. I thought perhaps that it was to obviate others drinking from the cup profaned by my lips, but in this I was entirely mistaken, as the same cup continued its course after it had come to me. The horse-' play ' of Arabia reaches its zenith in the hunting of the gazelle with *Slugi* hounds—a fine sport. Hawking is of course well known, but I saw little if anything of it, though in the Mesopotamian borderland it is much indulged in. Hare-coursing with *Slugis* is of course the common sport of the country.

Apart from the decline of horse-breeding, the general economic situation was a subject of constant discussion between my host and myself. In spite of all appearances the Qasim was by no means self-supporting. In a normal year dates had to be imported from the Hasa to supplement the 'Anaiza produce, which was inadequate to meet the requirements of the population of the city and the *Badawin* dependent on it. The same applied to Buraida, and at Riyadh the situation was such as to call for special rules. The *Badu* were allowed to purchase fresh dates there without restriction during the first month of the season, after which the sale of *Ratab* to them was prohibited in order to facilitate the laying up of supplies for the winter. The market was, however, again opened up to the tribes towards the end of the season.

The Qasim, like the other provinces of Najd, pays the usual *Zakat* to the central treasury, but, at any rate at the time of which I write, the administration of the area reabsorbed practically the whole revenue. The bulk of the state expenditure was accounted for by doles, presents and subsidies to all and sundry in accordance with a recognised scale and by the cost of the ecclesiastical establishment of *Qadhis*, *Nawwab*, *Muadhdhins*, etc. Ibn Sa'ud reckoned that, excluding the receipts from the Hasa and the seaports, no less than 70 per cent. of the whole revenue of Najd itself—from the Qasim to Wadi Dawasir—was reabsorbed in this way, leaving only 30 per cent., the total amount of which it would be difficult to assess, for public purposes.

At this time the prices of the ordinary necessaries of life ruled low in the Qasim, which had formerly done a flourishing transit trade with Hail and whose old Shammar customers now entered its markets at their peril. At Hail on the other hand everything was at famine prices in spite of occasional leakage of goods from 'Iraq. Rice, for instance, sold at 4 *Sa's* to the £T1 as against 2½ *Sa's* to the *Riyal* at Buraida. 'Adwan [1] Ibn Rimal, who had recently visited Ibn Sa'ud bringing with him as gifts a fine mare and *Dhalul* which had been refused, had begged in vain for permission to take away with him just enough for his own family's requirements in the matter of piece-goods and food-stuffs. To all such applications Ibn Sa'ud had but one answer : ' So long as you remain in the North you shall have nothing that I can prevent you having, but move down to the Bashuk waterings and thence to the Tawal Mutair and you shall be even as we are.' Another Shammar *Shaikh*, Ibn 'Ajil, had recently got away with 200 loads from Shinafiya, and Shammar agents continued to smuggle goods out to desert *rendezvous* whence they were taken up and sent to Hail. But Ibn Mu'ammar had, or was said to have, his spies at Hail itself, and Najdi smugglers doing business there were liable to summary punishment by the confiscation of their properties at home.

The great difference between the two great cities of the Qasim was always represented to me as being that, while the citizens of 'Anaiza—and those of Shaqra were of somewhat similar calibre—were enterprising business men on a large scale, the leading families of Buraida were only cameleers by profession. The former, accustomed to trade with great commercial centres like Baghdad and Basra, 'Amara and Kuwait, Bahrain and Bombay, were constantly in touch with the great world ; while the latter moved only between the interior and the coast as carriers of merchandise and only

---

[1] He was of the Ghafila subsection of Sinjara and was accompanied by his cousins Shati and Salim, sons of Fahad Ibn Rimal, and Naif Ibn Muhairit Ibn Rimal. Others of his party were : Shali'an Ibn Mustalih of the 'Aqni and Khashara Ibn Sa'di of the Kharsa subsection of Jarba' ; Miyah Ibn Falih Ibn Shilqan ; Salbi Ibn Manzil ; and Hadhdhal Ibn Khaima of Al Ja'far.

touched the fringes of civilisation—revelling in its vices and luxuries for a few brief weeks at a time and reviling them at home lest the truth should be suspected by their own folk.

Nevertheless they sometimes brought back unimpeachable evidence of their contact with a laxer morality in the shape of diseases here properly called 'foreign.' Dr. 'Abdullah was always insistent on this point and claimed that all venereal cases could be traced directly to the coast. A case he had recently seen and treated with partial success had originated fifteen years previously at Kuwait, and he declared that in Najd he had never come across women of the towns suffering from the disease, though he had known it in *Badawin* women infected by their husbands. He worked intermittently as a doctor, having several cases of rheumatism on his hands during these days of our sojourn at Buraida and many 'eye' cases too—these were very common.

As at 'Anaiza the playground of the Buraida children was the public streets, and so far as my experience went they were entirely devoid of the crabbed rudeness of their elders. As a rule they gaped at me awesomely as I passed, but they never showed any inclination to molest or even crowd round me. A large proportion of them seemed ever to be girls, charmingly pretty children ranging down from seven years to babyhood. They wore no more than a single smock of crimson with or without the full sleeves of their mothers' garments ; generally they went bareheaded, their hair being gathered up in half a dozen plaits heavily greased and smeared with henna. Long hair is perhaps the best appreciated of all feminine charms—' her head is so long,' they say of women who surpass their sisters in this respect—and it is at about the age of seven or eight, when they begin to wear the veil for the first time, that girls are marked down in the streets and bespoken by would-be husbands or fathers-in-law, as one might purchase yearlings at a horse show. Of the grown women themselves one saw but little in the streets except their ample outer garments, though at times, rounding a corner, one might catch a glimpse of the smock below—generally red though sometimes black and, more rarely, green or other colours—and the shapely figure outlined by it before the veil was hastily drawn across. The women, like the men, seemed to have graceful figures, firm and well-knit without any tendency to corpulence.

An important accession to the *Wahhabi* cause materialised during our last few days at Buraida in the arrival of one Salih Ibn Jabr of the Rashid family, who had become disgruntled and disgusted at the difficulties attending life at Haïl. He brought down definite news of the safe arrival and subsequent despatch on a mission to Jauf of an important enemy agent [1] who had been reported killed in the course of Lawrence's operations on the Hijaz railway, and he also reported that Ibn Rashid had recently received as a gift from the Turks 45 camel-loads of goods from Damascus, 20 of these being of piece-goods, ten of ammunition, and the rest of miscellaneous articles, including coffee, sugar and money. Salih had come down to the Qasim with a man from 'Ajaimi's camp—whether a refugee or an emissary I did not discover —which was at the wells of Hazil. Colonel Leachman, commonly known in the desert as Injaiman, and Mit'ab, the son of Fahad [2] Beg Ibn Hadhdhal, the great and aged chief of the 'Amarat, had been harrying 'Ajaimi's bands, and matters in the enemy's country were so unsatisfactory that Ibn Shuraim, an important *Shaikh* of the 'Abda and either cousin or nephew of Ibn 'Ajil himself, was reported to be contemplating desertion to Ibn Sa'ud.

Other arrivals from Haïl—refugees or pretending refugees with ulterior commercial designs—included a number of persons who had not long since been at Damascus and therefore had or were believed to have recent and accurate news of the front. The Germans, they said, had made arrangements calculated to secure Syria from serious danger, but were not in a position to advance. The Turks had been at their last gasp when we had advanced to and occupied Salt, but timely German assistance and the unaccountable withdrawal of the British had saved them from complete disaster. The economic position in Syria was very serious, and a famine threatened unless the Hauran crops could be made available for the Turks—yet the Germans were already diverting large quantities of the grain of that district

[1] 'Abdul Hamid al Masri.

[2] He died at an advanced age in July, 1927, at Baghdad.

to Europe. Jamal Pasha ' the great,' as he was called, had vacated the command-in-chief in Syria to become Minister of Finance at Constantinople, while his namesake, known as ' the little,' commanded in his place, and a Turkish official had replaced the former *Wali* of Syria.

The desert between Syria and the Qasim was, according to these people, so insecure that Rushaid Ibn Laila, who was still at Damascus, was experiencing considerable difficulty in arranging for the forwarding of his stores and guns—three of the latter—to their destination. The caravan of 45 camels already referred to, though fully franked through with *Rafiqs*, had to buy its way through to the tune of £1000 and a box or two of ammunition. Nuri al Sha'lan of the Ruwalla was coquetting outrageously with both parties and was making a fortune by franking Syrian agents through to 'Aqaba as his personal retainers authorised to buy and bring up stores to Jauf—their real destination being Damascus. The impression that at this time Nuri's territory was the main source of supply to the enemy was confirmed independently by a native of Buraida, Sulaiman al Rashudi, who had been in Syria since the early days of the war and had now come back by a direct route [1] involving a leisurely journey of thirty days. He seemed to have no idea that in visiting me he was guilty of a solecism, and he made no bones about accepting the cigarettes which I offered him. Occasional supplies had from time to time filtered into Damascus from Haïl, though he had not himself passed or seen the large caravan of a thousand camels already mentioned. But 'Aqaba was the most important source.

Another casual acquaintance of this period was destined to be my companion for many days thereafter. This was Hamād Ibn Mash'ān Ibn Hadhdhal, an *'Anazi* of the 'Amarat and distantly related both to Fahad Beg and Fahad al

---

[1] The stages of his journey were given by him as follows : First day, Damascus to Dumair ; three days on to Al Halba ; four days on to Mat (rested three days) ; three days on to Maqarr al Naqa ; three days on to Judaida (? 'Ar'ar) ; two days on to Maqarr al Ghadhari (halted one day) ; three days on to 'Aqailat Ibn Sukhail between Hazil and Hazam al Ma ; three days on to Haiyaniya (halted one day) ; three days across the *Nafud* to Shu'aiba ; three days on to Qusaiba ; two days thence to Buraida. The journey occupied thirty-five days, including thirty days of actual marching.

Dughaim.   A grizzled beard and weather-beaten features
made him look older than he was, but he certainly seemed
to me to be nearer 50 than the 40 years which he admitted.
He had come down to Riyadh, where I had once seen him,
with a present of horses from Fahad al Dughaim, but had
met with disaster on his way back to the 'Amarat pastures.
Travelling with a single companion he had fallen in with an
Aslam raiding-party at or near the Hidaqa wells, and the
pair had been stripped of all their belongings even to their
shirts and sandals.   Such treatment is considered scandalous
among the northern *Badu*, he said, but the rest—from the
Shammar southwards—have no such scruples.   Yet these
raiders refused to admit or disclose their identity or their
destination, which he judged to be the Ruwalla camps.
Naked and miserable Hamad and his companion had betaken
themselves to a *Sulubi* encampment near by, and with the
kindly assistance of the gypsies had found their way back
to Buraida to refit.

At Zibira they had met a convoy of 100 camels—30 loaded
with piece-goods and the rest with coffee, rice, sugar, etc.—
under 'Abdul 'Aziz al Bassam, nephew of Muhammad, a well-
known merchant prince of Damascus and himself the son
of Doughty's friend 'Abdullah of 'Anaiza, on their twelfth
day out from Kuwait *en route* for Haïl.   And near Hidaqa
he had seen the traces of a caravan of 300 camels, which had
a day or two before passed down in the reverse direction to
bring up more provisions.   With it had ridden the 'Ajman
Shaikh, Ibn Munaikhir, with his daughter, whom he had come
up to fetch away after her recent divorce by Ibn Rashid.
Hamad, who subsequently became something of a bore, had
at this stage all the appearance of being a desirable addition
to my little *côterie*, and I soon obtained Ibn Sa'ud's permission to keep him with me.   The very next day he was of my
party ; ' but,' said he, doubtless hoping for monetary compensation for the loss of his reputation, ' the tongues of
Buraida have already begun to wag against me.'   I assured
him there was no adequate cause for nervousness on that
score, but he replied with a proverb [1] and absented himself so

---

[1] ' *Idha surt gharib sir adib*—i.e. If you are a stranger in the land be
modest.'   Perhaps this is as near as the Arabs get to ' When in Rome do
as Rome does.'

completely from the evening meal that a search-party failed
to find him—he rejoined me later for my wanderings and was
always full of curious desert lore picked up in years of
constant movement over the whole of the Northern *Hamad*
from Aleppo to Madina. He had often come across the *Oryx*,
whose spoor, he said, is as that of cattle. And even when it
rains they drink not, being *jāzi*[1] all the year round like the
desert gazelles, though the latter are, he declared, known at
times to come down in great herds to the sea and to drink
their fill, whereupon they become completely dazed and are
easy of capture. Hamad had frequently met with the ostrich
and spoke also of the wild ass as existing in the Jazira, though
too wild, even when they have been in captivity since early
youth, to be broken in for riding purposes.

As I wandered with him to the crest of the *Nafud* ridge to
have perhaps a final view of Buraida, we saw the faint
crescent of the new moon over the western horizon. On the
morrow there would begin the movement for which I had
laboured so long, and I knew already that I was myself to
see nothing of it. I had had a long interview with Ibn Sa'ud
in the afternoon, and I had urged that there was only one
solution of his difficulties—an immediate move against Haïl.
' Well,' said he, ' you shall see. There are 20,000 men camped
in this district, and all yearning for the martyr's reward.
You shall see. To-morrow I ride.' ' And I with you,' I
replied. ' No,' said Ibn Sa'ud, and after long argument he
had dismissed me with a hint I could not ignore. ' We have
quarrelled greatly to-day—what is the time ? '

5. A Tour of the Khubub

At dawn on the 9th September, 1918—the sixteenth day
of my sojourn at Buraida and the third day of the last
month of the one thousand three hundred and thirty-sixth
year of the Muhammadan era—the war-flag of Ibn Sa'ud
went out through the city gate northwards. The die was
thus cast for a struggle which was to decide the fate of
Arabia probably for a generation and possibly for much

---

[1] *Jāzi* would seem to denote ' subsisting on the moisture of the pastures
without recourse to actual drinking.'

longer, and which raged over the face of the desert in the
desultory fashion of Arabian warfare until 23rd December,
1925, when the green banner of *Wahhabi*-land was hoisted
for the first time on the flagstaffs of Jidda. Peace was then
at long last to descend upon the great peninsula which had
known not peace from the beginning of time, but in September, 1918, one could only look down an endless vista of
war without knowledge of what lay beyond it. And for ten
long months it had been my single-hearted endeavour to
direct the steps of Ibn Sa'ud into that dreadful avenue.
The stakes were big. The hegemony of Arabia would be
the winner's prize. But my purpose was to bring yet another,
though a small, hammer to work on the red-hot anvil on
which world-peace was being fashioned in the forge of hell.
So I rejoiced when they brought me news that the army had
gone forth.

Ibn Sa'ud himself would set forth later in the day to catch
it up at Tarafiya, and I went to plead with him again for
permission to accompany the army. It was all in vain.
Triumphantly I demolished all the arguments he adduced—
all except one. My company would definitely destroy the
illusion of a *Jihad* on which he ever played to fan the enthusiasm of his followers. He always maintained in public
that my presence at his court was occasioned solely by
blockade and Sharifian problems, and that I had no special
interest in his campaign against Ibn Rashid. He would tell
them, nevertheless, that he had invited me to accompany
him, and that I had refused on the ground that the Hail
business was no concern of mine. I was anxious, he would
say, to depart, but it was he himself who insisted on my
staying until all difficulties of a political nature had been
settled. Whether such dust was sufficient to dim the dull
vision of sour fanatics I could not tell, but Ibn Sa'ud had
made up his mind and argument was useless. All that he
would agree to was that I should rejoin him at Tarafiya or
elsewhere after the first assault, and, hoping that the *rendezvous* might be Hail, I took my leave protesting against his
decision.

Our interview had been punctuated by diversions necessitated by the constant need of Ibn Sa'ud's personal attention

to the details of administration. The whole fabric of the *Wahhabi* state rested on his shoulders. He had some days before dictated a letter to *Shaikh* Salim of Kuwait, which I characterised on seeing it as somewhat provocative or at any rate as lacking in any indication of a real desire for harmonious relations. He had reconsidered and redrafted the message, of which a fair copy was now brought in for his signature, which he withheld until I had read and approved of the text. The secretary then whispered something in his ear, to which he replied, ' Let him come in.' A moment later the slim figure of Fahad Ibn Jiluwi darkened the doorway timidly and I became the sole witness of a strange scene. Ibn Sa'ud suddenly seemed to become as one possessed. He rose swiftly from the ground and in a moment was towering majestically over his young cousin and laying about his slim shoulders with his riding-cane, blow upon blow, in merciless wrath. At first the boy was too dazed to think of self-defence or escape, and then, recovering from his stupor, he closed with his sovereign, clinging to his neck, and a moment later he was fleeing incontinently from the room pursued by Ibn Sa'ud. I felt uncomfortable until the latter resumed his seat by me as if nothing had happened and told me with a smile that the same morning the boy had dared to strike one of the *Zigirt*, an offence he would tolerate from no one, and one which he himself only committed under the gravest provocation, very rarely. The royal bodyguard was privileged.

Ibn Sa'ud, accompanied by his escort, left Buraida during the afternoon. All day long odd parties of stragglers dribbled out towards the trysting-place, and towards sunset I ascended the central tower of the *Qasr* to watch them wend their way across the desert until, group after group, they passed beyond the horizon or into the dusk. The general direction of the march was north-north-east. Below me in the Jarada lay some 200 camels still waiting for their riders, and the rear was to be brought up by the Buraida contingent under Fahad Ibn Mu'ammar, which would start at dawn on the morrow. During Fahad's absence the governance of the city would be in the hands of his brother, 'Abdul Rahman. That day and the next I remained at Buraida trying to forget my disappointment in the trivialities of conversation and exploration, but I had Ibn Sa'ud's permission to spend the time of waiting at 'Anaiza.

'Abdullah Effendi was left behind with me and Hamad of the 'Anaza. The latter was full of desert tales, and in reply to my questions confirmed the existence of a primitive tribe of which Talaq the 'Ataibi—father of Nasir who was of my party to Wadi Dawasir—had spoken to Shakespear in 1914. Hamad could not say whether it was a section of the 'Ataiba but gave its habitat as the hill country along the sea coast, a country partly of mountains and partly of sand somewhere to the right of Mecca and left of Egypt ! The young men and women of the tribe go naked, the latter wearing their hair long and loose over their breasts. Before marriage the girls wear a sort of sporran (*mirka*) suspended from a string round their waists and also cups (*Qubba*) over their breasts. The men wear no head-dress. I have often since those days tried to verify this tale, but have never found any reason to think it really applies to any Arabian community. Perhaps it is only an echo of some traveller's yarn of experiences among the Nuba highlands.

Hamad had seen something of the Yazidis, among whom, he said, the *Wahhabis* would have short-shrift with the stock expression of their moments of boredom : *A'udhu billah min al shaitan*. And he had had experience of hunger and thirst in the desert, which led to talk of feats of abstinence from food and drink. He had once gone seven days without food in the rainy season when water was plentiful, and Dr. 'Abdullah told of a *Dausari* who crossed the eastern desert from Riyadh to the Hasa on foot carrying neither water-skin nor provisions, but trusting to rain pools for water and to chance meetings with human beings for food. In the extremity of hunger the *Badu* will cup [1] their camels and bake the blood into clots for food, and a Mutair raiding-party is said to have existed fifteen days on nothing but the hump fat of a single camel, each man having a lump of it as big as a fist, not to eat but to rub at intervals on his lips and over his face and chest. 'Aïdh, the *Qahtani* companion of my first ride to Riyadh, came in as we sat chatting. He accepted my

[1] *Yufassidun.*

invitation to join us at dinner that night and failed to keep
the tryst, but next day he came back with Gharib, who insisted on planting a kiss upon my forehead. And we talked
pleasantly of that first journey and of the southern desert
beyond it.

Another visitor during these last days was Muhammad al
Sulaiman of 'Anaiza, who had come hither in connection
with an inheritance case which he and the other party had
agreed to place before Ibn Salim, the *Qudhi* of Buraida, for
arbitration. He brought me a large quantity of peaches and
pomegranates, together with an invitation to lodge with him
at 'Anaiza on my return thither. Dr. 'Abdullah was included
in the invitation, which to me was the more welcome for the
opportunity of living in the town and wandering about freely
at all times.

On 11th September we started. The latest news from the
north was that Ibn Rashid had left Haïl some days before
to raid the Harb at Nabhaniya, but had turned back on his
tracks on receiving news of Ibn Sa'ud's intentions. Rumour
had it that he was but weakly supported, as the bulk of the
Shammar were away on the 'Iraq border and the only
important *Shaikhs* present in the Jabal were Ibn Shuraim
of the 'Abda and Ibn Rimal and Ibn Rakhis of the Sinjara.

The summer was now definitely in its decline, and though
the thermometer still showed readings of 104° and 105° there
was generally a breeze to keep the air fresh and cool. And
the sun was back again within range of my sextant's arc,
enabling me to get observations for time and latitude. The
usual delays attended our start in spite of all the assurances
of the previous night that camels and guide were ready. I
woke at dawn to hear that Rushaid had gone to fetch the
animals and to find that breakfast was being prepared.
Muhammad Shilhub, the Treasurer, tried to cheer me with
the news that this time an excellent guide had been found
for me, who knew every inch of the Qasim, and after breakfast Rushaid triumphantly announced that all was ready.
But Hamad had been overlooked—he was not very popular
—in the provision of *Dhaluls*, and I vetoed an unseemly
suggestion that he should ride pillion to one of the others.
Further delay ensued, and in an hour's time the necessary

mount was found. And, after a final and unsuccessful appeal from 'Abdullah to travel by the ordinary route instead of going by the *Khubub*, we actually mounted soon after 9 a.m. and in a few minutes were outside the north gate. I had developed a heavy cold and headache, but took heart of the prospect of 'Anaiza before us after an inhospitable sojourn in the surly, dour atmosphere of its northern rival.

Our course was north-westerly at first over a gently undulating plain of light sand and gravel bounded on the west by the *Nafud*, along whose edge lay the palm strip of Shamas [1] with its sprinkling of cotton plants and *Ithils*, its lucerne patches and few mud huts. We crossed the site of the ancient village, leaving the tower to our right, and shortly afterwards entered the *Nafud* area. The first of the *Khubub* was a trough lying south-east by north-west with the palms of Ghaf at the southern end with huts and subsidiary cultivation as at Shamas—the ordinary type indeed of the *Khabb* settlements. ' What is the name of that patch ? ' I asked of Ghazi, our guide, a man of the Harb tribe. He gave me some answer at random, to which I replied with another question : ' Where is Ghaf ? ' ' Ahead of us,' he answered, ' some distance off.' ' No—this is Ghaf.' ' Who says so ? ' he asked. ' The people living in it ! ' I replied. And it so happened that two men riding on asses were coming from the direction of the huts, bound for Shiqqa. I sent Mirwij to make enquiries, and their answer came to us loud and clear : ' Ghaf.' Ghazi now began to shuffle. These *Khubub* were miserable little spots whose names were of no concern to anyone. The country he did really know lay beyond Nabhaniya, and that lay well beyond the limits of our present programme. Our guide seemed to be letting us drift too far to the north-west towards Shiqqa, and as he appeared to have no very clear idea of the course we ought to be shaping, I turned south-west. The *Safra* or gravel plain—the lowest steppe of the Sara wilderness—lay beyond the sands about a mile to our right. On our path lay Quai', another *Khabb* whose main section lay half a mile to the south-east. We touched an outlying patch of cultivation surrounded for

[1] This patch was also named to me as Matrafi, which is probably the name of one of its wells. My present guide called it Jurda—probably wrongly.

protection against the onslaughts of the sand by a young
hedge of *Ithils* and guarded by a single *Qasr*. The *Ithil* hedge
is a characteristic feature of the Qasim.

Beyond this we came to a single *Qasr* and a thin line of
Ithils called simply Al Khabb, with the palm patch of
Huwailan a mile away to the south. Further marching over
a tract of scattered sand dunes brought us to the extensive
oasis of palm-groves and *Ithil* plantations called Muraijisiya.
Backed by a sand ridge of some height its groves lay em
bosomed in bays of encircling sand, and though it was barely
11 a.m., I decided to halt in protest against this aimless
wandering without a guide. My tent was pitched before a
beautiful carpet of rich green lucerne by a small but dense
palm-grove with a thick fringe of *Ithil*. They called it Jariya.
Its wells, some six fathoms deep, were worked by camels—
two to each well—for the irrigation of a considerable field
of sprouting millet. By fasting and phenacetin I brought
my aching head under control towards the evening after a
day of idleness.

Next morning Ghazi was superseded in the post of guide
by an uncouth lad from Muraijisiya. 'Ali was not more
than fifteen, and his experience was circumscribed by narrow
frontiers, but within those frontiers he was an expert. He
had been as far as Buraida, but had never seen 'Anaiza.
Westward he had ranged as far as Bukairiya, but he had never
actually visited Shiqqa, easily visible from where we lay—his
home. For him Muraijisiya was the hub of a small universe
—a village of 500 souls perhaps, buried in a palm-grove. Its
man-power contribution to the territorial forces of the
Wahhabi realm was no more than six strong, but in this
respect it claimed a superiority over Busar and Dharas—to
be visited during the day—which provided respectively four
men and three, complete of course with rifle and *Dhalul*.
The composition fee in lieu of service was 70 dollars a head,
and in any case the *Khubub* were not called upon except in
the case of general mobilisation for great forays. The land
tax is calculated at five per cent. of the annual produce of
the palms. The population of Muraijisiya is of mixed stock
—Harb, Mutair, Shammar and other elements.

Half a mile beyond Jariya lay the hamlet of Himar, two

palm-groves with 50 souls to tend them. West of it was Hamlan, a long straggling patch of palms and *Ithils* supporting 50 persons in a few *Qasrs*. A lofty ridge of deep soft sand divided this depression from that of Niqra, a thin strip of *Ithils* with a few *Qasrs*. Muhabil lay to the right in the same trough which debouches on to the gravel plain of Butain, and 'Araimdhi to the left. On the average these lesser *Khabbs* seemed to have a population of from 20 to 30 souls.

The next ridge looked down on a wide sandy depression in which lay Dharas, extending for a mile along our right flank and backed by a high sandy ridge, perhaps 150 feet above the level of the depression. Around it at various intervals lay Hilwa, Suwailimiya and Daïsi, typical lesser *Khabbs*. The palms of Dharas, dotted with many *Qasrs*, were of considerable density and the village itself of some size, unwalled and of mean mud huts with a single turreted *Qasr* of better mien in the centre. It boasts a population of 300 souls, mostly Tawajir—a section of 'Anaza—under an *Amir* called Waïl. In this oasis citrons and vines added distinction to the ordinary features of *Khabb*-land.

Khabb Raudhan lay next in our path with lucerne and vegetable cultivation of some richness and walled groves in an oval depression surrounded by high dunes. It had three or four *Qasrs* and a population of 100 souls, whose military contribution was one man. Then in turn we passed Khabb Dirija, where ten persons eke out their lives in a single *Qasr* on the produce of scanty palms, and Nakhalat—four *Qasrs* and forty souls cultivating lucerne, and at this time preparing for an extension of cultivation by the planting of an *Ithil* barrier round a patch of light sandy soil.

The summit of the next sand-ridge gave us a splendid view of the surrounding country. Far away in the plain to the west out of a vast flat without other excrescence rose the conical hill of Saq. Very little to the west of north lay Shiqqa, with its two watch-towers keeping guard over the three or four palm-groves nestling at the base of the *Safra* cliff. Westward of it extended the *Mamlaha* or dry salt lake, on which the Qasim draws for its salt. Northward of a line drawn west from our position the landscape was a vast flat gravel plain. To south and south-west all was sand, wave after wave, with the little oasis of Mansi and its *Qasrs* at our feet, and the village of Busar, the most westerly oasis of the Khubub district, standing out in front of its extensive palm-groves.

From here the track passes between the walled groves of Mansi, where we found a masonry drinking-trough fed from a well and pumpkins growing in addition to the usual items of cultivation. Then we reached Busar and halted by one of its wells with good water near an outlying group of huts. It was only 9 a.m., but we were in no hurry and the charm of the place and its people induced us to abandon all thought of resuming our march till the morrow. In fact we had no particular plans for the future, and I was aiming vaguely at visiting Bukairiya and possibly even Khabra and Rass. But the news imparted to us at Busar was unfavourable to the development of my plans. Ibn Rashid's raiding-parties were abroad, it was said, and that very morning two men of the village had been robbed of their *Dhaluls* on the return journey from Bukairiya. I suspected that the culprits were probably Harb elements taking advantage of the unrest caused by Ibn Rashid's excursion to do a little highway robbing on their own account. In either case we were not numerous enough to risk such an adventure, and decided to march as straight as possible for 'Anaiza.

Our camp was pitched within a ring of *Ithil* trees near the well, which like the other wells of the oasis was about seven fathoms deep, lined with masonry and provided with a reservoir from which runnels of stone-work led away to the cultivation. In the palm-groves, denser than any I had seen in these parts except at Sabakh, the air was moist and tepid with a tropical richness reflected in the luxuriant under-growth of garden crops. And all day long the weary watchers let off their ancient matchlocks to frighten away the preda-tory fowls of the air. Those that fell were gathered for the pot of some frugal household, but these were few, for the guns were amazingly inadequate—one I saw was a strange weapon five feet long, and another had been bought for no more than four dollars. There is but little wheat or barley cultivated in the *Khubub*, the main corn tract of the Qasim

lying round 'Ain Ibn Fuhaid and the Asyah region. But
here was an abundance of vegetables with vines and citrons
and the inevitable lucerne.

The population of Busar may be about 400 souls drawn
from the 'Ataiba, Subai', Suhul and Bani Khalid, to which
last belonged the *Amir*, Muhammad Ibn Muhaimid. Another
Muhammad—throughout the day I did not come across any
local man whose name was not Muhammad—of the poor folk
of the oasis insisted on the honour of entertaining us, being
the owner of the well by which we were halted. He led us
to a cabin of mud and seated us on the *Nafud* sand which
formed the floor of the smallest and dingiest parlour I had
seen, a room about fifteen feet long and seven feet broad with
rough mud walls and a roof of untrimmed palm logs and
Ithil rafters, all black with a sooty grime. His coffee was
very poor, but he made amends with excellent dates and his
hospitality was only limited by his means.

The afternoon we spent in a delightful excursion through
the thickest part of the oasis and up the lofty sand ridge
behind it, which rises like a hog's back to a summit worn to
a thin edge by the wind. Below us to the south lay the little
oasis of Ghammas—all else was sand with the *Safra* behind
and its sentinel Saq and the towers of Shiqqa. At our feet
was the oasis of Busar with its village of perhaps 80 houses
near the centre, disposed in two groups close together.
Here we sat and talked on the summit of the *Jurda*, as they
call the ridge. And as the afternoon wore on we began to
be thirsty, whereupon young 'Ali went bounding down the
steep sand-slope like a stag. ' It is the season of *Ratab*—fresh
dates,' said Ghazi the *Harbi* ; ' it acts on the townsman even
as the spring with its plenty of camel-milk affects the *Badu*,
making them strong and cheerful.' Ghazi himself, I noticed,
wore the *Ikhwan* chaplet, and was indeed the son of one who
had settled at Artawiya. He was deeply religious, but his
soul, restricted by the village life, pined for the desert, and
his father had given him permission to go forth on his own
account. He had been about to hie after Ibn Sa'ud when he
was detained for my service by the *Amir* of Buraida. As
a guide in these parts he proved useless, but in other respects
I found him a delightful companion, quite without bigotry,

proud of such knowledge as he possessed and ready to impart
it. And that night I struggled with him in a partly successful
endeavour to get a record of the sections and subsections of
the great tribe to which he belonged, ranging from the
Dahna to the Hijaz. The Bani Salim and Bani 'Amr he
allotted to the west, Bani 'Ali, Al Wuhub and Al Farida to
the east.

In Busar there was no appearance of fanaticism, and during
the morning one of the villagers—Muhammad like the rest
of them—came into my tent and asked for tobacco on the
strength of having been appointed as our guide to 'Anaiza.
And during the day whether in the village or in the gardens
I found the people friendly and polite. I should have liked
to dally here other days, but by the evening of the morrow
Busar was far behind us—probably never again to be seen
by me. From it our course lay southward or somewhat eastward of south past the dense walled oasis of Muwaih Shu-
wai'ar about a mile from Busar. Its walls were in somewhat
ruinous condition, and its four *Qasrs* supported a population
of some forty souls. At its further end was a straggling
patch of *Ithils*. From the next ridge we looked down on
'Aqul close by to the west with four *Qasrs* and descended to
Ghammas, already seen in the distance from the ridge behind
Busar. It was a long straggling settlement with a number
of palm-groves linked together by patches of lucerne and
vegetables. In it were some dozen *Qasrs* with a population
of about 120 persons, the family and dependants of 'Abdullah
al Ghammas of *Dausari* origin, the *Amir* and apparently sole
owner of the settlement. The wells here were only four
fathoms deep—an indication of our approach to the line of
the *Wadi*. Beyond its mile-long expanse lay a miserable
little oasis called Sabakh, apparently of recent creation and
supporting some thirty inhabitants in six mud huts. Here
we left the Khubub district with its high ridges and deep
troughs behind us to enter upon a tract of low sandy downs
with a greater profusion of *Nafud* vegetation. Here for the
first time in the Qasim I came across the graceful *Ghadha*,
which is most plentiful to the eastward of Buraida and has
gradually disappeared from central Qasim under the depredations of man and beast. The *Qirdha* broom was more

plentiful here than elsewhere in my experience, showing
obvious signs of much grazing, and besides these two were
the ordinary plants of the sand desert in plenty.

The well-worn track passes across a highly saline depression
called Nimriya, at the further end of which we came upon a
patch of *Ithils* and two long-abandoned wells. The salt,
which lies in a brilliant white streak in the centre of the
depression, had apparently proved too much for an incipient
settlement. Westward of this line the *Nafud* extends
without interruption to the neighbourhood of Bukairiya,
where it degenerates into a plain of light sand in which lie
the settlements of Rass, Khabra, Budai'a, etc. We were
on the edge of a desert tract in which raiding-parties might
be about. We marched cautiously, and the darker line of
the 'Anaiza *Safra* ahead was the only relief in the monotonous
expanse of dunes. And then, coming across it, we saw a
solitary old woman riding a donkey homeward to Ghammas
from 'Anaiza. She seemed to be untroubled by dreams or
imaginings of lurking foes. Yet a few moments later I
noticed to our right a marked depression coming through
the sand which I took to be the *Wadi*. Our guide, who had
had the tobacco of me yesterday, appeared to be taking us
too far eastward, in which case we should cross the *Wadi* at
a point already known to me. In answer to my question he
stoutly denied that the depression to our right had anything
to do with the *Wadi*, but I was sufficiently confident of my
bearings to defy his expert knowledge, and turned aside
with some caustic remarks about guides in general and him
in particular. At this he appeared to take offence and asked
permission to depart, which I immediately granted, whereupon he slipped without further ado from his pillion position
behind 'Aiyadh and made off on foot without even suggesting
that a partial payment of his partial services would be
becoming. This certainly surprised me, but I understood
when 'Aiyadh came up to say that, when I had turned off
westward, the guide had whispered that I was heading
straight for the danger-zone. That information increased
my interest in the horizon, but I rode on into the depression,
which is known as 'Adaïm al Falq and apparently constitutes
a former channel or back-water of the *Wadi*. It was encircled

with sand on all sides except the south-west, from which direction came an arm of the main channel. A few moments later we crossed a well-marked track running east and west between the *Wadi* settlements and Khabra, and from it we looked down on the *Wadi* itself. The solitary building of Qasr Ibn Jabr linked up my position with the rest of my wanderings, and afar off beyond the channel and the sands we could just see the palm tops of 'Anaiza. Continuing along the track we came into view of the most westerly plantations of the *Wadi* oasis and the *Sangars* on the *Safra* behind 'Anaiza. We struck across the channel at this point, where it makes a wide bulge to the north near the bushes of Ruwaidha, and soon crossed the actual torrent channel, whose general direction seemed to be from south-west to north-east. From here I could see the valley to westward, about half a mile wide, for about five miles back to a range of pink ridges of the *Nafud*, where is an *Ithil* patch and well called Hufaira.

As we approached Qasr Ibn Jabr we saw a large herd of grazing camels whose herdsmen, taking fright at us, proceeded to drive them off out of our track. I sent Mitrak forward to reassure them, and the stampede ceased. Such are the alarms of a border tract when the states on either side are at war. At the *Qasr* is a single well, and we passed on to the *Nafud* beyond, from whose first crest we saw the palms of Malqa ahead, with those of 'Anaiza beyond, the groves of the *Wadi* settlements being to our left. Passing Juai' we topped the next ridge to find the great city displayed before us, and in half an hour we were admitted to the house of our host, Muhammad al Sulaiman al Hamdan, where we were to spend the time of waiting until it should please Ibn Sa'ud to summon us north.

6. LIFE AT 'ANAIZA

I plunged headlong into 'Anaiza society. Muhammad at our arrival was in the act of making coffee for other guests, including an old acquaintance of mine in Fahad al 'Aqaili, *Amir* of Mudhnib, who had been all this time at Buraida with Ibn Sa'ud and was now on his way back home. I sat down by his side and entered into conversation on the ordinary topics of the day. The *Wahhabi* forces had left Tarafiya before dawn of the previous day (12th September), and Ibn Sa'ud would thus be practically certain of encountering Ibn Rashid in the open on his hurried way back from the neighbourhood of Jabal Aban, where—it was now definitely known though details were wanting—he had latterly been in conflict with the Harb of Ibn Nami, recently his own subjects but now converted to the cause of his rival. So we talked on very pleasantly until Dr. 'Abdullah, who had stayed back to see to the baggage and our accommodation— having himself a very pretty idea of the requisites for comfort —joined us, whereupon Fahad turned to me. ' Are you, then, Philby ? ' he asked. ' *Wallah !* I didn't recognise you, and have been wondering who the strange *Baduwi* was, but of course you were with 'Abdullah and now I remember. Forgive me.' And then we resumed our talk about all things and sundry. Sturdily orthodox he was without fanaticism, and more enlightened than the extent of his travels would seem to promise. He had made the pilgrimage to Mecca in 1915, the last *Hajj* of the Turkish *régime*, but had not gone on to Madina. Otherwise he had never been out of Central Arabia, not even to Kuwait or Bahrain. Of his hospitable reception of guests in his castle at Mudhnib I have already written.[1]

The coffee-drinking done with and Fahad departed, 'Abdullah and I ascended to the rooms reserved for us—the same rooms as Ibn Sa'ud had occupied when staying recently as Muhammad's guest. The main room or parlour was about 25 feet long, 10 broad and 18 high, with a plain white gypsum frieze, picked out at the top in a stepped pinnacle-pattern, reaching up about two-thirds of the height of the walls. In the latter were numerous shallow niches with simple moulding and pointed arches, while in the west wall were two windows, five feet high and three wide, with shutters of decorative woodwork and, of course, without glass. The door was of plain *Ithil* timber ochre-coloured, and the coffee-hearth in the north-west corner of the room near the entrance was of plain gypsum, raised above the floor level. Rugs were spread on

---

[1] p. 147, *ante.*

the floor over a foundation of Calcutta matting. It was a comfortable room though airless, for the windows looked out on to a narrow courtyard backed by a high blank wall, in which the family live-stock had their being—two cows, half a dozen sheep and fowls of a bantam breed. A touch of humanity was added to the household by the presence of two fine gazelles, fully grown with inward curving horns about ten to twelve inches in length, which enjoyed the free run of the house. They wandered prettily in and out of the rooms and up and down the stairs seeking something to devour. They had a *penchant* for paper and tobacco, and soon taught me to keep my possessions inside my boxes. And with the gazelles ran the hopes of the house of Muhammad, two charming little boys of friendly mien and without shyness, who came in at frequent intervals to suggest that I might like coffee or, as often as not, simply to look at me. 'Atiq was a very beautiful child of some eight years with the slender oval face and braided locks of a girl, while Sulaiyim was definitely masculine, a sturdy little fellow of five or six with close-cropped hair and no pretensions to good looks.

Adjoining the main chamber of our suite and on a slightly higher level was a sort of retiring-room, about ten feet square and richly furnished with carpets and cushions. Texts mostly Quranic and advertisements of the industrial products of Europe—particularly noticeable in such surroundings being two tin plaques extolling the merits of Player's ' Navy Cut ' tobacco—adorned the walls. Cheap and horrible coloured glass-ware of Austrian origin decorated the niches and an ochre-stained wooden shelf. While we were admiring the contents of this room we were summoned to breakfast, which was served in another chamber of the suite, whose brown clay walls were without decoration. The meal, prepared by the ladies of the household, was simple but dainty—rice and meat in various delicate guises and fruit— and a welcome change after the feeble efforts of 'Abdullah's cook, Buraih, a half-witted fellow with but an elementary idea of his art.

After breakfast news was brought to us that the dowager-*Amir*, 'Abdul 'Aziz, was taking coffee with a neighbour and would be glad to see us. We repaired thither and I found that

our host was Ibrahim Ibn Hamad al Sulaim, now an old man
of wizened countenance, but, unknown to and unsuspected
by himself, made immortal in the *rôle* of villain by one whom
forty years before he had escorted and betrayed. It was he
that had charge of the butter caravan with which Doughty
travelled on the road to the Hijaz,[1] and, with time softening
the memories of that memorable occasion, he seemed to have
forgotten the uglier incidents of the journey, in which he
figured none too creditably, and even claimed that his efforts
had saved the life of Khalil from the menace of the mad
Sharif, to whose tender mercies he had abandoned him at
'Ain Zaima. In those days he ' was a manly young sheykh
of twenty years, of a gallant countenance,' but the ' Waháby
rust was in his soul.' Now he was an old man, taciturn and
unprosperous, living in a mean house, whose parlour was on
the ground floor and without the usual wall-plastering of
juss. And by a strange coincidence I met him again in
January, 1926, the month of Doughty's death, when he came
down with old 'Abdul 'Aziz by the same way of the old butter
caravans to Jidda to offer congratulations to the new
Wahhabi king of the Hijaz. And again we spoke of *Khalil*,
neither knowing then that he lay on his death-bed, nearly
half a century after the adventure which had so nearly ended
his life in this very Hijaz.

'Abdul 'Aziz was full of gracious cordiality. ' I have done
now with this world,' he said, ' and have no more wish to see
it outside 'Anaiza or to be worried with worldly cares.' Yet
he asked news of the War, and when I praised his city he
asked me slyly if I did not prefer Buraida. I freely expressed
my opinion of that town and its churlish inhabitants,
and his pleasure was indicated by a half-stifled chuckle.
'Abdullah, the *Amir's* henchman, who had been in attendance on me before, now appeared with an invitation to the
governor's house, and we went off with him through the
crowded *Suq*. On all sides I was politely greeted by old
acquaintances and strangers alike, and I marvelled happily
at the great gulf which seemed to divide this little island of
humanity from all its neighbours. It seemed to me that,
apart from the greater intimacy of its citizens with the great

---

[1] *C.M.D. abr.* ii. 241, 267.

cities of the outer world, the historic independence of 'Anaiza
in its sand-girt oasis has been partly responsible for its greater
sympathy with the stranger within its gates.

'Abdullah, the *Amir*, was out when we arrived, but we
seated ourselves upon the cushions set round the open court
of his *Majlis* to await his coming. His greeting was very
friendly, and we fell to talking of the War. ' It is the War,'
he said, 'that has brought us here in Arabia a great prosperity.
Formerly the great nations kept their immense hoards of
wealth to themselves, trading one with another, but now they
pour them forth without stint and we, who were poor before
and without the amenities of life, have become rich with a
glut of money, arms and the like. We care not here if the
War should last for ever. When Shakespear passed through
here,' he continued, ' he asked us how we, Arabs, could
endure this life of continual strife and insecurity. And yet
before many months were out it was your European
civilisation that became the victim of strife on a scale
altogether appalling. We have after all but little to complain
of.' I asked if the *Amir's* residence, in which we then were,
was the selfsame building in which the great Zamil had lived
in Doughty's time. ' No,' said he, ' this is not our own
property but rented, and Zamil's *Qasr* is in the great *Majlis*
(market-square), only used now as a storehouse and public
guest-house. This house was built anew in those days of
which you speak.'

After a quiet afternoon spent in the seclusion of our own
quarters, Dr. 'Abdullah and I sallied out to call by invitation
on Salih al Fadhl. On the way we passed the now dilapidated
mansion of the Khunaini family in which Doughty had spent
so much time.[1] And later in the day I was introduced to
'Ali Ibn Salih al Khunaini, the nephew of Doughty's friend,
'Abdullah of that ilk, whose brothers were Salih and Muhammad. Another member of this family, Muhammad Ibn
Hamad, the grandson of 'Abdullah, I also met during the
day—a lad of about seventeen. The family had bought up
extensive palm-grounds at Basra, which had recently been
requisitioned by the British military authorities at a price
of Rs. 40,000 as a site for an electric power station. Muham-

[1] *C.M.D. abr.* ii. 166.

mad, the last surviving brother, having died the previous
year, his share of the money had been held in deposit pending
the production of an inheritance certificate. And 'Ali, who
had no desire to journey to Basra, was perplexed about the
steps needful to secure the release of his patrimony. I
volunteered, in gratitude for the hospitality and cordiality
that had been meted out to me at 'Anaiza, to arrange for
the rapid settlement of the case. And so another link was
formed in the chain of goodwill which Doughty had forged
in the friendly house of Khunaini.

Salih al Fadhl was deeply concerned for his son and nephew
at Mecca, thrown into prison on a trumped-up charge by the
tyrannous *Sharif*. I had forwarded pressing representations
on their behalf, but we still had no news of their result, and
Salih bore his trouble with hopeful philosophy. He was an
old man of courtly manner and great charm with an outward
effusiveness uncommon in the Arabs of Najd. To me he
always seemed the very type of that class to which so aptly
Doughty applied the term ' patrician.'

From his house, after the usual rounds of tea, coffee and
incense, we strolled out of the town by way of the Dhulai'a
suburb to the old fort of Qasr Kharshit, so called on Arab
lips after the Turkish commandant, Khurshid Pasha. Its
ruddy clay walls were in ruinous condition and the building
only of moderate dimensions—I searched in vain for antiquities. The present circuit-wall of the oasis, said to have
been built some ten or twelve years before in replacement
of one whose ruins still stood much closer to the city, a
broken-down secondary line of defence, runs outside these
ruins, separating them from the remains of the old Turkish
barracks, which seemed to have been loosely constructed of
stones and rubble cemented together with a white *juss*
mortar. The old wall had in fact circled the whole oasis as
it then was, but the extension of cultivation on this (eastern)
side had necessitated the throwing forward of the wall.
And at this time even this wall by no means contained the
whole oasis, outlying patches of palms and cultivation being
either unprotected or fenced about with subsidiary walls
joined up to the main circuit. According to local accounts
the oasis, the city and the population had grown enormously

during the preceding forty years. Yet the 'Anaiza of Doughty
was not other than the 'Anaiza of my day.

Near the *Qasr* lay the deepest well of the whole oasis, fifteen
fathoms to water here against only six in the wells of Khuraijiya. The slope of the basin lies from north-east to south-
west, where is the lowest lying ground. The well cultivation
is divided up into *Haudhs* [1] or little rectangular patches no
more than five paces by four, and our cicerone, the same
'Abdullah, reckoned an average of from 300 to 500 such
patches to a well. It seemed to me that ten acres was about
as much as such wells could irrigate in the intensive fashion
of the district. Asses and cows are used for draught purposes,
but more commonly camels.

After dinner at Muhammad's house we betook ourselves
to the house of old 'Abdul 'Aziz for the last function of the
day. Zamil's grandson, 'Abdulrahman Ibn 'Abdul 'Aziz, was
there and rose in friendly greeting as I entered the out-of-
doors *Majlis*, and also his cousin Sulaim and 'Ali al Khunaini.
The conversation turned on the respective merits of Buraida
and 'Anaiza, and I found an appreciative audience for my
strictures on the former. ' Were not the houses better built
at Buraida ? ' they asked, ' and are not its broad streets more
elegant than ours ? ' ' Yes,' I replied, ' their streets indeed I
have seen and learned to know, but as for their houses—apart
from the *Qasr* and the *Amir's* residence, I have only seen the
inside of one and that by night. Their streets,' I added,
' are fine and broad for the passage of camels, but its people
are *Jammamil*—caravaners.' The style of a not dishonour-
able profession is frequently used as a delicate insult, and
these good folk of 'Anaiza, proud of their city and their
hospitable reputation, smiled their appreciation of my
verdict.

Ibrahim Ibn Hamad was another that I met that day, the
grandson of Ibrahim al Saif, who admitted Doughty to his
house on the outskirts of 'Anaiza at his first arrival. The
story of that episode, like all legends, has become clouded
in its details, but was raked up for my benefit, as he remembered it, by one who had heard it from his father, who was
doubtless one of ' the three or four young men, sons of

[1] Or ' basins.'

Ibrahim,' who pestered the stranger at the prayer hour. Doughty, as the story is now told, had unwittingly lain down to rest in the mosque unchallenged, but shortly afterwards Ibrahim, a godly man, had roused him to join in the prayers of his household. The guest explained that he was a Christian, whereupon : ' *Nasrani !* ' exclaimed the old man, ' *Audhu billah !* I seek refuge in God,' and would have struck him had not one Yahaya of the house of Dhukair intervened.[1]

That night Dr. 'Abdullah and I slept out on the roof over our main room, and having given instructions that nobody should wake me in the morning, I composed myself for a long sleep after a day full of hospitable entertainment. But the six-foot wall round the roof kept the breeze off an enclosure which had been baked all day by the sun, and the stuffiness of the atmosphere made it impossible to sleep. Then the dawn *Adhan* woke me from an uneasy slumber and, dosing again, I was roused by the gazelles, who had discovered the note-book by my bedside. And later the sun, creeping over the parapet, forced me to flight. A bathroom had been specially prepared in our suite for Ibn Sa'ud, and both the previous day and this morning I enjoyed the luxury of a really good bath. The privy was inconveniently situated in the private part of the house, where one risked encountering the women of the household, and where at all times the servants and children were about, the former officiously accompanying one, ewer in hand, for the ablutions. The guest is without privacy in the Arab household, for there is privacy only in the seclusion of the *harim*, which is denied to the stranger.

Our first visit of the day was to the house of 'Ali Ibn Salih al Khunaini. A large courtyard with a spread of clean sand serves for the evening coffee-drinking when the sun is down, and the day-parlour adjoins it, a large plain room with bare walls and a sandy floor and a few rugs and cushions. Here we met one of 'Abdullah's patients of our first days at 'Anaiza, a syphilo-paralytic wreck reclining feebly on a cushion, but much better for the treatment he had received. He confessed to having spent some months a dozen years before at Cairo and Damascus, whence he had brought away the fell disease

[1] *C.M.D. abr.* ii. p. 160.

of the foreigner. Formerly he had received some relief from
some sort of iodine treatment. Later in the day another
patient thrust himself upon 'Abdullah, his left hand im-
mensely swollen with an abscess, which the doctor proposed
to cut. But he had no instruments and I offered him the use
of my razor !

The pleasure, honour or duty of providing entertainment
for us this second day (14th September)—involving both
the midday meal and dinner—had been claimed by the ex-
Amir 'Abdul 'Aziz, to whose house we repaired after the
coffee-drinking at the Khunaini house. The meal was served
in a portico adjoining the open-air *Majlis*, the tray being
brought in and spread before us. Seasoned rice and stuffed
chickens formed the body of the meal with dishes of delicious
vegetables and bowls of broth and bread and excellent
junket. Peaches too there were of supreme excellence and
dates of four [1] kinds, and when I called for water they brought
me cow's milk cold as ice. We had no sooner finished than,
in accordance with custom, we took our leave with only a
' God reward you' to our host, seeking the Dhukair household,
whither we had been bidden for coffee. On arrival we were
mildly reproved for our lateness by our hosts Sulaiman and
'Abdul 'Aziz, sons of Yahaya al Dhukair, who most of all
regretted that their old uncle Muqbil, who was in failing
health and had specially come round to see us, had been
unable to stay. This family has considerable property and
a thriving business at Bahrain, where at this time it was
involved in a mild controversy with the British Political
Agency. With the ' efficiency' characteristic of all British
institutions in the East, the Agency was anxious to drive a
straight road diagonally across some Dhukair property
against the will of the owners, who alleged that it would
adversely affect the building value of the land. I undertook
to represent their view in the proper quarters, but never
learned what happened in the end. Conversation had filled
up the interval between our entry and the completion of

---

[1] *Hilwa* (a large red date), *Shaqra* (the staple date of class at 'Anaiza),
Qattar (a small brown date) and *Umm Hamam* (a large brownish fruit).
Sukari is another much prized product, though better dried than fresh.
A globular yellow variety called *Rathan* was a favourite these days in the
Laun or half-ripe stage.

the coffee-brewing—an elaborate and often tedious process. Then the coffee was poured round with a round of tea, and then more coffee, at which one rises to depart, only to be detained for the *Tib* or incense, after which one can go.

No sooner had we got home, hoping to enjoy a quiet after-noon before embarking on the engagements of the evening, than our hopes were dissipated by the entrance of 'Abdul 'Aziz Ibn Qunaiyir, a near neighbour and connection by marriage of our host. We had perforce to accept his pressing invitation and accompanied him across the street to his house, where in a parlour on the ground floor, neat and cleanly, we resigned ourselves to more drinking of tea and coffee. The child 'Atiq came in and sat by my side, the talk turning on education, for which there was but scanty provision at 'Anaiza, none indeed but the *Quran*-teaching *Madaris*. The boy could read or spell out the sacred text with some difficulty, but was unable to write. Our host had two sons, the younger of whom could read while the elder had not even reached that standard—neither could write, and they marvelled to hear that my son, two years younger than 'Atiq, frequently wrote letters to me.

Our first engagement of the evening, about 4 p.m., was to drink coffee with old Muqbil al Dhukair, whom we had missed in the morning at his nephews' party. With him we found his elder brother, Yahaya, four years his senior and hale and hearty at eighty years though deaf as a post. That shortcoming did not affect his cheery good humour, and he took an active part in the conversation with the help of his son, who repeated to him everything that was said in a voice of thunder. The deaf man produced for my inspection a metal ear-instrument which he had long discarded as useless, and made fun of his infirmity, alleging that he had had the use of his ears for more years than most people lived. Muqbil himself was slightly deaf and had suffered much sickness latterly, in consequence of which he had returned to his native town after an absence of twenty-five years to recuperate from the effects of the pestilent climate of the Persian Gulf. For more than forty years he had directed the fortunes of his family's business at Bahrain, visiting India and 'Iraq, the Gulf ports and even Jidda. They were a delightful and

charming couple, worthy citizens of a worthy city, a veritable
Tweedledum and Tweedledee in an Arabian setting, now,
alas ! gathered to their fathers full of years and honour.
Muqbil produced a small-calibre sporting rifle of German
make in the hope that I might be able to replenish his low
stock of ammunition. He thought the weapon was English
as the inscriptions on it were in that language, but I had to
tell him that he would have to wait for his ammunition till
the end of the War. On either side of the breech was stamped
the mark of the Lion and Sun, and the weapon, obviously
of Persian provenance, had been given him by Colonel Ross,
the first consul of his memory at Bahrain. ' Why,' he asked
me, ' do you not go forth and shoot hares ? ' I said I had
seen but few, and he assured me they were very plentiful
in the *Nafud* about Wahalan. I had noticed a number of
black and white rabbits, perhaps hares, both in private
houses and on sale in the *Suq*. They told me these came from
'Aridh. The gathering, at which lime-juice was served
round in addition to tea and coffee, was broken up by the
arrival of Fahad al Bassam in search of 'Abdullah. His
little daughter, Fatima, had sickened of a fever overnight,
and the old man was full of a wistful grief lest the worst
might befall.

Leaving 'Abdullah to accompany him, Muhammad al
Sulaiman and I looked in on one of whom he had previously
spoken to me. On entering the parlour of 'Ali Ibn Hamad al
Markham, a room scarcely ten feet square and dingy and
grimed with smoke, we were confronted by the strangest of
sights—as it were the show-case of a watchmaker's shop.
Spread out in rows before us were some 200 clocks and
watches of various kinds, clockwork and other lamps, a
Naumann sewing-machine from Dresden and other mechanical articles. Early in life 'Ali had displayed an interest in
clockwork products and had been sent to Mecca to learn more
about such things. After two years in the holy city he had
returned to set up as a watch repairer at 'Anaiza, and five
years later he had gone to Basra, where during a sojourn of
two years he had interested himself in phonographs. Then
he had returned home and collected an extensive *clientèle*
extending to Buraida, whence, even as we sat with him, came

a messenger to enquire whether a batch of watches entrusted to him for repair was ready for delivery. Until then I had no idea that watches were in such common use in Arabia, but he assured me that practically the whole of his collection belonged to clients, and always maintained its numbers though he was always sending back mended timepieces to their owners. Buraida was not wholly without watchmakers, but 'Ali was clearly in a class by himself. He had a curious talent in such matters which, under professional training and in a wider field, might have earned him a great reputation. Yet he seemed to be perfectly happy surrounded by dozens of cheap or ancient watches scarce worth the trouble of repairing, and he confessed to me that his special joy lay in studying the secrets of any mechanical novelty that came his way. He would pore over them with his unaided eyes, and as soon as he felt that he had grasped the principles of any bit of mechanism, he would test his theories by dismantling and reassembling it. In that way he added laboriously to his store of knowledge and experience—a type seen but rarely in Najd, the secular scholar. And his mind rejected the narrow fanaticism of the *Wahhabi* faith, of which his father was as it were a lay-priest. He smoked openly in his little den and rolled cigarettes for us as he talked enthusiastically of his beloved science. In appearance he was quite amazing. Without a hair on his face, he seemed to be about 22 or perhaps 25 years of age, for his visage retained all the freshness of youth, but he claimed to be not less than 38, and the playfellows of his boyhood were already, he declared, grey-beards.

Dr. 'Abdullah now rejoined us with an idea that we had accepted an invitation to coffee with Ibrahim Ibn Hamad al Sulaim, who, as it turned out, was not expecting us, though he insisted on our staying to drink the coffee he was preparing for himself. And he smoked cigarettes without offering us any. Besides Doughty he numbered Charles Huber and, I think, also Euting among his European acquaintances of days long ago. But the conversation flagged, as our host appeared to have another engagement on his mind and did not like to say so, while 'Abdullah was feeling annoyance at his mistake. The appearance of 'Abdullah Ibn Rashid, the *Amir's* hench-

man, created the necessary diversion, and as there was still
some time before dark, I went off alone with him through
fields and palm-groves to the ancient hamlet of Janah,
nowadays little more than a comparatively modern village
on an old site. Parts of the old wall were to be seen here and
there, but the only section of any length was that which
once served to defend the settlement from the now dominant
'Anaiza. Several hundreds of yards of this wall now screen
one side of an extensive palm-grove, through which ran a
raised earthen aqueduct from a neighbouring well. Part of
the wall of the old mosque, now partly enclosing a patch of
cultivation, and the site of the *Majlis* of the former elders
of Janah were pointed out to me by 'Abdullah, and then in
the cheerful gloaming we returned through the wards of Qa'
and Hufuf to the house of 'Abdul 'Aziz, who was expecting
us for dinner. This was served at once in a gallery on the
upper floor, and we departed after a round of coffee in
the open-air court below for a brief visit to the *Amir*
'Abdullah.

New arrivals from Madina, who had travelled by way of
Rass, had brought in further news of Ibn Rashid's raid on
the Harb. The sufferers had been some subsections of the
Madarin and not Ibn Nami's people as originally reported,
and a battle had taken place at Humailiya, after which Ibn
Rashid had withdrawn with a booty of 30 camels towards
Samira, his main camp being at Faid. He had lost eight
men and a score of horses killed out of a total force of 600,
including about 50 cavalry. We hoped that Ibn Sa'ud with
his greatly superior force would try to cut off his retreat, and
it was rumoured that at a council of war Al Duwish had
counselled such a course against the general feeling of the
Ikhwan, who were for pouncing on the Shammar camps at
Baqa'a, north-east of Hail.

At the ex-*Amir's* house we had encountered yet other links
with the days of Doughty and Zamil, two men of humble
standing but greatly trusted in the *Amir's* service. These
were Sha'aithan, brother or more probably cousin of the
negro, 'Ali al Sha'aithan, at whose house Doughty had first
knocked and who thereafter regularly accompanied him
abroad under the orders of Zamil ; and 'Ali, grandson of that

'Ali.[1] ' How great is the difference,' said they as they accompanied me through the streets that evening to the house of Zamil's grandson, 'Abdulrahman Ibn 'Abdul 'Aziz, ' since those days. Old 'Ali accompanied Khalil even as we now go with you, but there are no rude children for us to beat away.' Indeed I had often noticed that the children here gave no cause for complaint. If they took notice of me they might line up as I passed and salute me gravely in the Turkish fashion with their hands on the middle of their foreheads, ending with an engaging smile. The little girls with their long plaited locks and bright garments—generally a smock of muslin and a pair of baggy pantaloons—were charmingly pretty as they played in the streets and open places like little butterflies doomed to a short career of gaiety. For five or six years only they enjoy an unrestricted liberty, running wild, before they are forced by a hard code to hide from the world within doors or behind the veil of sombre black. At twelve they become marriageable—many being marked down by would-be husbands or would-be fathers-in-law from the days before their withdrawal from the streets. Frequently they marry at fourteen, but often it happens that, if a girl be not fully developed at her marriage, her husband leaves her yet a year or two untouched. They seldom bear children before seventeen, but the lot of women is hard in Arabia with marriage thus thrust upon them prematurely. Here green smocks or black are the fashion for women, but red is rarely seen.

It was a charming hour we spent that evening in the parlour of Zamil's grandson. Lemonade of fresh limes from the adjoining garden was provided besides coffee, and cigarettes went round freely—I smoked as always my pipe. Here there was no bigotry, and it was already a good half-hour beyond the evening prayer time before we realised that we might be outstaying our welcome, though in the buzz of conversation nobody had heard the call. ' The mosque is close by,' said 'Abdulrahman, ' no need to haste away—any time will do.' The talk was of locusts and their dreadful visitations. The *larva*, called *Dibba*, hatches out from the egg, they say, in fifty days. Shallow trenches (*Zibbiya*) are

[1] *C.M.D. abr.* ii. 162.

dug out to catch them and there, being unable to crawl out,
they perish. Sometimes this method proves completely
effective, at others the locusts come all the same—presumably
from distant parts. These are dealt with by the beating of
drums which frightens them away. According to the
Traditions of the Prophet the locust will be the first creature
to disappear on the approach of Doomsday. And considerable consternation was caused in the time either of Abu Bakr
or 'Umar by the total absence of locusts for a series of years.
There was no great desire for the world's end in the Arabia
of those days, and great was the public relief when a newly-
captured specimen was produced before and certified as a
locust by the ecclesiastical authorities. The locust and the
fish alone of creatures require no formal ceremony of killing
to bless them as food, and the locust found dead is also
lawful food.

'Abdulrahman had a fund of simple knowledge, a genuine
seeker after enlightenment, and a mildness of address which
strongly recalled Doughty's description of Zamil. Even so,
I thought, must have been the great prince of 'Anaiza's
heyday. ' You should come with me,' I said, ' and see some
day our English country, and I will show you Paris and
Europe.' He objected that he might find difficulties there
in the matter of praying, but I assured him we had a few
mosques for *Muslim* worship. ' No,' he replied, ' some day
when the world is at peace I would fare to Madina and take
thence the train to Damascus. Beyond that I have no wish
to go.' Some years later our paths crossed for a brief moment
in the streets of Jidda. ' Do you know me, oh Philby ? ' he
asked. ' I do indeed, oh Zamil,' I replied, ' how fare you
and what brings you hither ? ' I was then in European
dress and without beard, and he had been told who I was as
I passed. He was unchanged. In his company, perhaps for
the memory of his grandfather, I always found great pleasure
at 'Anaiza.

Our last function of the evening was a visit to Fahad al
Bassam. His house and several others of his family abutted
on the great *Majlis* in a graceful crescent which added charm
and distinction to the high wall face with its tiny casements.
In the same square is the chief mosque and Zamil's old *Qasr*

with a square turret at one corner dwarfed by the tall tapering minaret. Fahad had the manner and appearance of a highly successful business man with a polished urbanity of the Turkish type, slightly hypocritical and more obviously artificial than Salih al Fadhl, capable of being very entertaining and probably the ablest man in 'Anaiza. Yet he was simple withal. He produced a bottle of Rose's lime-juice cordial for my inspection before sending it upstairs to be mixed for our benefit—he insisted on our drinking two glasses of it each, and here is no gentle sipping of cooling beverages as in Europe. You must drink it down at a draught, and the servitor stands before you to take the empty or half-empty glass, offering you a towel to dry your lips and fingers. Two of his sons were of the party, one a youngster of about seventeen with a blear left eye and the other, 'Abdullah, a child of six or seven. There was also Ibrahim, a boy of about thirteen, the son of 'Abdulrahman al Bassam, at this time deceased, who had ridden in Doughty's butter caravan to the Hijaz.[1] Fahad, with his Turkish facility of compliment, was good enough to prophesy a distinguished diplomatic career for me ! ' I can judge that,' he said, ' from the high esteem in which Ibn Sa'ud holds you.'

And so the day ended, a typical day of kindly entertainment by persons who had not allowed their faith—to which they were loyal enough in all essential points—to obscure their vision of a world of which some of them had had glimpses beyond the borders of their desert land. To that world they owed the material prosperity which for all its evanescent character they valued not a little. The great drawback of their social gatherings was the absence of air. In the open courts there was little to complain of, but in the parlours gently scented by the soft fumes of their *Ghadha* fires and incense the eternal rounds of tea and coffee induce a gentle trickle of perspiration which with but few intervals persists through the livelong day and would be intolerable to a community busily engaged in the world's work. But 'Anaiza is the Paris of Najd, a city of leisure and pleasure where no labour is envisaged more exacting than the dilatory discussion of business deals, whose settlement may as

[1] *C.M.D. abr.* ii. 238.

well be to-morrow as to-day, over coffee and tea and cigarettes.

The following day (15th September) was in general outline a repetition of its predecessor, but the social life of 'Anaiza is never dull. Here is not the dreary silence of the normal coffee-parties of Najd. Conversation is the favourite art of an idle folk keenly interested in the world about them. By our reckoning it was the ninth day of *Dhil Hijja*, the season of the great pilgrimage at Mecca, which would culminate in the *'Id* of the sacrifice to be celebrated not only at 'Arafat and Muna but throughout the Islamic world. A hot *Simum* from the south—by agricultural reckoning it was the beginning of the *Sfiri* (? *Safari*) season—made the midday hours sultry and irksome, for the high buildings of the city kept the wind out of the gardens and courtyards but sucked down the heat of the sun. But the *Suq* in these days of preparation for the *'Id* was full of activity, busy crowds thronging the shops, where dates, vegetables and melons were displayed in profusion with coffee, pomegranate-rind and salt—both of the white and pink varieties—and other things to tempt the housewife. Two rifles were being sold by wandering auctioneers. One had reached 40 dollars, a German Mauser of 1916 pattern, and the other 38, a new English short rifle, rising after six hours of desultory bidding to 46. We passed the brothers Sulaiman and 'Abdul 'Aziz al Dhukair sitting on a shop ledge talking while a group of black sheep near by was arousing the interest of a large crowd. The price of a sheep at that hour was from six to seven dollars, black fleeces all of them as far as I saw, and a brisk business was being done, each customer selecting his fancy with expert hands, kneading the soft parts of every animal before deciding. By the evening the price had mounted to ten dollars, and those who had bought betimes rejoiced. All the better class men wore *Aqals* of Mesopotamian type, heavy bands of loose camel wool jointed at intervals with bands of silver thread. Some wore head-bands of plain black and the kerchief was either white or the red check as among the *Badu*. Their *abas* were brown or black of light summer stuff, transparent but very durable. Wending our way homeward we passed a group of little girls disporting their holiday garments. Their cheeks were slightly rouged and they stood at gaze for us to admire them, bursting into merry laughter at their success with the *Inglizi*. Their garments were of soft transparent silk stuffs of various colours, and most of them wore head-bands of gold thread decked out with turquoise beads over their plaited hair plastered with grease. Very charming they looked.

'Abdullah the *Amir* was responsible for our entertainment this day and we went to breakfast after a preliminary call on 'Abdullah Ibn Hamad al Sulaim, a brother of Doughty's Ibrahim, who was with his brother in the caravan which Huber joined. He was a tallish, well-preserved man of about sixty-five, looking much younger than his years on account of the black dye of his small, trim beard. He had reached Poona ten years before on a pleasure trip, and of course he knew Baghdad, Damascus and even Cairo. In his courtyard was a foal, said to be from the 'Iraq country and recently purchased by him from the *Badu*.

The *Amir*, now in the prime of life, had spent some years in exile from 1891 to 1904, during which period he engaged in commercial ventures which took him as far as India. He had, however, no further ambition to roam. He had seen enough of the world and now prized leisure above all things, counting work a painful though inevitable interruption of the ideal. 'To-day for instance,' he said, 'I have no work on hand, and when we have done breakfasting I shall retire to my couch as is my wont.' I told him that in Europe anyone acting on his principles would soon die of starvation. He was interested in the monetary situation. The great difficulty, he thought, in the way of introducing a stable silver currency into the country in supersession of the dollar and Turkish small silver would be the mass of such coins to be called in presumably at a loss. The dollar must there-fore remain the basis of the Arabian currency. Two-thirds of the gold transactions of the *Qasim* were in English sovereigns and the rest in Turkish *Liras*. The Napoleon, called *Binto*, was seldom seen, German gold never and Russian gold coins only to a small extent. He wondered why the Maria Theresa dollar of Austrian provenance was called a *Fransawi* (French), but he had not noticed that, though

THE TOWN OF 'ANAIZA.

To face page 253.

these coins are currently manufactured according to the
needs of the market, they always bear the same date—1780.
As for the progress of the War, they had long ceased to put
faith in the papers. The evidence of their eyes was good
enough. Nothing could be much amiss with 'Iraq securely
in British hands. I suggested that with most of Belgium
and a large part of France in German hands his argument
was not altogether sound though his conclusion was in fact
correct.

It is customary at 'Anaiza to begin every meal with a
couple of dates by way of grace—after that there is no fixed
order of assault on the varied contents of the tray. Hamad
Ibn Hadhdhal was, however, guilty of a solecism in ladling
the curds on to his portion of rice and mixing the two
together. According to the ' Traditions ' this is an execrable
breach of table manners in the best (*Badawin*) society, though
it is normally practised by the primitive Ma'dan of 'Iraq
and even by the boorish *Zigirt* [1] or household retainers,
mainly of Bani Khadhir origin, in Najd.

We went on to call on Ahmad Ibn Suwal'ar, recently
returned from Mecca, in his dingy, smoky parlour, twelve feet
by ten with a pent roof. There entered an old man of seventy,
a connection by marriage (*rahim*) of our host, seeking of
Dr. 'Abdullah some remedy for his failing eyesight—a sore
hindrance to his work during the past two years. He was
Ibrahim Ibn Salih, the leading architect and builder of the
city. Starting life as an apprentice to a builder without other
education than what he gathered through his eyes, he rose
rapidly to fame and had built the tall minaret of the *Jami'*
Masjid 28 years before—it was 50 *dhra'*, he said, or nearly
80 feet in height. He also built the *Amir's* present residence,
that of Muhammad al Sulaiman in which we were lodged,
and in fact all the best houses in 'Anaiza. None of his
monuments, he asserted proudly, had ever collapsed, and
yet all had been built without any kind of design or plan,
without line or plummet, in fact with nothing to guide him
but his eye and his experience. ' Look,' he said, ' at the
Rafi' *sangar* which I built round and compare it with the

---

[1] This word is derived by the Turkish from the French ' sécurité,' which
in normal Arab mouths becomes ' sacurta.'

square of the Ibn Sallum one, mine has lasted the better and will stand yet for many a day.' For building the great minaret, for which the earth and mortar were delivered to him on the spot, he received the sum of forty dollars. He would readily undertake to build one twice as high, but would of course build it on a wider base. I asked him how the curved [1] façades of the 'Anaiza houses came to be developed—a very conspicuous and beautiful feature of the local architecture, though not apparently to be found elsewhere in Arabia. He claimed it as his own creation, easier to build and more enduring. A few days before I had noticed a tall minaret in the *Qa'* quarter. ' Who built that ? ' I asked. ' It leans to southward,' was his curt reply. Latterly he had taken to well-steyning without previous experience of such work, but he was now an acknowledged authority, though his failing eyes interfered seriously with a task requiring more than ordinary precision.

The afternoon was passed partly at 'Ali al Khunaini's and partly at Yahaya al Dhukair's, the ex-*Amir* being present on both occasions. On being offered a cigarette by 'Ali, I turned to 'Abdul 'Aziz to ask if he minded my smoking. ' Not a bit,' he replied, ' I used to smoke myself.' He had formerly been a constant victim of a sort of headache whose symptoms he explained at great length. In India he had found a sovereign remedy in a concoction including hyena's bile,[2] but in Najd itself, perhaps for some climatic reason, that same remedy seemed to be of no avail. In Najd, so soon to be visited by the dreadful scourge of influenza which is said to have carried off 25,000 settled folk and *Badawin* innumerable, disease was rare except the smallpox, which was even then raging in the town though less intensely than the previous year when at the *'Asr* prayers were daily read for four or five children gone before their time. He became interested in a discussion on vaccination, and I undertook to send for a supply of lymph for 'Abdullah to administer. One objection to vaccination was the fact that fresh supplies are not always available, and disaster had not seldom ensued

---

[1] The word is *mubram*, apparently applied indifferently to convex and concave curves. The latter also appears to be called *muk'ab*.

[2] *Murair al Dhaba'*.

from the use of old lymph by the many quacks who made
their living out of the people's need. Yahaya and Muqbil
were again in good form. The former was blessed with a
prodigious corporation, and always seemed to be in great
distress as he reclined upon his cushion under an avalanche
of fat. That and his deafness might well have embittered
him, but his temper was charming, and he took it in good
part when 'Abdullah twitted him : ' I can do nothing for
your ears, but if it is a tonic (*i.e.* an aphrodisiac) you want,
come to me.' ' *Alhamdu lillah*,' said the old man, ' the time
is not yet come for that.'

We dined at 4.30 p.m. at the *Amir's* special request, and
ate enormously in spite of the hour and the heat, but we
were glad to creep away to the solitude of our quarters, and
settled down in the hope of an undisturbed evening in the
cool of our roof. ' Come and look ! ' called Dr. 'Abdullah
to me, and as I followed his eyes out across to a neighbouring
roof, lo and behold ! a trio of young women of great loveli-
ness. Mere girls they were indeed, virgins ready for the
marriage market and keenly sought after, it was said, by
numerous suitors, among whom was Ibn Suwaidan, who was
reputed to be as uxorious as he was outwardly fanatical—it
often seemed to me that his fanaticism was only skin-deep
and he was thought to be a secret wooer of the forbidden
weed. 'Abdullah had already attracted their attention, but
they disported themselves without bashfulness before our
eyes and flinched not when 'Abdullah brought my binoculars
to bear on them. They were very beautiful, justifying the
boasts one often heard of the beauty of the women of Qasim.
One has indeed but to see the children to be convinced of the
justice of their boasting, if only the women retain in maturity
the promise of their childhood. The more the pity that they
are hidden away in senseless seclusion for the delight of
individuals, without education or training for the service
of society. The eldest girl was decked out as a bride in gay
apparel with profusion of gold ornaments which flashed in
the setting sun, while her sisters, engaged in tiring and admiring her, were in plain red smocks—the first time I had
seen this colour at 'Anaiza. In the gloaming they disappeared from our gaze and we were left wondering whether

we had witnessed the preliminaries of a bridal night or merely the trying on of holiday garments for the approaching 'Id. The latter explanation received some support from the occurrences of the following evening. Returning at sunset from a walk in the oasis I found 'Abdullah already on the roof renewing the pleasures of the previous evening, and he told me that the three girls had been treating him to an exhibition of their dancing. On this occasion, as I saw in a brief glimpse of them before darkness blotted them out, they were all in festive attire, in dresses of soft satin of an old-gold tint. And they were lovelier than ever. This second appearance in redoubled splendour, highly reprehensible according to local standards of decorum, was certainly not accidental. Marriage was their object in life and the approach of the 'Id was perhaps sufficient excuse for a minor lapse fraught with momentous possibilities. Their mother or aunt—for they were the orphan daughters of one Salihi deceased—maybe connived at or encouraged the exhibition of their beauty, and doubtless others than 'Abdullah feasted their hungry eyes on the fairness of their forms. The next evening, of the 'Id itself, the three had been reduced to one and the mystery was solved. The two eldest had gone to their husbands soon after we had seen the last of them, and the youngest alone, decked out in bridal glory, stood on the roof that night awaiting the call to her bridal couch. A transparent shift fell gracefully over a tight-fitting bodice and ample pantaloons. A light mantle of black completed her attire, and her face and braided locks were uncovered. The three sisters had been married off to three brothers of the house of Qublan and were no more seen of us.

The morning of 16th September found everybody too busy with 'Id preparations for the morrow to entertain the coffee-guests of normal days. 'Abdullah and I accordingly settled down to a quiet day as members of Muhammad's household, beginning with a frugal breakfast of rice cooked with currants and spiced onions, sliced melons (both musk melons and water) and dates. The melons generally seemed of poor quality here and quite tasteless, but latterly there had been some tendency to import seed from Zubair. Conversation turned on Wadi Rima, whose watershed Muhammad, who

had never heard of Wadi Hamdh though he had been to
Madina, placed somewhere between the latter town and
Yanbu'. He would have none of my suggestion that it rose
in the Harra north-east of Madina, and the matter was left
to be decided some day by a *Harbi* expert, whom he undertook
to produce to convince me. Each was to wager his mantle
on the issue. Up to about fifteen years before this time the
Wadi had been subject to regular floods, coming down as
often as five or six times in a year and often converting the
Zuqaibiya depression into a great lake in which water frequently remained throughout the year till the next floods.
More recently, however, the floods had more or less failed
both in regularity and quantity, but the previous year there
had been good floods and Zuqaibiya had filled up. This
year there had been none.

We passed into a geological discussion, my host taking
up an unassailable position behind a barricade of Quranic
evidence, from which it was impossible to coax him. For
him the age of the world was 5000 years at the outside, and
Noah's animals were the ancestors of all living creatures
now on earth. I happened to have by me the *Encyclopaedia
Britannica Year Book*, which I produced to argue that of all
the world's countries South Africa had stood longest above
the sea. ' Nonsense,' he said, ' we have it in God's own Word
that Juda was the first land to show itself above the waters
of the universal flood.' By that name they know Ararat.
But even as we were speaking something occurred to shake
his confidence in the scientific methods on which he relied
so implicitly. ' We keep the '*Id* to-day,' cried one of the
servants dashing into the room, ' the *Shaikh* has proclaimed
it, and to-day we sacrifice, the prayer will be said to-morrow
morning.' I turned triumphantly on my audience : ' Did I
not tell you yesterday from my books that to-day would be
the '*Id*—I, a mere infidel—and you *Muslimin* would not
credit me, while your wise men now believe the mere statement of some wild *Baduwi* with sharper eyes than most or
perhaps from some spot where the sky was not obscured by
clouds. You must have a human witness of things beyond
the power of man.' ' *Wallah !* ' said Muhammad, who was
slightly deaf and a little slow of comprehension, ' you did

indeed tell us.' On this occasion, of course, the dispute did not
turn on the sight of the moon the previous night, as the Day
of Sacrifice is the 10th of the lunar month, and the late
arrival of the news that the new crescent had been seen the
day previous to that on which 'Anaiza and its neighbourhood had seen it argued that it must have come from a
considerable distance—perhaps from the coast or from
Basra.

That afternoon—the sacrifices having been accomplished
and much meat distributed to the poor—we visited Muhammad Ibn Ahmad al Dhukair, whose father, long since
dead, was a younger brother of Muqbil and Yahaya. His
sister, residing with him, was still on the active list of Ibn
Sa'ud's harem and had recently borne him a daughter,
Jauhara by name in compliment to the chief queen. In his
large well-furnished parlour I noticed a large rocking-chair
of iron which he had bought some years before at Bombay.
Conversation turned on the subject of jewellery suggested
by the name of Ibn Sa'ud's infant daughter. Besides pearls,
the most popular gems are turquoises from Persia and rubies
from Burma, but diamonds are rare though occasionally
worn as ear-rings. My view of the Wadi Rima watershed
here received some support, but they displayed extraordinary
ignorance of the course of Wadi Hanifa, on which I was able
to give them authoritative information. Their geographical
ideas were puerile to a degree, and in the towns their idea
of the compass points did not seem to be as good as in the
average Indian. But they seemed to have an instinctive
perception of the fact that one goes up westward and down
eastward. We were joined here by Ibrahim Ibn Zamil, a son
of the famous prince, but of fanatical sort—the first specimen
of the type I had met with. He bore himself well in good
clothes and heavy woollen *Aqal*, but he ostentatiously
withheld his greeting from me, and I rose equally ostentatiously to go.

Before us went old Yahaya waddling along with such
speed as his great burden supported on short legs of prodigious girth would allow him. He greeted us warmly as we
passed and went on his way to some coffee-gathering. At
the door of our house we met a near neighbour, an old man

called Sulaiman al Sa'aiyid, who stopped to converse with us
and declared his anxiety to invite us to a meal. We protested
that it would be sufficient if we drank coffee with him, and
as the 'Id celebrations—the visits of mutual congratulations
following on the congregational prayer—would make such
a visit difficult on the morrow, we agreed to visit him at once,
allowing him just enough time to go home and light his fire.
In a few minutes Muhammad, 'Abdullah and myself, accompanied by little 'Atiq, attired in holiday raiment—a kaflya
of delicate pink silk, a great little Mesopotamian Aqal, a
black Aba and cane—repaired to his comfortable parlour,
in which we found another old man of more than seventy
summers like our host. This was 'Abdul 'Ali al 'Ali, originally
of Zilfi, who had come to settle here about the time of
Doughty's visit and remembered him well.

Old Sulaiman had started life as a merchant and had
spent twenty years at Basra in that capacity until about
sixteen years previously when, on the death of his father,
the only medical practitioner at 'Anaiza, he had returned
to succeed him in his profession, apparently without other
qualification for the post than the accident of being his
father's son. He had nevertheless applied himself energeti-
cally to the practice of his profession, covering the whole
Qasim, but complained that there were neither scope nor
prospects in this country. The only occasion he had received
payment more substantial than a ' thank you ' for his services
was when he had attended Mubarak Ibn Subah in his last
(fatal) illness, and had not only been paid by the old Shaikh's
heirs but had been provided with a stock of medicines on
which he had existed ever since.

I invited his opinion on the subject of evil spirits and the
cure of possessed persons. ' Possession,' he said in all
seriousness, ' is a common affection very easy to diagnose,
the Jan [1] being creatures of human form except for their
eye-slits, which are vertical instead of horizontal. They
enter their victims always by way of the great toe. But in
almost all cases I have succeeded in casting them out by
reciting spells min Kalam Rabbi—from the Word of my God
—over burning incense.' He obviously had shortcomings

[1] Pl. of Jinni.

as a doctor but none as a host, and I felt at the time that, even in my experience of 'Anaiza, I had never been made to feel more at home than in the parlour of this aged crack-brained physician. He excused his failure to invite us earlier on the ground of illness. ' However,' he continued, ' I go out but seldom, and you will be very welcome whenever you care to visit me, and you, 'Abdullah, be not shy of coming here—we are brothers ' (in physic). He claimed to have known Doughty, but made it quite clear—he spoke of him as the vaccinator—that in fact he had not seen him, and this impression was confirmed by 'Abdul 'Ali. To complete his entertainment of us he produced a tray, on which he set four bowls of the most delicious dates I had yet tasted in the locality, including two new kinds : a very large light brown variety called *Khokha* here and known elsewhere as *Diqla,* and a large reddish-brown date called *Hamar al Mudhnib* from its reputed place of origin.

Leaving our host we came to a secondary *Majlis* or open space towards the Dhulai'a end of the town—a space preserved for ever from encroachment by the builder by reason of its being *Waqf lil sabil (Allah),* devoted to the service of God. An irregular oval surrounded by houses set at every angle to its circumference, it appeared to be used as a timber and fuel mart to judge by the piles of wood of many kinds which encumbered it. Passing now out of the town through a series of lanes traversing the walled date-groves we reached a garden, some four or five acres in extent, belonging to Fahad al Bassam. Formerly it had been a show spot with a profusion of great trees, but consistent neglect had reduced it again to what it was—a mere palm-grove with a score of well-grown limes and lemon trees. Its chief feature was a fine well of masonry, some ten fathoms deep and of oblong shape with five wheels on which camels drew up the water-skins all on one side, to discharge into a large masonry reservoir, 100 feet long and six wide with narrow masonry channels leading into the various parts of the garden from a series of outlets. The water stood in it to a depth of about two feet, largely covered with weeds. Muhammad took advantage of it to perform his ablutions for the *'Asr* prayer, which he and 'Abdullah said in the garden while I wandered

to and fro.   We returned through the Dhulai'a hamlet,
passing through part of the main *Suq* to reach home.

Later the same afternoon I issued forth with Hamad,
'Aiyadh and Mirwij by way of Al Qa', which was still as in
Doughty's time a considerable open space piled high with
the refuse and rubbish of the town, surmounted by the
bleaching bones of camels and sheep slaughtered for the
market.   In one corner of it outside a garden wall stood a
large deep stone trough for the watering of animals, a gift
by way of *Waqf* from the owners of the garden, some members of the great Bassam family.   We then followed the north
road, walled on either side, which from the beginning of the
Malah hamlet onwards is identical with the main *sail*-bed—
a fine broad thoroughfare leading to the great cemeteries
about Dhabat, from which, taking a track at random, we
wandered through lucerne fields and market gardens and
walled groves until we reached the *Nafud* near a large well
close by an open gap in the circuit-wall.   The well [1] was of
eight wheels worked by four camels on one side and three
cows and a donkey on the other—lined with masonry and
some nine or ten fathoms deep.   Skirting the wall on the
outside we re-entered the oasis by another similar breach
and returned homewards through the Janah tract, meeting
Fahad al Bassam on the way as he issued from a garden
belonging to one of his relatives.   As we walked together the
conversation turned on Doughty, who had suggested to
'Abdullah al Bassam the conversion of the midden of Al Qa'
into a public garden for the recreation of the citizens of
'Anaiza.   The younger 'Abdullah al Bassam of those days—
I was to meet him later—was still alive, he told me, though
living a life of retirement in one of the gardens ; but old
Shaikh Nasir had long been dead.   Arrived at the great
Majlis he turned aside to pray in the chief mosque, and I
went home through the main *Suq*.

Formerly, they told me, the celebration of the *'Id* used to
be kept up for three days with dance and song and general
revelry, including military displays and dancing by *Badu*

---

[1] This well and the dense garden it served, known as Mu'aiwiya, were the
property of the Khunaini family, the garden being mentioned by Doughty,
who visited it.

women. But since Ibn Sa'ud's occupation of the Qasim it had reverted to being a purely religious festival of prayer and sacrifice, and the only remnant of the old paganism was a hideous din of songs and noise kept up throughout the night by the boys of the town, each quarter having its own gang of budding citizens parading its alleys and jealously keeping out all rivals if need be by the simple process of fighting them. Each brotherhood of boys would collect subscriptions to provide themselves with sweets and refreshments for the occasion, and the din they made was enough to keep me awake through part of the night.

Meanwhile I had spent the evening with Nasir al Shubaili —of an 'Anaiza family with considerable interests in the rich date groves of Basra—and some of his friends on a narrow roof-space connecting his two houses on either side of the street. This was greatly preferable to the usual stuffy parlour, and there was a fine spread of fruit—excellent peaches and melons—between rounds of coffee and cigarettes. The party struck both 'Abdullah and me quite independently as being more Mesopotamian than Arabian, the almost exaggerated though natural refinement of 'Anaiza being tempered with something of the breezy vulgarity of Basra. Nasir had been away recently on his property called Zubaida in the *Wadi*, where a new spring had been monopolising his attention. He therefore apologised for his apparent neglect of us, and without further ado plunged into the subject to which we had owed his present invitation. Some of his date land at Ma'qil had been taken up by the British military authorities at what he considered to be an inadequate valuation. I created something of a sensation by admitting that I was the culprit responsible for the assessment, which was made of course on the basis of a fair pre-war value, and not on the enhanced values arising out of the military occupation. At the same time I commented on the fact that he had not apparently appeared before me, as invited by public notice, to contest the valuation. He replied that he had done so a year later before my successor, when the fantastic plan of permanent acquisition of large areas had been abandoned and the question had reduced itself to one of compensation for actual damage done. In the end I suggested that he

could always test the validity of the assessment in the
courts, and he dropped the subject with an offer to take me
some day to see his plantations in the *Wadi*.

Next morning I was up before the dawn and out with
'Abdullah and my camera, carefully concealed under my
'Aba, to see and photograph the *'Id* service, which took
place on a low sand slope south of the south-west *Sangar*.
This, though the regular place of worship on such occasions,
was indistinguishable from the surrounding *Nafud* except
for a three-stepped *minbar* or pulpit not more than three feet
in height. On our way to our vantage-point, a sand peak
near the Khuraijiya garden, we passed through vast throngs
of people all hastening in the same direction, and among them
I noticed a good proportion of women in smocks of greenish-
blue and black *'Abas*. From the south and south-west gates
dense streams of people converged on the ' *Masjid*,' where
behind the pulpit sat an ever-growing phalanx of men,
behind whom at a reasonable distance gathered a similar but
smaller crowd of women. And all through the service late-
comers dribbled in on foot or on horseback to swell the congregation, the horses being parked together in front of the
left extremity of the prayer lines. Soon after sunrise a
procession of more imposing appearance than the loose
streams of humanity which had hitherto occupied the scene
emerged from the south-west corner of the oasis, and the
whole congregation rose as the *Imam*—Salih al Qadhi, cousin
of Ibrahim al Qadhi—proceeded to his place before the
pulpit. Without further ado the preliminary service of two
Rik'ats was begun, the thin clear voice of the *Imam* sounding
musically over the clear *Nafud* air—*Allahu akbar, Allahu
akbar !* And as he stood and bowed and bent and knelt and
prostrated himself, so did the whole congregation after him.
This over he mounted the pulpit, facing the seated audience,
many of whom from the wings crowded forward to take up
places on the ground nearer the preacher, while yet others,
having satisfied the minimum demands of a formal religion,
hastened off townwards to see to the preparation of the
feast and the provision for the poor. And now in a sing-song
chant, as if reciting rather than preaching, the *Imam*
delivered the *Khutba* or sermon in imitation of the annual

sermon on the mount of 'Arafat, which is the culminating ceremony, of the great pilgrimage of Mecca. And as he told the story of how Abraham would sacrifice his son Ishmael [1] the women and even many men among the congregation fell to sobbing aloud in sympathy with a father so God-fearing. He came then to an explanation of the practical aspect of the sacrificial ceremony. Of the animal to be sacrificed by each householder one-third should be set apart for the poor and needy, one-third should be distributed among the neighbours, and one-third might be kept for the needs of the household. About half-way through the sermon there was a distinct pause, of which a considerable part of the congregation took advantage to get away to their duties. The *Imam* then continued to the end, when there was a wild hurrying and scurrying homeward ; but I noticed that the women of the congregation stayed behind after the men had gone and crowded round the pulpit, continuing their devotions in postures of abject humility and adoration. Perhaps there was virtue in touching the very ground and pulpit on which the preacher had stood. And some, as they prayed, sobbed and wept bitterly.

As we returned by way of the south-west gate I noticed spread out before the doors of several houses in the dusty street reed-mats set about with dishes of porridge-gruel [2] and *saman*, round which guests sat eating. But in these I noticed no meat—possibly the humble contribution of the poor themselves to the penniless. At any rate on that day no one starved at 'Anaiza, where the holiday was celebrated with the only recreation known to its citizens, an endless round of visits to offer mutual congratulations and drink coffee. For me it was an occasion for the distribution of gifts among my host's children and servants, and our neighbour, 'Abdul 'Aziz al Qunaiyir, brought along his little son to receive a dole. Not content with this he told me of another son who was not at home at the moment, so I added a small contribution for the missing child. ' And what about myself ? ' said their father. That was strange behaviour for

---

[1] In the *Islamic* tradition it is of course Ishmael and not Isaac whom their father was called on to sacrifice.

[2] *Jarish.*

'Anaiza, and 'Abdullah, who heard his request, blushed with
shame. I turned away the demand with a jest, and 'Abdul
'Aziz retired disappointed but not ashamed.

Salih al Fadhl was our first visitor with courtly greetings
and an invitation for the morrow. And then came 'Abdulrahman al Bassam, brother of the younger 'Abdullah of
Doughty's day. This was my first meeting with him, and,
as if by way of excusing himself for not having called before,
he deplored tho ' wildness ' of the people. I deprecated such
a term in reference to 'Anaiza, but he insisted that there had
been an increase of bigotry in the town since Doughty's time
and expressed the hope that I would visit him some day in
his garden outside the town. He told me his brother,
'Abdullah, had busied himself for many years collecting
manuscript notes on many abstruse matters to form as it
were an encyclopaedia for his personal use. We broke our
fast by invitation at the house of 'Abdullah al Hamad al
Sulaim, where we with a number of other guests not known
to me sat round a frugal meal of rice spiced with onions,
bread, curds, melons and dates. Immediately after breakfast
we rose to take our leave, though our host made a formal
effort to detain us to smoke a cigarette. This rule of immediate departure after a meal always seemed to me the only
churlish trait in all their hospitable entertainment.

The talk had turned on the subject of Armenian women
in Arabia. Some 120 of them, possibly including some
Circassians, had drifted down into the Qasim the previous
year on the flood of persecution which had devastated their
homelands. Most of them came destitute and had been taken
to wife by sundry *Qusman*, finding in their new religion the
comfort and in some cases luxury denied them at home.
And the ecclesiastical authorities had recognised their special
need of protection by issuing an edict forbidding divorce
except on the condition that an ample monthly sustenance
for life should be provided by the husband. Some had been
sent down to Ibn Sa'ud as gifts, and by him had been passed
on to favoured courtiers. One had been offered to Muhammad al Sulaiman, who declined the dangerous gift for fear
of offending his actual spouse. And they told us of another
of bewitching beauty recently widowed, whose ambitious

mother was aiming at a splendid marriage coupled with the condition that she herself should enter the domestic service of her son-in-law. These Armenian women were reputed to be good cooks and well versed in the arts of housewifery.

After the midday prayer we sallied out to offer our greetings to old 'Abdul 'Aziz, the ex-*Amir*, whom we found sitting on the floor with a small party of visitors in the passage leading to his outdoor place of reception. He was poring over a slender volume entitled *Taqwim al 'Uyuni*, a sort of meteorological calendar prepared by some scholar of the Hasa to show for a period of 150 years, of which eight had already passed, the dates on which and the stars under which the various agricultural seasons began. We were now in the *Kharif* [1] according to this work, and the *Wasm* or *Safari*, the period of the *Wasmi* or most profitable rains, was due to begin on Muharram 10th, just a month ahead. He was trying to discover an explanation for the heat spell which at this time was certainly very oppressive in the town—the temperature before sunrise on this day of the *'Id* being 80° *Fahr*. The conversation then turned on travelling and education, and an old man of the Bassam family, nearly blind, asked the audience to take note of the great progress in this direction which the English had brought with them to the East.

On our way to keep an appointment with Sulaiman al Dhukair we fell in with another son of the great Zamil ; but Muhammad, like his brother Ibrahim, had been taken with the canker of bigotry. Sad to think that I was thus debarred from more than a passing acquaintance with the sons of one so renowned for tolerance in the great days of the past. Muqbil, Yahaya and 'Abdul 'Aziz al Dhukair were of the party at Sulaiman's, at whose door we entered simultaneously with the younger 'Abdullah al Bassam of Doughty's acquaintance. He was now an old man of over sixty, but well preserved, straight of carriage, with a well-trimmed beard whose grey was completely disguised with black dye—a regular old dandy in appearance and something of a pedant in character. He monopolised the conversation, talking loudly—mainly about medicine. On one occasion Doughty

[1] *See* pp. 60, 108, 167.

had administered a dose or pill of croton-oil to cure his
stomach, and so vigorously did it work that for some hours
he was practically a prisoner in his closet. A little later he
swelled all over, but the physician assured him there was no
ground for alarm, and next day he found himself in better
health than he had ever enjoyed before. And much to the
delight of old Yahaya, into whose deaf ear Sulaiman shouted
the story with considerable embellishments, I told the tale
of the man who had allowed or caused his mother to swallow
at one draught six doses of some stuff Doughty had given
her to effect a quicker cure, and how the latter, hearing
what had happened, told the man to run home as fast as he
could and, if he found his mother sleeping, administer the
contents of the coffee-pot ! Yahaya's only experience of
the outer world had been some fifty-three years before when
he visited Cairo with some merchandise, returning *via* Jidda
and Mecca. Since then Muqbil had conducted the family
business.

Our dinner, like our breakfast, was at the house of 'Abdullah al Hamad al Sulaim, whither we repaired about 5 p.m.
Our host had once visited India, but having dallied on business at Bahrain and Maskat, had found himself too badly
broken in health to enjoy Karachi and Bombay. Speaking
of Doughty he said : ' Really, I cannot but think that he
was lacking in wisdom. If, when called to pray, he had risen
with a " *Hallat al baraka*," [1] he would have had a very
different reception, and God himself would have been as well
pleased with him. Why, there was a certain great person of
Madina—a *Muslim* of course, but not of the *Wahhabi* sect
—who came to Najd and, finding his society not congenial
to the company, began to talk about sparrows.[2] Seeing that
his unwilling hosts considered the bird a delicacy by no means
easy to come by he began to talk big. " Wait till you come
to Madina, where I grow a peculiar kind of millet with spikes
in the seed which kill the birds. I get them by the thousand
and will give you a banquet of sparrows." " Go," said the host

[1] God's blessing on it.

[2] *Asfur*—in this case it probably referred to some other small bird,
though of course sparrows are eaten in Najd as elsewhere, where they are
served up as ortolans.

to a servant, " kill a fine sheep and see that a good dinner is prepared for our noble guest." That,' ended 'Abdullah, ' is the way to get on in the world.'

Dinner was served in an open gallery on the upper floor and our host, following a custom commoner at 'Anaiza than elsewhere, sat at meat with us. The great difference between the standard of life at 'Anaiza and other parts of Najd is due, he said, to the fact that citizens of the former are to be found in all the great commercial centres around Arabia, not as mere passengers but as permanent settlers. And there is no doubt of the civilising influence of mixing with the varied streams of the great world. The people of Buraida, for instance, are, it is true, to be met with at Baghdad, Damascus and elsewhere, but only as seasonal visitors whose permanent homes are in Najd. I told the story of the young churl for whom I had brought money entrusted to me by a relative in Baghdad and who never even invited me into his house. ' 'Anaiza,' I said, ' has so pleased me that I feel it is my home. Would you accept me if I wished to settle permanently among you ? ' ' Certainly,' he replied,' and we will find an 'Anaiza girl for you to marry, and if you accept the religion, so much the better.' ' No,' said Dr. 'Abdullah, ' not at all, he must choose between *Islam* and the abyss.' [1] Our host, who had at our first meetings been somewhat difficult to get conversation out of, had developed rapidly on better acquaintance, and on this day had shown his capacity as a hospitable and entertaining individual. This evening he absolutely insisted on our remaining for a round or two of coffee and cigarettes before departing, and his dinner had been excellent though simple.

At our departure it was still only sunset, and we visited one of the lesser persons of 'Anaiza, one Muhammad al Hamad al Khuraifani—a young man of Shammar origin who had spent seven years at Cairo and had visited Basra. He and his cousin, Muhammad al Hamad al Khardani, lived together, occupying one of the smallest and grimiest parlours I had seen—about six feet square. Time was, however, running short, as 'Abdullah was in a hurry to catch a glimpse of the young ladies on the roof, and we took our leave after

[1] *Al Hawiya.*

a single round of coffee. The day finished with a short and formal call on 'Abdullah the *Amir*, with whom we found 'Abdulrahman Ibn 'Abdul 'Aziz al Zamil, Sulaim and others. I was plied with questions as to the success of my photographic proceedings during the *'Id* prayer, and I was surprised to find how many persons had noticed me sitting alone on the sand peak and knew the purpose of my being there. I heard no word of even veiled criticism of my conduct during the day, and when I said I had been too far off to get a really effective picture, I was asked why I had not approached nearer. ' It would have been unseemly,' I replied, and my delicacy evoked a murmur of appreciation. Each day of my sojourn at 'Anaiza increased my gratitude for the ever-increasing kindness of all who had anything to do with me. For even at this hour we were accosted in the street by Muhammad and 'Abdullah, the sons of 'Ali, son of Zamil, whose pressing invitation to a final cup of coffee we deferred to another day.

I was scarcely awake next morning when visitors were announced, and I had to hurry over my bath and dressing. Descending to the reception-room I found the ex-*Amir* with Ibrahim al Qadhi and others inhaling perfume from a censer which had been brought in to dilute the overnight atmosphere of stale tobacco. My camera came in for close examination, as also my aneroid, for these folk had a natural inquisitiveness about scientific apparatus which argued great possibilities of intellectual achievement—blighted partly by the natural sloth of man living in a labour-discouraging climate, but mainly by the Arabian religious ban on too close prying into the secrets of the Creator. 'Ali, my host's son, was of the party, just arrived from the Hasa where he was in business with Indian connections. And a member of the Ribdi family from Buraida brought news of the recent arrival there of a caravan from Kuwait, with the sad news of the death at Zubair of Hamad al Muhammad, an old member of the Bassam family.

That morning we happened to be invited to breakfast with Fahad, whose messenger now came to fetch [1] us. Muhammad al Sulaiman went forward as we entered and, kissing our host

---

[1] *Yastalhaq* = he is coming to fetch.

on both cheeks, expressed sympathy for the family in their bereavement, saying, ' May God increase your reward,' [1] *i.e.* by patience in enduring the blow. And Fahad replied in mild tones of formal piety : ' May God recompense you and settle him in Paradise.' And, returning good for good, he added : ' May your eye be bright ' [2]—in reference to the return of Muhammad's son to his home. Then we talked of the latest War-news brought by the party from Kuwait. Russia had declared war on the Allies and Germany had carried hostilities eastward by way of the Caspian. British ships were pouring troops into various Persian ports, and a million men were already assembled in a nameless mountain, causing anxiety in Germany. ' Surely,' I said, ' you have forgotten to mention that Baghdad has been recaptured by the Turks.' Kuwait under Salim was a prolific factory of intrigue and propaganda against Great Britain, and Fahad knew that all the news he retailed was false, but there was a spice of malice in him—he was pro-Turk—and a childish belief that the retailing of obvious falsehood was not a bad way of eliciting the truth—or a counter-falsehood between which and the original his intelligence would enable him to strike a happy mean. And I had but little news of what was happening outside Arabia.

Fahad's mansion fronted on the great *Majlis*, a flight of stairs leading up from his front door to the coffee-parlour, but on this occasion we entered by the back door from some obscure street, whence a gypsum-plastered corridor led to the same parlour. Breakfast was served on a great tray, round which we sat on cushions, in a room with bare clay walls ; and Fahad waived the honour of sitting next to me —I wondered whether it was out of the humility which accompanies the hospitality of these parts or whether in his heart of hearts, making a rapid calculation of the ultimate risk, he sought thus unostentatiously to avoid feeding out of the same little dishes as a *Nasrani*.

We passed on to call on 'Abdulrahman Ibn 'Abdul 'Aziz al Zamil, at whose house the young Zamil, son of Salih al Zamil, a friend and fellow-victim at Jarrab of Shakespear, was reputed to be lying sick. Dr. 'Abdullah thought he ought

---

[1] *Adhdham Allah ajrak.*   [2] *Qarrat 'ainak.*

to see him in case he could be of any use. We found the door
bolted from within, and it was after a considerable delay
'Abdulrahman himself opened to our untimely visit, for we
had deprived him of the pleasure of breakfasting in his wife's
company and his wife of her breakfast, to which we were
hospitably bidden in her stead. 'Abdullah and I excused
ourselves from such sacrilege on the plea of having but
recently eaten, but Muhammad al Sulaiman joined our host
and between them they left nothing but scraps of a meal at
once frugal and distinguished. A large bowl of dates and a
bowl of milk was the mainstay thereof, and 'Abdulrahman's
own prowess with his gun had supplied the rest from his
palm grounds—an assortment of little birds, including
doves (*Hamam*), a bird of yellow plumage known as
Safara and a long-necked creature called *Qarnuq*.[1] The

FIG. 9. DIAGRAM OF ARAB BIRD-TRAP.
Explanation.—*a.* slab of stone; *b.* twig to prop *a.* over *c.* pit for
grain or water; *d.* low parapet to conceal *e.* the fowler; *f.* string
pulled to remove *b.*

Safara, said our host, was supposed to be the bird which
God made to descend from Paradise for the sustenance of
Bani Isra'il during their wanderings in the desert. I told him
that according to our tradition the bird in question was the
quail, which descended not from heaven but, as it still does,
from our own fair lands of Europe. The trapping of birds
is a common pastime of those who have no gun, and some
weeks later at Shamasiya I saw an ingenious contrivance.[2]
The fowler sits in a hole scooped out of the ground with a
breastwork to conceal him from his victim, holding one end
of a long string which at the other end is attached to a piece
of wood, about six inches long and propping up a slab of
stone set slantwise over a small pit, to which the birds come
down either to bathe after rain or to eat seed deposited
therein. When the bird is in, the string is pulled and the
slab descends on the pit, imprisoning it. It sounds a tedious

[1] This was of whitish plumage, possibly a Paddy-bird.
[2] *Vide* Fig. 9.

process, but may well be as absorbing as the fisherman's craft.

'Muhammadan tradition,' said 'Abdulrahman, who was commonly addressed as Zamil—a sweet name at 'Anaiza— 'has it that God sent down wisdom and philosophy to only three races, the Greeks, the Chinese, and the Arabs ; but from what I have seen of your people and heard of your country I would add a fourth—ay, I would add the *Inglis*.' 'We have,' I replied, ' but garnered in what we have from the store that the Arabs have long neglected, and to this day we use many Arabic words in the vocabulary of science—in mathematics and astronomy and the like. We took from you and have improved on what we took.' ' Are there, then, still among you,' he asked, ' folk who study the stars ? Yet there is one thing we have, we Arabs of Najd, more perfect than you will find it elsewhere, and you know what I mean.' ' Yes,' I answered, ' your religion, and your religion of 'Anaiza is more perfect than that of the rest of Najd, for you temper it with humanity and tolerance, which I have not found elsewhere.' And so we talked on pleasantly until it was time to go. The company of this grandson of Zamil was always a charming experience, and the mild hospitality and frank friendliness of his bearing always suggested to me the picture which Doughty drew of Zamil himself, though they said that physically the nearest living approaches to the great man were his son Muhammad and his grandson Zamil Ibn Salih, whom we had come to see though he was unfortunately not at home and fortunately not sick though in delicate health. 'Abdulrahman was full of a gentle, almost womanly solicitude for his cousin, who was also his half-brother—the two being the sons of two brothers by the same mother. I asked about available histories of the period in which Zamil lived and was recommended to study Ibn Ghannam and Ibn Bishr, the latter the author of a complete history of Najd under the Sa'ud dynasty up to the date of his own death in A.H. 1250.[1]

The afternoon found us again in a Zamil atmosphere, our hosts being his grandsons 'Abdullah and Muhammad, aged about thirty-five and thirty respectively and sprung from his second son 'Ali, who was killed at the battle of Mulaida

[1] About A.D. 1834.

in A.H. 1308.[1] The two brothers sat behind the coffee-hearth,
myself close up by the elder with another visitor, 'Abdul 'Aziz
Ibn Maiman, on my left—the last-named a citizen of 'Anaiza
whom I had not before met.[2] 'Abdullah had travelled little,
but from his conversation seemed to be entirely devoid of
all bigotry, while his younger brother had seen a good deal
of the eastern world and was shortly setting out again for
Basra and India. He complained that in these days it was
difficult to get permission to go to Baghdad, which he wanted
to include in his tour, and rejoiced gratefully when I volunteered to overcome the obstacles in his way for him—a
slight return for the hospitality I had enjoyed in his native
town. We naturally talked much of Zamil, an honoured
name, as I said, among the British. He had, they told me,
ten sons[3] and six daughters, the eldest son, 'Abdullah, being
mentioned by Doughty as a churlish cub. 'Ali al Sulaim,
the fanatical executive *Amir* of Doughty's time died an
octogenarian in A.H. 1314,[4] and I had met one of his sons,
a greybeard himself, at the *Amir* 'Abdullah's reception the
previous evening, though I did not then realise who he was.
Another victim of the battle of Mulaida was the *Amir's* own
father, Khalid al Sulaim.

As they helped me to sugar with my tea Dr. 'Abdullah
checked them, saying I preferred it unsweetened, at which
half incredulously they passed me a cup of the bitter stuff,
as they call it, and expressed amazement at my drinking it
so. The Arab loves sugar, and if one may believe them their
excessive use of it does them no harm.

Returning homeward we chanced to pass by an open door
at which the host was seeing a guest off. '*Tafadhdhal*,' he
said hospitably to us and we entered. This was 'Abdul 'Aziz
al Tamimi, whose courtyard, partly roofed over, served as
parlour. There was only the soft sand of the *Nafud* to sit

[1] About A.D. 1891. Zamil himself was killed in the same battle.

[2] He was in fact our next-door neighbour.

[3] I was only able to get the names of seven, as follows : 'Abdullah ; 'Ali,
killed at Mulaida and survived by his sons, 'Abdullah and Muhammad ;
'Abdul'Aziz, father of 'Abdulrahman ; Salih, killed at Jarrab and survived
by his son Zamil, aged fifteen ; Muhammad and Ibrahim, both living and
bigoted ; and Yahaya, who died childless.

[4] About A.D. 1897.

on. We had been accompanied here by 'Abdul 'Ali al 'Ali,
the old man already mentioned, and the only other guest
was 'Abdullah al Hamad al Sulaim. The talk turned on
horses, of which a batch of fourteen had recently been collected by a dealer, Muhammad Ibn Shamlan, to take down
to Kuwait for shipment to India. I saw them later in the
day in company with 'Abdullah al Hamad, who introduced
me to the dealer's brother, Nasir, and to 'Abdullah al Tamimi.
It seemed to my inexpert eyes a pleasing selection of animals,
though most of them were somewhat on the small side.
The majority of them were bays (*ahmar*), including the best
of the lot, an animal bought from the Dhafir, and therefore probably Mesopotamian rather than *Najdi* by origin.
Another fine animal was from the 'Ataiba, who with the
Harb and Mutair were the main suppliers of this particular
market. All were stallions—one a dark chestnut (*ashqar*),
two greys (*asfar*) and two flea-bitten greys (*rummani*). The
Indian market had come to a standstill owing to the War,
and this was said to be the first batch collected for some time.
'Anaiza, whose climate, they said, resembles that of Bombay
—being comparatively damp—has a special reputation as a
Marbat or collecting centre, but is not itself a breeding-ground.
The main supply divisions known to Indian buyers are, they
said, Jazira, *i.e.* Upper Mesopotamia, Gharraf or Lower
Mesopotamia, Al 'Ajm, by which is meant Persia or Kurdistan,
and Najd. The leading Arab horse merchants of Bombay
at this time were Jarallah Ibn Talib of Mausal and Ibn Faris
of Zubair. Formerly there was Ibn Mani', a native of Shaqra
and possibly the man referred to by Doughty, who had died
some years before. Jarallah's brother, 'Ali, had befriended
the British prisoners from Kut al Amara on their way through
Mausal, and at General Townshend's request had advanced
them £500. This was afterwards refunded by the Indian
Government to Jarallah, together with presents for all the
members of the family and the thanks of the Government.
'Abdullah al Tamimi told the story in my presence one day
to a very appreciative audience as an instance of British
gratitude for services rendered.

Reaching home, where our host's charming children ran
out into the street to greet us as they often did, Dr. 'Abdullah

found a patient seeking relief for the epileptic fits to which he was subject. And another soon arrived, Zamil Ibn Salih, accompanied by 'Abdulrahman. He was a pleasing type of young man and seemed in good enough health though liable to malarial attacks, for which Dr. 'Abdullah gave him a supply of quinine. It was then, though only 5 p.m., time to sally out for dinner, which, like that day's breakfast, was at the charge of Fahad al Bassam. On this occasion, owing to a manœuvre, perhaps deliberate, of Muhammad al Sulaiman, Fahad was left with no choice but to sit next to me, and he even went so far as to select choice morsels from here and there to place in my section of the dish, but, carefully as I watched, I did not observe him eating out of any of the dishes where my fingers had been at work. That may have been accidental, but when I asked if I might photograph him he declined on the ground that it would be *haram*. ' But,' he added, ' I would like to have a photograph of the *'Id* prayer.' His religion was definitely Ottoman rather than *Wahhabi* of complexion, and his politics Turkish rather than Arab in outlook. His brother Muhammad was at this time—as he still is—one of the leading merchants of Damascus, where, according to Fahad, he had been harbouring English spies. The Bassam family had favoured Ibn Rashid in the days of the struggle for the Qasim between him and Ibn Sa'ud, but Fahad himself had kept clear of that treachery—doubtless having shrewdly satisfied himself as to the probabilities of success on either side—and had remained staunch to the cause of 'Anaiza and Ibn Sa'ud, with the result that he alone of the family was allowed to remain after the latter's final victory. The other members of the family had drifted back since then.

At Muhammad al Sulaiman's suggestion and without seeing any particular point in it, I asked Fahad about a certain Ibrahim al Qadhi, not the man of that name I had met but his cousin—he was also a cousin of the chief priest Salih and a maternal uncle of Fahad. He had a reputation for great learning, though said to be fanatical and somewhat effusive in his loyalty to Ibn Sa'ud. Muhammad's somewhat curious object, as I afterwards learned from him, was to contrive that Ibrahim should hear that I had enquired about him in the hope that this circumstance might induce him to try and be friendly with me. Fahad, being notoriously a social busybody, was certain to let him know, but all he said in reply to me was that the object of my enquiry was indeed a man of great learning but one who seldom went out—a clever *riposte* to a manœuvre which he probably saw through.

His young cousin, 'Abdul 'Aziz al Bassam, had for some time been in our bad books by reason of his activity in smuggling goods through from Kuwait to the Turks *via* Hail. I twitted him on this and was surprised at his taking the matter quite seriously—denying that it was so. But Hamad, who had told me, disconcerted him not a little by telling the story of his meeting 'Abdul 'Aziz in a caravan bound for Hail. I let the subject drop when he asseverated that the man was still at Kuwait, but felt that, Fahad being for commercial reasons so anxious to stand well with all parties to the conflict, a gentle hint that his family was suspect in certain quarters could do no harm. I felt increasingly that he did not improve on acquaintance, especially when he dabbled in war-scandal. His further enquiries had elicited the information that an official news-bulletin had been posted up at Kuwait that King Constantine had been reinstated as Czar of Russia by the Germans and had declared war on the Allies. Such was the prattle one heard in these days in the best intellectual company of 'Anaiza. On another point, however, if he kept a diary as I did, the laugh will be on his side, for he told me that Mr. Lloyd George had somewhere expressed the opinion that the War would end that year, to which I replied sceptically that in my opinion it would last another four years. He agreed deferentially that I was doubtless right.

Having made a *détour* on the way home to see the horses, which were in some fields beyond Malah, I got back about sunset to find little 'Atiq all decked out in his *'Id* finery and surrounded by a bevy of young ladies of his own age playing some game of which he appeared to be the hero. Merry laughter greeted my appearance, and I passed on up to the roof, where Dr. 'Abdullah was wistfully gazing out on to the empty scene of the revels of the three belles. In fact he had not drawn entirely blank, for the three girls accompanied by

a fourth had actually appeared for a few moments. And he
declared thay had made signs at him and shouted at him
though he could not hear what they said. The fourth was
apparently an elder sister of the other three, who some years
since had been given in marriage to our next-door neighbour,
the octogenarian 'Abdul 'Aziz Ibn Maiman. The latter already
had two wives well stricken in years, but the girl, only about
sixteen or seventeen at the time, immediately asserted
herself and presented her old husband with an ultimatum,
as the result of which the two old wives were turned out of
the house. Such is the great tragedy of the Islamic marriage
laws—the stranding of derelict women when they cease to
serve the main purpose for which men wed. Those who are
childless when their turn comes are indeed worthy of pity.
Again the following evening Dr. 'Abdullah and I found that
we had not been altogether forgotten by the young ladies,
though on this occasion only one of them—apparently the
youngest, a mere girl of thirteen and the last of the three to
be married—appeared on the roof. And she was in all her
bridal finery, a flame-coloured gown with a filmy veil of
mauve thrown negligently about her shoulders and later
discarded altogether to show her braided locks crowned with
a small flattened tiara of gold and turquoises. Without any
pretence of bashfulness she stood forth to be seen to the best
advantage while she carried on a conversation with somebody
invisible to us. Certainly she was very beautiful—a picture
of typical Oriental grace and glamour—and she was almost
a child by our ideas.

After the evening prayer we called on Salih al Fadhl and
passed a pleasant hour in his outdoor parlour. After a round
of coffee a raspberry-flavoured sherbet was passed round in
long glasses set on a clean white china tray with a nickel rim.
Clean white towels were handed to each of us on which to
wipe hands and mouth, and there followed sliced melons
served with the same regard to cleanliness. Salih's wife,
though herself of 'Anaiza, had spent many years at Madina
and had not forgotten the lessons learned in the highly-
polished Turkish society of the place. The general standard
of housewifery is high at 'Anaiza, though there were some
notable exceptions, but Salih's was unquestionably the model

establishment. Dietz and other lamps with glass globes were to be found commonly in these houses, but the usual type was a clockwork globeless lamp, which was quite efficient and dispensed with the serious necessity of replacing broken glasses. Hurricane-lamps were also in common use and by far the most useful type. One never seemed to hear of houses catching fire in these parts, though doubtless such occurrences were not altogether unknown. Salih had a specially soft place in his heart for Madina and seemed even to regret the ' improvements,' which the Turks were being enabled to carry out in the matter of street-widening by the great reduction of the population due to emigration and other War causes. They were said to be extending the railway right up to the neighbourhood of the *Haram*, from which they had already removed the whole of its ' pious spoil.' The general opinion was that Fakhri Pasha would be able to hold out indefinitely unless the strong fortifications were carried by storm, which was most unlikely. The flight of the inhabitants had resulted in a large area of palms being neglected for want of labour. For lack of water they would slowly perish.

On 19th September came the first detailed news of Ibn Sa'ud's movements, which will be set forth in the next section of this chapter. Meanwhile the duty of entertaining us for the day having been allotted to 'Abdullah al Bassam and his brother, 'Abdulrahman,[1] a special treat had been arranged for us by them in the shape of a visit to the ' country.' About 7 a.m. Dr. 'Abdullah and I, accompanied by Muhammad al Sulaiman and a young nephew of his, whose father was a merchant in the Hasa, sallied out on foot *via* Malah and, leaving Dhabat to our right, struck across country from the main road until, after passing under a *Qantara* or aqueduct of palm trunks, we came to the garden of Rumaihiya, a magnificently dense grove of tall, fruit-laden palms with a rich undergrowth of fig-trees, limes, etc., belonging to 'Ali al Bassam, whom we met as we passed through. This garden was unwalled and was adjacent to the walled-in property of Muhairiya, to which 'Abdullah al Bassam had bidden us for

[1] Two other brothers had died respectively twelve years and one year previously.

breakfast. Before entering it, however, we turned aside to inspect a group of wells sunk to a depth of 8 or 10 fathoms into a pocket of sweet water and serving for the irrigation of a large number of gardens. One of them had a super-structure of ten wheels, five a side, half of which were being worked at the time by camel-traction. The 'Anaiza camels are mostly black, though other colours were not wholly absent, the most common being a darkish dun.

'Abdullah and his brother—my next meeting with the latter was to be in London in 1926 !—welcomed us most warmly on our entry into their garden, where, now wandering about, now coffee-drinking or breakfasting in a summer-house of palm branches with a spread of soft red sand from the *Nafud* in lieu of carpet, we remained till it was time for us to wend our way back down the north road about midday.

This was reputed to be the best garden in the whole oasis, in spite of some deterioration in recent years, for at one time, said 'Abdullah, there was a thick undergrowth of fruit trees, whereas at this time the splendid palms stood in gaunt rows over a carpet of green millet. The soil was a light sandy loam necessitating frequent manuring,[1] and the garden covered an area of six *jaribs* or three acres. In its centre was a ten-fathom well from which the water was discharged by camel-draught into a masonry basin, from which it flowed into an enclosed bathing-pool—a delightful touch of civilisa-tion. Thence it passed on either side into long masonry reservoirs, from which distributary runnels convey it to every part of the property. Near the entrance is a row of mud-huts for the labourers and their families, while the summer-house stands at the edge of the palms, which, planted in straight rows, occupy about two-thirds of the whole area, the rest being devoted to the cultivation of lucerne. The summer-house itself consisted of several rooms—a parlour, a dining-room and apartments for 'Abdullah and his brother and their families when they come out for a change from their town-house. 'Abdullah's son, Muhammad, did the honours at the coffee-hearth, but otherwise took no part in the proceedings. The picnic began with the service of melons

---

[1] *Samad* (pl. *asmad*) is manure in general, while *dimal* is applied only to camel and other animal dung. Sewage is regarded as unclean and not used.

in the parlour, after which we moved to the dining-room for breakfast, which consisted of plain boiled rice and mutton with an assortment of small birds, including the *Safara*, which was somewhat tasteless, and with many small dishes of meat in richly-spiced gravy almost like curry. And there were of course dates in amazing variety—about a dozen different kinds, all from the garden, which in fact contained some twenty-eight different varieties. These 'Abdullah claimed to be fully representative of the whole oasis, for he had never failed to establish in his own garden any new kind that was brought to 'Anaiza, and he himself had imported many varieties from 'Iraq. Here, for the first time in Arabia, I tasted the *Buraim* and *Hasawi* from Basra and the *Barhi* of similar origin, and he proudly showed me the first palm of the last-named species which ever came to 'Anaiza, a tall stem planted thirty-five years before. The oldest palm in this garden was thirty-seven years old, the garden itself having thus come into existence since Doughty's time. Other varieties which I saw or tasted on this occasion were : the *Sukari*, the *Umm al Khashb*—so-called from the circumstance that its heavy bunches of great red fruit have to be propped up with poles lest they break, and this variety is not gathered as other dates, for the whole branch is severed from the palm and hung up throughout the winter, the fruit remaining fresh all the time—the *Hilwa*, the *Qattar*, the *Rusainiya*, reputed the most delicious of all—a delicate light-brown fruit of medium size—the *Umm al Hamam* and many others. Throughout the garden I walked barefooted on sand or soft grasses.

Both on this occasion and later at dinner in their townhouse, when 'Abdul 'Aziz, who was present, waxed enthusiastic on the subject, we talked of ways and means of increasing the water supply, of motor-driven pumps and artesian bores ; and they thought perhaps that my present visit might ultimately prove fruitful in this direction, though, so far as I know, 'Anaiza is still irrigated in the old way while Madina has for years had its pumps. I suggested that it would be uneconomical to set up a pumping plant for a small garden, but 'Abdul 'Aziz looked at the matter from the labour-saving point of view. ' Why,' he said, ' we could use it for an hour a

day and let it lie idle the rest of the time.' I advised that
they should select half a dozen intelligent boys to send to
India to study such machines, but ' that,' he said, ' is beyond
our intelligence. You English are full of energy, but we are
mere clods of clay. The Arab has brains, but they care not
to use them.' We talked also of medicine, a subject in which
the great citizens of the town were all interested and had a
smattering of knowledge. 'Abdullah took us out to see a
second walled enclosure of his on the north flank of his
garden. This he allowed to run wild with a growth of *Ithils*
to form a bulwark against the encroachment of the *Nafud*
sand. Here he pointed out a low spreading weed called
Jalab, whose roots are boiled to form a powerful emetic.
This and another plant he afterwards from his encyclopaedia
identified respectively as *Ipecacuanha* [1] and *Jaborandi*, from
which *Pilocarpin* is extracted. And he told us that near
Jidda he had discovered the *Caffeine* plant known in Arabia
as *Ruh al Qahwa*, though he had not since come across it
elsewhere. In the *Nafud*, he said, grows a plant called
Ghalqa, which no animal will touch, for it is deadly poison.
As for the *Datura* they agreed that it does not occur at all
or only very rarely in Najd, and they confessed to complete
ignorance of the plant mentioned by Palgrave as producing
fits of giggling in those rash enough to try it. I was surprised
at both my hosts submitting to being photographed without
any reluctance, and we left them in their garden to see them
again in the evening in town.

Their parlour was large with bare clay walls somewhat
grimed with smoke—no plaster and no attempt at the usual
decoration. Fahad was there too and again sat next to me,
but had taken the precaution of dining at home and merely
toyed with a dish of *blanc-mange*. After dinner 'Abdullah
produced a handsomely-bound volume in which was inscribed
by his hand, page after page of it, the complete genealogical
tree of the Bassam family to date—a subject to which he had
devoted much attention and labour. To my delight he
allowed me to take it away to copy its contents.[2] The tree
went back from the youngest members of the living generations to Hamad, the first of the family to migrate to 'Anaiza

---

[1] *Cephaelis ipecacuanha (Rubiaceae).*   [2] *See* Appendix I.

in A.H. 1173 [1] from Wushaiqir owing to local disturbances. Thence it was traced back through Bassam, the eponymous ancestor, to Tamim and further to the point where the line branched off from the stock of which the Prophet came. And thence finally through the realm of pure legend to Alyas and beyond. Incidentally he told me that *Qasr Bassam* in the settlement of Barud had no connection with the family, its name being derived from a man so-called who was in no way related to them.

On our way back from the Bassam garden and when passing through the *Suq* we had met old Muqbil al Dhukair sitting on the raised sill of an unpretentious shop, his place of retail business—all wholesale transactions being usually conducted here in private houses. In response to his invitation we proceeded to his house later to foregather with his sons and brother. The ex-*Amir* and the *Amir* 'Abdullah himself were also of the party, and the conversation turned on the subject of inheritance rights in connection with the recent death of Hamad [2] al Bassam, over whose estate some dispute had arisen in the family. The *Shar'* rule is of course followed here, giving one-eighth of all the property of a deceased person to his surviving wives between them and dividing the residue among the children in the ratio of two shares to each son and one to each daughter. In the present case there were no heirs of the first degree in question, but only the children of nephews, and the dispute was as to whether daughters of nephews had any claim. The prospective male beneficiaries were contesting the equitable and generally-shared view that the daughters had a right to shares, and, well-to-do as they were, were trying to exclude a family of comparatively indigent women from anything but a mere pittance. ' Such is the world's way,' sighed the kindly old ex-*Amir*, ' the strong have no shame, fearing not God, and the weak go to the wall.' In all such gatherings 'Abdul 'Aziz always took precedence over those present, and on this occasion the *Amir* 'Abdullah, being offered the second cup of coffee, pointed to me, but as the man approached to pour out for me I deprecated the honour and 'Abdullah with mild words accepted the homage to his

---

[1] About A.D. 1760.   [2] *See* above, p. 269.

rank. Such were their gentle dignified manners—a charming relic of an old world. As one rose to go the host would always detain one a little longer ; ' *tutaiyib*,' [1] he would say and then, producing the censer,[2] would prepare the embers and incense [3] himself for his guests, who after the solemn ceremony would be free to go.

In the evening we visited Muhammad Ibn Sulaiman al Shubaili, who, like his cousin Nasir, was more Mesopotamian than *Najdi*, of somewhat unnatural bearing and obsequious. He had married at Baghdad in A.H. 1318 [4] and spent most of his time there and at Basra, where his grievance was not the assessment of compensation for his lands—he thought it was quite reasonable—but the occupation of his family residence near the Whiteley Bridge. At 'Anaiza he was residing temporarily in a hired house pending the rebuilding of his own. And at his hands we experienced a departure from Najd customs, having rose-water sprinkled over our heads after partaking of melons and a very sickly sherbet.

The following day, Friday, 20th September, was spent comparatively quietly, and the task of entertaining us fell on Sulaiman al Dhukair. Before going to him for breakfast Muhammad al Sulaiman and I called on Sulaim, whose parlour was a model of cleanliness and neatness. Abul Faraj, a substantial merchant of Madina though ruined by the War and now for some time resident here, was of the party though he talked but little ; and also Sulaiman al Qublan—probably husband of one of the three beauties—but he was quite silent. Sulaim's three-year-old son, Yahaya, sat by my side and, having the previous day seen Khalid, the ex-*Amir's* son, aged eight, and heard from him that he had just had his first lesson in shooting, I asked him if he could shoot. And the conversation turned on rifles and game-shooting. According to Sulaim the cutting and paring down of the long military rifle produces no appreciable effect on the accuracy of the weapon, whose lightness is a paramount consideration for those who fight on horseback—a rapidly-disappearing feature of Arab life. I said that I had not yet had the fortune to meet any Arab who could really be called a good shot, and he retailed a story of such an one ' with a splendid eye,'

[1] ' Take incense.'   [2] *Midkhan.*   [3] *'Ud.*   [4] About A.D. 1900.

who, while travelling with some companions, came upon five gazelles grazing together. Thereupon, warning his friends not to shoot on any account, he loaded his rifle and with five shots bagged the lot. The short British service rifle is known as *Sharfa* and the long one as *Samha* or *Umm Ahad'ashar* ; the Enfield carbine is known from its ' crown ' mark as *Umm Taj* ; while the old and new pattern Mauser are called respectively *Umm 'Ashara* and *Umm Khams* from their magazine capacity ; the Winchester Repeater is the *Umm Sab'at'ashar*—the ' Mother of seventeen.' Of these the *Umm Taj* was most highly prized, with the new Mauser a good second and the *Sharfa* next, the last-named coming in these days exclusively from the *Sharif*, who dished them out indiscriminately to the *Badu* to be sold in turn by them in the interior. The *Sharif's* officials also made a good thing out of this business of selling rifles meant to be used against the Turks to the followers of one who was to be in the near future their master's successful rival. Only a few days before this an 'Anaiza man had brought away some twenty boxes of ammunition and taken them down to the Hasa, where Ibn Jiluwi agreed to buy them. While the contents were being counted the man, who must have strained his heart in moving the heavy boxes, suddenly fell down dead with streams of blood pouring out of his mouth. He was removed, in the hope that his life could yet be saved, to the house of Salih al Sulaiman, but, though the blood continued flowing all through the night, he never recovered. Sulaim, now about thirty-five, had as a boy accompanied the rest of his family into exile and had traded at Maskat, whence on one occasion he had accompanied his father and a consignment of rifles to Kuwait.

At breakfast, which was served in the open on a low roof shaded by the palms of an adjacent garden, Yahaya and Muqbil were present besides our host, while at dinner we were honoured with the company of the ex-*Amir*, and Muhammad al Sulaiman's son, 'Ali, was also present. The latter I had visited during the day in his new house in the same street as ours, recently purchased in view of his approaching marriage—the main object of his present visit to 'Anaiza—for 600 dollars. It was worth, they said, quite 800,

and would easily fetch a rent of 40 dollars a year. The
parlour decoration was elaborate with various Quranic
inscriptions and a chronogram, elucidated by figures, for the
date of the building, A.H. 1328.[1] 'Ali had spent four years
in business at Bombay, six months at Jubail and two or
three years in the Hasa, where he had learned something of
the pearl trade. Pearls are sold by weight under a complicated system for the division of the proceeds between all
concerned in their getting the largest buying organisation
being represented by M. Rosenthal of Paris, known to the
Arabs as Habib. According to him Jubail was a *Baduwi*
settlement with a good harbour, obstructed to some extent
by a bar,[2] but not so badly as the 'Uqair entrance. It was
superior to Qatif in having deep water right up to the wharves
in place of shallows necessitating the use of lighterage for
nearly a mile.

Muqbil again aired his minor grievance in connection with
some property of his at Bahrain, of which mention has
already been made. In the time of Major Trevor, then
Political Agent, a compromise had been effected by which
the road was to be made straight across, and since then
the land had lain vacant. Recently, however, a plot had
been sold for building purposes and an office clerk, a Persian
with a spite against Muqbil, had revived the old controversy
about the diagonal road, with which the proposed building
was alleged to interfere.

Religion was the topic of conversation at the evening meal.
' I notice,' said 'Abdul 'Aziz, ' that you say *Inshállah*, but that
is surely not the way of the English. I have been aboard
your ships often, and when I have enquired when we were
expected to arrive the captains have always answered with
an air of absolute assurance : " We shall be there at such or
such a time." ' I explained that in England a Latin formula
with the same meaning as *Inshallah* is not infrequently used,
and added, to their great amusement, that experience had
even taught us to associate the weather with the Deity in such
circumstances. ' If God wills,'' the old man went on, ' Philby
will become *Muslim*, we would not have him go to the fire.'
' I will wait,' I replied, ' till the coming of Christ, which your

---

[1] About A.D. 1910.   [2] *Riqq.*

books assure us of, and if He confirms the preaching of the
Prophet, I will join you.' 'But,' retorted 'Abdul 'Aziz Ibn
Yahaya, ' it will then be too late, for salvation is only for
those who have put their faith in Muhammad.' Fear of the
fire is very real in the devout Arabian, and the ex-*Amir* with
a sigh quoted the *Hadith* [1] about the sects of the Jews,
Christians and Muslims, all destined for the fire except one.
He was genuinely gratified at my taking him up and finishing
the quotation—sure sign that I was studying the teachings
of the Prophet—and he was still more delighted when I
quoted again from the same source : ' There is none born but
is born within the fold, but their fathers make Christians of
them or Jews or Mages.' Old Muqbil spoke of the Gospel of
Barnaba, in which he had seen foretold the coming of a
Prophet called Ahmad,[2] and in soft impressive tones quoted
a long passage from the *Quran* about the Ministry of 'Isa.
In doing so he omitted the essential preamble : ' God says,'
and, meekly submitting to the ex-*Amir's* correction, began
it all over again. He referred to the disciples of Christ as
Al Hawariyin.

After the evening prayer we brought our day's activities
to an end with a call on 'Abdullah and Muhammad, sons of
'Ali al Zamil, with whom was Nasir al Shubaili. 'Anaiza was
eagerly waiting now for every bit of news about the progress
of Ibn Sa'ud's campaign, and at every gathering the subject
came up. In one of his books 'Abdullah had come across a
passage which reminded him of Shakespear. ' Was it our
Shakespear ? ' he asked, ' or perhaps his brother or father ? '
The reference was to our great dramatist. The Sulaim family
derives its name from Zamil's grandfather, who had five sons
—'Abdullah, Yahaya, Ibrahim, Muhammad, and 'Ali, the
last-named [3] being, as 'Abdullah agreed, a harsh man without
tact or good sense. 'Abdullah was supposed to resemble
Zamil physically more than any of the living members of the
family ; yet when he smiled in his gentle deprecating way I
thought I saw the characteristic smile of the *Amir* 'Abdullah.
Among other things he told me of some non-Arabic inscriptions on the face of the *Safra* cliff to the right of the *Rafi'a*

---

[1] *See H.A.* vol. i. p. 112.   [2] *i.e.* Muhammad.

[3] ' Executive *Amir* ' of 'Anaiza in Doughty's time.

Sangar, but I never had an opportunity of investigating them properly, though Dr. 'Abdullah and I made an abortive expedition the following day, to find nothing but a few *Wasms* and a short Arabic text [1] or name which we could not decipher.

He was again of the party next morning when Dr. Abdullah and I called on Sulaiman al Sa'aiyid, the witch-doctor, who, as on the previous occasion, overwhelmed us with hospitality, insisting on our partaking of dates, melons and curdled milk, in addition to which he produced a bowl of melon-juice to

FIG. 10. INSCRIPTION ON A ROCK IN THE 'ANAIZA *Safra*.

which I did not feel equal at that early hour. Ghazi, the *Harbi* member of my party, had lately been showing signs of a ' devil ' within him, and the previous day over some trifling dispute he had drawn his sword on one of the others. Dr. 'Abdullah and Muhammad al Sulaiman were strongly for his instant dismissal, but I suggested it would be better to hand him over to our host for treatment, to which Sulaiman enthusiastically agreed. Very modestly he protested at 'Abdullah's not having visited him more often, as he had hoped, he said, to increase his medical knowledge by converse with him, and the latter answering somewhat rudely, I thought, as he often did when not interested, I came to our host's rescue : ' At any rate in one matter you have nothing to learn from 'Abdullah, who is powerless against sprites.' The old man was delighted, though I thought that perhaps

[1] *Vide* Fig. 10.

some of his seriousness over his pet subject may have been an affectation.

We afterwards spent the time before breakfast in strolling through the gardens immediately south of the town. Passing Fahad al Bassam's property of Munaihiya, we ended up in a fine, large garden of perhaps eight or nine acres belonging to 'Abdulrahman al 'Abdul 'Aziz al Zamil, in which there were many fig-trees, now practically destitute of fruit, and quantities of tomatoes and egg-plants. This area is irrigated from a well about 8 or 9 fathoms deep, which also supplies a long narrow masonry reservoir shaded by a double row of fig-trees, and is adjoined by a garden belonging to Ibrahim al Zamil. The gardener told me that the bunches of dates are always left on the tree until the first shower of rain, when, whether ripe or not, the fruit is collected and stored. The date, however ripe, does not fall to the ground—*pace* Palgrave—but merely shrivels up in its skin.

On the way to the house of Nasir al Shubaili for breakfast we came upon a group crossing the lesser *Majlis*, in which were Ibrahim al Qadhi, 'Abdullah al 'Ali al Zamil and others, whom I obtained permission to photograph. After the operation I had to demonstrate the working of the camera, and Ibrahim in particular was like a child in the pleasure he took in looking through the view-finder. Nasir looked somewhat perturbed as we entered and hurriedly whispered something in Muhammad al Sulaiman's ear. As I afterwards learned he had only expected three of us, but in so doing he was entirely in the wrong according to local etiquette, which laid upon him the duty of entertaining the whole retinue of a guest. A long delay accordingly supervened before breakfast was at length served, and then there was enough to feed fifty persons, peaches forming a welcome and luxurious addition to the ordinary light menu.

I walked home with 'Ali al Sha'aithan, whom I met in the great *Majlis*, and found Fahad al Bassam and Salih al Fadhl waiting for me or rather for the latest war-news, having heard that the courier from Kuwait had brought me a mail. There was nothing of importance, but I passed on copies of the Arabic *Basra Times* to them to peruse and send to the *Amir*. We then called on our octogenarian neighbour,

'Abdul 'Aziz al Maiman, who received us warmly in his spacious but simple parlour, whose walls were adorned with a dado of white *juss* picked out with stepped pinnacles at the top. A slight variation of the usual theme was a thin white line [1] running round the top of the pinnacles—somewhat suggestive of the cornice of the Petra façades. Above the dado the walls were of bare clay, except for a chronogram giving the date of the building as A.H. 1334.[2] Coffee was prepared in the ordinary way at the hearth and then two

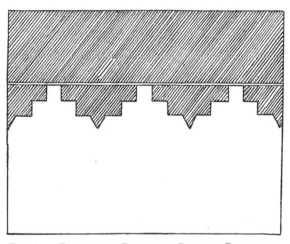

Fig. 11. Dado with Fringe of Stepped Pinnacles
surmounted by white line (as cornice) in house of 'Abdul 'Aziz al Maiman
at 'Anaiza.

trays were brought in, one loaded with glasses and the other with three teapots, the tea, which had been specially prepared for us by his wife, the eldest of the four Graces, being of two kinds—black or Indian and white, also known as *Istambuli*, being Russian tea imported *via* Constantinople. Tea had only been in regular use in Central Arabia for some thirty-five years, before which a hot lemon concoction with sugar had been in vogue. Another charming attention of the young wife, who may or may not have known who her husband's guests were, was the dropping of a bundle of fans from an upper invisible window into the sand-strewn courtyard, whence our old host fetched them to distribute among us.

[1] *Vide* Fig. 11.   [2] About A.D. 1916.

He was suffering from eczema or some other horrible affection of the skin, his right hand being raw with the malady and his nose disfigured with an enormous scab.

We passed on to the *Amir* 'Abdullah, whom we found engrossed in the *Basra Times.* He confessed he had no very clear idea where the Caspian might be, and, getting at a tangent on the subject of gold, told us that years ago gold-bearing ore of a glistering red colour had been found in the mountain of Hulaita two days' journey S.W. to S.S.W. from 'Anaiza. A *Baduwi*, commissioned by somebody at Basra, had carried away several sacks of it, but since then no more had been heard of the matter. At the same place are said to be ruins of an old town—perhaps a mining centre of ancient times.

Dinner was at the Shubaili house, and in the course of conversation about ancient inscriptions somebody volunteered the information that at about an hour's journey from 'Anaiza, apparently in the *Safra*, there is a hill called Qarat al Kis. This is said to contain a cavernous underground chamber or corridor which, starting from an entrance about the height of a man, increases in size and has never been properly explored owing to local fear of *Suknis* or sprites. On every occasion of an attempt to enter it hurricane-lamps had been suddenly extinguished. I expressed a desire to succeed where others had failed, and was promised an opportunity of making the attempt, but circumstances dictated otherwise. Dr. 'Abdullah, feeling tired, had not wanted to come out to dinner, but after half agreeing with my suggestion that there was no need to do so, he decided to come with us on the ground that it would not be seemly for a male guest to remain behind when his host and all male members of the family had departed, leaving only women in the house. ' But,' said I, ' that happened to me on Friday when you all went out for the *Juma*' prayer.' ' With you,' he replied, ' it is quite a different matter.' On our way home we called in to say good-night to the ex-*Amir*, in whose parlour I noticed the *Amir* 'Abdullah seated in the humblest place, and as I went towards him to offer my greetings, he smiled as if deprecating my paying him any attention in the presence of his senior. On such occasions all the members of the family

—Ibrahim al Hamad and Sulaim and 'Abdulrahman were also present—occupy the lowest places and only strangers sit with the host. Polygamy was the chief topic of conversation, the *Amir* 'Abdullah venturing the opinion that Europe's losses of men during the War would compel her to abandon her monogamous basis both in order to make good the actual deficiency in the population and also in fairness to the women otherwise deprived of all chance of marriage. ' Do you people of Europe indulge in bigamy at all ? ' he asked, and I explained that it was among us a criminal offence, though rare cases of secret bigamy might be found. ' No,' intervened Dr. 'Abdullah, who was possibly not feeling at his best, ' quite ten per cent. of the male population of England live in a state of bigamy.' I pressed him for the evidence on which he based the statement, and it turned out that among the very small number of Englishmen he had known at Constantinople and other places before the War there was one bigamist. He then withdrew the charge as being too sweeping. Fornication and adultery, I was told, was not so rare in Najd as I had imagined, though they were only indulged in in the strictest secrecy—for death to both parties was the penalty for detection.

At Salih al Fadhl's next day we found Fahad al Bassam and 'Ali al Sulaiman, the son of our host—a pleasing young fellow with very grave face and demeanour, coupled with a low drawling intonation which at times had a charm of its own. Fahad explained that his tale of Russia's re-entry into the War on the side of the Central Powers had merely been his own deduction from an ambiguous and mischievous Kuwait interpretation of a Reuter report of a speech by some member of the Soviet, who maintained that it was absolutely necessary for Russia to take an active part in the War. In the Arabic translation this was rendered in such a way that one might believe that Russia had actually been forced into the War.

We passed to lighter subjects such as the advantage of regular physical exercise, a champion of which was 'Abdullah Ibn 'Abdul 'Aziz al Bassam, who, though well over sixty, practically lived in his garden estate and from it made regular daily excursions on foot into the rolling *Nafud*. Talk of swimming, for which they seemed only to use the word denoting bathing [1] in general, led to fish stories—of sharks in the Shatt al 'Arab, and so to a tale by Muhammad of a whale which some years before had penetrated as far as Qurna, and being caught by the retreat of the tide had become stranded and blocked the fairway. I ventured to be sceptical and told how in a narrower part of the river the Turks at the beginning of the War had failed to block the channel by sinking the *Ecbatana* and two other ships, whereupon the whale story was slightly modified—the river, true enough, continued to flow on either side, but the passage of ships was temporarily impeded, and the whale being killed by rifle fire from the banks, the atmosphere was polluted by its stench until it was hacked to pieces and removed.

In the afternoon Dr. 'Abdullah and I strolled out past Al Qa' and westward through the palm-groves until we came to a high sand-bank which had formed in a gap of the circuit-wall by the fine gardens of Haifa—the property of the Yahaya branch of the Sulaim family, all of whose surviving representatives were either at Hail or in 'Iraq. While we sat there, taking our ease on the soft sand, a cheerful-faced youth of the peasantry joined us, chatting about his life. He had been at the taking of Qunfida by the *Sharif's* forces, and spoke affectionately of the British, whose cause and ours, he said, is one—*Halna wahid*. Formerly he had followed the profession of pearling on the east coast, but with the decline of that industry during the War he had thought to vary his life by service under the *Sharif*. And, wearying soon of that, he had decided to return to his native land, which he did in company with Ibrahim al Jumai'a and his party, ' who were returning from Jidda after they had seen the Consul off to Egypt—I did not myself meet the latter.' I left him in ignorance that I was the ' Consul ' in question. We watched the folk at work on the plots of cultivation around us—a group of men were busy digging over a patch of ground while an old woman opened the sluices of the irrigation channels to release streams of water on to the thirsty lucerne. Egg-plants with their attractive fruit of dark purple stood in

[1] *Sabah.*

rows on either side of the channels. A number of wells were in full work, the camel-teams being driven up and down their inclines by women who hastily drew up their fallen veils as we passed them. As the sun sank behind the *Nafud* we wended our way slowly homeward through the walled lanes between the groves ; and, reaching home, we sat down to a homely meal on our roof, just our host and ourselves— a welcome change from the unceasing entertainment of the preceding days.

After dinner 'Abdullah al Hamad al Sulaim, who had come to see if Dr. 'Abdullah might have a wash for the sore eyes of his little son, sat with us till it was time for the *Akhir*. I told him that we proposed going shortly to Buraida for a change, as indeed we intended doing if only to relieve the hospitable folk of 'Anaiza of the burden of our presence. ' Why,' he replied, ' why go back without cause to a place where your hearts will be straitened ? ' And he told us of a certain *Baghdadi* (Ibn Salih, I think, was his name) who came to settle in Najd and first lighted on Buraida, which he found quite intolerable. So he came to 'Anaiza and eventually passed on to Riyadh, loudly proclaiming everywhere his adverse opinion of the people of Buraida in spite of the advice of his friends to remain silent where he had no good to say. Such is the wisdom of the Arabs—to bear in silence with everything except irreligion. And, the talk turning on Doughty, he continued : ' We of 'Anaiza are indeed proud to honour anyone who is honoured by Ibn Sa'ud—though it be to give him the very mantle off our shoulders—while if any be not honoured of the *Imam*, why—we do not desire him, though he be our own father. Khalil erred in coming as a poor man without recommendation, and if you had come likewise we should have rejected you. Huber came in style from Ibn Rashid and found honour, as you too have found it, coming similarly. Khalil should not have come as he did unless he were prepared to profess the common religion.' He told also of a *Nasrani*—apparently a European though he had no recollection of his name—who lived at Riyadh for ten or twelve years in the days of Faisal, professing the faith of his forefathers and even preaching in the mosques and honoured. Years afterwards Ibn Mani', the horse-dealer,

while walking along a street in Bombay heard himself hailed
by the same man, though the latter had to recall the facts
to his memory before the dealer recognised him. I thought
perhaps that the story might be an echo of Palgrave, but the
facts as told did not fit in with such a theory. 'Abdullah al
Hamad, during the time of his exile at Kuwait in company
with other members of the Sulaim family and the Sa'uds
and Muhannas, accompanied a raiding-expedition organised
against the 'Ajman and 'Awazim by Mubarak, whom he
characterised as an old tyrant. There were three *Bairaqs*
representing respectively Kuwait itself, 'Anaiza and Buraida,
and the country of the east coast, through which they passed,
was full of ruinous sites—oases and settlements. ' That,'
he said, ' is the country of ancient habitation, while here in
Najd there is nothing very old.'

September 23rd was my last full day at 'Anaiza, and we
began it with a coffee-party at 'Abdullah al Hamad's. As
we were expected, the place of honour nearest the hearth had
been left empty for me, and I found myself next to a member
of the Ribdi family of Buraida, whose identity I only discovered accidentally through a chance remark, though I
had realised he was not of 'Anaiza and sensed a lack of
cordiality in his manner. No suitable opportunity occurred
of airing my opinion of his native town, as a direct approach
to the subject would have been beyond the pale of good
manners. So we sat for the most part in stolid silence while
'Abdullah himself made the coffee and prepared the hot milk
which in many households takes the place of tea at this early
hour—it was but little past seven o'clock. The desultory
conversation embraced the latest news of the Haïl campaign
and of happenings further west where the *Sharif* was again
becoming ominously active.

'Aiyadh and I then strolled out to the *Sangar* Rafi' to
enjoy the fresh wind from the north and to get some photo-
graphs of the oasis which, owing to vigorous entertainment,
I had left to the last moment. As we were about to re-enter
the oasis by the east gate we were hailed by an old peasant
busy with the irrigation of a melon-patch called Mughitha
just outside the walls : ' Come through the greenery,' he
called to us, and selecting two ripe melons from his patch he

handed them to us to take away. Twice daily he irrigated his little garden, which contained mostly melons of the local sort—somewhat tasteless—and a small area of the small-leaved sweeter *Furaiduni* variety originally imported from Zubair. From the east gate—or rather perhaps south-east —a track leads to the Dhulai'a suburb, just in front of which on the right hand lay a raised slag of black rock, suggesting the presence of iron or coal.

Having breakfasted quietly at home we went off soon after noon to have coffee with 'Abdul 'Aziz Ibn Qunaiyir, where we were interrupted by the arrival of good news from the front and letters from Ibn Sa'ud for the *Amir* and myself. And the rest of the day—our determination taken to leave 'Anaiza on the morrow—was spent by me in preparing letters and telegrams to go by courier to Kuwait with news of the latest developments. At the hour known as *Bain al 'ashawain* (*i.e.* between the sunset and evening prayers) we sallied forth to say our farewells at the house of the ex-*Amir* 'Abdul 'Aziz, where we found the *Amir* 'Abdullah and others of the family. There was joy abroad at the news of a ' victory,' which left me sceptical and deferred the realisation of my hopes to another day. I little realised that the friends, who had been so hospitable and of whom I took farewell with genuine sorrow, would not greet me again till the little ripple of initial success had expanded north and west embracing the vast territories of all the enemies of the *Wahhabi* monarch. It was at Jidda that we next should meet in January, 1926, the death-month of Khalil and the month of Ibn Sa'ud's acclamation at Mecca as King of the Hijaz. By then the old Arabia known to Doughty, which I myself had seen, had passed away and the new Arabia stood forth as a giant re-freshed to run its course. And among the first who came down to see the miracle, of which we had often talked at 'Anaiza, was Doughty's faithless guide, Ibrahim al Sulaim, and the fair-spoken grandson of his loyal friend, 'Abdulrahman Ibn 'Abdul 'Aziz al Zamil.

7. THE FIRST BLOW FOR ARABIAN SUPREMACY

From time to time during our sojourn at 'Anaiza news or rumours came in of the progress of Ibn Sa'ud's campaign

against the rival dynasty of the North. The preliminary
concentration at Tarafiya, whither he had ridden from
Buraida, was followed by a more business-like one at Qusaiba
on the northern frontier of the Qasim, where the belated
contingent of Ghatghat joined the rest of the army—now
consisting of the royal bodyguard of citizen troops about
three hundred strong and seven *Ikhwan* contingents as
follows :

			Strength in men (with camels or on foot)		Strength in horses.
'Artawiya	-	-	1000	- -	100
Ghatghat	-	-	800	- -	100
Dahina	-	-	700	- -	80
Furaithan	-	-	700	- -	75
Sajir	-	-	500	- -	65
Mubaïdh	-	-	500	- -	58
Dhaba'a	-	-	300	- -	50
Ibn Sa'ud's bodyguard	-		300	- -	300
Total	-	-	4800	- -	828

A force of five thousand men is about as large as can be
conveniently kept in the field at one time in the Arabian
deserts, and Ibn Sa'ud was thus as strong as he could wish
to be for any operation short of an assault on the battlements
of Haïl itself. His obvious aim was to catch Ibn Rashid,
who was known to be raiding the Harb, in the open and to
force him to a fight. With this intention he launched out
from Qusaiba a few days before the '*Id* with provisions for
six days. Marching north-west for 70 miles as the crow flies
they reached the wells of Ajfar, 50 miles due east of Haïl, on
the day of the '*Id* itself (16th September). The patrols
(*Sabur*), thrown out well in advance, returned the same day to
announce that the Arabs previously reported as being at the
watering of Sidr north of Ajfar had decamped towards 'Idwa
at the eastern extremity of Jabal Salma. ' *Hajju*,' [1] said
the *Mutairi*, who was himself one of the patrols and the
first messenger to 'Anaiza, ' *wajadna hujujhum*.' Another
item of news they brought—and one of vital importance—
was that Ibn Rashid himself was celebrating the '*Id* at

---

[1] ' They were gone ; we found (tracks of) their going.'

Sab'an [1] north of Jabal Salma and west of 'Idwa. It was clearly within Ibn Sa'ud's power to force his rival to battle, but to do so he would have to fight with his back to Haïl and run the risk of having his retreat cut off in the event of failure.

In these circumstances he held a council of war to seek the advice of the chief men of his force, and Ibn Lami of the Mutair was the first to speak ' winged words.' ' We have come out,' he said, ' for your honour, for the honour of the *Ikhwan* and for the honour of the Qasim. We are your servants. Command and we obey.' Then up and spoke Duwish : ' I will answer for the *Ikhwan*. We have come out to attack Ibn Rashid and we are sworn not to return until we have done so. Let us go forth and settle accounts with him.' And Ibn Sa'ud replied : ' I am indeed well pleased with your advice and sentiments, but I warn you we are in for serious business this time. Swear now to me by God that you will follow where I lead and not return until we have fought it out with Ibn Rashid. Whoso craves a martyr's death let him come with us, the rest can return to their wives.' Thereupon the *Ikhwan* raised up their voices weeping and swore loyalty even unto death, for which they straightway prepared by the ceremony of mutual absolution for all wrongs committed and suffered. And finally each man dictated his last will and testament, the documents being collected and sent back to their various homes.

Ibn Sa'ud now formed three advance parties, respectively under the command of a nephew of Fahad Ibn Mu'ammar, of Mishari Ibn Musaiyis of the Mutair and of Al Firm, *Shaikh* of the Harb. These had orders to tempt Ibn Rashid out of the fortifications of Sab'an either by a direct challenge or by a feint on Haïl itself, while Ibn Sa'ud himself followed with the main force in reserve to take advantage of any situation that might arise. Our *Mutairi* messenger and others had been left behind because their *Dhaluls* had broken down, and the last they saw of the main force after its start on 17th September suggested that Ibn Sa'ud was aiming to get to the northward of Haïl. The news, so far as it went, was hopeful enough, and there seemed every prospect of Ibn

[1] A group of *Qasrs* with cultivation.

Rashid being forced to battle in the open or being cut off from Haïl, which might in that case be opened to the invader by the hands of treason.

The following day further details dribbled in. Ibn Sa'ud had watered his animals at a well called Sidr and Ibn Rashid had attacked the Harb encampment at Humailiya without much success at a moment when practically all their camels were out grazing far away in the *Nafud*. The tribesmen lost some eight or ten men killed and thirty camels captured in this skirmish, while Ibn Rashid not only suffered greater losses but had to decamp with all speed on receipt of the news of his enemy's movements in the Haïl district, and the Harb were thus able to recover their raided camels. To us, waiting on tenterhooks of expectation at 'Anaiza, the drama was rapidly drawing to a climax. And, at last, on 23rd September one of the usual coffee-parties was suddenly broken up by the arrival of 'Ali al Sha'aithan with the good news that good news had arrived from the front. We had to possess ourselves in patience for details until we could arrive at the *Amir's* house, where we found the *Bashir*,[1] Rushaid al Hamazani, a *Shammari*, the carrier of letters for the *Amir* and myself from Ibn Sa'ud. The letters contained the news of the ' victory ' and an invitation to me to rejoin the victor at Qusaiba, where he preferred to rest awhile on his laurels.

Ibn Rashid had made good his entry into Haïl and, leaving the bulk of his army there within the walls, had himself gone to the redoubtable stronghold of Mu'aiwij Baqa'a some four or five hours to the N.E. of the capital. Ibn Shuraim had remained with his Arabs at Sab'an, while the Bani Yahraf— a shepherd tribe in general charge of the flocks and herds of Ibn Rashid and standing in much the same relation to him as the Sukhail subsection of the Matarifa section of 'Anaza did to his rival—occupied the space between these extreme points in a semicircle behind Haïl with their main concentrations at Dhab'a, 'Akkash and Sufaila, the last only two miles north of Haïl. Keeping the citizen troops and a considerable force of the *Ikhwan* in reserve, Ibn Sa'ud launched the main body of the latter at the Bani Yahraf, who were duly ' taken ' at Sufaila with great loss. The booty

---

[1] ' The bringer of good tidings,' cf. *Mubashshir* = missionary.

was reckoned at 2000 camels and sheep innumerable, and the *Ikhwan* galivanted in triumph round the very walls of the capital, from which they were fired on, though it seems that no artillery was used. The question now was what to do next—whether to press the attack on Ibn Rashid's stronghold or not. A council of war was convened at which the *Muslimin*, delighted with their booty, ' *ma rau dhalik*,' *i.e.* did not like the look of the sterner business now proposed. ' We have no quarrel,' they urged, ' with Ibn Rashid personally, and we have got what we wanted—so let us get home.' And such was the decision of the council. The only creditable incident of the campaign took place during the process of withdrawal, when three men of the *Wahhabi* force, acting as scouts in the rear of the column, came upon an ammunition train of five camels on its way to Ibn Rashid. The four men in charge fled at sight of them, and 10,000 rounds of ammunition were brought in to Ibn Sa'ud's camp at Sidr, where the night of 20th September was spent. Next day the army moved to Ajfar and on the 21st they marched back to Qusaiba. Rushaid, the *Bashir*, who was sent on ahead to bring us the news, could say nothing of future possibilities except that, unless Ibn Rashid came out to fight for his lost animals and thus forced Ibn Sa'ud to stand or turn back on him, the latter contemplated retiring further to Tarafiya and thence to Buraida. Thus the initiative was tamely surrendered to Ibn Rashid and, as events were yet to prove, the great opportunity of eliminating the Shammar power from the scheme of things Arabian was thrown away, not to recur until 1921. As things stood, however, it appeared likely that the contest thus begun by the throwing down of the gauntlet would continue. ' *Wataina al dira*,' said the triumphant *Ikhwan*, ' we reached the city itself.' And it seemed unlikely that Ibn Rashid would sit down quietly under the insult—the first time that the arms of the house of Sa'ud had ever reached the city walls since Haïl became an independent power. It seemed certain that Ibn Rashid would send forth messengers to rope in the Shammar from far and wide to resume the disengaged battle, and in my disappointment at the meagreness of the results achieved I recorded the consoling conclusion that my campaign was

at any rate launched in real earnest and was no longer
dependent for continuation on the will to war of Ibn Sa'ud.
To my mind the whole future of Arabia was dependent on
the issue of this struggle between irreconcilable tissues in its
very heart. Until that heart beat evenly and in complete
harmony with itself it could not hope to control and invigo-
rate the palsied flank of the great continent, which the
doctors—British doctors—were so busily patching up into
the semblance of a living body with splints and stitches.
The unification of the two sections of Najd was an essential
step to the unification of Arabia, and in those days it was
counted ridiculous to speak, or even think, of Arabian unity
in terms of a *Wahhabi* domination. Yet in September, 1920,
when I next met Ibn Sa'ud at 'Uqair, whither he came down
to meet Sir Percy Cox, then on his way to assume the post
of High Commissioner in 'Iraq, I found that the Haïl campaign had remained where it was at the end of September,
1918, and that the *Wahhabi* monarch was more prone to
cavil at the undue partiality of the British Government for
the Sharifian dynasty—in spite of Turaba !—than to set his
hand to the obvious remedy within his reach. And I told
him then that the British Government would never take him
seriously until he had eliminated Ibn Rashid and the Shammar dynasty from the picture of Arabia. ' All will be as you
wish,' he replied, ' if God wills.' Haïl fell in the following
August, and within three years Ibn Sa'ud was practically
master of all Arabia.

8. A NIGHT MARCH TO BURAIDA

Ibn Sa'ud's invitation confirmed me in my resolution to
leave 'Anaiza forthwith, and it was decided that we should
start as early as possible on the morrow. The rest of the day
was spent in writing reports and letters for Baghdad, but
for some reason—the inevitable indolence of the Arabs—no
courier could be found to take them to the coast that evening,
and as I could not leave till they had gone, I awoke on the
morning of 24th September determined to imitate the dila-
toriness of my friends and to show no anxiety to make a start.
Accordingly, I rose late to find old Muqbil and Salih al Fadhl

waiting to say good-bye and whiled away a pleasant hour in
final converse with them. On their departure I went for a
last walk in the pleasant gardens with 'Abdullah al Rashid,
who had studiously avoided me all these days owing to my
passion for long excursions, but had presumably thought it
time to put in an appearance at the eleventh hour to secure
any bounty that might be going for the sake of past services.
Our walk brought us to the Khunaini garden of Ma'aiawiya,
which we entered at a venture to find three members of the
family—'Ali and Sulaiman, sons of Salih, the brother of
Doughty's friend 'Abdullah, and Muhammad Ibn Hamad al
'Abdullah. They received us with a warm welcome and
showed us all over the garden, which excelled all others in the
oasis in the matter of fruit trees, and at length we sat down
to rest awhile under the drooping branches of an enormous
peach tree, breakfasting on fruit by the side of a slender
rivulet from the neighbouring well, of which we drank,
lapping up the cool water with our hands. The peaches and
pomegranates they set before us were certainly the finest I
had tasted in Arabia, and we ended up with *Subaihiya* dates
dripping with luscious juice. This garden was about fifteen
Jaribs in area, of which a third was devoted to palms—say
some 500 stems whose produce this year, excluding what was
taken by the owners and tenants for their own use, had been
sold for 4000 *Riyals*, shared equally by owner and tenants.
A similar division of profits between owner and tenants
applied to all the produce of this particular garden owing to
its extraordinary productiveness, though in most gardens
the tenants' share of others than the date crop was as high as
two-thirds or even three-quarters. There were about 100
pomegranate bushes and about the same number of peach
trees, both from Taïf, while the owners had recently imported
and planted half a dozen cuttings of a special apricot from
Basra. Apart from these there was a considerable number
of lemon and fig trees, the latter throwing their rich shade
over an oblong masonry tank through which the water of
the nine-fathom steyned well passed to a miniature weir over
which it fell in a clear cascade to the irrigation channels below.
The garden was full of the murmuring of running water
and the music of the well-gear—a delightful pleasaunce of

rivulets and greenery in every shade, the dark palms over
crops of little millet with rich patches of lucerne in the open
spaces. The owners were pleased with their handiwork, but,
like their fathers before them in the time of Doughty, still
had their thoughts on the tube-well and machine-pump
which would bring it to perfection.

On our way back we passed one of the Bassam gardens
which the *Amir* 'Abdullah had rented on the very favourable
basis of only one quarter of the produce to the owner—the
tenant of course paying the whole cost of maintenance.
Apart from his hereditary joint-interest in the ex-*Amir's*
town-garden the *Amir* had no landed property in 'Anaiza.
And as we continued on our way homeward we fell in with
a party returning from a shooting competition in the *Nafud*,
the target being a piece of paper stuck up at a range of 400
yards. One of them had a short British service-rifle and
another a German Mauser, the latter being valued at about
£11 or £12—roughly double what the former would fetch in
the market.

I whiled away the rest of the forenoon and most of the
afternoon reading an Arabic translation of some light French
erotic novel, which I found among the few volumes which
constituted my host's library. And then I announced that
I was ready to start. Then occurred the inevitable delay
attendant on the bringing of the camels. Dinner was served
for us at 4 p.m., the camels were loaded, and at 5.45 we
started without a guide.

In ten minutes we were clear of the north gate and proceeded in a north-westerly direction along a well-marked
track running between the palms of Sufaila—the northern
extremity of the oasis—and the lofty sand masses of Musabbih on our right. The direct road, which we had missed
owing to the absence of a guide, lay more to the right, running
due north, but our track towards Wadi al Janah was an
alternative route. In a short while we reached the crest of
the *Nafud*, whence the track descended in gentle undulations
amid vegetation of *Hamdh* and *Adhir*. To our left lay the
settlements of Sha'ib Malqa, while behind us lay the great
mass of the 'Anaiza oasis dark emerald in hue, and in front
of us appeared the palms of the *Wadi*. A mile out from the

north gate we passed on our right the shallow depression of
Raudhani with a score of scattered palms and *Ithils*, a
single well with some patches of lucerne around it and a
lonely hut. A little further on, on our left, lay the Niqra
depression with a fenced-in patch of lucerne and some *Ithils*
and a well. And so we came down the slope into the bed of
Wadi Rima about 200 yards to the right of the hamlet of
Wadi al Janah.

By now it was dark and we set a course diagonally across
the *Wadi* to make Al Jasar, where we would strike the main
road, but it was impossible to direct our march with any
precision. At first we followed a well-marked track running
now between palm-groves and now in the open, but soon we
found ourselves in a maze of irrigation channels with no
apparent exit. Here I decided to halt a while to send out
scouts to reconnoitre, but they had gone only a short distance
when they were challenged, and at the same moment a man
loomed up out of the darkness but a short way off enquiring
who we were. ' Friends,' we shouted in reply, ' come here.'
' Don't you go, Ibrahim,' shouted a female voice near by,
but he, disregarding his nervous spouse, approached. Simultaneously our scouts had created a panic in another part of
the settlement—for we had apparently stumbled into the
large hamlet of Wadi Abu 'Ali—and in a moment the still
night air was shrill with the ululations of women and the
gruffer challenges of men. ' *Jauna, jauna*—they are on us,'
screamed the women, assuming that some enemy, perhaps
one of Ibn Rashid's patrols, was at their doors. Meanwhile
Ibrahim, who had reached us, shouted back an assurance that
we were harmless travellers, erring from the right road, but
it took some time for the tumult to die down, while he
guided us through the palms and channels and put us once
more on the road. Such were the alarms of daily life in
Arabia during those days. In the darkness we lost our way
once more, and it was not without much difficulty that we
found the Jasar causeway and passed over it to the first ridge
of the Buraida *Nafud*. And here, deciding to wait for the
moon, we lay and rested on the soft sand till 9.30. Very
pleasant was our march thereafter on the beaten track over
the cool sand-waste lit up by the moon. At first we moved

briskly, chatting among ourselves and singing to the night air, and then, as the hour grew later, a silence fell upon us, broken only by the padding of the camels. It was a pleasant experience to march by night as the Arabs love to do—a pleasure which I had always deliberately eschewed in order to see as much as possible of the country. On this occasion we were travelling over ground already traversed, and I could give myself up to enjoyment of the moment without thought of compass and note-book. The Pole Star led us on through the night past the dark groves of Al Khadhar and the black fringe of the Sabakh palms silhouetted against their ridge of sand. At midnight the great clay city itself loomed up before us in the moonlight and a quarter hour later we stood before the east gate demanding admittance. ' Who are ye ? ' came the challenge from within, to which they replied, ' The companions of the Englishman.' The gate was borne back to admit us, and the good steward, Shilhub, had dinner ready for us. We were to resume our march before dawn, and I was glad, after making sure that all was ready, to lie down on the roof of our dwelling for a few hours' sleep.

9. NORTHERN QASIM

Soon after 4 a.m. we were roused from our slumbers and an hour later we were on the move over the gritty plain lying to the north-west of Buraida between the *Nafud* on the left and the sandstone wilderness of Al Butain on the right. For half an hour or more our course was the same as that followed on the way to the *Khubub* past the ruinous tower of Shamas and the palms of Ghaf ; we then diverged from it in a north-westerly direction, entering the *Safra* itself, a low rolling plain, on which we encountered a large party of the 'Abadilah [1] Mutair returning from the ' victory ' at Haïl with about 200 camels representing their share or what they considered their share of the spoils—the animals taken by themselves. Their leaders were 'Alaiyan Ibn Dhamna, whom we did not see to speak to, and Dhaidan Ibn Darwish, with whom we chatted for a few moments, a courtly, fair-spoken man of about forty, who was unex-

[1] Bani 'Abdillah.

pectedly cordial to me—he and his followers were not yet reckoned among the *Ikhwan*. It afterwards transpired that these folk had without permission driven off their booty in all haste from the field of action to keep them out of the regular division of the spoils prescribed by the *Shar'* law, according to which Ibn Sa'ud's treasury was entitled to take one-fifth, though in fact his rule in such cases was generally to sell his share and divide the proceeds among the members of his bodyguard who were without opportunities of securing spoil for themselves. So the Mutair had eventually to disgorge a share of their booty greater than they would have had to give up according to the rules. Parties like this returning from an expedition are known as *Manakif*.[1]

The winding edge of the *Nafud* here returns to within a quarter mile of the *Safra*, and far away to the right appeared the grey cliff of Watta', on the hither side of which Sha'ib Wudai' runs down towards the Buraida plain. A solitary *Qasr* stood on the edge of the *Nafud* close by and another a little further on where the sands reached right up to our track. And ahead of us lay the palms of Shiqqa backed by a tower-crowned cliff of the *Safra*.

Having marched about seven miles from Buraida we entered a sandy depression in which lay Sufaila or the lower section of the Shiqqa settlement, the cliff with its two small towers being to our right behind a walled palm-grove of some extent. A few smaller groves dotted the space between this and the little hamlet of some four hundred souls, including the tenants of the outlying groves—an unwalled group of small mud-huts, outside which, drying in the sun, lay the oval blocks of brownish salt brought from the salt-pans of Qara'a. The latter lay dazzling white at some distance to the west, and seemed to me nothing like as extensive as the *Mamlaha* of 'Aushaziya, though their salt is reckoned superior by the *Qusman*.

The *Nafud* falls back in a wide semicircle to the south of the Sufaila-Qara'a depression, and as we continued our march to the north-west with the cliff on our right hand, we passed scattered groups of huts and *Qasrs* with patches of cultivation about them. In one place we found a dry pond

[1] Meaning ' those sent back or returning.'

obviously artificial with masonry-lined banks and aqueducts leading into it from the cliff—no doubt a reservoir for the use of the inhabitants and their animals. We then topped a slight rise in the ground to enter the depression of Rafi'a or the upper settlement, overlooked by three towers on the cliff. This depression, like that of Sufaila, drains down to the salt-pans, from which there seemed to be no outlet. The main hamlet of Rafi'a is an unwalled collection of modest mud-huts, containing with outlying *Qasrs*, etc., a population of about two hundred souls. Another smaller hamlet in this section was in ruins and apparently deserted, and a number of palm-groves lay scattered along the foot of the cliff.

The last well of the Shiqqa settlement, which from beginning to end spreads over an extent of about three miles, lay in the neck of a rough valley descending between *Safra* cliffs from the north-west towards the depression. Here we halted for a while to draw water and partake of a meal of dates. The well, about six fathoms deep, stood in a four-acre patch of *Mulaisa* and pumpkins,[1] the water being drawn up by camels into an unlined reservoir from which channels carried it into the crop. In one of these channels was a small drop over which the stream fell clear and bubbling to water a *Mulaisa* crop some distance away. The soil here and in the valley, up which we marched after our brief halt, was of a soft reddish sandstone with a considerable sprinkling of black rock, which increased as we advanced up the valley. The latter was about half a mile across, the banks on either side being flat-topped. About a mile up the valley we came to a *Qa'* or mud-flat, sun-cracked and littered with fragments of black rock, the first of a series of such flats known collectively as Qi'an Ablaq, from the single deserted building of Qasr Ablaq in the second or third of them, formerly the scene of well-cultivation of the usual Arabian desert type. This series of flats, divided from each other by tongues of *Safra* and light sand, appeared to form a continuation of the valley, which we had entered at the Shiqqa well and whose banks continued without interruption though more widely apart for a distance of some six or seven miles. There were some five or six flats in all, the largest being about three-

---

[1] *Qara'*.

quarters of a mile across, and every now and then we came across segments of what was obviously a continuous stream bed. Black rock was much in evidence, in some parts like great masses of slag, but there was little to diversify the monotony of the march until we, quite suddenly and almost with a gasp of amazement, reached the head of the valley and found ourselves on the edge of a desert ocean. Before us stretched a wilderness, immense and unimaginable, utterly barren and featureless, absolutely flat but for a scarcely perceptible swell. In my memory it has always remained as the very abomination of desolation, the very archetype of the perfect desert of human imagination, of which even Arabia can surely boast but few examples. The floor was of brown-grey gravel like the Dibdiba with a meagre scattering of withered *'Arfaj*, *Shih* and grasses and an occasional patch of mud-flat. Here there was nothing living except ourselves—a cheerless dreary waste in which it would be easy to lose oneself by straying from the beaten track, for there was no landmark of any kind to steer by except a few cairns marking the camping-grounds of the 'Anaza who occasionally come down, as they had done the previous year, in search of grazing. All this wilderness is reckoned part of the Butain and is generally accounted to the range of the Harb.

After marching for about four miles over the desolate scene there appeared far off to the north and north-east a coast-line as it were of higher ground, so far away that it seemed featureless. In all probability it was the *Safra* of Qa'ara in the direction of Tarafiya, though some said it was the Asyah *Nafud*. It was at any rate a cheerful though distant companion as we plodded steadily and drearily on over the unending desolation. And at last it came to an end as, after six miles, we entered and crossed a shallow grassy depression trending north-eastward and, half an hour later, came upon a small group of *Sidr* bushes said to be one of a number of similar groups collectively named Raudha Dakmaniya. From here until we reached the head of a broad grassy valley called Khannasa four miles further on, the desert was full of life, swarming with the grazing camels of the Firm Harb—camels in calf, others in milk with youngsters frolicking beside them. Black and white were the prevailing colours, and I had never seen so many white animals together, the great beasts looking for all the world like tents in the distance.

The flat desert now began to be rougher and more folded to form the Khannasa, which we entered near its head and followed down between its low *Safra* banks in a N.N.W. direction towards the Qusaiba depression, into which it spills. Further down the valley became choked with outcrops of *Safra* and black rock, through which ran a slender *Sha'ib* about twenty yards wide. Having marched for about three miles down the valley we struck up its left bank, from whose summit we had a fine view of our goal—the palms of Qusaiba standing out of the far side of a great mud-flat against the background of a gaunt cliff, some 150 to 200 feet high. Descending towards the depression we recrossed the Khannasa channel and, leaving the palms to our left, continued up and down over the rough ground at the edge of the depression towards two *Qasrs* called 'Amudiyat. Then, descending on to the saline mud-flat, we continued for another half-hour to the *Qasr* and walled palm-grove of Mashquq, where Ibn Sa'ud's war-camp was spread out among the sand dunes.

It was just over twenty-four hours since we had left 'Anaiza the previous afternoon, and in that time we had marched some fifty-four miles with only three hours' sleep. Long sojourning at Buraida and 'Anaiza had relaxed my riding muscles, and I was stiff in every limb and aching all over. But custom demanded an immediate visit to my host. The first person I met on entering the camp was his brother, Sa'ud, who came forward with a very cordial welcome. Ibn Sa'ud himself was holding a *Majlis* in his tent and, seeing us through the glasses ever ready at his side, beckoned us to approach. He greeted me very warmly, and was obviously in the best of tempers owing to his recent success. And a moment later he was brimming over with gaiety. Some letters were brought in with news—still news to him though we had heard it already at 'Anaiza—of Shakir's last attack on Khurma and the annihilation of his force. ' Why,' said he laughing, ' did you not fire your rifles as you came in with

THE OASIS OF QUSAIBA.

To face page 308.

such good news ? Go, so and so and so and so, and tell the *Ikhwan* that their brethren of Khurma have annihilated the Sharif's army. And tell them,' he added, ' it is the *Sahib's Bishara* ! ' And I had further good news for him in my Government's approval of the issue to him of 1000 rifles, 150,000 rounds of ammunition and some tents. Sunset being near I took my leave, and as my tent had not arrived, lay down on a carpet, dead tired, to sleep or doze in the cool evening air till dinner should be served—a welcome meal of rice and camel meat of the spoils of war. I then lay down again to resume my slumbers, but was wakened by the arrival of two batches of mails—from Kuwait and Bahrain respectively—which must have just missed me at 'Anaiza. I glanced hastily through the official letters in case there might be anything of urgent import to communicate at once to Ibn Sa'ud, and, leaving the rest for the morrow, slept again a deep and refreshing sleep.

The dune area on which we were encamped was of considerable extent, forming a disintegrated projection of the *Safra* on the east side of the Qusaiba basin, whose main section, about a mile wide from east to west and more than twice as long, lies S.E. by N.W. Between the dunes and the western *Safra*—a steep and lofty cliff behind the Qusaiba oasis itself, but becoming less imposing as it extends northward—there is a secondary and somewhat indeterminate projection of the main basin in a north-north-westerly direction to a point about two miles from Mashquq, where stand the *Qasr* and hill of Suwwal, while at a point half a mile south-east of this *Qasr* a valley runs up north-west into the *Safra* between low slopes towards Saqiya, some miles distant—apparently also a *Qasr* with some cultivation around it. The surface of the depression, sloping gently to west and south, is like that of the typical *Qa'* of these parts with a strong tendency to salinity and much sun-cracked in parts as the result of flood water.

The two *Qasrs* of 'Amudiyat, about two miles south-east of Mashquq, have already been mentioned in connection with our march to the latter, whose single *Qasr* is of quaint and attractive architecture, and exists for the protection of a three-acre grove on the edge of the dune area. The grove is irrigated from a spring in the dunes, from which the water is conducted to it, and also to the *Qasr*, by an underground *Kariz* with occasional apertures covered over with slabs of stone.

About two miles south of Mashquq across the mud-flat lies the thin oasis-patch of Qusaiba itself protected from surprise attacks from the west by a line of five small watch-towers along the summit of the high cliff behind it. The oasis extends for about a mile from south-east to north-west with an outlying grove and *Ithil*-patch further on in the latter direction, but is disappointingly meagre, consisting of a very thin and straggling line of palms with but few dense patches. Its situation at the foot of an imposing cliff is certainly very picturesque, and the effect of ruggedness is enhanced by the craggy nature of the cliff-face from which aprons of detritus descend to the edge of the palm-belt. The oasis is blessed with numerous springs bubbling up at the ground-level to give birth to the running streams which irrigate the palms, while in some cases, where the ground-level has risen or the water-level has sunk, irrigation by lift is resorted to—the depth to water varying from three to six feet.

At intervals between the foot of the cliff and the palm-belt lie the three hamlets of the settlement, of which the middle one is altogether in ruins. The largest is the southern, and the whole population of the oasis cannot exceed five hundred souls, mostly *'Abid* or ex-slaves. The quaint architecture of some of the *Qasrs*, with the great cliff towering above them on one side and the palms on the other, gives a pleasing effect ; but I was most of all struck by the number of graves— almost all of a dozen or more bays between the aprons of detritus were occupied by cemeteries—which seemed to be out of all proportion to the numbers of the living population. Qusaiba is indeed renowned for its unhealthiness. ' By God's will,' said one of my companions, ' illness comes upon them and they die in numbers.' Perhaps this accounted for the fact that only *'Abid* appeared to inhabit the place. Ibn Sa'ud had lent me a pony with Arab saddle and bridle and no stirrups to visit the place on, and we had had an enjoyable ride out, but there was something in the atmosphere of

PALMS AND BUILDINGS OF QUSAIBA.

To face page 310.

Qusaiba which made one glad to get away from it, and though I regretted not having time to visit the cliff towers and look out on what lay beyond, I felt a real relief as my pony, galloping for home, increased the distance between me and a miserable community rotting to death for the sake of the produce of a few palms. Such was Qusaiba, the most northerly outpost of the Qasim and the northerly limit of my wanderings in Arabia at this time. Some years later I was to see Jauf and the desert around it, coming from the north, but to this day Fate has not vouchsafed me a glimpse of the ' promised land ' of Jabal Shammar, the province on which all my thoughts and energies were concentrated during the year of my first sojourn in Arabia. Of Ibn Sa'ud's territories, as they then were, I had seen practically everything from Wadi Dawasir to Qusaiba, from east to west, but my march to the north had left me with one vivid regret— 'Uyun [1] was away from the track and my companions would not risk a diversion in that direction lest Ibn Rashid's warriors should be on the warpath.

The force encamped at Mashquq was reckoned at between 5000 and 6000 strong, made up of the various *Ikhwan* contingents and Ibn Sa'ud's own following of *Zigirt*. He was now sending out orders for a general muster of all the citizen contingents of Central Najd to carry on the good work he had begun. Meanwhile during the two days I spent in the camp there was great activity in the collecting, parading and division of the spoil, which, apart from sheep slaughtered on the battle-field to be eaten at once, consisted roughly of 900 camels actually present at Qusaiba, about 300 taken away furtively by their captors to avoid their inclusion in the common pool, and about 300 young animals. One camel was set apart for every hundred men to be slaughtered for food, the general ration being otherwise limited to dates as rice was only for the few. Half a dozen horses had also fallen to the victors, and besides the ammunition train already referred to, the tents, saddlery and other articles captured from the Bani Yahraf had fetched 4000 *Riyals* at auction and some £400 or £500 had been taken in cash. One of the *Ikhwan* had come up to Ibn Sa'ud with £200 in his hands to surrender to

[1] *See H.A.* vol. ii. p. 140.

the pool. 'Who saw you take it ?' he asked, incredulous of such honesty. 'None but my God,' was the reply.

It was said that, at the first onslaught of the *Wahhabis*, the Bani Yahraf were under the impression that it was Ibn Rashid come out to punish them for some offence. 'Why come ye, then, like this ?' cried an old woman of the tribe ; 'if you come to punish, you have but to pronounce sentence and we submit, oh Ibn Rashid !' 'But we,' said one of the *Wahhabis*, 'are not from him, we come in the name of Ibn Sa'ud.' 'Ibn Sa'ud !' shrieked the hag, 'oh Muhammad Ibn Rashid ! where, where are you ? To think that Haïl has come to this !' Many of the women were found sitting quietly in their tents. 'Get up,' said the victors, 'what are ye sitting on ?' Most of the captured cash had been taken thus, for the women had buried the money and sat upon it in the hope of saving it. Bags of rice marked 'Kuwait' were found in the camp—damning evidence against Salim—and the dates were from Khaibar. The whole of the booty—Ibn Sa'ud foregoing his share—was divided up among the army, *Ikhwan* and *Hadhr* alike.

During these days I naturally saw much of Ibn Sa'ud in his spare moments. On one occasion he was just settling up a case as I entered, and I noticed that the plaintiff, one of the *Ikhwan*, addressed his master indifferently as '*Ya al Imam*' or simply '*Ya Akhi*.' The case related to the recovery of a sum of 62 *Riyals* jointly from sixteen defendants, against twelve of whom the claim was remitted by the plaintiff on the ground that they like himself were *Ikhwan*. Of the four that remained on the list one was dead. 'You say 62 dollars,' said the judge, 'and sixteen debtors. Well, that,' after careful consideration, 'makes three dollars apiece ; and twelve, you say, are *Ikhwan* ; that leaves four.' 'But one is dead,' interrupted one of the defendants. 'Yes, but your party is responsible for his debt. But, let me see, the share is not three but four dollars each less a fraction, and four times four is sixteen—dock two for four times the fraction. That leaves fourteen, so pay fourteen dollars and there's an end of it.' At one stage there was an argument as to whether the non-*Ikhwan* were only four or more. 'You say,' said Ibn Sa'ud, 'there were only four.' 'There were only

IBN SA'ŪD'S CAMP AT MASHQŪQ.

To face page 312.

four,' replied the defendant. ' Say : " By God, only four," '
pursued the judge. ' By God, only four,' and that point was
disposed of.

One of the *Ikhwan* had recently told him of a dream he
had had, seeing five moons together in the sky. Two of them
were in the west, very dim and near their setting—the Sharif
and the Turks. Another stood low and nearly set, though
brighter than the others, over the northern horizon—Ibn
Rashid. The fourth shone with great brilliancy overhead
on the meridian, shedding lustre over all the earth ; and the
fifth moon was also one of great splendour rising rapidly from
the east ; and these two moons made a treaty of friendship
for two hundred years, and the earth had peace and prosperity. And he told me of another dream he had dreamed
himself. He saw himself in the *Suq* at 'Anaiza, and a big
snake came out to attack him. He turned to slay it when
somebody called out : ' Leave the big one alone—he is
harmless, but look at that little one. Kill him first, for he
is dangerous and his bite is deadly.' So he turned again and
slew the little viper, and then dealt with the big snake at his
leisure. ' Ibn Rashid,' he explained, ' is the real danger, and
I need not fear the Sharif.' Nevertheless he warned me
seriously on this point. ' The Sharif is mad and will have
reason to regret his conduct towards the people of Khurma.
You mark my words, they will be in Taïf before long and, if
God pleases, they will put an end to the Sharif himself. As
for Shakir, if they have caught him this time, they will
assuredly not spare him.' Shakir was reported on this occasion to have had two guns and two machine-guns, which had
presumably been captured by the *Ikhwan*. Ibn Sa'ud also
stoutly maintained that there was a secret understanding
between the Sharif and Ibn Rashid, the latter being encouraged to resist the *Wahhabi* attack, launched with the
active approval of the British Government, by promises of
a Sharifian attack on Ibn Sa'ud's flank. Such an agreement
was far from being unthinkable, though for the moment
there was no tangible evidence of it. But it was certain that
the relations of our two Arabian allies were dangerously near
breaking-point. And, apart from Ibn Sa'ud's determined
and very natural disinclination to accept the Sharif's

suzerainty in any form whatever, I could not see any ground
for attaching any responsibility to him for so unsatisfactory
a state of affairs. In no case had he been the transgressor,
and there could be no reasonable doubt whatever that
Husain was deliberately trying to provoke some action which
in the circumstances of the time would force the British
Government to intervene on his behalf. At Mashquq I was
indeed among the host of the Lord, surrounded by the
Ikhwan in every direction. Even Tami,[1] who was among the
Zigirt, avoided my company, and those who had the mis-
fortune to be attached to my service were looked upon
askance by the righteous, who neither greeted them nor
returned their salutations, and on occasion came ferreting
round their tent in the hope of catching them smoking.
On one occasion two of the *Ikhwan* were walking along
towards where Manawar was sitting. ' Shall we greet him ? '
said one. ' No,' replied the other, ' turn your face the other
way, he is of the party of the *Ingrez*—it is not right.' So
they passed on without looking at him. And on another
occasion Manawar, when passing a tent of the *Ikhwan*, had
looked in to ask for a drink of water. ' No,' they replied,
' you are an infidel and the servant of an infidel.' ' I did not
come to discuss that,' he replied, ' I asked for a drink of
water, give me to drink.' So they poured out to him, and
when he had drank he said : ' See, I have drunk from that
bowl and I have but just now come from dipping my hand
in the same dish of rice as the *Ingrez*—you had better break
the bowl, for it is unclean.' And they cursed him as he
walked away chuckling at his little joke. As for myself I
never had anything to complain of, and was left alone in my
tent to smoke and indulge in any other abomination at will.

Ibn Sa'ud, having sent out his orders for a fresh muster in
force, decided to await his reinforcements at Buraida. In

---

[1] Tami as a matter of fact was in disgrace and under sentence of dismissal
from Ibn Sa'ud's service, which may have accounted for his avoidance of
me. During the recent operations he had been sent out scouting and,
observing the ammunition train of five camels (subsequently captured)
on their way to Ibn Rashid, had lost his head and, rushing back to camp,
warned Ibn Sa'ud that the enemy was upon him in force. When the nature
of the alarm became known Ibn Sa'ud had him beaten till he shrieked for
mercy and then dismissed him. So Tami disappeared from the scene—in
disgrace—to die a year or two later in the service of the Sharif at Madina.

accordance with this plan the camp at Mashquq was struck and we were on the move before sunrise of 28th September. Marching south-east over the gently undulating dune country we left the two *Qasrs* of 'Amudiyat to our right and struck up a steady slope with low cliffs converging from either side towards a gap in the eastern *Safra*. Round the *Qasrs* lay some 400 to 500 tents of the Firm, which seemed to be disposed anyhow without any attempt at symmetry, though perhaps the passage of our large army through them may have operated to enhance the effect of haphazardness. So far as I could see all their sheep were black. The Firm are a family of Bani 'Ali,[1] to which also belong the folk [2] of Ibn Shariyan, who was encamped with about 300 tents under the hillock of Suwwal. Another Harb group, the Ibn Sa'da family of Al Wuhub,[3] was also gathered in the Qusaiba district, perhaps 300 tents in all—so that the Harb, not counted in the army, were not less than 1000 tents strong, fully committed to the cause of Ibn Sa'ud, and likely from their geographical position to be the first to feel the brunt of any movement of Ibn Rashid.

Exactly an hour after leaving camp and soon after passing a low conical hillock on the sand slope whose width from cliff to cliff was here about half a mile, we scrambled up a rough steep incline to the lip of the *Safra* wilderness—all reckoned still to the Butain, an immense sandy plain here covered with rough shingle and rock *débris*. The *Gom* here made a splendid picture marching on a front of not less than two miles—the *Bairaq* to the left and a little in advance, Ibn Sa'ud himself and the *Zigirt* in a solid block in the centre, and the masses of *Ikhwan* on the right. Mansur Ibn Rumaih, famed with his brothers throughout Arabia for their knowledge of the camel, exchanged greetings with me as he passed. He had assessed the value of the camels taken at Haïl at 60,000 *Riyals*, and at this figure they had been taken over by Ibn Sa'ud, who had distributed the amount in cash to the members of his army. And Sa'd al Yumaini, hurrying up to join the bodyguard, had time in passing to tell me of his feats of valour in the recent fighting—a tale of four men

---

[1] Of the Kharashif subsection.   [2] Wuld Muraid subsection.
[3] Of the Madhyakh subsection.

killed and some booty. And then the young prince, Sa'ud,[1] second son of the *Wahhabi* ruler, whom, at our camping, I was able to provide with some ammunition for a Mannlicher sporting rifle, of which he had run short. And finally Ibn Sa'ud himself sent back Fuhaid to invite me to join him, and for the rest of the march till our halt for breakfast I rode with him at the head of his army.

At breakfast the host swarmed over the level plain like locusts, and a hundred fires told the merry tale of coffee-making. Our meal was of cold camel-meat, rice and dates. Among the party was Muhammad al Khalifa of a branch of the Bahrain ruling house deposed long since by the British when they installed 'Isa, who was in turn to suffer the indignity of deposition at the hands of the British Government as the reward of over fifty years of faithful service. The recent history of Bahrain forms no part of my theme, but it is difficult to mention the name of its veteran ruler without suggesting that few episodes in our imperial history have given us greater reason to blush. And Arabia, seeing and understanding, marvels not at our blushing but at our blundering. Jasim Ibn Rawwaf, suspect of blockade-running, and my Buraida friend, 'Abbas al Fallaji, were also there ; and Mansur Ibn Rumaih already mentioned ; and the redoubtable warrior-governor of Buraida, Fahad Ibn Mu'ammar ; and Faisal Ibn Rashid, gloating over the recent discomfiture of a dynasty, whose prerogatives his own branch had for a brief space usurped a decade or so before ; and Sa'ud al 'Arafa, by birth the senior member of the house of Sa'ud ; and others, not least among them the fanatical Faisal al Duwish.

Breakfast over, the march was resumed and I started off ahead to leave my host to his freedom. And as they passed me a short while after I heard the camp-chaplain, Al 'Uqairi, declaiming some passage from the ' Traditions ' for their souls' uplift. We marched over the dreary plain with its withered stumps of *'Arfaj*, *Shih* and *'Aushaz*, and afar off to the north-east, perhaps seven miles away, the ridge of Qa'ara broke the level monotony. During the previous spring, they said, the

[1] Now heir apparent to the Dual Monarchy of the Hijaz and Najd and its dependencies.

rains had been favourable and all this tract had been green
with herbage. Now all was dry and the barley-like *Sama*
grass was dead. The northern extremity of Qa'ara is called
Mudarraj.

There were but occasional undulations in the vast plain,
and it was not till we had marched some five miles after
breakfast that we came to a palpable feature, a *Niqra* or
depression called Naghabij lying north and south for a
distance of four miles, and containing a single desert well.
Travelling along this we rose again to the bare wilderness
and soon after halted for a midday rest in a nameless and
scarcely perceptible depression, where there was some dry
'Arfaj for the camels to browse on.

Just before we arrived here and while the front of the army
was narrowed to pass through the Naghabij depression a
slight incident had occurred which is worth recording. I
was riding along with four or five of my own party and happened to pass a small group of *Ikhwan* about a hundred yards
away when one of them, without any sort of provocation
other than the sight of me, cried out : ' I call God to witness
my hatred of you.' [1] The insulting remark—the first I had
actually heard during all my sojourn in the country—was
probably meant for my companions on my account rather
than for my own ears. They at any rate immediately took
up the challenge and were beginning to shout back abuse
when I cut them short : ' Leave them alone. Would you
answer every dog that barks at you ? ' But the Arab, and
more particularly the negro, is irrepressible when labouring
under a sense of wrong, and I soon noticed that Manawar
had dropped back to open a fire of abuse on the *Ikhwan*. I
rode on ignoring him and determined to get rid of one with
so little self-control lest his company and any resulting
controversy might result in Ibn Sa'ud declining to have me
with him in the campaign about to begin. Another member
of my party, the *'Anazi*, Hamad Ibn Hadhdhal, had taken
his leave of us before we left Mashquq, where he was within
comparatively easy reach of his home pastures in the
northern desert. He had proved less interesting than I had
hoped and at times was a terrible bore, so I was not sorry to

[1] ' *Ashshad Allah 'ala bughdhakum.*'

get rid of him ; and he had failed to wheedle a further cash
gift and my Mannlicher rifle, which he had been using temporarily, out of me.   In fact we left him there without mount
or saddle or arms and with nothing but a box of matches, a
pipe with a tin lid and whatever remained to him of a gift
of fifty dollars I had given him at 'Anaiza.

Just before 2 p.m. I was thinking of settling down for an
afternoon siesta—the temperature in my tent was 108° *Fahr.*
and the day was certainly at its hottest—when word went
round that the *Bairaq* was unfurled for the resumption of the
march.   So I had to follow suit, wondering at the strange
unreasonableness of Arab ways.   Had a long march been
the object of such a manœuvre it would have been intelligible
and excusable, but in point of fact we marched that afternoon
for little more than an hour before camping for the night.
Doubtless Ibn Sa'ud had been unable to sleep and had suddenly become bored with sitting still—a mere whim which
caused everybody an hour's unnecessary discomfort and
added little to the total of the day's progress.

During that hour or rather more we travelled about four
miles over a plain slightly more undulating than before with
humps of stony ground alternating with patches of bare earth
and here and there little sandy channels with some vegetation.
Afar off to the left the Qa'ara ridge limited our view, converging slowly and steadily on our course until, at some distance short of it, we camped in an extensive shallow depression called Al Baiyid [1] with plenty of *'Arfaj* for the camels.

During the day the extended front of the marching army
put up a large number of hares, many of which were duly
bagged after exhibitions of skill and energy which were
altogether admirable.   I saw four captures with my own eyes
—all by Arabs on foot chasing the animals and heading them
off from one to another with great efficiency until they sat
down exhausted and merely required to be picked up.
Otherwise life was conspicuous by its absence, though in our
camp on the sand dunes of Mashquq *Jarbu's* had been plentiful, actually coming into my tent during the night, attracted
by the lamp, and I had the satisfaction of killing a scorpion
which seemed to be searching for my feet.

[1] ? 'Ubaiyid.

Ibrahim al Jumai'a, whom a sore eye had prevented from active participation in the recent battle, was among my first visitors this evening, though he seemed to have but little to say and was perhaps chilled by a none too enthusiastic reception. And later Sa'd al Yumaini foregathered with Rushaid and myself to while away the evening in idle chatter. Circumstances brought the conversation round to the subject of tobacco. On one occasion during the previous year, said Rushaid, Ibn Sa'ud was about to start out on a raid. Just before the appointed hour he had without any warning summoned six persons to stay behind with him and gave the order for the rest of the *Gom* to march. ' Listen to me,' he said to the six, ' I have no reason to complain of you or dislike you, but you smoke—there are your *Dhaluls*, your swords and rifles, and now, God be with you, take them and leave my territory.' And the six with one voice declared that, if smoking was indeed their only sin to which he took exception, they would forswear it rather than forsake him. With that they produced their pipes and tobacco and destroyed them before him. The sentence of banishment with honour was withdrawn, and four of the six had kept their vow honourably ever since. The other two had continued in their evil ways without so much as the break of a day. They tried to pump me about the future plans of Ibn Sa'ud, and told me the common rumour—based on the overhearing of part of my conversation with him—that the force would now disband and go home to prepare for a general muster for a regular *Jihad*. ' There is none here,' said Sa'd with his usual frankness, ' except yourself who has the least desire to capture Haïl or who is in any way interested in its fate.' That was probably true, for the great majority of the force encamped around us and it seemed that a further long delay in operations was inevitable if the idea of a disbandment was to prevail. As a matter of fact the general muster did take place late in the same year in circumstances very different from those prevailing at the time of this conversation. Its objective was then not Ibn Rashid but the Sharif, and its result was Turaba, fought in May of the following year—one of the most decisive battles ever fought in Arabia.

Sa'd had during the day heard two of the *Ikhwan* talking

about me. ' Where is the fellow ? ' asked the one who had
never seen me of his companion who had, ' I have seen no one
about here wearing a *Kabbus*.' [1] ' No,' replied the other,
' he wears clothes like any Arab.'

As we were talking a rifle shot rang out in the still night
air and then another and another—news doubtless from
Khurma. And so it was. A *Qahtani* who had taken part in
the last affair rode in with tidings of the great victory of the
Muslimin, who had captured four guns and five machine-
guns. Official confirmation of the victory was yet to come,
but there could no longer be any doubt of the truth of the
news. What more humiliating to one who claimed to be
King of the Arabs than three successive defeats in the open
—with heavy losses in men and the loss of eight guns and
ten machine-guns—by a little village like Khurma !

It was only 2 a.m. when I was awakened on the morrow, but
Ibn Sa'ud, the *Bairaq* and the whole force were on the move
long before we could get ready. We therefore followed at
leisure, travelling by moonlight over a scene that was as
monotonous as that of the previous days. Just before dawn
my companions halted for prayers at a point where the
Qa'ara ridge, coming from the left, seemed to peter out in
the plain, disclosing as it did so the dim line of the Tarafiya
Nafud behind it, while the plain to our right ran up to a
low indeterminate ridge, between which and the *Nafud* lay
a pass—at first five miles wide but rapidly narrowing to only
half a mile. Our course lay through this natural passage.

As daylight gradually overcame the pale light of the moon
we found ourselves steadily overtaking the *Gom*, and passed
Ibn Sa'ud's party, which, having turned aside for the morning
prayer, was enjoying a few moments of sleep. As we passed
they began to stir again, but had marched only a little way
when again they broke off for breakfast, while we continued
on our way intending to arrive at Tarafiya for our first meal.
As we passed close by a group of marching *Ikhwan* one of the
churls called out in loud rasping tones of bigotry : ' Why
do you bring this infidel near us ? ' [2] ' Remember God ! '
replied Sa'd al Yumaini, who had ridden with us from the
start and happened to be nearest the offending man, who

[1] Hat.   [2] ' *Laish tajib hal kafir yamna ?* '

replied : ' There is no God but God.' By this time we had
passed by and could hear no more, but Mitrak, Mirwij and
'Ayadh showed signs of retorting and I had to growl at them
to keep silent. In the circumstances only one of two courses
was possible—either to ignore altogether the idle vapourings
of ignorant bigots or to make a big fuss by taking the matter
up with Ibn Sa'ud, and I had excellent reasons for not
adopting the latter course. Some distance further on I was
dismounted to have my saddle readjusted when two men
passed by apparently discussing me and, as they passed, one
of them went solemnly through the motions of raising a rifle
to his shoulder, taking aim and pulling the trigger three or
four times. While Sa'd was busy with my saddle I kept my
eye steadily fixed on the clown, who turned away abashed
and out of countenance like a naughty child.

And so we continued down the valley, whose surface was
sandy with patches of hard mud, and whose width varied
between a mile and a quarter mile as the *Nafud* came forward
and receded. In the midst of it lay a low mound of friable
sandstone with a low but marked escarpment in process of
disintegration into sand, and at length we ascended on to
the *Safra*, which here throws out a tongue of rock to within
a hundred yards of the *Nafud*. Crossing it we re-entered the
valley, which now runs south towards Tarafiya, and Sa'd
pointed out to me about a mile away to the east the scene
of the great battle, usually known as Sarif, which was fought
in A.H. 1318.[1] Ibn Rashid—'Abdul 'Aziz Ibn Mit'ab, the
successor of the great Muhammad—lay encamped at Sarif,
some distance back in the *Nafud*, with his Shammar and a
loyal contingent from Buraida which had revolted from his
allegiance and closed its gates. Mubarak Ibn Subah lay at
Tarafiya with his allies—Sa'dun of the great Muntafik tribe
of 'Iraq ; 'Abdulrahman, father of the present *Wahhabi* ruler,
with a *Najdi* contingent and a contingent from Buraida.
Ibn Rashid sent out a small cavalry patrol to reconnoitre the
enemy and a brisk fire was opened on it by a similar force
operating from Tarafiya. On hearing the sounds of firing
Ibn Rashid gave the order to advance, and Ibn Subah doing
the same, the battle took place on the first slope of the *Nafud*

[1] About A.D. 1900.

and on part of the Tarafiya plain. Ibn Subah was decisively
defeated and the enemy occupied his camp, while he and his
allies took to flight and were only saved from the attentions
of parties sent out in pursuit by the victor by a timely and
very heavy fall of rain. The slaughter had been heavy during
the encounter itself and the flood, they say, ran blood-red,
carrying before it the corpses of the slain and depositing them
in rows on the edge of the wide *Sabkha* depression extending
along the east side of the Tarafiya basin. 'Abdul 'Aziz Ibn
Sa'ud, still a mere boy, was simultaneously laying siege to
Riyadh, but raised it as soon as he received news of the
defeat and withdrew to Kuwait. Meanwhile Ibn Subah fled
via Zilfi, and the *Najdis* were remorselessly pursued as far as
the confines of 'Aridh, many villages being sacked and burned
by the pursuers. Ibn Rashid himself marched straight on
Buraida, whose gates were opened to him by treachery, and
taught its people the dreadful consequence of rebellion by
executing 180 of its citizens and exacting enormous fines from
the rest—families like the Ribdi and Sharida being mulcted
in 10,000 *Riyals* apiece. But the harsh and vindictive treatment of the vanquished by the victor had made the name of
'Abdul 'Aziz Ibn Rashid hated throughout Najd, and 'Abdulrahman, safely arrived at Kuwait, had foretold that Najd
would soon return to its rightful rulers—a prediction whose
fulfilment began in the following year at the hands of a son,
for whom destiny had so much in store.

Reaching the top of the rise we found ourselves on the rim
of the great self-contained basin of Tarafiya enclosed on one
side by the *Safra* and on the other by the *Nafud* and about
two miles in diameter. The east side of the basin is occupied
by the *Sabkha* already mentioned, towards which the sandy
surface of the rest of the depression slopes down gently from
the *Safra*. In a few moments we were encamped close to a
Qasr in the centre of the basin with a few palms and *Ithils*
about it ; this was one of about fifteen similar habitations
accommodating about a hundred souls of the Tawajir section
of 'Anaza who originally came here from Majma'a. Two
other patches of *Ithils* completed the picture of present
desolation which has overtaken a settlement which appears
at one time to have been much more prosperous.

Soon after we had arrived in camp Ibn Sa'ud rode in followed by the solid phalanx of his escort, and I immediately followed him to his tent for an audience, which proved very dull as he was as sleepy as myself. The young princes, Faisal and Fahad, who had been left behind in camp here during the expedition, immediately came in with the kiss of welcome for their father on both sides of the nose and on top of it, and then took their places in the audience-tent with becoming gravity. Ibn Sa'ud then enquired of their health in the most formal manner as if they were honoured strangers rather than his *own children* yet to reach their 'teens—no doubt a part of the educational routine designed to teach manners and deportment by practice rather than precept. I left them soon afterwards to return to my tent in the hope of an hour or two of sleep to make up for my early rising, but I had first to attend to an unexpected guest—Sultan Ibn 'Abdul 'Aziz al Hasan, who sat talking and smoking for half an hour, and later in the afternoon reappeared with his brother, Hasan. Neither of them seemed to have any matter of interest to discuss with me, and it was perhaps only a fellow-feeling of exile in the wilds of Arabia and the obvious opportunities for a quiet smoke that had made them seek me out.

Tarafiya figured a second time in history in the year A.H. 1326,[1] when a battle was fought at the southern end of the *Sabkha* patch between Ibn Sa'ud and Sultan Ibn Rashid, who had Al Duwish of the Mutair and the Buraida people with him. Between Sarif and 1906 'Abdul 'Aziz Ibn Sa'ud had substantially justified his father's prophecy by recovering Riyadh and all the provinces south of the Qasim. In the latter year 'Abdul 'Aziz Ibn Rashid lay at Raudhat al Muhanna after a long march, when Duwish and others warned him to be on his guard against an impending attack. He disregarded the warning, and next day at dawn Ibn Sa'ud was upon him and a furious battle took place, in which Rushaid, who had also been with Ibn Rashid at Sarif, and the cavalry in which he was serving carried all before them in their sector of the battle, while the day went against the Hail force as a whole and 'Abdul 'Aziz himself was killed. The latter's son, Mit'ab,was placed on the throne, but troubles

[1] About A.D. 1908.

soon broke out at the Shammar capital, where the 'Ubaid branch of the dynasty usurped the functions of the infant ruler. It was Sultan of this branch who met Ibn Sa'ud at Tarafiya two years later, the latter, being himself wounded in the shoulder, gaining a decisive victory. Sultan fled, leaving his half-brother, Faisal Ibn Rashid—who was with us on this march—to hold Buraida, which Ibn Sa'ud attacked unsuccessfully, suffering a reverse near Sabakh.

Ibn Sa'ud having business to transact at this, his base-camp, we remained at Tarafiya over the last day of September—a day of complete inaction so far as I was concerned. In the early hours of the morning I sat in my tent watching the *Ikhwan* troop past, many of them scowling furtively in the direction of the infidel's abode, to a provision dump near by, whence in turn they drew a month's ration of rice, coffee and other necessaries. Some of them carried back the sacks allotted to them on their heads, while others had brought their camels along to bear the heavy loads. And later the monotony of the morning was varied by the appearance of an aged woman of the *Suluba*, who sat at my companions' tent-door offering dried venison for sale and keeping up a vivacious banter of ribaldry with Rushaid, who was always in his element among the dregs of society. I found it very difficult to piece together the voluble conversation of the old hag, who quoted many snatches of verse and even joined in a familiar song. In the end I purchased a couple of gazelle horns from her and a tasselled purse made from the throat of a deer with a simple decorative design in black paint.

One of the *Ikhwan*, passing unknowingly by the tent in which 'Abdullah was sitting alone at the time, looked in and greeted his astonished host, who however uttered words of welcome and entertained him with conversation for some minutes as if there was nothing unusual in the occurrence. At length, and perhaps disappointed at the absence of coffee, he rose to go, and at a little distance was accosted by fellow-*Ikhwan*, who had seen him come out, with questions as to why he had visited the tents of the *Inglisi*. Horrified at his unwitting crime he turned towards us and made public atonement by spitting in our direction. Ghazi, our *Harbi* guide of the Khubub excursion and now once more in my

service—he had almost taken the step of becoming an *Akhu*
but had withdrawn before actual admission, though he
always wore the prescribed chaplet—told me that he had
been informed by a cousin of his in the 'Artawiya camp that
the brethren had sworn to entreat him evilly for his sin of
being with me, should he put in an appearance among them.
And Rushaid told me that an *Akhu*, with whom he had been
in conversation the previous day, had seriously admonished
him for the excessive length of his pantaloons, which according to the rules should not descend further than half-way
down the calf. He had solemnly promised to be more
meticulous in future, and the man had gone off happy at the
thought of a service rendered to a fellow human being.

Ibrahim al Jumai'a honoured me with two visits, one in
the morning and the other in the evening, when we discoursed
pleasantly enough on the great battles of the past. And I
whiled away part of the afternoon skimming through an
Egyptian Arabic translation of a penny-dreadful entitled
' *Fatat al nihilistiya* ' or ' The Nihilist Girl,' which with a
number of similar works formed the bulk of Muhammad al
Sulaiman's library at 'Anaiza. An uneventful interview
with Ibn Sa'ud was followed by a dinner of rice and mutton
—a welcome change from our recent diet of tough camel.
Water is plentiful and good at Tarafiya, particularly in two
wells, the rest having a slightly mineral or saline tendency.

On starting next morning I had intended to go by the
direct road to Buraida, but Dr. 'Abdullah and Rushaid, who
had promised to get me a competent guide for the march,
had failed to do so, and I showed my annoyance by striking
off on a track which I knew was well to the east of the proper
road. Rushaid suggested feebly that the direct road was
more to the right, but I merely replied that, as we had no
guide, I could not take his word for it and continued on my
way. Whereat, much perturbed at the prospect of a long
march, he hied off to a *Qasr* to seek a guide, and finding one
without difficulty, as he could have done before if he had
exerted himself, he shouted out, ',Come this way ; I have
found a guide.' I continued on my way and eventually
Rushaid and the guide caught me up. ' Here's the guide,'
he said, ' and there's our road over there.' ' Where does this

track lead to ? ' I asked, turning to the guide, who replied guilelessly : ' To Raudhat al Ruba'iya.' Whereupon, to the obvious anguish of the whole party, I said : ' Very well, this will do us very well now that we have come so far.' And it so happened that it was one of the hottest days we had had recently ; the *Nafud* blazed like a furnace and there was no wind. 'Abdullah was completely out of temper with the world generally and with me in particular, while Rushaid, in spite of a splitting headache, made amends for his original sin by being the only cheerful member of the party through-out the day except myself, and I seized every opportunity of blessing the chance that had resulted in my seeing so much more of the country than I had expected to. ' And,' I added, ' I propose to do as I did to-day whenever I find that there is no competent guide to direct us.' As a matter of fact our new companion, an old man of eighty called Sulaiman, was exceedingly competent and entertaining, for he regaled us with tales of old wars and battles and recited snatches of verse to while away the time. And at the end of the day he called down on me all the blessings of the Almighty in return for a cash present which had exceeded his wildest imaginings.

We started off from camp soon after 6 a.m. and almost immediately came to a walled grove of some fifty palms, some *Ithils* and a *Qasr* lying astride of and completely blocking the Tarafiya *Sha'ib* which runs down from the *Safra* to the *Sabkha*. The length of the *Sha'ib* is dotted here and there with isolated *Qasrs* and wells in which the depth to water is from four to five fathoms. Passing by another *Qasr* and small grove of palms and *Ithils* on our left, we entered an extensive tract of cornland with scattered *Qasrs* and wells and finally, a mile from our starting-point, came to the largest of the *Qasrs*, a small hamlet indeed enclosed by a formidable turreted wall with only a single gate, so far as I could see, on the north side. Beyond this, after passing some ruins of an old village on the cliff forming the left bank of the *Sha'ib*, we entered and crossed the *Sabkha* tract, extending perhaps a mile on either side of us to north and south.

The *Nafud*, on to which we passed out on the other side, runs at this point about due north and south and eventually

WĀDĪ RIMA EAST OF BURAIDA.

To face page 327.

curls round the southern extremity of the *Safra* until it
passes out of sight to the south-west. For a mile and a half
we laboured up and down the *Nafud*, which is dotted at
frequent intervals with shallow depressions and has a rich
vegetation of *Tarfa* (in the hollows), *Ghadha*, *'Arta* and other
typical growths, until we came to the single well of 'Usailan,
one fathom only in depth and exceedingly briny, in a hollow
with a single *Hish* bush. Beyond this the *Nafud* ridges were
steep, high and generally bare. We passed another well,
Haisiya—briny and shallow like the last—in a depression
more or less shaped like a horseshoe, like the *Falj* pits of
which they tell in the great northern *Nafud*, though I never
heard the term applied to such depressions, which are generally known as *Niqra*.

Reaching now a high ridge of sand we looked back on the
Sabkha of Tarafiya, which shone again like a lake of quick-
silver. Beyond the ridge lay a trough with *Tarfa* bushes, and
from the next ridge behind a veritable ocean of sand billows
appeared the sandstone ridge of Raudha Ruba'iya. For the
next hour we struggled grimly up and down the steep waves
of the *Nafud*, until suddenly we found ourselves in the
channel of Wadi Rima, a bare clay-bottomed passage from
20 to 50 yards wide meandering amid a maze of sandhills
from south-west to north-east and distinguishable only for
a mile or so on either side of our line of crossing. Beyond the
Wadi the same succession of sand ridges continued, from one
of which we had a clear view of the serpentine channel
running at first north-east and then north-north-east until
it was lost again in the sands. About a mile beyond the
Wadi we had to negotiate a very lofty and steep sand slope,
from whose summit we looked down on the palms of
Raudhat al Ruba'iya backed by the escarpment of the ridge
already seen in the distance. In a quarter hour we reached
a small unwalled hamlet right under the escarpment, on
whose summit stood a watch-tower.

North of this point lay a group of walled palm-groves
extending to a distance of a quarter mile, while the main
portion of the oasis consisting of some dozen groves extended
southward for nearly a mile along the base of the escarpment,
which itself runs north for about three miles to the *Wadi*

channel and south for nearly ten miles towards Shamasiya, a similarly situated settlement. Eastward the *Safra* extends about 10 or 12 miles to the sands of the Thuwairat *Nafud* towards Zilfi—forming as it were an island of rock completely encircled by an ocean of sand.

The trough in which the oasis lies has an average width of half a mile between the escarpment and the *Nafud*. In it about a mile to the north lie the single *Qasr* and palm-grove of Ruwaidha or Ruwaidhat al Zayidi, so named after Ibrahim al Zayidi, its owner, a citizen of Buraida though of Dawasir origin. A second watch-tower on the escarpment about a mile south of the first and a number of scattered *Qasrs* in the palm-groves, all of which are walled, complete the picture of a charming settlement buried away from the world. The largest of the *Qasrs* in one of the largest groves near the south extremity of the oasis belongs to the local *Amir*, 'Abdullah Ibn Bazi, of Shammar origin, who lords it over a population of some four hundred souls, mostly of *Tamimi* stock. The palm-groves contain, as everywhere, a fair sprinkling of *Ithils* and considerable areas of lucerne. From the northern watch-tower to which I ascended for a view of the surrounding country there was nothing to be seen but the *Nafud* and the darker line of the 'Aushaziya *Safra*.

On returning to where I had left our camels and the rest of the party I found we had been invited to coffee by one of the villagers, and we forthwith entered his parlour, whose smoke-grimed walls bore quite an elaborate scheme of decoration in white paint,[1] while the clay cupboard by the side of the hearth was ornamented from top to bottom with a shark's-tooth moulding in high-relief. A number of the inhabitants soon gathered in the parlour to hear the latest news of the recent expedition, but it was on the whole a dull and spiritless entertainment, from which we were glad to escape as soon as the coffee had gone round. Of their bounty they produced dates to appease our hunger, but they were quite the worst and driest fresh dates I had ever tasted. Of local gossip there was none, though for some reason the conversation turned on timepieces and I was told there was not a single watch of any kind in the whole village.

[1] *Vide* Fig. 12.

Resuming our march soon after midday we marched
south along the flank of the oasis to Ibn Bazi's garden at the
end, from which we turned south-west into a bay of the
Nafud, in which lay their cornfields.   Entering the sands we
found ourselves on the well-marked Buraida track which
negotiates the *Nafud* at a lower and easier level than that on
which we had laboured earlier in the day.   About one mile
out from Ibn Bazi's garden we topped a low ridge to find

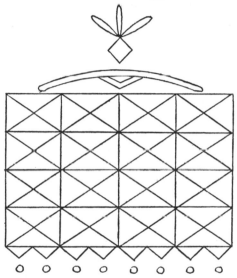

FIG. 12.   MURAL DECORATION IN HOUSE AT RAUDHA RUBA'IYA.

ourselves once more confronted by the Wadi Rima channel,
at this point splayed out in an immense circular mud-flat
known as Al Dahura and apparently completely surrounded
by sand ridges.   The circle may have been about two miles
in diameter, and its hardened surface was here and there
diversified by sandy patches with *Rimdh* and other vegetation which appeared to mark roughly the general course of
the main flood channel.   To the south-west as we advanced
lay the dozen or more abandoned *Qasrs* of Taumiya backed
by the line of the 'Aushaziya *Safra* and its prolongation in
the Itaiyima *Nafud* strip.   The main line of the channel
seemed to come up from the south-west past this point, and
the distance covered by us diagonally from the point at

which we entered the Dahura to that at which we climbed up on to the first slope of the Buraida *Nafud* was about seven miles in all. Another three miles over the ridges and hollows of the *Nafud* brought us to the depression of Khabb al Qabr, whose palms, interspersed with a few huts, extended on our left for about half a mile along the lea of the sand ridge, while the single *Qasr* and two palm patches of Niqar al Thanna lay half a mile to our right. Passing a watch-tower on the next ridge we came next to a large *Qasr* and hamlet called Rafi'a, which, thirty years before when Muhammad Ibn Rashid camped there for a considerable time after his victory at Mulaida, was said to have been a flourishing oasis. Two miles away to the north-north-west lay the palms and *Qasr* of 'Auda between the *Nafud* and the *Safra*, while immediately to our left lay 'Ajuza, a similar group. Next came Khudhair and Suwair to our left and 'Ukairsha, one of the biggest of the Buraida *Khabbs*, to our right. And so at last, after a weary day and passing well to the right of Wahtan, we came to Sadda and the wells of Saqa'a between it and the corner of the great city which we entered by the east gate.

Fahad al Mu'ammar was holding his court, as we arrived, in the usual place outside our dwelling, and I sat awhile with him on the earthen bench along the wall, drinking coffee and talking of the recent fighting, in which by all accounts he had greatly distinguished himself—having killed nine men in mounted combat and he blind in one eye. Retiring for a while to rest I was soon summoned by Fahad to join him at dinner, and, famished as we were, we did justice to the excellent meal of rice and mutton which he placed before us, served on a higher platter than any I had ever seen elsewhere. And, dinner over, I retired to the cool of my roof to rest and read until it was time to sleep.

CHAPTER IV

HOMEWARD BOUND

1. A BOLT FROM THE BLUE

OCTOBER 2nd dawned as fair a day as one might wish for, with a cool breeze from the north fanning the palms of Buraida under a brilliant sky. Yet for me it was a day of vexation and bitterness. Ibn Sa'ud was not yet arrived from Tarafiya, and there was nothing in my circumstances to suggest that my sojourn in Arabia was drawing to a close.

'Abbas al Fallaji came to see me in the morning in connection with a projected visit to Baghdad, where he would be in need of letters of recommendation. I parried his demand in the hope of enjoying more of his society in the days to come. I would visit his house and perhaps gain admission to the houses of his friends. He himself was too obsequious to be likeable, but I wanted to break the ice that lay over the still waters of Buraida society, disguising the sweetness which one knows well enough in the streams that spread therefrom to the ends of the earth—Baghdad, Damascus and Cairo. I took him aback with the frankness of my accusation that Buraida had not treated me with the consideration or courtesy due to the representative of a Great Power on whose hospitality and protection so many of its citizens depended for their prosperity. ' Ya sa'adat al Sahib ! ' he replied, ' your excellency knows that all of us are not alike—and least of all myself.' I was prepared to try out the new experiment, and our conversation was interrupted by the arrival of a mail-bag from Kuwait. We never met again, and I know not if he ever went to 'Iraq.

The contents of the mail-bag were the most startling and depressing letters I had received since my mission began. Indeed the orders I received were, unless substantially modified or cancelled outright, tantamount to the termination of that mission. I was thunderstruck and raged impotently against the folly of my government. His Majesty's Government had decided that they no longer wanted Ibn Sa'ud to proceed with the campaign against Haïl lest his success should ruffle the temper of King Husain. The argument was presumably that his ill-temper might jeopardise the progress of Lawrence's campaign in Syria, but we know now that that argument was untenable, as Lawrence and Faisal had quarrelled with the old tyrant over the telegraph wires from Abal Lisan and had tacked themselves on to Allenby's army. Be that as it may, His Majesty's Government had arrived at this decision and had accordingly further decided to withdraw a present of 1000 rifles and corresponding ammunition already handed over to 'Abdullah al Nafisi, Ibn Sa'ud's agent at Kuwait, in replacement of an earlier gift of worthless Winchester repeating-rifles, at which the *Wahhabi* monarch had looked frankly in the mouth to the discomfiture of the donors. For such a proceeding as the withdrawal of a gift already given there could be no excuse. And finally the High Commissioner at Cairo was reported to be stoutly resisting a proposal, which had commended itself to the British Government, to send a British Commission to examine and settle the Khurma boundary question. In view of subsequent developments during an eventful decade it is well for Ibn Sa'ud that the counsels of the British Government at this stage were directed by ignorance and prejudice.

By the time I saw Ibn Sa'ud on his return later in the day he had received and read his Kuwait agent's account of the sequestration of the rifles, and was not in the best of moods to be offered the cup of bitterness which I was instructed to press upon him. He railed bitterly at His Majesty's Government out of the fulness of his heart. 'Who after this will put their trust in you? I wanted not to attack Haïl and you pressed me to do so. And now you tell me to stop. And you hold me up to the ridicule of my own people by supplying me with worthless weapons, while now you add injury to insult by withdrawing the serviceable rifles you offered me in exchange.' And so we covered all the old ground of earlier discussions again with no secret made of Ibn Sa'ud's disgust and mortification, the while I had no leg to stand on and nothing to reply. My long struggle to present a fair and true picture of *Wahhabi* Arabia had ended in defeat, but there was no doubt in my mind that His Majesty's Government, laying their plans behind a smoke-screen of misrepresentation, had entered upon a course of error which would lead them into undreamed-of consequences. There was only one hope of avoiding those consequences, but that hope lay in using British troops in Arabia, a course which, but for a slight lapse in 1919, never commended itself to those in authority. For the time being my course was clear. I could not accept as final or satisfactory the policy which I was instructed to communicate to Ibn Sa'ud. I proposed to repair at once to Baghdad to see what could be done and my host concurred in my proposal. ' And if your Government declines to modify its policy,' he added, ' it is of no use your coming back. I will show them what I can do. *Wallah !* it is the Sharif who is responsible for this blow at me—he has utterly deceived the rulers of Egypt, and I will attack him if, to humour him, your Government persists in treating me so ill.'

And so I went forth from his presence with my departure fixed for 4th October. The following day my interview with Ibn Sa'ud was deferred till late in the evening, and took place on the roof of his private apartments in the *Qasr.* He avoided all discussion of the matters which had occupied us the previous day, and after some conversation of a general character he sent for Rushaid and Mitrak, who were to be in charge of the march to Kuwait. I took but little interest in the detailed instructions given for their guidance, as I knew that, subject to such obstruction as I might receive from my companions, the order of march would be at my discretion. I left Ibn Sa'ud to complete my packing and the following morning I was awakened at dawn.

I had no desire but to get started, and I was ready before 6 a.m. Two hours later I was still waiting patiently while the camels were being collected and loaded up, and at this stage I was summoned to my farewell audience. This took place not in the large new hall, where Ibn Sa'ud normally

received visitors, but in a room known as the ' old *Majlis,*
an airy apartment open to the breezes on the north side
where there was a pillared verandah. We were alone, and
Ibn Sa'ud, with a courtesy so characteristic of him and so
charming, sent for breakfast, which we ate together—a
frugal meal of buttered rice and dates. And then we discussed affairs of state in real earnest, for Ibn Sa'ud's final
representations were deliberately conceived in the manner
of an ultimatum. His whole future was at stake, and he
genuinely desired to follow the path of friendship with Great
Britain.

' Impress upon them,' he said, ' on my behalf that His
Majesty's Government must adopt one of two lines of policy,
for there is no alternative that will satisfy me. Let them,
if they wish, leave me to myself under guarantee that all
states in alliance with them will refrain from encroachment
on my rights or territories—I wish for no better than to
remain in peace in my own dominions, and if I am left in
peace I undertake for my part to remain quiet. Or let them
maintain the present active alliance between us against their
enemies and my enemies and I undertake to give them
satisfaction in return for arms and money. But as for Ibn
Rashid, I cannot bind myself to inaction in that direction
unless your Government is prepared to guarantee me against
attack by him or his tribesmen—but remember, the guarantee
must not be of the kind I know so well from my experience
of the aggressions of the Sharif and the 'Ajman. With
regard to the former I gave my guarantee long since to the
people of Khurma that they would not be attacked again,
and the Sharif has attacked them. So now I will carry out
my promise of support unless the British Government is
prepared to accept one or other of the alternatives I have
explained to you. *Li khatar min riayaï,* remember that, I
am nervous of my own subjects, for hitherto I have stood
alone against their natural inclinations, persuading them that
British friendship was to their ultimate advantage. But
what can I say to them now ? Who will trust you again after
this ? '

And then, relaxing the strain of his pent-up feelings, he
turned to speak charmingly of myself, expressing regret at

my departure in terms of touching friendliness and an earnest wish that I might return again to him after setting things to rights with the British Government. ' But if you cannot arrange these matters come not back, for I can no longer hold out against the reason of my own people, and I will not accept another representative.'

I replied that I would do my best and took my leave of him with a heart that was heavy with disappointment at the catastrophe which had shattered the work of a year at a moment when every obstacle to success seemed to have been surmounted. It was, for all I knew, perhaps a final farewell that I bade him as I went forth from his friendly, majestic presence to the camels that waited outside to carry me on what would perhaps be my last journey in Arabia. When things were going well I had scarcely been conscious of the fatigue and worry which had accompanied my task in a land of fanatics who, by studied aversion and often by unconcealed expression of their hatred of the infidel in their midst, had made my life a lonely and depressing one, only relieved and made endurable by the steady friendship of Ibn Sa'ud, by the feeling of success which that implied, and by the excitement engendered by opportunities of work in the service of science—opportunities which had enabled me to traverse the length and breadth of Wahhabiland, from east to west and from south to north. But now I felt weary and glad to think that my goal was home. In the open space of the Jarada I found but three of my escort party ready to start, and being in no mood to brook delay, I mounted and set out with them, leaving the rest to follow if they would. It was not till we had halted for the first evening's rest that the main body of the caravan joined us, and by that time the routine of marching and geographical work had soothed me into oblivion of other worries.

2. ZILFI

My three companions on this first stage of our long march were : Mirwij, a slave of the royal household and formerly of Haïl, who had now been in regular attendance on me for some three months ; Khuzaiyim, a *Shammari* of the Aslam

subsection, who was to vouch for us in case of contact with
raiding-parties of his tribe ; and Rashid of the Rashidi, a
tribe with affinities with the Mutair under *Shaikh* Adh'an,
in the double capacity of guide and *Rafiq*. These two men
were unknown to me before.

We left Buraida by the east gate, travelling in an easterly
direction towards the Rafi'a watch-tower, beyond which,
traversing ground already covered during my journey of a
few days before from Tarafiya, we passed through the palms
of Khabb al Qabr on to the mud-flat beyond. We now came
after an hour's marching to the first ridge of the real *Nafud*,
which lay in waves of soft sand between us and the Rima
valley. From the second ridge we saw the *Qasr*-granges of
Taumiya in the valley itself below us somewhat to southward
of east, while far ahead beyond a great sea of sand appeared
the darker lines of the Mustawi and Khartam rock-ridges,
the latter somewhat to right of our direction while the former
marked the position of our first goal—the oasis of Shamasiya.

From the last regular ridge we descended a gentle slope
into the firm soil of the valley bottom, where the track was
well marked as it passed between scattered outlying hummocks of *Nafud* sand. About three miles to the S.S.E. lay
the few huts and palm-grove of Dhulaiyim under the lea of
the Khartam ridge where the latter abuts on the *Wadi*.
Then passing at a distance of about a mile from the Taumiya
Qasrs we entered upon an area of *Rimdh*-covered dunes
through which we struck obliquely across the valley, from
whose right bank patches of sand covered with black pebbles
intruded across our path. The channel seemed on the average
to be about three-quarter mile in width, varying in places
between a few hundred yards and two miles—its greatest
width being in the great mud-flat basin of Dahura, which
appears to be the meeting-point of not less than two different
channels. The surface of this basin became rougher with a
slight efflorescence of salt as we proceeded eastward towards
the Sa'afij *Nafud*, on to which we finally passed out of Wadi
Rima. This belt of *Nafud* sand forms the right bank of
the *Wadi* between Dhulaiyim at the north extremity of the
Khartam ridge and Nabjiya at the northern end of the
Mustawi. Southward it extends unbroken, they say, between

these two *Safra* tracts to the watering of Shuraimiya, some thirty miles south of Shamasiya, where the sands of Nafud Thuwairat, lying east of the Mustawi ridge, join it to form the sand-belt known as the Shaqra or Batra *Nafud*. The whole of this Rima valley country is of sandstone disintegrated or disintegrating into sand. For a couple of miles we marched over a rolling down liberally covered with the graceful *Ghadha* bushes and patches of briny *Rimdh* and knotty *'Arta*, until we entered a tract of higher and barer *Nafud*, lying north and south but ribbed with cross-ridges of sand whose axes were east and west, exposed to the north wind. In this part there was vegetation in scanty patches only in the hollows. From the summit of this *Nafud*, or rather from somewhat beyond it, the first palms of Shamasiya came into view backed by the dark barrier of Mustawi, which was now seen to consist of a stepped cliff with a flat ledge, about a quarter mile wide, connecting the summit of the first section with the foot of the second. The oasis itself lay in a trough between the *Nafud* sands and the former.

Shortly after 2 p.m., having marched about 15 miles, we camped in the middle section of the oasis, and were entertained to coffee in the parlour of a freedman resident of the village, a dingy apartment of clay walls grimed with smoke and without ornament. Our host and a few friends who came in to see us were exceedingly cordial and expansive. The people of the settlement, they told us, were mostly freedmen tenants of Bani Tamim landlords originally from Washm, the local *Amir* being one Ibn Fauzan. The population may have numbered some five hundred souls scattered about in a number of hamlets over a distance of about a mile. At the northern and southern ends of the settlement lie small hamlets more like overgrown *Qasrs*, walled and turreted, while the central hamlet was without wall and of mean mud huts. The palm-groves seemed to be less flourishing than those of Raudha Ruba'iya and of more recent planting, their chief product being the *Maktumi* date, of which we bought a *maund* for a dollar. The southern section was the most prosperous part of the settlement, the wells varying from ten to fourteen fathoms in depth, sunk into the rough sandstone rock of the subsurface with stone limning only for some six to ten feet down. The water is good and plentiful, camels and cows being in general use for drawing it up for irrigation purposes, while the best well, by which we camped, appeared to be served by hand only for the exclusive supply of drinking-water. The irrigation well-pits are generally rectangular, about 12 feet by 6, and carry two or at most four wheels in the superstructure. Fodder for the well-animals was plentiful, being for the most part the excellent *Nussi* grass of the Thuwairat *Nafud*, of which we bought a full camel-load for eight dollars.

A number of scattered granges at various distances from the main settlement may be counted as suburbs of Shamasiya —namely Ruwaidhat, a group of *Qasrs* in a tract of cornland half a mile to the south ; the *Qasrs* of Barjisiya, two miles away in the same direction ; and those of Duwaihara, a mile further south, through which runs the caravan-track from 'Anaiza to Zilfi. All these outlying farms are cultivated by the people of Shamasiya itself, who also manage two patches of cornland about a mile to the northward, in which are groups of *Qasrs*. A watch-tower called Al Abraq, not visible from our camp, stands upon the cliff two miles off in the direction of Raudha Ruba'iya, and a similar turret overlooks the southern extremity of the oasis.

The settlement is said to be older than Buraida itself and to derive its name from the now ruined village of Shamas outside the city walls to the north. Presumably, therefore, it was the freedmen tenants who came from there at the invitation of the owners of the land and brought with them the name of their own village.

I had hoped to make an early start the following morning, but the sun was well up before we moved off for a full day's march of some 26 miles. The ascent of the first cliff presented no difficulty, but the second could only be negotiated in single file up a steep incline sprinkled with small loose boulders of sandstone. In a quarter hour we had gained the summit of the ridge, whence a wide view of a somewhat dreary landscape presented itself to our eyes. Below us lay the neat rectangles of the Shamasiya palm-groves and hamlets, and beyond them the *Nafud* stretching into the distance, broken in its midst by the trough of Wadi Rima. Before us

lay a flat bare plain of sandstone rock with a worn calcareous
surface, broken up here and there in boulders, and beyond it
appeared the long yellow line of Nafud Thuwairat.

The wilderness sloped gently eastward, traversed by a
narrow runnel of a torrent-bed which trended back to the
Shamasiya trough. Beyond it the surface became a hard
rough ' *pat* ' with scattered patches of stone and shingle to
vary its monotony. And, as we advanced, this gave way to
a rolling down tract with ridges of rock and bare stony
depressions, whose direction was generally from south to
north into Wadi Rima or eastward into the Mustawi trough
ahead. We passed by a mound of great black boulders and
followed the depression of a stony valley, 200 yards wide,
running through a series of cross-ridges, each somewhat
lower than the preceding. And in its midst we came upon
a spot known as Rujum al Shuyukh, where once many years
before Ibn Sa'ud had pitched camp in the course of some
raiding expedition against the Shammar. His temporary
coffee-hearth of desert stones still remained to tell its story,
and the raised circles marking the sites of tents or shelters.
Occasional outcrops of black rock varied the scene as we
descended, crossing and recrossing a petty *Sha'ib* bed, into
the Mustawi valley at the black hillock of Bruma.

The Mustawi is in fact not so much a valley as a plain,
about three miles wide and forming a transition from the
sand rock of the *Safra* behind us to the *Nafud* sands ahead.
Our crossing was in the neighbourhood of a low watershed
from which the plain drained respectively north and south
towards Wadi Rima,[1] and a bushy basin about 15 to 20 miles
southward known as Armah. The surface, showing in parts
signs of former floods, is of a sandy loam strewn with black
shingle and fragments of sandstone with outcropping black
ridges, in which are patches of a deep red rock.

As we approached the *Nafud*, which lay ahead in a far-flung
arc whose extremities outflanked us, there was a thin covering
of sand over ruddy clay with plentiful bushes of *'Arfaj*, among
which we breakfasted on the first low sand-ridge. For the
first two miles the going was easy enough and the sea of sand
was dotted with islands of black rock and reefs of bare low-

[1] One of the *Sha'ibs* trending in this direction is the Rakham.

lying clay. We then passed into the *Nafud* proper of ruddy
sand, wave upon wave, in the midst of which we came upon
a group of Suluba, who had come from Majma'a, men and
women toiling through the laborious sand on asses of their
peculiar breed. And with them was one Abu Hamza, an old
man of some local repute as a professional beggar and a
citizen of Rass. Whither they were bound I did not discover,
for we dallied with them no longer than it took to distribute
a few dollars for luck to him and some women who came with
him to beg alms. In return they told us of the little settlements embosomed in the sands of this *Nafud*—the palm
settlements of Thuwair, from which the sand-waste derives
its name of Thuwairat, and Mansaf and Qusaiba between us
and the great *Wadi*, and the wells of 'Artawiya (not to be
confused with the *Ikhwan* settlement of the same name) and
Hamudiya respectively southward and northward of Zilfi.[1]

Then we went on up and down ridge after ridge of the deep
sand, red and bare, passing frequent depressions of clay.
In general the axes of the waves seemed to lie north and
south, but there was an absence of mathematical regularity
which produced a sense of confusion until, after the afternoon
prayer, we entered the highest and grandest section of the
Nafud—the Zulaighif tract of lofty ridges of pure red sand
parted from each other by deep valleys trending south-west
to north-east. The crests stood some 300 feet above the
valley bottoms, and our course followed the latter to the
passes leading between the high hummocks from one into
another. And so we came to and halted at the little palm-
grove of Nukhail al 'Abd in a circular clay bottom.

Here a few mud turrets served to shelter the score or so of
tenants cultivating these 15 acres of palms for the benefit of
owners residing at Zilfi. Some of them joined us to drink
coffee and brought us a supply of the local *Khadhri* dates,
reputed to be heating. Our baggage animals, by reason of
the heavy going, arrived long after ourselves, but we were
able to procure a goat from a local herdsman for our dinner,
at which we had the company of two new-comers who had

[1] Other settlements named to me were : South of the main road : 'Aqla
and Marr, both palm-patches with a *Qasr* or two ; northward Zahlula,
Ithila, Rijmiya, Ruhaiya, Hadhiya, Umm 'Arta, Baidha Nathil, Harrar,
Quai' and Abu Tarfat.

A DROVE OF SHEEP ON THE NAFŪD BETWEEN BURAIDA AND ZILFÏ.

To face page 340.

caught us up with a message from Ibn Sa'ud during the day.
One of these was Zubara, an old *Harbi* friend of my journey
to the Hijaz, and the other a surly *Mutairi*, Dabbi by name,
who had been sent to join me as an additional *Rafiq*, but,
whether from innate sourness of temper or by reason of
religious prejudice, had studiously avoided me all day and
would not even sit down in my company to the meal—he
had only himself to thank for missing the best of the meat.
Rashid, who had guided us so far, was little versed in the
geography of the region, apart from the road itself, and
Rushaid listened obsequiously to my frequent appeals to be
provided with competent guides without any intention of
meeting my requirements. On the whole this day of marching
through the *Nafud* had frayed all our tempers, and I felt a
little weary of my companions.

Apart from the main circular palm-patch already mentioned the settlement of Nukhail al 'Abd comprises a diminutive group of palms close to it on the north with a picturesque
watch-tower on the sand slope separating the two sections.
The subsoil water is here so close at hand that the palms,
tapping the moisture with their roots, need no irrigation,
while drinking-water is drawn up from *Thamaïl*,[1] unlined and
not deeper than a fathom. A queer little settlement it is,
like many others, in the heart of a *Nafud* as grand and formidable as any to be seen in Arabia. Its saving grace for the
traveller is that the high-road, lying for the most part in a
depression or series of depressions with but few ridges to
negotiate, presents no difficulty. Its total width along the
line of the road from the Mustawi plain to that of Zilfi is some
16 miles, of which we had some four still before us when we
mounted to continue our march next morning.

About a mile beyond our starting-point and separated
from it by a low pass over an intervening sand ridge lay two
straggling patches of palms and vegetables in a shallow
depression to the left of the high-road. This was Hamdhiya,
which differs from Nukhail al 'Abd in enjoying artificial
irrigation from wells about three fathoms deep surmounted
by the ordinary *Suwani* superstructure. The mouths of these
wells, otherwise unlined, are fortified with rough brushwood.

[1] Pl. of *Thamila* = water hole.

and cattle, working up and down a short incline, draw up the water-skins to empty into the irrigation ducts, along which melons and pumpkins are grown. A considerable area of new palm-stems had been put down in this settlement the previous year and seemed to be flourishing. As we passed by towards another small palm-patch a quarter mile distant a man working on one of the wells ran up to us with a gift of pumpkins.

So we now came to the highest part of the Zulaighif, whose great naked peaks of sand furrowed by the wind lay all about us. Ahead the summit of the Tuwaiq escarpment came into view, and a few minutes later as we debouched from the *Nafud* into the Zilfi plain the settlements of the oasis lay scattered before us backed by a line of cliffs extending from the northernmost headland of Khashm Jazra until it disappeared into the far horizon of the south.

In ten minutes we had arrived before the walls of Zilfi Shamaliya, the more northerly of the two main villages, and proceeded to camp under the curious but silent gaze of the village children. For the next hour or so there was much going and coming between the village and our camp, grass and millet-stalks being brought for the camels, a sheep and other articles of food for ourselves, the while I tried conclusions with Dabbi, who was still apparently determined to have nothing to do with me. In answer to a direct challenge on this issue he protested that he had intended no discourtesy, but I told him I had no further need of his services. Half an hour later he returned to reopen the discussion. ' Look you,' I said, ' you object to me for being an infidel. I was created like that and, if God wills, shall remain so. And praise be to God! But I have no need of your deceit and disloyalty, though it is rather to Ibn Sa'ud that you are being disloyal. How can I agree to your remaining with me in these circumstances ? ' At that I left him to ruminate the position, and I had his answer soon afterwards in the *Amir's* house, where he sat by me to eat dates off the common platter.

The *Amir* of Zilfi, Salman Ibn Baddah, was absent from home on a visit to Ibn Sa'ud together with his predecessor in the office, 'Uthman Ibn 'Uthman, of whose summary dismissal I have written elsewhere.[1] In Salman's absence his brother, Bijad, had been left in charge, and it was he who now summoned us to take coffee with him, complaining hospitably of our failure to send notice of our coming to enable him to prepare breakfast against our arrival and inviting us to dinner in the evening—an invitation which I gladly accepted, as I had decided to spend the day exploring the various settlements of the Batin, as the plain is called. His parlour, though of fair size, was exceedingly plain and dingy with untrimmed clay walls black with smoke and without furniture other than mat-strips of Hasa make laid over the floor of sand. Our host told us of a new spring (Saih by name) of sweet water, which had recently been discovered to the great advantage of folk who had lived long years on the bitter water which had alone been known in these parts ; and it certainly seemed to me that the water he gave us was as good as any in Arabia. After a round or two of coffee Bijad with his own hands brought in a mat piled up with great bunches of fresh *Hilwa* dates, reddish in colour like the *Khadhri*, but of better repute. In this neighbourhood they were already cutting down the date-bunches from the palms, though in the Qasim the normal practice was to wait for the first rain of the season. And here the autumn season or seasonal subdivision known as *Wasm* was reckoned not to have begun, though in the Qasim a fortnight of it had already passed. Whether there is any natural justification for this difference of nearly a month—for the beginning of *Wasm* would be ten days hence—in the classification of the seasons by such close neighbours I cannot say with authority, but I had no doubt that some actual change of conditions had taken place. As if by magic summer had disappeared in a night. My thermometer recorded an early morning temperature of under 62° *Fahr.*, the lowest experienced since the previous spring. And the midday heat had become appreciably milder in spite of the *Nafud*.

Zilfi and the settlements round it in the Batin plain form a separate and independent district with affinities both with Qasim and Sudair [2]—the latter beginning properly at Ghat

[1] *H.A.* vol. i. p. 362.
[2] Majma'a, the capital of Sudair, lies towards the eastern extremity of Tuwaiq some 15 miles east or south-east of Ghat.

some 15 miles to the south at the mouth of a gorge of Tuwaiq.
The village of Shamaliya is the oldest of these settlements,
and the population of the district, as at present constituted,
is said to date back for five generations. It is composed
almost entirely of 'Ataiba elements, to which the families of
both the *Amir* and the ex-*Amir* belong. Shamaliya with a
population of some 1500 souls is roughly circular in shape,
and enclosed as by a wall by the contiguous backs of its
houses. At salient corners it is provided with turrets, and,
apart from the back entrances to various houses, there are
four regular gates, on the north, east, south and west sides
respectively. Inside there is an extreme regularity as of
scientific town-planning, with streets straight and from ten
to fifteen feet wide. A large building like a fort stands at
the south-east corner, but for the rest the houses are poor and
unpretentious. We entered the village by the west gate to
go to the *Amir's* house, the *'Id* prayer enclosure—a regular
clay-built mosque with colonnades in contrast with the open
spaces usual elsewhere—being outside the same gate and not
far from our camp.

As we sat round waiting for coffee an ancient member of
the Mutair tribe came in and sat down next to me, but a few
moments later, having apparently taken stock of the situation, he rose abruptly and took his seat on the further side
of the coffee-hearth—whether out of deference or of fanaticism
I had no means of knowing. In any case other residents who
came in to join the party at the call of the pestle and mortar
conversed freely with me and seemed devoid of any objection
to my presence, though they did not specifically greet me on
their entry. And on my return to our tents Rushaid,
conscious of past shortcomings in his capacity as my guide,
philosopher and friend, brought in a small boy of the village
who claimed to be five years old and was certainly not more
than seven. He was something of an infant prodigy, and,
sitting down before me, proceeded to recite poem after poem
in most amazing fashion. To my shame it must be confessed
that I understood but little of his recital, but I was fascinated
at his manly rendering of extracts from an apparently
unlimited repertoire and disgraced myself by giving him a
princely gift of five dollars after he had gone through as

THE *SUQ* AT ZILFĪ.

To face page 345.

many ballads. Rejoicing greatly he darted out of the tent exclaiming, ' *Allah yaghnik*—God keep you from want ! ' and, so exclaiming, tripped over an unseen tent-rope to burst into tears. The poor child was soon consoled for his hurt and ran off to the village happy as a skylark.

After the midday prayer Bijad came in person to conduct me to the house of one Sulaiman who had met me in the morning and invited me to coffee. Skirting the village to the north gate we found our host's house in the main street leading therefrom to the *Suq*, an irregular square with forty-five shops which catered for the wants of all the Zilfi settlements. His parlour was clean and well built with walls of unadorned clay, and a cushion had been specially provided for me on the floor mats, which with the coffee utensils were all the furniture of the room. Coffee, tea and incense passed round at frequent intervals as my host and the acting *Amir* talked to me of their circumstances. Life had become very expensive at Zilfi owing to the War, for no caravan had come in from Kuwait during the past three months. They were anxious to know when the War would end, and I little suspected then that an optimistic answer would have been justifiable. The bulk of the trade of Zilfi was of a forwarding nature, the place being a sort of clearing-house for a district of considerable extent, including the *Nafud* settlements and those of the Hamada, which is a southern continuation of the Batin. But the prospects of agricultural development in the latter were apparently a subject of constant speculation here. Apart from the new Saih spring already mentioned they told me of surviving remains of an old irrigation system at the edge of Tuwaiq some five miles to the north. Such remains argued the presence of a spring, but all efforts to bring it to light had ended in failure. Then, proceeding further afield, we discussed whether it would be possible or advisable to touch the great *Ikhwan* colony of 'Artawiya—as big, they said, as Buraida and ever growing—and with one accord they all advised against it. Even the Kuwait caravans are not allowed to pass through it or even to draw its water, much less to pass a night there. And the rumour of an infidel might well bring out this nest of hornets about our ears. On the whole I could scarcely go against such a verdict, and resigned myself to foregoing even a passing glimpse of a place so notorious.

Later in the afternoon I sallied forth to visit the palm-groves and villages to northward of the Shamaliya scttlement. The camels, which had had so lean a day in the *Nafud* that this morning they browsed in desperation on the green but unpopular *Adhir*, had had a good feed during the morning and stepped along gaily over the sandy *Rimdh*-covered plain. A ride of twenty minutes brought us to the beginning of an extensive patch of young palms, melons, pumpkins and some cotton extending northwards to a main clump of full-grown palms. This was the plantation of Saih irrigated from numerous spring-fed wells varying from three to five fathoms in depth and said to have been discovered accidentally some fifteen years before by a man burrowing after a *Jarbu'* which had gone to earth. Since those days the settlement had been greatly developed, and extended for about a mile along the left bank of Sha'ib 'Araira,[1] which descends from the Tuwaiq upland at the small palm-patch of 'Araira with a few *Qasrs* in a fold of the escarpment and runs across the valley to the *Nafud*. This plantation enjoys an advantage over all its neighbours in having water comparatively near the surface, the general depth elsewhere being ten fathoms.

Following now the shingly bed of Sha'ib 'Araira we came after another mile of marching to a group of four large groves known as Al Liqa, whose main body rested on the edge of the *Nafud* with two of the groves in front of it and separated from each other by a narrow interval. Passing between these palm-groves—the one on our right was surrounded by a high wall with two turrets—we came to the main grove, in which were spread out at intervals a small hamlet, a much larger hamlet, and finally at the northern extremity another big hamlet, the whole population of the three being about 800 souls.

We were now at the northern extremity of the Zilfi cultivation except for a couple of *Qasrs* in a straggling palm-patch, known as Qusur al 'Abd, about two miles due north ;

[1] A similar *Sha'ib*, Samnan by name, issues from the escarpment further to the south near a small palm-grove of the same name. This also flows across the valley and turns south.

VILLAGE OF AL LIQU NEAR ZILFÏ.

To face page 346.

and turned southward over a well-marked track running through the settlement and beyond it towards Zilfi. Here we met a very old man who greeted us in a weak tremulous voice, and was said to be a hundred years old. He was formerly *Amir* of the Liqa settlement, his name being Ibn Farhud, but had long been superannuated in favour of his cousin, Ibn Dahash.

About a mile or more beyond these groves we saw some old ruins of the ancient settlement of Manzila, consisting of a large *Qasr* and numerous wells about half a mile to our right. The local tradition is that this and Qusur al 'Abd were the original settlements of this tract and were constantly at feud. Whether their water supply failed or for some other reason both villages were abandoned in favour of other sites, Zilfi (*i.e.* Shamaliya, which is seldom used in local parlance) being colonised from Manzila and Al Liqa from its rival.

This completed our tour of the outlying settlements and we returned to camp, leaving 'Aqda, or Zilfi Janubiya, to be visited on the resumption of our march on the morrow, and contenting ourselves with only a distant view from camp of a nearly unbroken series of groves along the line of Sha'ib Samnan. From east to west these are Thamaïl, Haitan with 'Aqda standing somewhat forward of its eastern extremity, and Lughaf nearest the *Nafud*, along which the *Sha'ib* turns south to the palm-patches of Ghaifa and Targhasha, about half a mile and three-quarter mile down-stream of Lughaf.

The experience of the infant prodigy of the morning had created a favourable impression on the youthful population of the village, several of the bolder spirits of a crowd, which dogged my movements in and around the village with a friendly inquisitiveness, coming up to me to shake hands— an unusual experience. But I did not reckon with the possibility of a second *Qassad* or ballad-monger of tender years in a community so small and, on the pretext of weariness, turned away one such pretender lest I might have to spend the evening listening to and paying a succession of them.

We dined with Bijad and did justice to his generous though simple feast of rice, lentils and mutton, talking of the ordinary facts and incidents of his village life. The *Hadra* or caravan which had set out for Kuwait from Shaqra when I was there to bring up supplies for Ibn Sa'ud's army had arrived during the day, its 500 camels making a splendid spectacle as they came over the edge of Tuwaiq and descended the slope towards the village. Next day they would continue the journey to Buraida, but for the time being Zilfi was full of life. The military muster of this district amounted, said Bijad, to 4000 men, but from what I saw and heard of the various settlements, that figure I judged to be a fairly reasonable estimate of the total population,[1] men, women and children. Round our camp I had noticed a number of old ruins with signs of gypsum cement (*juss*), but the modern building seemed to be mainly of clay with some houses of masonry leeped with mud. Timber was or had been plentiful, but large demands had been made on the *Ithil* plantations of the Batin by the rapidly-growing town of 'Artawiya, which now went as far afield as the Qasim for its roof timber. A good stout beam of *Ithil* wood might now fetch as much as thirty dollars.

Having returned to camp from our dinner-party I sent Bijad a present of fifty dollars, about half of which was to cover the cost of fodder and other supplies, and a pair of inferior field-glasses. He was so overcome by such recognition of his services that he came round post-haste to ask whether he could do anything more for us, and next morning he came over to see us off. Altogether he left a charming impression of friendliness on my mind—a man of good heart and good appearance, taller than the average and well built, perhaps under forty years of age.

Next morning we were off at the crack of dawn and in a quarter hour reached 'Aqda, a square village walled about and about 350 yards long and broad. The join of the walls on north and east was surmounted by a turret, and other turrets dotted the walls at intervals, while about the middle of the village rose a tall square minaret slightly tapering towards the top. An archway under the central turrets of the north and east walls gave entrance on those sides to the settlement, and I judged that there might be similar entrances on the other two sides. 'Aqda seemed larger than Zilfi in

[1] Zilfi 1500, 'Aqda 1000, and Liqa 800, leaving about 700 for the numerous petty settlements.

superficial area, but its houses were less crowded upon each other.

From here a quarter hour's march up the tributary *Sha'ib* of Umm al Dharr [1] brought us to the foot of the Tuwaiq escarpment after we had passed a masonry dam built to divert the flood through a double-arched culvert into the main stream. A short scramble over broken ground in which we disturbed a covey of game birds,[2] which ran away crouching to the ground but would not rise, and a scramble up a steep rocky path brought us to the summit of the escarpment, not more than fifty feet high at this point, where we halted for a few moments to take a last look over the Zilfi plain. And then we set off again towards the east.

3. 'ARTAWIYA—THE *IKHWAN* FOUNTAIN-HEAD

At the coffee-drinking in the *Amir's* house the previous morning I had begged our host to procure me a really competent guide for the rest of the march, but Rushaid intervened : 'Don't worry about that ; God has produced the very man you want—he knows every tree and stone between here and Kuwait.' 'What is the use of your saying that ? ' I replied ; ' you have said the same almost every day since we left Riyadh, and I have seen but few good guides.' ' Leave this talk,' he persisted, ' wait and see, it is a *Sulubi* I have found.' And I began to think, though not without some scepticism, that my words had borne fruit, especially when, later in the morning, Rushaid brought in a man who vouched for the omniscience of his uncle, our guide to be. So we arranged that the latter should sleep in our camp to be ready for an early start.

I was myself just thinking of going to bed when the *Amir* and Rushaid came into my tent and sat down, I thought, for a last chat. ' Tell him,' said Rushaid nervously, and my suspicions were aroused. The guide had understood that we would be travelling by the main track known as Manshariha,

---

[1] This flows into Sha'ib Samnan.

[2] These were doubtless *Sisi* and not partridges, as I had imagined until my error was exploded by the experts—*vide* R. E. Cheesman's *In Unknown Arabia*.

and it was only to that route that his claim to omniscience applied. The more southerly route we intended to follow was unknown to him, and in any case he would lie with his wife that night. He would join us in the morning in the hope that we would have changed our minds about the route for the pleasure of having his omniscience at our disposal. I replied that I would go by any route he liked—they were all new to me—but that he must come to our camp at once to be ready. The *Amir* went off, I thought, with a heavy heart, knowing that he was merely deferring an inevitable disappointment, but even he was not prepared for what had happened in fact. At any rate I had been sleeping for half an hour when the sound of whispering by my bed-side awoke me. Bijad had been to the man's house only to find that he had saddled up his *Dhalul* and fled without further thought of his wife's embrace. ' Would you,' said the *Amir*, ' have me have his house burned down ? I am ready to punish the man as you direct.' ' No,' I replied, ' why should he accompany me if he doesn't want to ? I merely asked Rushaid to find me a guide, and this is what always happens when I ask a service of him. All he can do is to talk loudly and vainly.' And then Rushaid did begin to talk about the strenuous efforts he had made. If now I would forgive Dabbi all would be well. But that I declined to do, and next day the pantomime was complete and I had an ample and satisfying revenge. Dabbi followed me like a whipped cur always within earshot, and my companions showed an astonishing interest in the geographical features of the march in the hope that I might find illumination in the loud answers of the discredited guide.

At first all went well. The Tuwaiq was Tuwaiq and could be nothing else—an arid calcareous plateau sloping gently up to a divide from which it sloped gently down. Behind us lay the long line of rose-pink sands which we already knew as Thuwairat. Some miles to the northward the beacon of Khashm Jazra marked the point where Tuwaiq had sunk for ever in a sea of sand. To our left front those sands rose in the great ridge of Nafud Dhuwaihi, continued southward by the rock wilderness of Hamada Mujazzal, beyond which the ridge of Mujazzal itself, with a ridge called Wudai'an

parallel to our course on the right and covering Majma'a.
At this point the width of the plateau was only three miles,
and we passed from it into a plain of loam-soil called Sibilla,
from whose covering of *Rimdh* and *Shih* a quail started up
in solitary terror, while *Jarbu'* played about from hole to
hole. Beyond a clump of *Talh* acacias we crossed the central
depression of the plain, a sandy stream-bed trending north-
east towards the *Raudha* of 'Aqla, in which is a water hole.
The depression was rich with vegetation and in it were
sheltering a pair of *Hubara* which flapped away lazily before
our approach.

Another stream-bed with a line of *Sidr* and *Salam* bushes
cut across our track trending northwards to the now parallel
Nafud, and then we passed into the Hamada wilderness,
where a fox slunk away over a surface black as it were with
a spread of cinders. A patch of *'Arfaj* bushes compelled a
halt for breakfast for camels and men, our portion being
dried venison (*Jalla*) bought at Zilfi and rice, with Zilfi's
excellent water to wash them down. We then continued over
a bare stony plain to a depression trending north-east,
Shubairima by name on account of the *Shubram* growth
which mingled with the desert sage, beyond which lay an
immense gravel plain. The low ridge of Mujazzal lay ahead,
with the hill and watering of Umm Ghur away to the right.

At length we reached the horizon of the ridge itself and
struck the head of a *Sha'ib* [1] valley which runs down through
it eastward, between low banks two miles apart. And Dabbi,
loudly questioned for the benefit of my apparently unheeding
ears, told us this was Sha'ib Butaira, which would lead us to
the wells of Dijani, our immediate goal. And so we continued
along the meandering course of the torrent-bed, crossing and
recrossing it, while the valley narrowed to half a mile or less.
Suddenly, towards mid-afternoon, we became aware of black
sheep grazing along the right bank of the valley and idly
wondered why or how they had come so far and whence ? And
then we marched through a small detached flock with women
guarding it, of whom we asked, ' *Wush ba'd al ma*—how far
the watering ? ' ' Near by,' they replied encouragingly, ' you
will be there before the sun-setting.' ' Is it Dijani,' I asked,

_____
[1] This was in fact the head of Sha'ib 'Artawiya.

' or Qai'iya ? ' And their answer created consternation in
our ranks : ' *La, ya rajjal—al dira* [1]—'Artawiya ! ' I
continued on my way without remark, but Dabbi, who was
behind, came up with obvious signs of embarrassment and
uneasiness. We had decided to avoid 'Artawiya like the
plague and he, our guide, prating of Sha'ib Butaira, had
brought us almost to the door of the lion's den. I continued
on my way in spite of his entreaties to turn aside up the slope
on our right, and it seemed to them that the disaster of a
guide's ignorance was going to be completed by my obstinacy.
By way of diversion—having not the slightest intention of
risking my skin in 'Artawiya—I reminded them that it was
time for their afternoon prayer, and couching my beast on the
soft sand of the *Sha'ib*, I took out and lighted my pipe. Then
they prayed uneasily and beseeched me to make haste to leave
that cursed track. I told them I would first finish my pipe.
' A fine guide you are,' I said, ' are you not ? For, had it not
been for those women we have just met, we should have been
in front of 'Artawiya by now. And won't Ibn Sa'ud laugh
when I write to him that Dabbi took us to 'Artawiya when
he thought he was going to Dijani ?'

By this time Rushaid was becoming distracted with fear
and I yielded to his entreaties. We breasted the slope to find
ourselves on a sort of down [2] and in the midst of grazing flocks.
Dabbi now had to ask his way of the shepherd folk, men now,
whose white head-bands proclaimed the ardour of their faith
though they seemed to find nothing amiss in us. The downs
seemed to be extraordinarily bare for grazing, though there
was some '*Arfaj* and occasional grasses in the hollows, from
which finally we rose to a plateau extending eastward for a
mile to a depressed plain in whose midst, in surroundings
utterly dismal and unattractive, lay the town of 'Artawiya !

Barclay Raunkiaer was apparently the last European to
pass this spot, and that was in 1912 when, it would seem, the
first house had not yet been built. Only six and a half years
had passed and there had grown up a town of not less than

---

[1] ' No, man ! the town.'

[2] From this point the course of Sha'ib 'Artawiya was visible for about a
mile trending north-east until lost in the folds of the plateau beyond which
it would emerge into the 'Artawiya plain.

10,000 inhabitants, which I was the first European to look upon from afar. Since then it may have become a veritable metropolis of narrow fanaticism, but no foreigner has visited it. The first *Ikhwan* colony to be founded, it is an epitome of the *Wahhabi* revival, which under the wise and skilful guidance of Ibn Sa'ud has brought the boon of peace, security and, in a measure, unity to Arabia. The town that I looked upon through my glasses from a distance of perhaps three or four miles was a landmark in history, already at this time dreaded through the length and breadth of Arabia, avoided even by *Muslims* professing the tenets of Wahhabism in its broader aspect, the subject of calumny, misrepresentation and hostile propaganda in the councils of the Hijaz and even in the ante-rooms of the Arab Bureau at Cairo. The triumph of the movement in spite of all the obstacles placed in its way and with no weapons but miscellaneous rifles and ardent faith is one of the most thrilling and decisive episodes of history.

The town lay N.N.E. of our point of vantage, comparable to Buraida as it lay astride of a ridge in the midst of an undulating plain—a great walled city whose western ramparts flanked by a great tower at either end were clearly visible, together with that part of the interior occupying the slope on our side. I could only see a section of the south wall, the rest of which was cut off by an intervening ridge which also prevented my seeing the other two sides. The houses seemed to be of clay, and a scattered suburb of *Qasrs* and hovels lay outside the walled town a mile to the north, doubtless about the site of the wells which formerly made the place an important halting-point on the route to Kuwait. Of vegetation there was no sign, though I was told that palms had recently been planted and that corn and vegetables were raised by the people to supply their wants. The *Nafud* lay about two miles beyond the town, while the Butain, as the valley is called, was an immense rolling plain between the Mujazzal plateau and the northernmost extremity of 'Arma —a mere low ridge.

Having feasted our eyes on the forbidden city we descended into the parallel valley of Sha'ib Butaira and camped for the night in its bed among a clump of *Sidr* bushes. For a length of nearly a mile up and down this valley are scattered countless unlined water-holes, some twenty or more of which contained water, though in most cases the water was foul and covered with a green slime. The cleaner wells produced remarkably good water, the depth to which varied from three fathoms in the higher ground on either side to as many feet in the *sail*-bed itself, which was of sandy grit and about thirty yards wide. The surface round the wells was black with the droppings of sheep and literally swarmed with large black ants which stampeded the camels at the watering. A solitary vulture brooded, bloated by some recent meal, over the scene and flopped away unwillingly only when I got close up to inspect it. The watering of our camels was facilitated by the discovery of a bucket and other gear in one of the disused holes—doubtless the property of some herdsman from the town—and the day closed for us with a dinner of rice and venison and on a note of nervous irritation due to the dissensions of the day. But I nursed in secret my joy at an unexpected view of an amazing town, of which we had further glimpses during the early part of our next day's march of only thirteen miles to Dijani.

After following the Butaira for a mile down to its exit from the plateau into the Butain we diverged somewhat to south-ward of its easterly course and, crossing the pebbly bed of Sha'ib 'Artawi, came in due course to a depression called Daban, which trending northwards coalesces with the two streams already mentioned to form the Majma'. This joins the Sha'ib 'Artawiya to form the depression or basin in which lie the wells of 'Artawiya itself.

Beyond Daban we marched monotonously over the downs until we came to the gentle upward slope of stony 'Arma, from whose summit, elevated not more than 100 feet above the Butain, we looked down on the wide circular basin of Qai'iya, two miles ahead of us and covered with the black tents [1] of the Bani 'Abdillah (Mutair) dancing in the mirage. We turned aside, however, along the crest of the ridge and then slanted gently down to the great circle of Dijani, at whose south-eastern edge we halted for the day.

[1] There were about 200 tents and the *Shaikh* in charge was Ibn Dhamna.

4. THE DESERT HIGHWAY

Until a comparatively short time ago Zilfi was the first inhabited place on the track of caravans proceeding from Kuwait to the great twin cities of Qasim. That honour now belongs to 'Artawiya, inhospitable as it is to the passing stranger, and the desert is thus contracted by about thirty miles. With the growth of the *Ikhwan* movement the depressions of Dijani and Qai'iya will in course of time bear their crop of houses, and the waterings to the east will similarly be converted into settlements of men. The terrors of the great desert journey between Central Arabia and the Persian Gulf are doomed to elimination by natural processes, and those processes will now be hastened by a comparatively recent product of man's industry—albeit the industry of western man. Motor-cars have crossed Arabia more often than Europeans !

But at the time of which I write the motor-car was unknown in Wahhabiland, and we were separated from the coast by 200 miles of unmitigated desert traversed by a number of alternative tracks converging on each other in the neighbourhood of their eastern and western destinations. The one we had chosen would next strike water at the wells of Qara'a, 85 miles distant, and then not again till Subaihiya, 95 miles further on within the confines of the principality of Kuwait. For such a journey the camels had to be well primed with water, and our early arrival and long day's rest at Dijani gave them every opportunity to graze their fill.

The circle of the Dijani depression was about a mile in diameter and the wells were distributed in two large groups known as Harmaliya (south) and Umm al Finajin (north). They varied in depth from ten to twelve fathoms, and contained good and plentiful water in roughly excavated, unlined shafts of three feet diameter, sunk through the limestone of the subsurface. Groups of sheep and goats lay about the wells throughout the day, and the tents of the shepherds dotted the depression, some seventy-five in all, Mutair *Badawin* and elements from Furaithan and even Ghatghat. Naturally we had no occasion to hob-nob with the denizens of the two *Ikhwan* settlements, but some of the Mutair visited us. They have a very characteristic and peculiar intonation in speaking, a slight check of breath in the throat which gives a pleasing musical softness to their speech, which I thought the softest I had heard in Arabia—a speech of feminine delicacy on the lips of men. They told us of a recent raid in the neighbourhood of the *Ikhwan* settlement of Mubaïdh near Majma'a, in the course of which a party of the 'Ajman had carried off some herds of camels and were probably by now well on their way back with their booty towards the Kuwait territory, in which they harboured to deliver their pin-pricks at Ibn Sa'ud. In a sense this was good news for us as the raiders were in front of us and not behind. We had been fortunate in not running across them the previous day, for our track must have crossed theirs, though they would probably have done most of their travelling by night. Nevertheless at this time both the Shammar and 'Ajman were liable to be on the warpath, and we had an anxious time before us as we approached the Kuwait frontier, one of the most unsettled parts of Arabia.

I spent the day for the most part quietly in my tents, and while strolling about in the evening came across two small shock-haired boys of the *Badawin* playing a simple game which seemed to keep them out of other mischief for hours on end. Each in turn would throw up a small tin disc into the air for the other to sling a stone at it, and, though it was only hit once in the five minutes I stood watching the game, it was clear that such practice in throwing strongly at a mark was an excellent preparation for the wild life of hunting and herding they would have to live. That evening we had an ewe for dinner, from whose womb a fully formed lamb had been removed at the killing—I had always imagined that the Arabs would not sell a pregnant ewe for butcher's meat. The carcase of the animal was trussed up on a pole stretched on the shoulders of two of the men while the rest set to drawing off the skin whole and cutting up the joints. Practically everybody took an active hand in the process, and when an old woman came up to beg of us she received the lamb *foetus*, the feet and the entrails of the sheep, an old worn *Qirba* and some dates and sugar. This miscellaneous assortment she bundled together in the folds of her dirty robe, and as she went off blessing us I noticed that the sheep's entrails were reposing on the sugar.

The following day, 9th October, I crossed the Dahna for the third time on a line somewhat to southward of that which I had followed on my journey down from Basra the previous April to rejoin Ibn Sa'ud. I had wondered then how he would receive the general whittling-down of the programme I had gone to the Hijaz and Egypt to discuss. Since then things had taken a favourable turn, and there had seemed to be every possibility of great developments. Yet now I was on my way back once more to the coast full of apprehension as to what would happen.

The tension between myself and my companions, which had arisen out of the folly of Dabbi, had continued through the day at Dijani and remained with us during the passage of the Dahna. Mitrak was of course not under the ban of my displeasure, but he seemed to have lost all interest in proceedings gone so awry in country which bored him—for he was of course a stranger to it, though he had traversed it often before. Besides, he was still suffering from the effects of a trick I had played on him at 'Anaiza on the day of the arrival of news of Ibn Sa'ud's victory before Haïl. I naturally wanted to get the news to Baghdad with the least possible delay, and having prepared my letters I sent for Mitrak. ' Look here,' I said, ' these letters are of the utmost importance. Mount at once and fail not to be in Kuwait within six days.' I did not tell him that among the letters was a request to the Political Agent at Kuwait to pay the bearer 100 dollars subject to his arrival within seven days. He made a show of great zeal and had his *Dhalul* saddled at the door and the letters in his hand when he suddenly remembered that he had neither food nor *Qirba*. My host had provided both on the instant, and then he admitted that his need was for money. At that I lost patience and told him he need worry himself no further, and two days later, though not directly from me, he heard of what I had written in the letter. Since then he had forgiven neither himself nor me, for he had wanted the money for frivolities at Kuwait and might have had more than amply sufficient for his amusement had he been less selfish.

Our *Hamla* [1] had left camp half an hour before the rest of us and it took us an hour and a half to catch it up. From that point we slowed down to a dismal pace of $2\frac{1}{2}$ miles an hour, for from now onwards it would be risky to scatter in case of raiding-parties liable to be found anywhere between us and the line of waterings known as Tawal al Mutair.[2] About a quarter hour after starting we topped a slight rise in the bare stony plain to see the long line of the Dahna far ahead of us in the morning dust-haze, its level being broken by great sand peaks, 32 in number within our view. And then we struck out along the well-beaten tracks over the undulating plain of northern 'Arma clad with *'Arfaj*, so continuing until we crossed the outlying sand ridge of 'Araiq Majda and beyond it converged on the Baihis road coming from Qai'iya in the trough of Lughaf before the first section of the Dahna itself. Here we halted for breakfast before beginning the well-known weary passage of the sands.

I had been riding alone ahead of the party when I came up with a solitary rider—a *Hashshash* or grass-cutter going to cut *Nussi* in the Dahna for his camels at Dijani. As I approached I noticed the white chaplet of the *Ikhwan* on his head, but greeted him nevertheless and he returned my greeting with cordiality. And we rode awhile together conversing about the country. When he saw that I knew something of it he exclaimed, ' *M'anta bahaiyin*—not a bad fellow you ! ' And then he added a suggestion that such a compliment deserved some practical recognition, to which I replied that my money was behind with the *Hamla*. He accepted the refusal with resignation and did not repeat his request in public when, as he passed, I hailed him to join us at breakfast. That invitation he accepted without ceremony, and having eaten he rose and rode off without thanks. He would spend that night in the Dahna and return on the morrow to his own folk. If he met me again he would probably neither greet me nor show sign of recognition.

The westernmost section of the Dahna is Jadhma, perhaps a mile wide, in which we encountered a flock of sheep, black without exception, in charge of a small boy with the usual ass carrying a full water-skin. The sheep water at Dijani in

---

[1] Baggage train. [2] Including Safa, Qara'a, Haba, etc.

the evening and march through the cool night to the Dahna grazing, where they remain through the day to march back and arrive at water the following dawn—and so on for ever, a hard and monotonous life for sheep and shepherd. As the animals moved about grazing I noticed a number of little yellow-breasted birds moving in company with them, one bird to each sheep taking advantage of its cool shadow.

Between Jadhma and the next section, Ardh al Ajal, lay a depression of firm sand with outcrops of rock, which 'Ayadh, who had formerly wandered in this country in the service of some Mutair chief, named to me as Khabb al Ridham, though Ghazi my *Aslami* guide of April had called it Khabb al Radhm, a name which 'Ayadh transferred to a later depression. Doubtless there are tribal differences of nomenclature in areas so monotonous without well-marked features, but perhaps in such cases one should in this tract follow the Mutair practice, as it is unquestionably their ground. A small party of that tribe passed us here coming from Qara'a—three men and one woman with four camels, one of which carried a load of *Nussi* for a good-looking mare which tripped along with the party unled.

Ardh al Ajal, a slightly undulating plateau of sand with *Adhir* and *'Arta* as the chief features of its vegetation, was half a mile across and parted from the third section by a narrow *Khabb*, a similar depression dividing the latter from the fourth section. Neither *Khabbs* nor sections were named to me on this occasion, but the fourth section was the first of the typical Dahna ridges with eight great sand peaks ranged along it at irregular intervals, while a group of nine such peaks showed up some ten miles away to the south of east—our course being north-eastward. Two grass-cutters passed us on their way to Dijani, their camels loaded high with *Nussi*, which is most plentiful in the central tracts. We now passed between two sand peaks and down a slope of deep sand into a broad depression dotted with grazing camels, on which our party made a wild scattered rush to enjoy the milk of full udders which no Arab can resist. The *Nussi* grasses shimmered daintily in the sun, and a little girl, apparently sole guardian of the herd, confirmed 'Ayadh's name of Khabb al Radhm for this depression, which had

formerly been named to me as Khabb al Naum. The line of
this *Khabb* and the sand ridges on either side lay from
north-west to south-east, and a subsidiary sand ridge
beginning a mile to our northward ran down the depression
as far as one could see with the solitary and well-known peak
of Niqa' Mutawwa' riding upon its back half a mile away.
It took us an hour and a quarter to cross the depression,
three-quarters of an hour to cross the fifth section, a tract of
sandy downs, and half an hour to negotiate the ensuing
depression, Khabb al Naum according to 'Ayadh, in which
the track is well marked in fifteen snaky lines.

Half an hour sufficed for the crossing of the sixth section,
the highest part of the Dahna, where the going was somewhat
heavy. From its summit we looked back on the great line
of peaks, the knotted backbone of the sand waste, a hazy
silvery white under the glare of the afternoon sun. A narrow
Khabb divided this section from the seventh and last, Jaham
by name, a low rolling sea of sand waves in the midst of
which I spotted a couple of white gazelles,[1] while Mirwij
without success tried his rifle on an eagle [2] seated on the
summit of a ridge. Over this tract we marched an hour to
its furthest edge, where we camped in the sand overlooking
the wide plain of Jandaliya backed by the low pink line of
'Araiq Duhul. A strenuous march, followed by an inferior
meal still of venison and rice, disposed us to sleep well on
the rich soft sand under the sky—for we did not pitch the
tents. The camels lay round us chewing their cuds with a
regular crunch-crunch, and my companions chattered or
snored, while I, writing up my diary by the light of a lamp,
was invaded by a host of beetles and other insects. The
Baihis road had proved easy enough going and belied the evil
repute of the Dahna, which to the traveller forms a respite
from the deadly bareness of the rock wilderness and for the
herdsman is a veritable Paradise of rich grazing.

It took us nearly two hours to cross the Jandaliya plain
and the 'Imar sand ridge (a southern continuation of 'Araiq
Duhul apparently, as the latter is said not to come down as
far as this) beyond it. And then we stepped on to the hard
desert of Summan, where the track, deeply scored in the

[1] *Rim.*   [2] *Nasr.*

surface, passes first over a flat plain and then through a
somewhat lumpy tract into the characteristic eternity of
ridges and depressions, set in circles and semicircles, of the
Summan proper. We plodded on monotonously, and I
amused myself testing my companions against their bellies.
We had started at 5.30 a.m. without food, and as the sun rose
higher and higher with never a sign of breakfast, spirits began
to droop visibly. But none spoke. Later they tried to catch
my eye, but I evaded them until at last 'Ayadh broke down
and wailed pitifully at me : ' *Ana juwai*'—I am a trifle
hungry.' ' Yes,' I replied, ' you are all ready enough to think
of your own and your camels' bellies, but what about the
hunger of my mind for knowledge ? And you leave me to
starve.' But I was myself not unready for food, and we
halted by low twin hills called Junaiah, some miles before
which we had passed at some distance to the north of a *Dahal*
or rock pool, dry at this season and said to be 30 fathoms in
depth—these measurements are made by the length of rope
let down into the well and drawn up again by a camel, the
distance traversed by which is then roughly paced. Near by
on our track was a cairn called Rijm 'Aqab on a low mound,
and before we came to Junaiah we passed through a depression with a clump of *Sidr* bushes.

At 10.30 we resumed our march and continued till 4.30
with half an hour's halt for the afternoon prayer.   Three depressions—Umm 'Adan, Jau Ibn Rashdan named after a
Mutair *Shaikh* of the Jiblan section, and Jau Marzuq marked
by two cairns—varied the monotony of the march, and a
flicker of amusement was raised by Rashid the *Rashidi's*
clumsy and unsuccessful attempt to kill a viper lying up on
the top of an *'Arfaj* bush to get the air—it was perhaps thirty
inches or more in length and half an inch thick with a pointed
head, and it escaped into a hole.

Soon after this we had an incident to stir us out of our
growing torpor. Topping a ridge we observed the heads of
a party approaching us which had descended into a hollow
ahead without seeing us. We had the advantage and stood
awaiting developments, each man disengaging his rifle from
the saddle. Half a mile separated us from them as they,
topping the ridge, became glued to the ground, surprised. A

led horse made them suspect, and for a tense moment we watched each other. We were ten and they apparently seven, so Dabbi and Rashid trotted forward to parley, while on their side a man mounted the horse and cantered forward. With a hundred yards between them they stopped and there was a loud exchange of explanations. Then they drew together with words of greeting, and at the sight thereof both parties advanced to fraternise. They had come from the wells of Qariya south of Qara'a, and were bound for the Qasim to see Ibn Sa'ud. One of them was Ibn Hallaf, a *Shaikh*, I think of the Dhafir, and another Ibn Mandil of the Bani Khalid, a connection of the *Wahhabi* monarch by marriage. They had no news to give us, and Ibn Hallaf, a man of middle age and good appearance, asked if I was the Englishman who had been campaigning with Ibn Sa'ud. ' *Anta alli ghazait ala Hail ?*—are you he who went raiding against Hail ? ' And he added to Rashid as we passed : ' *Wallah ! Baduwi !* '

Somewhat before this incident we had crossed the tracks, two days old, of the thirty 'Ajman raiders, who had raided the camels from Mubaidh and were apparently making for Hafar al Batin. About five miles to the north lay a conical hillock called Umaitha and another landmark was the cairn of Rijm al Dab. Otherwise the landscape was featureless, and we camped in a shallow depression off the road to avoid accidental encounters. Our water was showing signs of running out and our stock of dried venison was reduced to negligible proportions, the whole lot being ostentatiously placed on my side of the dish. I scattered it over more fairly and myself dined on rice alone liberally mixed with onions. Again we slept in the open, and the insects were nothing like so plentiful as in the Dahna, though there seemed to be a good many flies, and the following day's march found them about us in great numbers.

All day long we rode tediously over the Summan, where the only variation on the general monotony was an occasional depression deeper than the rest or distinguished by a name. Our camels performed wretchedly and during the afternoon were mute with thirst—yet they seemed to eat readily of such shrubs as they found, deriving perhaps some portion of liquid therefrom. Our breakfast was a concoction of scraps —rice, venison, onions and coarsely-baked bread—and the water in our skins was dark brown and full of impurities but cool. I had but two draughts during the day for economy's sake, though more would have been welcome, for the wind, though not hot, was dry and parched one's lips. The Arabs drew their kerchiefs over their mouths—they think this prevents thirst, and it may be so if one is used to the habit.

After an hour's march we caught up the *Hamla* in the depression of Bazm, and then our course lay over undulating country with little scattered basins called *Sibgh*,[1] beyond which lay a ridge with a cairn on its summit, Rijm al Rajd. Another depression, Faidhat al Haml, marked a transition into the Sulb section of the Summan, a sort of steppe descending gently from ridge to parallel ridge. Umm Sudair with a single *Sidr* bush to justify its name and Faidhat al Sulubi, where we saw a couple of vultures scavenging on the site of an old camp, and occasional other depressions with *Sidrs* in greater or less plenty were stages on the way to breakfast. The *Sidrs* were partly in bloom and beginning to form their unattractive berries. Then a monotonous down brought us to a high ridge lying N.W. by S.E. across our path with a cairn on its top, Rijm al Shuyukh, commemorating an occasion when Ibn Sa'ud, in whose train was Mitrak, ' took ' the Mutair concentrated in the broad Khamma depression below to the tune of 245 killed.

The track to Haba wells diverges to the right in this great depression, which is three miles long and half a mile wide with a copse of *Sidr* in its midst. We kept on, and rising on to the desert beyond passed through a series of depressions, including that of Junaina, to a ridge with the cairn of Rijm al Majlis, beyond which we traversed the lumpy plateau of Dhaharat al Dhabi. Beyond that lay a gravel country, gently undulating, the Dibdiba, in which we found and took charge of a stray camel in an extremity of thirst. A halt for prayers, a further march over a broken plateau, Huzaimat Sadawi, of limestone, and the passage of the Majhara depression brought us to the top of a gentle slope in which lay the head of Sha'ib Sudaira, a valley half a mile wide running north along the

[1] Pl. *Sibugh*.

eastern escarpment of the ridge, about 30 feet high. The right bank of the *Sha'ib* was a low ridge and near its head were two rock-cut reservoirs or *Malzams* for the capture and storage of water in flood time. We camped in the midst of a *Sidr* copse.

All through the day we had seen no signs of man, but here the *Sha'ib* was full of sheep and their attendants, and we were able to procure enough water from the latter to replenish our depleted stock. We also bought a sheep for only five dollars, whereas we had paid ten at Dijani, and had a good dinner of mutton and rice, at which a number of the shepherds assisted us.

During the day, while travelling with the *Hamla*, I had entered into conversation with one of the servants whose un-Arab or rather un-*Najdi* features had aroused my curiosity. In point of fact he claimed to be a *Yamani*, and probably had other blood in his veins, a short sturdy lad with a plump rounded face, Muhammad by name and surnamed the *Bey* on account of his foreign appearance. He was a native of San'a and the son of a shopkeeper who wanted him to take service in the Turkish *Dhabitiya* gendarmerie, but, having other ideas for his future, he absconded from his home with a coffee-caravan which in 45 days arrived *via* Najran at Sulaiyil, where he had seen me. Later he came up north to join the household of Ibn Sa'ud. Another snake was killed during the day by Khuzaiyim the *Aslami* and a number of *Hubara* were seen, of which one was bagged by a second rifle-shot after it had been wounded by the first. The ' protective ' colouration of this great turkey of the desert is very remarkable. On the ground, whether still or moving, it is well-nigh invisible against the grey-brown desert surface, and it is only when it rises above the sky-line that it can be readily spotted. Even then its lazy flight carries it away from the fowler with astonishing speed. *Dhabbs* or horny-tailed edible lizards were also seen in plenty, but none were captured.

A short march of eight miles down the length of Sha'ib Sudaira brought us to Qara'a next morning. The valley between its ridges expanded here and narrowed there, running at first north and then turning north-east. In its bed was plenteous vegetation of many kinds, and as we approached the wells a long line of camels came past us breasting up the valley on the way to the high Summan behind us for grazing. During the long drought of the summer they had clung to the well area of Tawal Mutair, moving to and fro between the various waterings, but they would now stay out the whole winter, coming in to water only occasionally should the rains be insufficient. With them went the herdsmen allotted to their care. That slow dragging procession of animals bored with existence seemed to me an epitome of Arabian life—a grim struggle of the animal kingdom against the two demons of hunger and thirst.

Qara'a has two wells, each some 35 fathoms in depth, and to all appearance perched on the summit of a flat-topped pyramid whose slopes outward and downward are rayed by camel paths worn by the padding feet of the draught animals as they go up and down drawing up and returning the leather bucket. These paths extended star-wise from the centre, there being eight to each well, allowing of eight camels to work simultaneously. Each group provides its own tackle of rope, bucket and pulley, as the wells are surmounted by no permanent structure.

The depression in which they lay was about half a mile in diameter, roughly circular and surrounded by low hills and knolls, a basin of light sand strewn with stones and pebbles and full of the tents of the *Badawin*. I counted 167 tents, large and small, belonging to various elements—Mutair of course and some Suluba and a group from the Shammar 'Abda of Ibn Jabrin's following. The flies were dreadful and the water was badly discoloured but otherwise not unpleasant.

Sha'ib Sudaira actually empties itself, not into the Qara'a depression as one might surmise from the presence of water in it, but into a waterless or well-less depression a mile or so to the north. Beyond it northward, marked by a long low ridge as seen from here and fed by Sha'ib Ashari, lay the Safa basin with three wells only 22 fathoms in depth. Haba to the southward has two wells of 35 fathoms, while eastward some eight or nine miles distant lay Qariyat al 'Ulya and Qariyat al Sifla, two groups of numerous wells with water as near as two or three fathoms, and south of the latter at a similar distance lay Abwab, which varies in depth to water from four fathoms in the summer to almost ground-level in the flood season. And far away to the south again is Anjabiya, completing the group of waterings loosely included under the district name of Tawal Mutair, whose northern counterpart is Tawal Dhafir beyond the Batin.

The soil and surrounding hillocks seemed to be of a gypseous limestone, in which the *Badawin* make their primitive cement-kilns. A hole is scooped out of the earth and filled with desert fuel, which is lighted and left burning for 24 hours, after which the limestone or gypsum ash is taken up for the construction of troughs round the wells. The Suluba had only goats with them. The Mutair camels were mainly black or dark brown, while those of the Shammar were fawn-coloured and white. These groups, including those who had gone up to the pastures [1] in the morning, had been on these wells for two solid months. The Jabrin folk were *Ikhwan*, though they had not yet settled down to a village life, and did not seem in any way resentful of our intrusion. Their leader was Muqbil.

The Mutair were represented by three sections of the 'Alwa group, to wit the Barasa under Manif al Sur, the Shuqair under Hakim Ibn Hazza', and a detachment of the Dushan, whose main body under 'Abdul 'Aziz, the young son of Faisal al Duwish, was at Safa with the Jiblan section under Ibn Shiblan. Some of the Buraih group sections were at the two Qariyas.

It was naturally enough the Suluba whose interest was aroused by our arrival, and their women and children swarmed round our camp all day in search of alms and unconsidered trifles. The scanty remains of our breakfast— there were but bare bones and a little rice—were carried out to a squatting group of women, who with their children consumed all greedily either from the dish or from the cauldron in which we had cooked the meal, while some used a fold of their dirty robes as a preliminary receptacle more spacious than a mouth. The bones were gnawed and licked clean, and one small child carried off the empty head to seek out lurking fragments of brain and offal. And again in the afternoon, when a sheep was being cut up for dinner, they

[1] *Nida* = to go to pasture, *Manda* = pasture land.

assembled to carry off the entrails and other rejected parts. And at the same time a few women and a large band of children assembled round my tent collecting pellets of camel-dung [1] and giving me an admirable opportunity for observation through the tent-flap. The children, and particularly the little girls, were of an extraordinary fairness and had a certain prettiness tinged with a gravity out of keeping with their years. They wore the common red gown, which as they moved discovered the slender, graceful forms within, and veils too of black, but so loosely that their faces were fully exposed. The small boys, circumcised like the *Muslims*, wore whatever rags no one else wanted. And the women seemed to be of goodly form and handsome though worn by hard living. Their features indicated the presence of two quite distinct types—the one of a typically gypsy appearance and of Semitic cast, the other plump and squat-faced and Mongolian. They wore veils, but without any attempt to keep them where they should be, and as they became accustomed to our society they bandied light-hearted banter with our men. Rushaid was in his element quipping ribald jokes with gusto. In the evening they gathered round like vultures watching to the end of the meal, after which they fell to in a free fight for the scraps, each dame or damsel rushing away with what she had seized like a dog to devour it in peace—and as often as not followed by a less successful friend.

During the day we were troubled by the persistent efforts of a half-wit *Mutairi*, stark naked except for a small loin-cloth, to enter our camp. He was treated with scant respect, being chased off each time by Rushaid or one of the others hurling stones at him and foul abuse of himself and his parents. But he renewed his attempt under cover of darkness and then, for the sake of peace and quiet, he was bound with ropes and left to lie among us till the morning incapable of molesting us. He accepted the treatment without a word of protest, for the previous day a woman, whom he had been pestering, had cut his jaw with a stone. His treatment recalled a minor incident of the morning's march when a dog ran across our path and one of our party,

[1] *Jalla.*

a *Dausari* named Muhammad, made as if to unsling his rifle for a shot. I remonstrated : ' Would you eat him ? ' And he replied shamefacedly : ' God give you long life ! No, but they eat the Arabs,' presumably by claiming a share in their scanty substance.

Our camels had gone 87 hours since their last drink and spent the day drinking and resting from their labours. Meanwhile I made arrangements with a Sulubi, 'Id by name, to take letters ahead of us to Kuwait ; and also arranged with one of his kind, Suwai'id,[1] to act as our guide for the rest of the journey. He was not of prepossessing appearance and created a bad impression by insisting that his wages should be fixed before starting. He probably lost over the deal, which was agreed to at 20 dollars—a large sum for him, but perhaps less than he might have got had he left it to me. In fact he proved to be an agreeable companion without any special competence to be a guide.

For 25 miles we marched over a wilderness that was the abomination of desolation, our eyes well skinned for an enemy on the sea-like horizon. But no enemy appeared and no sign of human life was seen that day after we had left the tents of Qara'a behind us. Suwai'id entertained me with his quizzical chatter, and his presence aroused my other companions to conversational advances, which started in the form of criticisms of his geographical contributions. Out of the general vagueness I pieced together in my note-book the results obtained from contradictory evidence. And the general improvement in the social atmosphere of the party was blessed by a remarkable meteorological occurrence immediately after our arrival in camp. A thin shower of rain descended upon us from a large heavy cloud that rose suddenly from a clear sky in the north-west—the first rain of the *Wasm* season, the first rain that I had experienced since 6th May. For more than six months the deserts had been dry, and we talked optimistically of the herbage which hereafter would reach to the girths of the camels.

Suwai'id talked of hunting and of his kinsfolk. ' Whence come ye ? ' I asked. And he looked at me meekly with a queer smile on his little gypsy countenance—he was of dark

[1] Diminutive of Sa'd.

complexion with a tint of burnished copper—and replied :
' They say we spring from you—from the *Angraiz*,' and I
pleased him by admitting that the rumour was just. ' We
are indeed cousins,' I said. Formerly they paid but little
heed to the customs of *Islam* in the desert, but now there
was greater conformity for fear of the *Ikhwan*. They pray
and practise circumcision.

Our exit from the Qara'a depression was by a valley
trending north-east between low ridges, Rish al Nadhim on
the right in continuation of the hills on the south side of the
basin, and Buraiqa on the left starting from the hummock of
Damigh a quarter mile north of the central well. Beyond a
little hill called Mazbur the valley splayed out to a width of
two miles and the low ridge of Munaisifat al Safa appeared
over the northern bank some five miles away, the half-way
mark between the two waterings. Beyond a small *Sha'ib*
ending in a bushy depression on our left we rose on to a
sandy plain, in which a quail started out of the scrub of
'*Arfaj* and *Alanda* and Suwai'id accounted for a poisonous
snake—it was about 15 inches long with greyish stripes on a
creamy ground and three grey bars on its head. All this
country is still counted to the Summan under the name of
Mashalif.

A group of basin-like depressions led to a series of channels
known together as Shaiyitat, the first of them being Shaiyit
Rawiyan, trending north-east. We halted here for breakfast
in a thick patch of scrub in a depression. In its lower course
the Rawiyan is joined by Shaiyit 'Atshan on its way to the
Wabra wells. The bed of the 'Atshan was of limestone slabs
and its right bank was a ten-foot cliff. We followed its
course almost up to its source and found ourselves on a vast
gravel plain with gentle undulations. Five miles to our left
was the ridge of Kara' ending in a knob called Faisal. In
the same direction was the ridge of Wirya and on our right
the low coast of Tuwaiyil Nadhim. I spotted a solitary
gazelle in the distance, and was surprised to find how few of
my companions could pick it up. The Wirya ridge converged
on us and in due course we ascended its gentle slope to find
that it was a vast gravel tract of many-coloured stones,
black, white, green, dark red and other colours. In it is a

wide shallow valley, Suban, lying cast and west. We
entered this near a *Raudha* called Sudaira, and marched
on a twin *Raudha*, Khubaira and Ramadi by name. And
beyond them we found ourselves on the Dibdiba near the
basin of Rijlat al Dhaba'. Its vast space was of sand and
grit with much vegetation, in which a flock of some 20
gazelles was seen. Our *Sulubi* tried a shot at them without
success, but killed an 18-inch thin and harmless snake which
he called *Zaruq*. And towards sundown we camped in a
depression at the ridge of Al Hamar. Our dinner was venison
and rice, and the possible presence of enemies made it necessary to shroud my lamp with sheets of the *Times*.

At Qara'a I had found my bed—in the open—saturated
with dew, and the air during the early hours of the day was
moist and muggy until the sun dried the desert surface. It
was the first time I had felt any dampness in the atmosphere
since the spring. At this camp too after the rain there was
dew, and we made an unusually early start for what proved to
be a march of about 33 miles. It was still dark and the false
dawn rose up like a great cone in the east, fading gradually
into the hazy yellow light of the real dawn. The Dibdiba
was vast with the gentlest swell as of a sea at rest. Its
surface of sandy grit overlies the limestone rock. Some
gazelles were again seen at dawn. The ridge of Dhaba' lay
afar off to our left and the Qara'a tract, like a ridge, far ahead.
We plodded on wearily, and I passed the time counting the
paces of several camels. My own, a fawn-coloured '*Umaniya*
which I had ridden regularly since leaving Riyadh, took 89
paces a minute, and Rushaid's, a large-limbed white shaggy
beast secured from the recent spoiling of the Shammar, took
88. Yet his walked away from mine with its longer steps.

We came to a spot where well-marked natural lines,
almost artificial in appearance, sharply divided the *Rimdh*-
covered Dibdiba tract from that of Qara'a, a cheerless,
bushless plain, a tract of light sandy soil on a loam foundation
with very gentle undulations and occasional patches of grit.
Not a bush was to be seen in its immense desolation, but it
was yellow with autumn grasses [1] and made glad the hearts
of our camels and their riders—all the latter except myself,

---

[1] *Nussi, Ramam, Hathra, Hulaiba*, etc.

for it was tedious goading on the hungry beasts as they obstinately writhed down their long necks towards the rich grass or hay. This tract swarmed with gazelles, of which large herds were in view the whole day, though our hunters went forth again and again in vain.

The necessity of keeping together for fear of enemies was irksome to Rushaid and Khuzaiyim the *Aslami*, who were always dropping behind to enjoy a quiet smoke. On one occasion I sent back a message by one who was not privy to the cause of these delays that anyone who wanted to halt for any reason should trot ahead so that we should come up with them. Rushaid was up with us in a trice growling at the slight conveyed in my message and marched sulkily until he could bear the abstinence no longer. He halted, dismounted, ostentatiously looked to his girths and helped himself to water. I marched on, but before we were out of earshot I caused 'Ayadh to cry out a formal proclamation to the effect that anybody wishing to drink water or smoke should go ahead before halting for that purpose. And I added that anybody in need of tobacco had only to apply to me. The announcement was greeted with roars of laughter, and Rushaid kept well ahead the rest of the day with very beneficial effects on our rate of marching. Just before reaching the Qara'a tract he had warned me that we should find no bushes for fuel ahead, but, scenting the probability of a clamour for an early halt if fuel was with us and hoping that the absence of it might produce a great effort to reach the Shaqq depression, I vetoed his proposal that we should load up with brushwood. The result was that we had no fuel that night except camel droppings and grasses.

During this march the advantages of keeping together were aptly illustrated by an alarm. Away to our left and about a mile distant a party was sighted on the march. Close inspection through the glasses resulted in its classification as a *Hadra* or caravan, and no sooner had that conclusion been arrived at than Rushaid and three or four others dashed off to get the gossip. I was not consulted, and to show my displeasure at this interruption of our march I halted the rest of the party and, lighting my pipe, proceeded to examine the other party through my glasses. It was a party of about twenty persons with rather more than that number of camels. Among them was Mansur Ibn Sharida of Buraida homeward bound from Kuwait and Barqash Ibn Jabrin returning to his folk at Qara'a.

This meeting produced an untoward incident. As I laid my glasses aside 'Ayadh took them up to examine the strangers, whereupon Dabbi, probably out of mere officiousness and with no idea of insulting me, reproved him. 'Ayadh answered hotly as the *'Abid* ever do, and the dispute had become somewhat heated when, on the return of Rushaid and the others, we resumed the march. It developed rapidly and 'Ayadh, spitefully using the argument that Dabbi had rebuked him for using the possessions of an infidel, declared that he cared nothing for such as Dabbi. ' I am here,' he shouted, ' under the orders of Ibn Sa'ud in the service of the *Angraizi*, and I am proud of that service.' All of a sudden— and I was not certain who acted first—the pair had unslung their rifles from their saddle-pegs and began circling round each other manœuvring for position. Hitherto merely an amused spectator of the dispute, I now thought it time to intervene. I rode at Dabbi and, invoking the curse of God on him for a mischief-maker, I shouted to Rushaid to disarm them both. He hesitated and things looked ugly. I promptly couched my *Dhalul* and, rating Rushaid in the choicest terms, announced my intention of staying there until my order was obeyed. Both were then promptly disarmed, and with a caution against the renewal of their chat I remounted, and no more was said.

A tract of *Rimdh*-covered plain now became inserted in the Qara'a under the name of Humaidha, in which the Buraih section of Mutair were thought to be pasturing from their centre at Wafra. With them were the relations of 'Ayadh and Mirwij, to whom I gave permission to go off in search. They rejoined us next day at the moment of our arrival at Subaihiya, having drawn blank for their friends, though they fell in with the grazing camels of the section. During the 24 hours of their absence they subsisted entirely on camel's milk. We camped that night in a broad shallow depression in the wilderness, disturbing a large herd of gazelles which went away westward on our approach.

The Qara'a tract stretched away before us apparently without end, and as there were rumours of men and camels about, I dispensed with my light and we composed ourselves for an early rest, determined to make Subaihiya next day if possible. All day long we had marched over a featureless plain, and I could not but admire the skill with which our *Sulubi* guide, dubbed Abal Khala or ' desert-man ' by our men, steered an absolutely straight course with nothing but instinct to guide him. He was of the Majid [1] section, and told me that with the advance of civilisation the Suluba were tending to prefer ordinary cloth wear to the deerskins formerly their sole apparel.

I had given orders for a very early start but was astonished to be wakened at midnight. This I took philosophically enough as we had a flat desert without relief to traverse, and for four hours we marched by the Pole Star in the dark. And at the end of that time we were still in the same desert that had wearied us the previous day. It was not till 5 a.m. that the distant coast of the Shaqq ridge appeared on our right front circling round across us. At 8 a.m., having the broken hills of Fawaris al Shaqq on the right, we reached the Shaqq depression and crossed its narrow line to the high ground beyond. We had done with Qara'a and broke our fast to celebrate the accomplishment, having marched for nearly eight hours with only a short break for the dawn prayer.

From here we traversed an undulating plain clad with *'Arfaj* and dotted with depressions. That of Shuqaiq we crossed after marching an hour—it runs to the north-west between low limestone ridges and apparently has no exit. An hour later we passed on our right the shallow depression of Radifat al Shuqaiq, and another hour of the monotonous undulations brought us into view of our goal, the low summits of the Burqan ridge which lay about half a mile beyond the Subaihiya wells. It looked delightfully near, for we were weary, but three hours of weary marching were still before us. To the north-east as we steered on the main sandy peak of Burqan appeared the black solitary cone of Wara. And, passing a depression called Thamila Turki, we found the surface scored with sandy runnels and sloping in steppes to-

[1] *See H.A.* vol. i. p. 268.

wards the Subaihiya basin. The depression of Thamila Turki drains into another called Majwa, after passing which we came into view of the wells lying before and below us, still a long way off over the deceptive sloping plain. Around the wells and approaching them from the pastures to the north we saw enormous droves of camels. The place was alive and we advanced towards it as rapidly as our jaded camels could carry us.

Suddenly we became aware that a sort of panic had set in among the camels nearest us, those approaching the wells. We made the usual signs to indicate our pacific intentions, and the camels resumed their march as if satisfied. But a shot fired at us from a great distance—it hit the ground beyond Mitrak, who was immediately ahead of me—made it evident that we were still suspect. We continued our advance, making signs of friendliness, while Rashid the *Rashidi* went ahead of us alone, but the occupants of the wells still refused to be convinced and desultory shots whizzed about our heads. We still advanced, but matters were becoming serious and the shots were getting uncomfortably frequent and near. Rashid was now well ahead with Rushaid, Mitrak and one or two others close on his heels. Some way behind and more slowly I followed with the main body, and the baggage train was a mile in the rear. Something was clearly wrong, and the shooting became a regular fusilade. I had no mind to be the victim of an accident on my last day in Arabia and slipped down from my saddle. The rest of the main body followed suit, and we couched the camels to await events. Khuzaiyim and another were ahead of me, and I just behind them standing up to watch the progress of our advanced body, when a horrid crack in the air, as of splitting lead, warned us to greater discretion. And we all sat incontinently down behind our barrier of camels. By this time Rashid had reached the wells and had begun parleying, but the firing, though more desultory, still continued for a space. It was not till Rushaid arrived that it stopped altogether and we received the signal that all was well. We soon reached the wells to camp and learn the reason of this strange assault. The camels belonged to a caravan of Kuwait townsfolk who had worked themselves up to a great state of nerves at the prospect of the long desert march before them. Owing to our own vacillating policy in allowing the *Shaikh* of Kuwait and his 'Ajman and Shammar friends to pin-prick Ibn Sa'ud without check the whole countryside was in a state of fear and uncertainty. The suspicion aroused by our sudden appearance created panic, and there was no one in the caravan to keep the nerves of the company under control. Had we been what they thought us, they had a disadvantage of position which placed them at our mercy. They were fools, and it was only their wild shooting that obviated an unfortunate accident, for which there would have been no reparation. And, strange as it may seem, it was the first time I had been under actual fire during the whole year of my sojourn in Arabia.

5. KUWAIT

Unblessed with telegraph or other means of rapid communication Arabia has ever been a land of rumours, flying across its desert spaces as chaff before the wind with ever and anon a grain of stray truth in its midst which falls unseen, unheeded. The probable one accepts as possible ; the impossible or highly improbable one brushes aside into the limbo of idle tales, wondering perhaps at the causes and motives underlying their invention. And that night of 15th October, 1918, at the wells of Subaihiya on the frontier of desert Arabia I wrote simply in my diary : ' The latest Kuwait rumour is that Damascus has been captured ! ' That gossip would go gently swelling into Arabia, and next morning a British officer of the Inland Water Transport Department at Shuwaikh, brown-faced, brown-kneed and clad in workmanlike shirt and shorts of *Khaki*, came to the doorway of his office-residence wondering at the couching of camels before his house. And he wondered more when a bearded stranger in flowing robes addressed him in his own tongue enquiring the whereabouts of the British Political Agent. It was then his turn to astonish the stranger. The rumour was but half the truth after all. Damascus and Bairut were in our hands. Allenby and Lawrence had crippled the Turkish armies in Syria by enormous captures of men and guns. Bulgaria after a series of decisive defeats was out of the War by unconditional surrender. Turkey and Austria were clamouring for immediate peace on pain of taking independent steps to secure it for themselves. And even Germany had put forward a tentative proposal of peace which was a clear confession of defeat. For all practical purposes the War was over, and within a month I witnessed the Armistice celebrations at Baghdad. But for me it is that day and night of 16th October that will ever stand forth in my memory, when, newly returned after seven months of wandering in the wilderness, I was greeted by news as unexpected, as dramatic and as joyful as any that has ever met weary traveller in the world's history. Yesterday was as the days of the weary years before with a burden of blood and terror on the conscience of mankind—in my own little sphere I was weary and despondent. To-day was the beginning of a new era of peace and goodwill, and the great news rang in my ears as the joy-bells of a world's rejoicing. My thoughts went out in waves of gratitude to the men who had fought through the horror of those years and particularly to those who were no more to enjoy the sense and fruits of victory.

The Subaihiya depression lies within the borders of the semi-independent British-protected principality of Kuwait, whose natural inland frontier lies roughly along the trough of Shaqq. In it are a large number of wells—more than fifty they told me—with plentiful brackish water at a depth of only two or three fathoms, the shafts being roughly hewn in the limestone rock in a series of circles of progressively diminishing diameter. There is no masonry lining to these wells, and the water, which is sweet in a few of the wells, is drawn up by hand. The atmosphere was that of the Persian Gulf coast, damp and clammy, and I was glad of copious water to wash away the stains of travel for the first time since our departure from Buraida. A change of clothing was not less welcome, and I lay down to rest hoping they would leave me in peace till the dawn. But Rushaid and his friends were impatient for the flesh-pots of Kuwait, and I did not resist their summons to start before 2 a.m. For two hours therefore we marched in the dark, and the order went round for the maintenance of absolute silence lest there might be enemies or raiders lurking about the approaches to the wells. For some reason they could not keep silence, and on one occasion I called a halt to remonstrate with their idle chattering. If they must talk, I said, let them talk in security, halted, lest we should walk into an ambush. Then we marched off again, this time in silence, over a broken, sandy plain, merging on our left into the bare gently undulating desert and bordered on our right first by the Burqan ridge and then by the low line of the coastal sand dunes called 'Adaïm. Not far off somewhat north of east lay the cone of Wara and some six miles to westward the low ridge of Manaqish.

After two and a half hours of marching—the plain is called Suda and has occasional outcrops of limestone rock—we passed, at a distance of a mile on our left, the wells of Mishash al Tawil, two, they told us, with brackish water at four fathoms. Round them lay a large flock of black sheep, but in the dim light of pre-dawn we passed unnoticed. We were off the main track, which lay about a mile to our left, to avoid chance encounters and passed fairly close to the wells of Malah in a *Sabkha* depression at the edge of the dunes. In this neighbourhood we crossed the comparatively recent tracks of a party of nine raiders proceeding in a north-westerly direction apparently from one of the numerous waterings to be found at intervals along the edge of the sand area, in the *Sabkha* strip which converged gradually on our course until in due course we crossed it—it was about a mile broad and seemed to end altogether about two miles further on to our left—by the tracks of the main road. Another track on our right crosses it to go *via* Malah to Subaihiya, while the main track, which we now joined, goes *via* Mishash al Tawil. The saline belt is called Barud or Bawarid.

The sand hills into which we passed undulated gently, with a sprinkling of 'Arfaj and a coarse reed-like grass called *Thandua* growing in tufts, and merged further on into a vast plain of white sand on firm soil, extending as far as we could see in every direction. Every now and then, as we topped a rise, we caught glimpses of the cliff-like surroundings of Jahra shimmering in the morning light far away to the north-west. During our short halt for breakfast we had a man out to watch against enemies, and as we remounted he called out that he had just seen five men mounted on *Dhaluls* apparently riding towards us though their movements were hidden by a slight rise in the ground. He remained on watch, and a few minutes later reported that they had turned away, and in any case their number was too small to cause us any anxiety, though in all probability it was a gang looking for mischief. We kept now to the well-marked track and I noticed the trail of brushwood dragged at the tail of the Kuwait donkeys for the fuel-market of the port.

At 9.30 a.m. came the climax of the march, and I looked out suddenly on a long string of blue-green oases in the trough of the desert. It was the sea ! And I rejoiced, with a tinge of regret, at the thought that my travels in Arabia were at an end. Half an hour later the topmost summits of the Kuwait buildings were faintly discernible, and from the next ridge the plain sloped down in gentle undulations to the still distant city now clearly visible in all its length and breadth, though veiled by a haze of dust and mirage. And there came up to meet us the myriad camels of the Buraih, breasting the slope in huge companies, laden with rice and dates for the tribesfolk at Wafra in the high desert behind us. And from each company as it passed we were hailed for news of the desert. ' Have you come by our tents ?' they asked, ' at Wafra ? and is it true, as they say at Kuwait, that Ibn Sa'ud fled precariously from before Haïl and reached Buraida only with a scanty following ? '

In these days false news was deliberately manufactured both at Kuwait and at Mecca for the discrediting of Ibn Sa'ud. Some of these Buraih camels had been captured in a raid on the hostile Shammar, but had subsequently been sequestrated by Shaikh Salim—to annoy Ibn Sa'ud, to whom the Mutair are of course subject—and had only been restored to their captors as lawful spoils under the direct orders of the British authorities on the basis of representations made by me. Little did these folk realise that they had me to thank for the recovery of their valuable booty. One of the *Shaikhs* with whom we talked was Tallah Abu Shuwairibat, head of the Birzan subsection, and another Sattam Abal Khail of the Jiblan section of the 'Alwa group.

We now struck off the main track to a group of new

masonry buildings called Shuwaikh put up as offices and residences for a group of British officers serving at Kuwait. There we were informed that the Political Agent, Mr. MacCollum, was in the Agency within the town, and in due course we had threaded our way along the sea front to the hospitable portals of that building. There I received a cordial welcome, and sending my desert companions round to Ibn Sa'ud's agent, 'Abdullah Nafisi, delivered myself over to the enjoyment of the amenities of modern civilisation. MacCollum's hospitality was on a princely scale, and I drank champagne that night after months of nought but desert water. And there were home letters and newspapers to read and much to talk about.

Next morning at an early hour Shaikh Salim, ruler of Kuwait and son of the famous Mubarak, anticipated the visit I intended to pay him by calling in person. It was my first meeting with one whose actions and attitude had been a constant source of trouble to me all the days of my mission. And I was favourably impressed with him for all my knowledge that he was inevitably cast for the *rôle* of a disturber of Arabia's peace. The charming courtesy of his calling on one who should have called first on him was in keeping with his general suavity and charm of manner and speech. By birth and breeding he was in the direct line of Arabia's best chivalry, but the canker of envy, hatred and malice had eaten deep into his soul. The heir of a great tradition which in the hands of Mubarak had fostered the genius and guided the steps of Ibn Sa'ud himself, Mubarak's son was doomed to a career of pettiness, and he had linked himself appropriately enough and ostentatiously with the losing cause of the Hashimite dynasty. Kuwait was to suffer in the process, but the future was still on the knees of the Gods and Salim's policy at this time, deliberately adopted, was one of pin-pricking hostility to Ibn Sa'ud. Both on this occasion and during the evening when I returned his call we discussed in as informal a manner as possible the most controversial topics, and he never for a moment departed from an attitude of calm argument, courtesy and even deference. And for my part I reciprocated his attitude, withholding blame or accusation, in the hope that some day it might fall to me to mediate in the cause of Arabian peace. That day never came for me, though it was at Kuwait six years later—after Salim himself had been long gathered to his fathers—that the peace of Arabia was shattered into fragments, to be restored only with the final triumph of the *Wahhabi* cause so detested by Salim.

The *Shaikh* was attended at both interviews by his confidential secretary, Mulla Salih, and at the evening meeting also by one of the leading merchants. The former was a short, dapper little man, clever and intelligent, and took a prominent part in the conversation, during which I was struck by the simplicity of Salim's demeanour and the entire absence of any tendency to formality. The *Shaikh*, who was about fifty years of age, was in appearance older than his years, anxious and careworn, but he had a pleasing conversational manner, smiling now and then almost covertly in his sleeve as if it were unseemly to show amusement without a deprecatory gesture. At our first meeting I still wore my beard and desert apparel, but Salim—a born *Baduwi* and an ardent *Muslim*—almost hinted that it was unseemly to be so decked out, perhaps a disagreeable necessity in the ignorant and fanatical atmosphere of Ibn Sa'ud's uncivilised realm, but the sooner got rid of the better. My enquiries about a barber were met by an eager undertaking to produce one without delay, coupled with a stipulation that I should be shaven and decently clad before calling on him in the evening. The barber not only rid me of my beard but reduced me to a tolerable semblance of a convict by cropping my hair to the roots before I realised what he was at. The shedding of my Arab garments and a bath completed a transformation at which, when I appeared, the ruler of Kuwait expressed unbounded satisfaction. It was no longer with an emissary of Ibn Sa'ud he had to do but with a British officer and gentleman. My companions of the march grinned from ear to ear at the horrible change.

Salim never lost an opportunity of protesting his unshakeable loyalty to the British cause, and doubtless the recent decisive turn of affairs in our favour made his protestations genuine enough. Nevertheless he had, as MacCollum and his predecessors had good reason to know, been consistently and deliberately disloyal from the moment that he succeeded to the throne of his ancestors. He had intrigued with the Shammar and, through them, with the Turks, and he had grown rich in the process. He had been lucky to escape peremptory deposition at the hands of the British authorities, who had always dealt with him generously and with long-suffering. In a vague way he spoke of his territories as including a good large slice of the Mutair country, embracing ' our Hafar, our Safa, our Qara'a and our Haba.' But in the same breath he deprecated the discussion of boundaries : ' Our lot is as one with the lot of the house of Sa'ud.' Ibn Sa'ud had often spoken in similar terms of the relations of Najd and Kuwait in the time of Mubarak, but those relations had suffered a set-back owing to Salim and a definite rupture was clearly inevitable and not far distant. In 1922 the boundaries of the Kuwait principality were definitely fixed under the auspices of Great Britain, whose aeroplanes had recently been to the defence of Kuwait against the threat of an *Ikhwan* assault.

Salim definitely accepted King Husain as his suzerain and regarded him in the existing circumstances as entitled to assume the Caliphate of *Islam*. But in all these matters his attitude was clearly dictated by a desire to be objectionable to Ibn Sa'ud, and there was very little doubt in my mind that, if the *Sharif* had been near enough to interfere effectively in his affairs, he would have resented any demonstration of his suzerain authority. And even in a recent exchange of telegrams between the two rulers a certain coolness had been apparent. King Husain had asked him to take steps to prevent ' my 'Ataiba subjects ' having access to the Kuwait market, and Salim had replied that no steps were necessary as ' your 'Ataiba subjects never come to Kuwait.' The point was subtle and wounding—an implicit refusal to recognise the Sharifian general claim to suzerainty over a tribe which was for the most part under the jurisdiction of Ibn Sa'ud.

The vexed question of the blockade was now happily of no account in the scheme of the future, and Salim declared that he had now made adequate arrangements for the prevention of the passage of raiders through his territory.

I mentioned the party we had seen and the fresh tracks we
had crossed, and I twitted him with our experience at
Subaihiya. Over the latter he became quite excited. ' If
you wish,' he said, ' I will have those folk punished at once.'
I deprecated any such action, knowing that the offenders
were subjects of Ibn Sa'ud. And finally he told me that
messengers had come in from Buraida that day with news
that Ibn Sa'ud had sent a delegation with peace proposals
to Haïl. Half an hour later from 'Abdullah Nafisi and the
messengers themselves I heard another version—the authen-
tic version—of the same story ; the delegation had come
from Ibn Rashid to propose peace to Ibn Sa'ud !

During the two days of my sojourn at Kuwait I had little
time or inclination to see much of the town or its denizens—
an immense city for Arabia with perhaps 50,000 inhabitants
at this time, the chief seaport of Central Arabia with a busy
boat-building industry. All I desired was to get away with
all possible speed, to return to Baghdad and, if possible, to
England, which I had not seen for ten years. So on the
morning of 18th October I boarded the little steamer
Kalika, and shook the dust of Arabia from my feet—with
many regrets and some relief, wondering whether it would
be my fate some day to penetrate again into the haunts of
that uncouth and fanatical desert people.

And, before I went, I had the satisfaction of informing
'Abdullah Nafisi that the embargo on the despatch of the
thousand rifles had been removed. They would now go
inland to Ibn Sa'ud, and with them went a letter, in which
I explained the details of the new situation which had arisen
and counselled patience in face of the difficulties that lay
ahead.

A TYPICAL ARABIAN GENEALOGY.[1]

THE genealogy of the Bassam family of 'Anaiza prepared and maintained by 'Abdullah Ibn Muhammad Ibn 'Abdul'aziz al Bassam :

Page 1.

List of Kings of the Hijaz from the Birth of Jarham.

1. Jarham Ibn Qahtān—the first who ruled over the kingdom of the Hijaz since the Arab occupation.
2. 'Abd Yālīl,   son of preceding.
3. Jarsham   do.
4. 'Abdul Madān   do.
5. Nafīla   do.
6. 'Abdul Masīh   do.
7. Madhādh   do.
8. 'Amr   do.
9. Al Hārith   do.
10. 'Amr   do.
11. Bishr   do.
12. Madhādh   do.

Page 2.

Bassām Ibn 'Aqba is the ultimate ancestor of us, the Bassāms of 'Anaiza and of Āl Fīrūz and Al Qudhāt and Al Hasānā and Al Kharāshā and Āl Bin Hasan of Wushaiqir and of Al Bijād and Al Quhaidān and Al 'Atīq and Al Muqbil and Al Haidān Ibn Muqbil of Wushaiqir and of Al 'Uthaimīn Ibn Muqbil of Qarāīn and 'Anaiza and their cousins, Al Hasan Ibn Muqbil, well known in Harma' and Majma'a, and of Al 'Inaiyiq and Al Dihān at Zubair and their branches joining them in Bassām Ibn 'Aqba.

And in this Raiïs we join, we, Al Bassām Ibn 'Aqba and Al Bassām Ibn Manīf, and also Al Qudhāt and Al Hasānā and Al Kharāshā, and those mentioned above descend from them, as also Al Mushārifa including Shaikh Muhammad Ibn 'Abdulwahhāb, and of them are the Kharāqā of Shaqrā (namely Mushrif Ibn 'Amr

Ibn Ma'dhad Ibn Raiïs) and the Mushārifa are numerous clans including Al Barādā and Al Khalīfa and Al Shināna and Al Nashwān and Al Sakrān and Al Mughāmis of Hudhāma in Sudair and Al Tawāl of Harīq and Al Muhannā of Harīq and Al Juraifa and Al Fākhirī at Harma' and they have many branches coalescing with them in Mushrif.

Pages 3 and 4 and the first four lines of page 5 are devoted to a sort of formal introduction, ending on page 5 as follows :

In the name of God the Merciful, the Pitying. ·

I have written this tree with my pen, I, 'Abdullah Ibn Muhammad al 'Abdul'azīz al Bassām, and it relates to our pedigree, oh Al Bassām dwelling in the town of 'Anaiza of the towns of the Qasīm —and that in the year 1322 of the *Hijra*, excellent and honoured, and all this I had collected in past years and now I have revised the writing of it this year in the city of Bombay of the cities of India in this book.

And these are the rulers of the Hijāz and the date of their ruling, each one according to Christian chronology, for they were before the mission of the Prophet Muhammad—prayers and peace be upon him—transcribed from the book of Edward Vandyk printed in the year 1310 A.H.

Thus said Ghīlān Dhawi 'lrima in his *Qasida* which was parodied by Hishām Ibn 'Amr 'ul Qais Ibn Sa'd Ibn Zaid Manāf Ibn Tamīm of the town of Marrāt of the towns of Washm, which was the first of them :

.   .   .   .

After this quotation the genealogy proper begins :

'Adnān   122 B.C.

|

Ma'add   89 B.C.

|

Nazār   56 B.C.

|

Madhar   23 B.C.

|

Alyās   10 A.D.

|

Madraka	43 A.D.	Tābikha	
Khazīma	86 A.D.	Add	
Kanān	109 A.D.	Murr	
Al Nadhar	142 A.D.	Tamīm	Qāsim
Mālik	175 A.D.	Zaid Manāf	Wahīb
Fihr	208 A.D.	Mālik	'Alwī
Ghālib	241 A.D.	Ibn Abi Sūd	Muhammad
Luwai	274 A.D.	Rabī'a	Zākhir
Ka'b	307 A.D.	Shihāb	Raiïs
Murra	340 A.D.	Zuhair	'Aqba
Kilāb	373 A.D.	Shaddād	BASSĀM
Qudhai	406 A.D.	Nahshal	'Abdullāh
'Abd Manāf	439 A.D.	Sunai'	Muhammad
Hāshim	472 A.D.	'Aqba	Ahmad, who migrated in 1010 A.H. from Malham to 'Aya-ina, where he became *Qadhi* and died about 1040 A.H.
'Abdul Muttalib	505 A.D.	Mas'ūd	
'Abdullah	538 A.D.	Mūsa	
Muhammad [the Prophet]			

Genealogical table (generations I–IX, read across the page):

I	II	III	IV	V	VI	VII	VIII	IX
'Abdullah, son of Ahmad, *Qadhi* of 'Ayaina	Ibrahim	Hamad settled at 'Anaiza 1174 A.H.	'Abdul'aziz	Muhammad Ibrahim Hamad Sālih	Hamad 'Abdul'aziz * 'Abdullah * 'Abdulrahmān * — Sulaimān 'Abdullāh Hamad	'Abdul'aziz * 'Abdulrahmān * Sulaimān * 'Abdul'aziz 'Abdullāh * Muhammad* Muhammad Muhammad Ahmad* (b. 1325) Muhammad 'Abdulkarim* (b. 1327) Sulaimān* (b. 1300) Sālih Muhammad* Hamad * Sulaimān * 'Ali 'Abdul'aziz Muhammad 'Abdullāh Muhammad 'Abdullāh * — Hamad Sālih 'Abdul'aziz —	Hamad* (b. 1328) Sālih* 'Ali — — Sulaimān 'Abdul'aziz * 'Ali * Hamad* (b. 1328) — — — —	| | | | | | | | | | | | | | |

I	II	III	IV	V	VI	VII	VIII	IX
			Muhammad	'Abdullāh	—	—	—	—
				Sulaimān	Muhammad	Sulaimān *	'Ali *	—
					'Ali	Muhammad*	'Ali *	
						Sulaimān *	Another *	
					'Abdullāh	'Abdulrahmān	—	'Abdullāh *
						'Abdul'aziz	Sālih *	
							Hamad *	
							Ibrahim	
							Muhammad	
						Hamad *	'Abdullāh *	
						'Ali *	'Abdullāh *	
						Muhammad*	Hamad *	
						Sulaimān *	'Abdullāh *	—
							Ibrahim *	—
							'Abdul'aziz *	—
				Hamad *	Khālid *	—		
					Muhammad			
					Ibrahim *			
					'Abdullāh *			
						Hamad	Sulaimān	—
						Sulaimān *	'Abdullāh *	—
						Muhammad	Hamad *	
					Sālih *	Hamad	—	
						'Abdullāh		
						Sulaimān *		
						Ahmed *		
						'Abdulrahmān*		
						Muhammad *		
						'Abdul'aziz *		

I	II	III	IV	V	VI	VII	VIII	IX
			'Abdulrahmān	Fahad *	'Abdullāh Ibrahīm * 'Abdullāh * 'Abdul'aziz * Hamad *	Fahad *	'Abdulrahmān * Another *	|
				Hamad 'Abdul'aziz Hamad 'Abdulmuhsin	'Abdullāh Hamad *			| | |
					Muhammad*	Sālih * Sulaimān * 'Ali * 'Abdullāh * Hamad * 'Abdulrahmān * 'Abdulmuhsin * 'Abdulrahmān * Muhammad * 'Abdul'aziz * Muhammad * 'Abdulmuhsin * 'Abdulmuhsin Ibrahīm * 'Abdullāh * 'Abdulhamīd * Bassām * Rushaid * Muhammad		
					Ibrahim			
					'Abdullāh *			
					'Abdulrahmān		'Abdulrahmān *	|

I	II	III	IV	V	VI	VII	VIII	IX
				'Abdullāh *	'Abdul'aziz	—	| |	| |
					Sālih	'Abdul'aziz *		
					Ibrahim *	'Abdul'aziz *		
					Fahad *	Muhammad *		
						'Abdullāh *		
					Sulaimān *	Hamad	| | |	| | |
						Muhammad		
						Another		
					Muhammad *	'Ali *	|	|
						'Ali		
						'Abdullāh *		
						'Abdul'aziz *		
						Ibrahim		
					Hamad	Ibrahim	| |	| |
						Ibrahim *		
					'Ali *	'Abdul'aziz *		
						Sulaimān *		
						Hamad *		
						'Abdulrah mān *		
					'Abdulrahmān	'Abdullāh *	| |	| |
						Muhammad *		
						Muhamdam		
						Muhammad		
						Ibrahim *		
				Muhammad	Sulaimān	Hamad *		
					Hamad *	—	—	| |
					'Abdullāh	Muhammad	'Abdullāh *	
						'Abdul'aziz *	Hamad *	

I	II	III	IV	V	VI	VII	VIII	IX
						Fahad *	Hamad *	Hamad *
							Muhammad *	'Abdullāh *
							'Abdul'aziz *	
							'Abdullāh *	
							'Abdullāh *	
					Sālih		Sālih *	
					Hamad	Sulaimān *	Muhammad *	
						Hamad	Hamad *	
						Sālih (d. 1328)	'Abdullāh *	
					Muhammad*	Muhammad *	—	
				Ibrahīm			—	
					'Abdullāh	'Abdulrahmān		
						Ibrahīm	Son *	
						'Abdullāh *		
						'Abdul'aziz	—	
						'Abdulrahmān		
						Sālih	'Abdullāh	
						Sulaimān *	Muhammad *	
						Muhammad *	Muhammad *	
					'Abdullāh	Sulaimān	'Abdullāh	
			Sulaimān	'Abdul'aziz	Sālih	'Abdulrahmān	Ibrahīm *	
					Muhammad		Hamad *	
					'Abdulrahmān *	'Abdullāh	'Abdullāh *	
					Sulaimān *	Muhammad *	—	
						'Abdul'aziz *	—	
						'Abdullāh *		

I	II	III	IV	V	VI	VII	VIII	IX
				Ibrahim *	Sulaimān	Muhammad *	Hamad *	—
					'Abdullāh	—	Ibrahim *	
					Muhammad *		*Another*	
							—	—
					'Abdullāh *	Muhammad *	'Abdullāh *	
						'Abdul'aziz *		
						Hamad *		
						Sulaimān *		
						Ibrahim *		
				Hamad		Hamad	—	
						Ibrahim *	Hamad *	
							'A·dul'aziz *	
						Muhammad *	Hamad *	
							'Abdulrah- mān *	
							Sulaimān *	
						Hamad *	Muhammad *	
						Sālih *	'Abdul'aziz *	
						Fahad *	Sulaimān *	
						'Ali *	'Abdul'aziz *	
							Mihammad *	
							'Abdul'aziz *	
							Sulaimān *	
							Sulaimān *	
							Ilrahim	
							'Abdul'aziz *	
							'Abdullāh *	
					Sulaimān	Hamad *		—
						Ibrahim *		Muhammad*
						Muhammad		'Abdulrah- mān*
							Hamad *	Sālih *

I	II	III	IV	V	VI	VII	VIII	IX
		Muhammad	Ibrahim	Hamad	Muhammad	Ibrahim		'Abdul'aziz*
						'Abdullāh *	Muhammad *	'Abdullāh *
						Hamad *	'Abdullāh *	Sulaimān *
			'Abdulqādir	Hamad	'Abdullāh	'Abdulrahmān*		Muhammad*
				Hamīd	'Ali *	'Abdullāh *		
						'Abdul'aziz *		
						Muhammad *		
					Sulaimān *	Muhammad *		
						'Abdul'aziz *		
					Fahad *	'Abdullāh *		
						Another *		
						Another *		
				'Ali	Sulaimān	'Abdul'aziz *		
					'Abdulmuhsin*	Muhammad *		
				Ibrahim	'Abdullāh	Muhammad *		
					'Abdulrahmān			
					'Abdul'aziz			
					Sulaimān	'Abdul'aziz *	Muhammad *	
						Ibrahim	'Abdullāh *	
Muhammad		Muhammad	Ibrahim	Muhammad	Muhammad	'Abdullāh *		
						'Abdul'aziz*		

— Denotes line finished.   * Denotes living in 1918.

APPENDIX II

SECTIONS AND *SHAIKHS* OF THE HARB TRIBE

A. Sections ranging about 'Ain Ibn Fuhaid and the Ja'la plain, Asyah
and the Dahna, but not extending beyond the Qasim westwards :

Section	Chief *Shaikh*	Subsection	*Shaikh*
I. Bani 'Ali	Muhsin al Firm	Al Kharashif	Muhsin al Firm
		Al Kalaha	Asim Ibn Juwai'ad
		Wuld Muraid	Naïf Ibn Ma'aiyan and Khalaf Ibn Shariyan
		Al Qurun	Sulaitan al Qarn
		(?) Al Madarin	?
		?	? Ibn Nami
II. Al Wuhub	Dha'ar Ibn Sa'da	Al Madhyakh	Dha'ar Ibn Sa'da and Muhammad Ibn 'Afair
		Al 'Uwaiyidh	Niqa al Maharwal
		Al Darabisa	Lafi Ibn Radhi
		Al Khalasa	Zuhaiyan Ibn Suran
		Al Sharathin	Daiyis Ibn Shuraithan
		Al Madhhan	Dha'ar Ibn Zabil
III. Al Farda (Frida)	'Ali Ibn Hammad	Al Hammad(?)	'Ali Ibn Hammad and Zaid Ibn Hammad
		Al Hidban	Hudhul Ibn Hudaib
		Al Furaid	Salih al Furaid
		Al Nauman	Muhammad al Nauman
		Al Dawamik	Hamad Ibn Damuk
		Al Khalifa	Naïf Ibn Nauman

B. Sections in Western Najd around Nafi, Haid, Dakhna and Western
    Qasim :

Section	Chief *Shaikh*	Subsection	*Shaikh*
I. Bani Salim			Hijab Ibn Nahit (at Dakhna)[1] and Hujar Ibn Nahil
		Wuld Salim	'Isa Ibn Naji
		Al Zuqaibat	'Ajjaj Ibn Mushal-wat and Nasir Ibn Zuqaibi
		Al Hubairat	'Id al Hubaira
II. Bani 'Amr		Al Dhuwaba	Hindi Ibn Nahis[2] and Mujhim Ibn Dhuwaibi
		Al Shutara	Barraz Ibn Shutair
		Al Baidhan	Nima Ibn Mushad-daq
		Al Ghirban	Nasir al Ghurabi
		Al Sha'b	'Id al 'Afaihij

[1] *i.e.* settled in an *Ikhwan* colony.

[2] His father, Nahis Ibn Dhuwaibi, was killed in a raid by the Mutair in 1918.

THE HOUSE OF SA'ŪD

Male descendants of the late Imam 'Abdulrahman ibn Faisal ibn Turki ibn 'Abdullah ibn 'Abdul'aziz ibn Saud ibn Muhammad ibn Sa'ud.

I	II	III	IV	V
Faisal (Sultan 1834-1867) of Najd	*'Abdullah, (died childless)			
	* Sa'ud			
	Muhammad (died childless)			
	'Abdulrahman (d. 1928)	†'Abdul'aziz (King of the Hijaz and Najd and its Dependencies since January 8th, 1926)	Turki (d. 1919)	Faisal
			Sa'ud	Fahad
				Sultan
				'Abdullah
			Faisal	
			Fahad (d. 1919)	
			Muhammad	Fahad
			Khalid	
			Sa'd (d. 1919)	
			Nasir	
			Sa'd	
			Fahad	
			Mansur	
			'Abdullah	
			Bandar	
			Musa'id	
			'Abdulmuhsin	
			Sultan	
			Mash'al	
		Muhammad	Khalid	Fahad
			Fahad	
			Sa'ud	
			'Abdullah	
			'Abdul'aziz	
			Faisal	
			Bandar	
		Sa'ud	Muhammad	'Abdullah
			'Abdullah	
			Faisal	
		'Abdullah	Faisal	
		Sa'd (killed 1916)	Faisal	
			Fahad	
			Sa'ud	
		Ahmad		
		Musa'id		

* Rival claimants to the throne of Najd during the civil wars which lasted from 1867 to 1891.

† Ruler of Najd since 1901.

INDEX

Butter, 35, 86, 238, 250, 334
Buttermilk, 168
Butterflies, 64
Buwāhil (Banī Tamīm), 143

C

Caffeine (*Qahwa, q.v.*), 281
Cairo, 3, 20, 38, 213, 242, 252, 267-8, 331-2, 353
Cairo, Zoological Gardens, 3
Calcutta, 237
Caliphate, 381
Cambridge, 10
Camel, 29, 31-3, 37, 52, 60, 62, 68, 74, 77-9, 89, 96, 100, 110-1, 116, 119, 123-5, 127, 129, 131, 144, 146, 155, 157, 176, 188, 198, 213, 220, 222, 226-7, 235, 241, 247, 261, 296, 298-9, 302, 304, 307, 311, 314-5, 318, 324, 328, 333, 335, 342, 346, 348, 351, 354, 359-63, 365-6, 368, 370, 372-5, 378
Camel-dung, 117, 367, 371
Camel-equipment, 205
Camel-graziers, 105, 235
Camel-meat, 93, 125, 200, 309, 316, 325
Camel (milch-camels, *v. Mish*), 22, 41, 54, 64, 130
Camel-milk, 124, 215, 232, 307, 359, 372
Camel-skin, 125
Camel, speed of, 71
Camel-thorn, *v. 'Āqūl*
Camel-trade, 113, 191
Camel (for well-traction), 35, 115, 122, 149-50, 194, 229, 241, 260-1, 279, 293, 306, 338, 365
Canopus, *v. Suhail*
Cardamum, *v. Hail*
Caspian Sea, 270, 290
Cat, 3, 26, 45, 167
Catholic, 4
Cawnpore, 112
Cemetery, 52-3, 92, 105, 115, 143, 150, 163, 175, 310
Cereals, 87
Chain *v. Silsila*
Chalk, 132
Cheesman, R. E., 349
Chicken, 168, 209, 237, 243
China (Chinese), 272
Christian (Christianity, etc.), 3, 23, 26, 29, 43, 77, 242, 270, 285-6, 293
Circassian, 108, 265
Circumcision, 367, 369
Citron, 116, 230, 232
Climate, *v. Temperature*
Clocks (Clockwork), 245, 278
Coal, 295

Cockchafer, 45
Coffee, 7, 10-1, 14, 34-5, 58, 63, 70-1, 81, 89, 96-7, 106, 119, 124, 128, 130, 136, 147, 158, 162, 164-7, 169, 184, 192, 200, 211, 220, 222, 232, 236-7, 240, 242-8, 250-1, 256, 258-9, 262, 264, 267-9, 277, 279, 289, 294, 298, 316, 324, 328, 337, 340, 343-5, 349, 364.
Coffee-hearth (parlour), 90, 105-7, 147-8, 162, 164-5, 202-3, 209, 236, 242, 250, 259-60, 289-90, 328, 337, 339, 344-5
Cokas (nickname of Sir P. Cox), 202
Companions (of the Prophet), 46, 72-3, 94
Concubines, 199
Constantine, King, 276
Constantinople, 17, 39, 98, 221, 289, 291
Cotton, 69, 205-6, 228, 346
Cows, 64, 115, 122, 168, 237, 241, 243, 261, 338, 342
Cox, the Hon. Sir P. Z., 202, 211, 300
Cremation, 53
Croton-oil, 267
Cunliffe-Owen, Lt.-Col. F. G., *v. Owen*
Curb (bit), 59
Curds, 253, 265
Currants, 256

D

Da'aij, Khālid ibn, 89
Da'ās, Dahhām ibn, *v. Dahhām*
Dāb, Rijm al, 362
Dābān depression, 354
Dabbī (of Mutair), 341-2, 350-2, 357, 362, 372
Dahal (water-hole), 361
Dehash, ? ibn, 347
Dahhām ibn Da'ās (? Daham ibn Dawwās), 34
Dāhina, 19, 85, 110, 296
Dahnā (Dahanā), 19, 30, 32, 48, 86, 129, 175-6, 233, 357-62
Dāhūra (Wādī Rima), 329-30, 336
Daīsī, 230
Dakhāinī (? *Datāinī*, date), 90
Dakhīl, 'Abdul Rahmān al, 201
Dakhīl, Muhammad ibn, 27
Dakhīl, Sulaimān al, 201
Dākina, 12, 15
Dakmānīya, Raudha, 307
Dalqān, Nafūd, 126
Damascus, 17-8, 29, 101, 220-2, 242, 249, 252, 268, 275, 331, 375
Dāmigh hill, 369
Damthī, 135, 140

418 INDEX

INDEX

Temperature, 38, 59, 79, 85, 108,
137, 227, 266, 318, 326, 343
Thādiq, 84
Thaila (Wādī Rima), 179-81
Thamāïl (Zilfī), 347
Thamām (grass), 127
Thamām, Sha'īb, 84
Thamīla (pl. *Thamāïl*, water-holes),
341
Thamīla Turkī, *q.v.*
Thandūa (grass), 377
Thanīyat al Raml, *q.v.*
Thanna, Niqar al, 330
Tharmānīya, 83
Tharmida, 85, 87-9, 92-4, 117
Thaur (pl. *Thīrān*, oven), 78
Thulaima (Mudhnib), 146, 150
Thulth Abū 'Alī (Wādī Rima),
181-2, 184, 303
Thunaiān, 'Abdul Qādir ibn, 39
Thunaiān, 'Abdul Rahmān ibn, 8
Thunaiān, 'Abdul Rahmān ibn
(brother of Ahmad), 39
Thunaiān, Ahmad ibn, 2-3, 22, 24-5,
27, 39
Thunaiān, Faisal ibn, 39
Thunaiān, Sa'ūd ibn, 39
Thuraiya (Pleiades), 60
Thuwair, 340
Thuwairāt Nafūd, 328, 337-41,
345-7, 350
Tīb, *v.* Incense
Timber, 260, 348
Tobacco, 26, 31, 35, 38, 65, 93, 207,
233-4, 237, 255, 262, 268-9, 319,
371
Tomato, 168, 288
Tonic, 255
Townshend, General, 274
Traditions (*Hadīth*), 46, 66, 249, 253,
316
Trans-Jordan, 215
Trevor, Major, 285
Tubailān, Sha'īb, 144-5
Tubaiya (early summer), 60
Tube-well, 302
Tulaiha, Sha'īb abu, 156
Turāb, Khashm, 80
Turaba, 40, 101, 213, 300, 319
Turaif al Habil, Nafūd, 80, 84-7
Turk (Turkish, Turkey, etc.), 15-8,
22, 24, 26, 29-30, 32-3, 39, 43-4,
56, 61, 84, 86, 92, 98-101, 104-6,
108-9, 112, 119, 154, 168, 170, 191,
207, 220-1, 236, 240, 248, 250,
252-3, 270, 275-8, 284, 292, 313,
364, 375-6, 381
Turkī ibn 'Abdul 'Azīz ibn Sa'ūd, 8,
17-20, 24, 32, 38, 59, 61, 191-4,
208, 211, 213, 216
Turkī ibn 'Abdullāh ibn Sa'ūd, *q.v.*

Turkī ibn 'Abdullāh ibn Sa'ūd (Al
'Arāfa), 49-50
Turkī, Sharīf Muhsin ibn, *v.* Muhsin
Turkī, Thamīla, 373-4
Turquoises, 258, 277
Tuwaim, 146
Tuwaiq, Jabal, 1, 11, 47, 70, 72, 74,
76-82, 84-6, 88, 342-6, 348-50
Tuwaiyil Nadhīm, *q.v.*

U

'Ubaid branch of Rashīd dynasty,
324
'Ubaid ibn Rashīd, Hamūd ibn, *v.*
Hamūd
'Ubaid ibn Lughaimish, *q.v.*
'Ubair, Sha'īb, 70
'Ubaiyid (? Al Baiyid), 318
'Ūd (v. *Tīb*, incense), 283
'Udhaij, Sha'īb, 122
'Ukairsha, 210, 330
'Ulamā (*'Ālim*, etc.), 15, 24, 29, 103,
123
'Ulyā, Qariyat al, *v.* Qariya
Umaitha (Summān), 362
'Umānīya (breed of camels), 68, 127,
370
'Umar (the Caliph), 249
Umm al Radhma, *q.v.*
'Uqair, 285, 300
'Uqairī, ? al (camp-chaplain to Ibn
Sa'ūd), 316
'Uqaiyān, Khabb al, 186
'Uqaiyān, ? ibn ('Ataiba), 122
Urdu, 113
'Usailān, 327
'Uthmān ibn Kharāshī, *q.v.*
'Uthmān, 'Uthmān ibn, 70, 342
'Uwaid, 201
'Uwaina, 58
'Uwainid, 81-2
'Uwainid, Sha'īb, 81
'Uwaisa, 173
'Uyūn (Qasīm), 311
'Uyūnī, Al (author of calendar), 266

V

Vaccination, 56, 254, 260
Venereal diseases, 219
Venison (*Jalla*), 48, 209, 324, 351,
354, 360, 362-3, 370
Vine, *v.* Grapes
Volcanic, 128
Vulture, 354, 363

W

Wabra (Eastern Desert), 369
Wadhna Kuhaila, q.v.

PRINTED IN GREAT BRITAIN
BY ROBERT MACLEHOSE AND CO. LTD.
THE UNIVERSITY PRESS GLASGOW

THE *Middle East* COLLECTION

Arno Press

Abbott, Nabia. **Aishah: The Beloved of Mohammed.** 1942

Addison, Charles G. **Damascus and Palmyra.** 1838. 2 Vols. in 1

[Adivar], Halidé Edib. **Turkey Faces West.** 1930

Baddeley, John F. **The Rugged Flanks of Caucasus.** 1940. 2 Vols. in 1

Barker, Edward B. B., ed. **Syria and Egypt Under the Last Five Sultans of Turkey.** 1876. 2 Vols. in 1

Bell, Gertrude Lowthian. **Syria: The Desert & The Sown.** 1919

Bowring, John. **Report on the Commercial Statistics of Syria.** 1840

Brydges, Harford Jones. **The Dynasty of the Kajars.** 1833

Churchill, [Charles H.] **The Druzes and the Maronites Under the Turkish Rule from 1840 to 1860.** 1862

Denon, Vivant. **Travels in Upper and Lower Egypt.** 1803. 3 Vols. in 1

Donaldson, Bess Allen. **The Wild Rue:** A Study of Muhammadan Magic and Folklore in Iran. 1938

Eton, W[illiam]. **A Survey of the Turkish Empire.** 1798

Forbes-Leith, F. A. C. **Checkmate:** Fighting Tradition in Central Persia. 1927

Fraser, James Baillie. **Narrative of the Residence of the Persian Princes in London, in 1835 and 1836.** 1838. 2 Vols. in 1

Fraser, James Baillie. **A Winter's Journey (Tâtar) from Constantinople to Tehran.** 1838. 2 Vols. in 1

Gobineau, Joseph Arthur. **Romances of the East.** 1878

Islamic Taxation: Two Studies. 1973

Kinneir, John Macdonald. **A Geographical Memoir of the Persian Empire.** 1813

Krusinski, J[udasz Tadeusz]. **History of the Late Revolution in Persia.** 1740. 2 Vols. in 1

Lane-Poole, Stanley. **Cairo:** Sketches of Its History, Monuments, and Social Life. 1898

Le Strange, G[uy], ed. **Don Juan of Persia: A Shi'ah Catholic, 1560-1604.** 1926

Leeder, S. H. **Modern Sons of the Pharaohs:** A Study of the Manners and Customs of the Copts of Egypt. 1918

Midhat Bey, Ali Haydar. **The Life of Midhat Pasha.** 1903

Miller, Barnette. **The Palace School of Muhammad the Conqueror.** 1941

Millspaugh, A[rthur] C[hester]. **The American Task in Persia.** 1925

Naima. **Annals of the Turkish Empire from 1591 to 1659 of the Christian Era.** 1832

Pasha, Djemal. **Memories of a Turkish Statesman, 1913-1919.** 1922

Pears, Edwin. **Life of Abdul Hamid.** 1917

Philby, H[arry] St. J[ohn Bridger]. **Arabia of the Wahhabis.** 1928

St. John, Bayle. **Village Life in Egypt.** 1852. 2 Vols. in 1

Sheil, Lady [Mary]. **Glimpses of Life and Manners in Persia.** 1856

Skrine, Francis Henry and Edward Denison Ross. **The Heart of Asia:** A History of Russian Turkestan and the Central Asian Khanates from the Earliest Times. 1899

Sykes, Mark. **The Caliphs' Last Heritage:** A Short History of the Turkish Empire. 1915

Sykes, P[ercy] M., ed. **The Glory of the Shia World.** 1910

De Tott, Baron. **Memoirs of Baron de Tott.** 1785. 2 Vols. in 1

Ubicini, M. A. **Letters on Turkey.** 1856. 2 Vols. in 1

Vambery, Arminius. **Arminius Vambery:** His Life and Adventures. 1914

Vambery, Arminius. **History of Bokhara.** 1873

Waring, Edward Scott. **A Tour of Sheeraz by the Route of Kazroon and Feerozabad.** 1807

NVENTORY 1983